'This is beautifully written and develops a thoughtful, innovative and interesting argument on a matter of considerable importance. The method used entails an unusual, multi-layered and deep analysis of well-trodden ground, leading to thought-provoking, well-reasoned conclusions and some pragmatic practical proposals.' – *Lizzie Barmes, Professor of Labour Law & Co-Director QMUL School of Law Centre for Research on Law, Equality and Diversity, Queen Mary University of London*

The English Judiciary, Discrimination Law and Statutory Interpretation

In 1856, the US Supreme Court denied Dred Scott, now free of slavery, his Constitutional rights, solely because he was black. According to the Court, when the Constitution was drafted, some 60 years earlier, its authors would not have intended that 'a subordinate and inferior class of beings' qualified as citizens of the United States. Thus, the meaning of language drafted over half a century before was frozen in time.

This case, perhaps more than any other, demonstrates that the matter of statutory interpretation is critical, technical, and, sometimes, highly emotive. The case is not a mere nugget from history to indulge our disgust with values of another age, and with it a satisfaction of our progress to today's higher moral ground. It is the unfortunate case that the senior courts of England continue to produce highly contentious interpretations of our equality and discrimination laws.

This book examines these cases from the perspective of statutory interpretation, the judge's primary function. The scrutiny finds the judgments technically flawed, overcomplicated, excessively long, and often unduly restrictive. As such, this book explains how the cases should have been resolved – using conventional methods of interpretation; this would have produced simpler, technically sound judgments. Rather like the case of Dred Scott, these were easy cases producing bad law.

Dr Michael Connolly is Senior Lecturer at the University of Portsmouth, UK.

The English Judiciary, Discrimination Law and Statutory Interpretation

Easy Cases Making Bad Law

Michael Connolly

Routledge
Taylor & Francis Group
LONDON AND NEW YORK

First published 2019
by Routledge
2 Park Square, Milton Park, Abingdon, Oxon OX14 4RN

and by Routledge
52 Vanderbilt Avenue, New York, NY 10017, USA

First issued in paperback 2020

Routledge is an imprint of the Taylor & Francis Group, an informa business

British Library Cataloguing-in-Publication Data
A catalogue record for this book is available from the British Library

Library of Congress Cataloging-in-Publication Data
Names: Connolly, Michael (Law teacher), author.
Title: The English judiciary, discrimination law and statutory interpretation : easy cases making bad law / Michael Connolly.
Description: New York, NY : Routledge, 2018. | Includes bibliographical references.
Identifiers: LCCN 2018019587 | ISBN 9781138324565 (hbk)
Subjects: LCSH: Judges–England–History. | Courts–England–History. | Discrimination–Law and legislation–England. | Law—England–Interpretation and construction.
Classification: LCC KD7285 .C66 2018 | DDC 342.4208/7—dc23
LC record available at https://lccn.loc.gov/2018019587

ISBN 13: 978-0-367-58623-2 (pbk)
ISBN 13: 978-1-138-32456-5 (hbk)

Typeset in Galliard
by Swales & Willis Ltd, Exeter, Devon, UK

Contents

Table of authorities

Cases

Statutes

Statutory instruments

EU legislation

Preface

In 1856, Dred Scott took himself, his wife, and two daughters from Missouri to the United States Supreme Court. He was seeking, as citizens of the United States, their Constitutional right to access to the courts. The Court rejected the petition, because they were black:

> We think they are not, and that they are not included, and were not intended to be included, under the word 'citizens' in the Constitution, and can therefore claim none of the rights and privileges which that instrument provides for and secures to citizens of the United States. On the contrary they were at that time considered as a subordinate and inferior class of beings, who had been subjugated by the dominant race.[1]

Thus, the meaning of language drafted over half a century before was frozen in time. This case, perhaps more than any other, demonstrates that statutory interpretation is critical, technical, and, sometimes, highly emotive.

Dred Scott's case is not a mere nugget from history to indulge our disgust with values of another age, and with it a satisfaction of our progress to today's higher moral ground. The reasoning of the decision represents the 'old school' of statutory interpretation, that the meaning can be divined from the framer's intent. This method happens to be prevalent these days in the political *and* legal discourse on the future of the Human Rights Act 1998 and the UK's membership of the Council of Europe. Thus, a way of thinking that led to such an abhorrent judgment in 1856 remains with us today. The point is that statutory interpretation has the potential to be as critical today as it was back in 1856.

This is none the more so, perhaps, than with modern-day discrimination law and the English judiciary. The definitions of discrimination provided by equality legislation are a measure of how far a society is willing to challenge deep-seated assumptions, attitudes, and patterns of inequality. The judiciary has a major role in shaping these definitions. This is evident from the antecedent American cases (dating from the 1964 Civil Rights Act) and those of the Court of Justice of

1 *Dred Scott v Sandford* 60 US 393 (Sup Ct 1857) 404–405.

the European Union, which worked with more aspirational than detailed legislative provisions. One might conclude that the legislation coming before the English courts was thus 'ready-made', presenting the judiciary with few interpretive difficulties. But on many occasions, this has proved not to be the case, with the senior English courts producing a number of highly contentious decisions. Commentators, heavily critical of many of these cases, tend to analyse them by reference to external understandings of concept, theory, or policy. This book offers a unique internal critique of the process producing the decisions subject to such academic scrutiny. It makes a textual analysis of leading English judgments on the definitions of discrimination, and does so through the lens of statutory interpretation – the judge's primary function. The scrutiny finds that these judgments are technically flawed in terms of the process of statutory interpretation and the definitions produced; it also finds them to be overcomplicated, excessively long, and often unduly restrictive. As such, it finds that these cases were better, and more easily, resolvable using conventional methods of interpretation, which would also shape the definitions better to reflect the policies underlying the legislation. Although highlighting inexpert reasoning, the textual scrutiny reveals other threads, particularly notable in the narrow interpretations. There is an adherence to the common law's notion of binary litigation, envisaging just two individual litigants (e.g. *a* worker and employer) necessitating a harmed individual and fault-based liability; this is at odds with the societal and group-based purpose of the legislation. One can also detect a lingering historical negative or indifferent attitude to matters of equality (which is explored), often realised nowadays with an assortment of personal predilections. The book concludes by offering suggestions for reform based around these findings.

The law is stated as correct on 10 April 2018.

1 Introduction

> [T]he right to criticise judges . . . may be one of the safeguards which helps to ensure their high standard of performance.[1]

Historically, notions of equality did not figure in the common law, and, by extension, in the process of statutory interpretation. In the 19th century, women were denied the vote because the statutory instruction that 'the masculine gender shall be deemed and taken to include females' was not enough to rebut the common law presumption against women's suffrage.[2] Non-Christian MPs could be prosecuted under an antique and defunct statute requiring an oath to made 'upon the true faith of a Christian'.[3] Into the 20th century, and as recently as 1986, a public kiss between two men led to their convictions of 'insulting' behaviour.[4]

Thus, it was for Parliament to address inequality and discrimination, enacting in the 1970s the first dedicated comprehensive anti-discrimination legislation.[5] The definitions of discrimination provided by this legislation (classified nowadays as 'key concepts' within the Equality Act 2010) are a measure of how far society is willing to challenge deep-seated assumptions and attitudes (apparent in these historical cases), as well as patterns of inequality. Yet the *interpretation* of this dedicated legislation has shown that the judiciary has a major role in shaping these definitions.

The key concepts, drafting, and judges today

There are three major policy decisions to be made when drafting discrimination legislation. The first is the areas of civil activity chosen for regulation (such as employment,

1 Salmon LJ, *Report of the Interdepartmental Committee on the Law of Contempt as It Affects Tribunals of Inquiry* (Cmnd 4078, 1969) 15.

2 *Chorlton v Lings* (1868) LR 4 C P 374.

3 *Miller v Salomons* (1852) 7 Exchequer Reports (Welsby, Hurlstone, and Gordon) 475; 155 ER 1036, affirmed, *Salomons v Miller* (1853) 8 Exchequer Reports (Welsby, Hurlstone, and Gordon) 778; 155 ER 1567.

4 Under the Metropolitan Police Act 1839: *Masterson v Holden* [1986] 1 WLR 1017 (QB).

5 Preceded by the relatively limited Race Relations Acts of 1965 and 1968.

services, housing, education), the second is the protected characteristics identified for coverage, and the third is defining actionable discrimination (the latter two being 'key concepts'). Once chosen, defining the activities is a relatively straightforward task, and has proved comparatively uncontroversial from an interpretive standpoint.[6] However, the definition of race has been subject to some interpretive disagreement; this has arisen when the definition has been tied to the meaning of discrimination itself,[7] over which there is much less consensus, with views typically ranging from a 'results-based' ambition (requiring quotas) on the one hand, to liability limited to blatant intentional discrimination, on the other.[8] This is the most challenging aspect of drafting the law. It is law rooted in morality and seeks to define conduct, sometimes inadvertent or subconscious, which society considers 'wrong', or at least worthy of a legal cause of action and remedy. If the law is to go further than merely address one-to-one acts of bigotry, and tackle patterns of disadvantage not ordinarily noticeable in workaday 'street level' life, it becomes more controversial. It asks the question of society, which generally does not see itself as prejudiced, of how far it is willing to go in putting its hands up and admitting that its institutional, inadvertent, subconscious, and sometimes benign conduct *causes* (or perpetuates) these patterns. As such, discrimination law becomes a tool of social and economic change, a challenge for the English judiciary, not renowned for its judicial activism.[9]

It was fortunate for the drafters of Britain's first comprehensive anti-discrimination statute – the Sex Discrimination Act 1975 – that the case law on the US Civil Rights Act 1964 had already given these matters some consideration and consequently mapped out two basic definitions of actionable discrimination to ensure that the legislation was effective. These were direct and indirect discrimination.[10] Accordingly, these definitions were adopted in some detail.[11] Similarly, by the mid-1990s, definitions of disability discrimination,[12]

6 See e.g. on access to 'private clubs' under the Race Relations Act (hereafter RRA in notes) 1968, *Charter v Race Relations Board* [1973] AC 885 (HL) and *Dockers Labour Club and Institute Ltd v Race Relations Board* [1976] AC 285 (HL). The precise boundary of 'employment' under the Equality Act 2010 (hereafter in notes EA 2010) has become controversial: *Jivraj v Hashwani* [2011] IRLR 827 (SC) [34], criticised by Baroness Hale in *Bates van Winkelhof v Clyde & Co LLP* [2014] 1 WLR 2047 (SC) [39].

7 For 'ethnic origins' see *Mandla v Dowell Lee* [1983] QB 1 (CA), reversed [1983] 2 AC 548 (HL), and *JFS* [2010] 2 AC 728 (SC), discussed below respectively pp 171 and 190.

8 See Chapter 3, p 56.

9 Most notably, perhaps, in the common law's adherence to the notion of freedom of contract. Commenting on the 19th century, Chitty states that a contract's 'validity should not be challenged on the ground that its effect was unfair or socially undesirable': *Chitty on Contracts* (31st edn) 1.028. The allegiance to freedom of contract was maintained into to 21st century. See e.g. *Photo Production Ltd v Securicor Transport Ltd* [1980] AC 827, 848 (Lord Diplock) and, most recently, *Cavendish Square Holding BV v Makdessi* [2016] AC 1172 (SC) [33] (Lord Neuberger PSC and Lord Sumption JSC).

10 Known in the US as disparate treatment and disparate impact. See, respectively, *McDonnell Douglas Corp v Green* 411 US 792 (Sup Ct, 1973); *Griggs v Duke Power* 401 US 424 (Sup Ct, 1971).

11 See Chapter 6, and Lord Lester's account of the transposition from US law of indirect discrimination, 'Discrimination: what can lawyers learn from history?' [1994] PL 224, 227.

12 Notably disability-related discrimination (either by proxy or by disparate impact) and reasonable accommodation. See further Chapter 7.

outlawed initially by the Rehabilitation Act 1973,[13] were well-developed by the American courts,[14] providing another touchstone for those drafting the Disability Discrimination Act 1995. This is not to say that the statutory definitions produced were flawless; they were not entirely free of uncertainty nor prepared for every scenario. That is apparent from many of the cases studied in this book. But they did reproduce definitions fleshed out by the American judges and legislators with somewhat more experience in dealing with the challenge of securing effective protection against discrimination. By contrast to the drafters, the *interpreters* of these statutes – the English judiciary – largely ignored the American antecedents and the obvious intention of the drafters to reproduce them.

Instead, for the English judiciary in many cases, the legislation was a vehicle on which to produce an abundance of independent views, or personal predilections, on what this or that definition should actually mean.[15] It is inevitable that at least some such opinions were technically flawed. It was also predictable that the same issues would return repeatedly to the appeal courts for the clarification they had failed to give hitherto. For instance, the House of Lords/Supreme Court alone has entertained eight cases over the issue of a benign motive 'defence',[16] and four on proving the necessary disadvantage to get a claim of indirect discrimination off the ground.[17] Although, as these numbers suggest, there may be little consensus on the detail, there is a general, but not overwhelming, theme of conservatism. Many of the decisions have been restrictive, or even retrograde, and certainly not purposive. Among these, there is a number of examples where statutory intervention was necessary to rescue the situation, using more detailed, precise language, which was less vulnerable to unduly narrow interpretations. The restrictive interpretations given by the Court of Appeal to two elements of indirect discrimination[18] were redressed by legislation.[19] A House of Lords decision on the definition of disability

13 See now the more comprehensive Americans with Disabilities Act 1990.

14 See e.g. *McWright v Alexander* 982 F 2d 222, 228, (7th Cir 1992) and the cases cited within.

15 Lord Neuberger once commented extra-judicially, that 'virtually every' appellate judge has been guilty of writing a 'vanity' judgment: 'Open justice unbound?' Judicial Studies Board annual lecture 2011, 16 March 2011, para 24, < webarchive.nationalarchives.gov.uk/20121206022550/http://www.judiciary.gov.uk/Resources/JCO/Documents/Speeches/mr-speech-jsb-lecture-march-2011.pdf > accessed 23 March 2018.

16 See further Chapters 4 and 5. The cases are: *R v Birmingham City Council ex p Equal Opportunities Commission* [1989] 1 AC 1156; *James v Eastleigh BC* [1990] 2 AC 751; *Nagarajan v London Regional Transport* [2000] 1 AC 501; *Chief Constable of West Yorkshire v Khan* [2001] UKHL 48; *Shamoon v Chief Constable of the RUC* [2003] ICR 337; *R (European Roma Rights Centre) v Immigration Officer at Prague Airport* [2005] 2 AC 1 (HL); *St Helens MBC v Derbyshire* [2007] ICR 841; *R (E) v Governing Body of JFS* [2010] 2 AC 278 (SC). In addition, the issues of knowledge of the protected characteristic, and (for two Law Lords) discriminatory intent, arose in *Lewisham LBC v Malcolm* [2008] 1 AC 1399 (HL). See Chapter 9, especially p 221.

17 See further Chapter 8. The cases are: *Orphanos v QMC* [1985] AC 761 (HL); *R v Secretary of State for Employment, ex p Seymour-Smith (No. 2)* [2000] ICR 244 (HL); *Rutherford v Secretary of State for Trade and Industry (No. 2)* [2006] ICR 785 (HL); and *Essop v Home Office* [2017] UKSC 27.

18 'Requirement or condition' within RRA 1976, s 1(1)(b): *Perera v Civil Service Commission* [1983] ICR 428 (CA) (discussed Chapter 8, p 154); 'Justifiable', under RRA 1976, s 1(1)(b)(ii): *Hampson v Department of Education* [1989] ICR 179 (CA).

19 See now EA 2010, s 19.

discrimination was effectively reversed by Parliament,[20] whilst another upset long-standing and efficacious orthodoxy on assessing the impact of a challenged practice in indirect discrimination claims.[21] At a lower level, several novel theories produced by the Court of Appeal had to be overturned on appeal.[22] Meanwhile, some prominent judgments[23] that could be characterised as purposive or progressive, or at least 'neutral', remain technically flawed and prolix.[24]

These 'troublesome' cases suggest that, first, the judiciary has been important in not only fleshing out the statutory definitions of discrimination but also shaping them; second, it has been ignorant of, or turned a blind eye to, instructional antecedents; third, it has had a less than technical mastery of the statutory definitions; and fourth, given that the troublesome cases examined in this book span a period of some 33 years (1983–2016), it would seem that the senior judiciary has learnt very little from decades of experience. The multiplicity of troublesome cases revisiting a single issue coupled with the numerous reversals and upsets raise a suspicion that something is wrong with the judges' interpretation of the discrimination legislation on the key definitions. One commentator suggested that the unsatisfactory decision in one particular House of Lords case was the result of 'judges not intimately acquainted with the statutory discrimination provisions'.[25] It would be easy to conclude that this excuse could be projected onto many of these judgments, or at the least those given by the Law Lords who presided in *Malcolm*. This book agrees that the problem in *Malcolm* (and other cases) can be attributed to the judiciary, but argues the cause is much deeper than a mere unacquaintance with the relevant legislation. The proposition is that these judgments, creating so much bad law, are at their heart technically flawed, as well as overlong and overcomplicated. It argues that they were relatively easy cases to decide correctly with the use of the basic tools of statutory interpretation, a feature noticeably absent in the judgments. This is not to say that *all* discrimination judgments are poor; there are cases correctly decided upon concise, clear, and technically sound reasoning.[26] But the cases under review in this work were in the senior courts on key definitions of discrimination, disseminating

20 *Lewisham LBC v Malcolm* [2008] 1 AC 1399 (HL). See now EA 2010, ss 15 and 19 (with 6(3)).
21 *Rutherford v Secretary of State for Trade and Industry (No. 2)* [2006] ICR 785 (HL).
22 See e.g. *Mandla v Dowell Lee* [1983] 2 AC 548 (HL); *James v Eastleigh BC* [1990] 2 AC 751 (HL); *Essop v Home Office* [2017] UKSC 27.
23 See *James v Eastleigh BC* [1990] 2 AC 751 (HL) and *R (E) v Governing Body of JFS* [2010] 2 AC 728 (SC); *St Helens MBC v Derbyshire* [2007] ICR 841 (HL).
24 See e.g. *R v Birmingham CC ex p EOC* [1989] 1 AC 1156 (HL); *James v Eastleigh BC* [1990] 2 AC 751 (HL); *St Helens MBC v Derbyshire* [2007] ICR 841 (HL); *R (E) v Governing Body of JFS* [2010] 2 AC 278 (SC).
25 A McColgan, *Discrimination, Equality and the Law* (Hart 2014) 166, commenting on *Lewisham LBC v Malcolm* [2008] 1 AC 1399.
26 Notable judgments were those of Morison J, clarifying the law in the early days of the Disability Discrimination Act 1995: *Goodwin v The Patent Office* [1999] ICR 302, 307 (EAT); *Vicary v BT* [1999] IRLR 680, 682 (EAT); *Ridout v TC Group* [1998] IRLR 628 (EAT). See also Baroness Hale's on clarifying indirect discrimination and age in *Homer v Chief Constable of West Yorkshire* [2012] ICR 704 (SC), on defining direct discrimination in *R (European Roma Rights Centre) v Immigration Officer at Prague Airport* [2005] 2 AC 1 (HL), and on indirect discrimination in *Essop v Home Office* [2017] UKSC 27.

mixed signals about the law's commitment to addressing patterns of inequality, as well as deep-seated discriminatory assumptions and attitudes. They thus encumber the development of this law, whilst their prolixity is of little use to those interested parties trying to understand it, ranging from the litigants concerned, legal advisors, prospective claimants, and even the citizen who wishes to understand the law, a requirement of the Rule of Law.[27]

The purpose of this work is to establish the technical shortcomings and offer some context, so to explain this slippage, to a degree at least. The cases studied highlight a number of relevant factors, such as a cavalier approach to the rules of statutory interpretation, an apparent lack of expertise in the legislation's technical definitions and novel purpose of societal advancement,[28] and the judges' 'binary' mind-set requiring an at-fault tortfeasor causing harm to an individual victim. As already noted, other features are apparent, such as personal ideological predilections and a lingering historical judicial negative attitude towards matters of equality.

The approach of this book

The central question for this book is why are these leading judgments on key concepts so poor? This is, of course, a leading question. And so it is necessary to establish that the judgments are indeed 'poor', by which it is meant that they are technically flawed and prolix. The 'technical' question especially requires an understanding of the concepts represented by the definitions, which should be expressed in a way to ensure their integrity and efficacy.

Meanwhile, the requirement of integrity expects that statutory provisions are interpreted in a way that does not jar with other elements of any particular definition, or the particular instrument under consideration, or indeed other legislation forming part of the same 'code', or scheme (statutes *in pari materia* or 'in the same matter').[29] Thus, without good reason, identical words or phrases in the same statute or legislative scheme ought to be given the same meaning. In the same vein, legislation should not be interpreted to render other parts of the instrument meaningless. For instance, where an Act provides that 'racial group', means 'colour, race nationality or ethnic or national origins', it would damage the provision's integrity to reduce the term 'ethnic origins' to a biological test, effectively assimilating the term with 'race' and thus rendering the phrase 'ethnic origins' otiose.[30]

'Efficacy' requires that a definition is interpreted to fulfil its purpose, informed by the statutory language deployed, as well as the generally agreed purpose, set

27 *Black-Clawson International Ltd v Papierwerke Waldhof-Aschaffenberg AG* [1975] AC 591 (HL) 638 (Lord Diplock). See further p 28, text to n 85. More recently, Lord Neuberger avowed that judgments should be 'clear and easily interpretable by lawyers . . . and non-lawyers': 'Open justice unbound?' Judicial Studies Board annual lecture 2011, 16 March 2011, para 5, < webarchive.nationalarchives.gov.uk/20131202164909/http://judiciary.gov.uk/media/speeches/2011 > accessed 10 April 2018.

28 See Chapter 3, generally.

29 See p 28.

30 See *Mandla v Dowell Lee* [1983] QB 1 (CA) (reversed [1983] 2 AC 548) interpreting RRA 1976, s 3(1) (see now EA 2010, s 9). Discussed p 171.

out in precedent, legislative history, or even scholarly literature. Thus, the word 'premises' in a 'safety Act' was interpreted to include a cave used for storing flammable material.[31] These notions of integrity and efficacy form this 'technical' benchmark by which the judgments are appraised.

The 'prolixity' question is addressed by asking if a case under review could have been resolved more easily. This is tested by identifying with acuity and clarity the actual issues in question. In order to identify these issues, an understanding of the legislation is required (thus the first two questions are inevitably connected). From there, the relevant legislative provisions, and their interpretation, are identified. If this can produce a shorter, less complicated, and technically sound judgment, then this aspect of the hypothesis is met.

One may sense at this stage that the first two examples (integrity and efficacy) carry a flavour of statutory interpretation, respectively representing the 'otiose' and 'mischief' rules[32] (the latter being deployed in the 'safety Act' case). Such a sense would be correct, as both of these matters are integrated into the major appraisal in this work, which is to test each judgment by the standard, or 'habitual', tools of statutory interpretation. The point of this approach is that it examines the judiciary's primary function in these cases, which is statutory interpretation. As such, it gets closer to the root of any technical shortcomings than an analysis by reference to, say, policy, concept, or theory. This third test utilises the judiciary's principal, well-known, and established tools of statutory interpretation. The test is met if this approach would produce a technically sound judgment, at the least. The result is enhanced if it would also produce a shorter and less complicated judgment.

Thus, this book offers a textual scrutiny of a body of case law on the key definitions of discrimination law through the lens of statutory interpretation, an '*internal* norm'. Reference points for all three sub-questions will include 'external' sources such as precedent (including antecedent US authorities and European Union (EU) case law), legislative history, and well-established theories, concepts, and aims of discrimination law. It is not surprising then that the principal literature under review comprises the judgments and the legislation on which they are based. It does not analyse critically the key definitions provided by the legislation, with, say, a view for reform. As noted earlier,[33] it assumes these are largely satisfactory. The critical focus is on the judgments. Being strongly doctrinal, this work's qualitative credentials are limited. This is deliberate and beneficial. It aids clarity, and achieving clarity (or avoiding prolixity) is one of the main features of the hypothesis. Hence, there is no attempt to discover, for instance, the job pressures,

31 See *Gardiner v Sevenoaks RDC* [1950] 2 All ER 84 (KB). The long title to the Celluloid and Cinematograph Film Act 1922 read 'An Act to make better provision for the prevention of fire in premises where raw celluloid or cinematograph film is stored or used'.

32 See Chapter 2, respectively p 25 'Other words and sections of the instrument', and p 22.

33 See p 1, 'The key concepts, drafting, and judges today'.

peer pressures, emotional input,[34] or social or political ideology[35] of any decision-maker studied here. The judges' thought processes *are* analysed, but only by their judicial language and legalistic references.

1 The selection of cases

The judgments selected for attention were leading cases on the key definitions of discrimination provided by this legislation (nowadays, the Equality Act 2010, classifying these definitions as 'key concepts'). The selection was upon the following criteria: (1) their importance to the meaning of discrimination; (2) they were written by the senior judiciary of England and Wales; (3) there is a range spanning a period from the early days of the domestic legislation to the present day; and (4) that they appear to be exceptionally troublesome.

On the first criterion, as noted earlier,[36] these key definitions are a measure of how far society is willing to challenge deep-seated assumptions and attitudes, as well as patterns of inequality, and thus represent the central philosophy of anti-discrimination law. As such, litigation over their meaning presents the judiciary with a significant interpretive duty.

On the second and third, these judgments were handed down by the Court of Appeal and the House of Lords/Supreme Court, where one would expect to find the senior (and, it must be presumed, *superior*) judges. Judgments of this status not only provide guidance for the lower courts and tribunals (which preside over the vast majority of claims), but also they signal more generally, to the legal world, interested parties, and the public, the standards and ambition expected by these key concepts. The cases span some four decades, ranging from 1983 to 2016 and present a 'mini-history' of the judiciary and modern discrimination law. This facilitates an analysis of any evolutionary features of these cases. Some of the judgments were reversed, overruled, or in the minority, but the purpose of this study is to examine how the senior judiciary has approached the matter of interpreting and defining these key concepts of discrimination law.

Fourth, from the cases that could meet the criteria thus far, there is a smaller cohort that, as suggested earlier,[37] appears troublesome. These were identified by their simple 'outward' characteristics of recurring issues,[38]

34 See e.g. D Robertson, *Judicial Discretion in the House of Lords* (Oxford University Press 1998); RJ Cahill-O'Callaghan, 'The influence of personal values on legal judgments' (2013) 40(4) *Journal of Law and Society* 596.

35 See e.g. JAG Griffith, *The Politics of the Judiciary* (5th edn, Fontana 2010).

36 See p 1.

37 See pp 3–4.

38 *James v Eastleigh* [1990] 2 AC 751 (HL); *JFS* [2010] 2 AC 728 (SC); *Chief Constable of West Yorkshire v Khan* [2001] UKHL 48; *St Helens MBC v Derbyshire* [2007] ICR 841 (HL).

persistent dissents,[39] reversals,[40] and the upsetting of established efficacious definitions.[41] No reading or analysis of a judgment beyond a headnote (at most) is necessary to identify these characteristics and raise a suspicion of a difficulty worthy of investigation. It is of course arguable that other cases match these criteria, but none could be said to be more important in terms of establishing the key definitions and the precedential status, or more useful in providing a historical perspective.

Those are the reasons (and limitations of space) that other possible candidate cases have not been prioritised for review. Some are considered below, by the definitions included in this work, and then by those definitions not included.

Direct discrimination, victimisation, and the benign motive 'defence'

Beyond those directly addressed in this book, other significant House of Lords' cases on the benign motive (or *but for*) question are *Nagarajan v London Regional Transport*[42] and *Shamoon v Chief Constable of the RUC.*[43] Both of these are subsumed into the discussion within.[44] In the Court of Appeal, *Owens & Briggs v James*[45] (on mixed ground cases) likewise has been subsumed into the discussion. The uncomfortable 'benign motive' decision in *Simon v Brinham Associates*[46] may well have been conveniently forgotten and/or impliedly reversed[47] but it has not been expressly addressed by the senior courts.

On the comparison for direct discrimination, the Court of Appeal in *Smith v Safeway*[48] arguably produced an inefficacious and unsymmetrical interpretation (on dress codes for men and women in employment), but the decision did not upset any established orthodoxy[49] and has neither been revisited nor reversed or overturned. In *Madden v Preferred Technical Group Cha Ltd* the Court made the rather obvious point that proof of less favourable treatment of a foreign national is not definitive proof of discrimination; the 'because' element must still be satisfied.[50]

39 ibid.
40 *Essop v Home Office* [2015] ICR 1063 (CA), reversed [2017] UKSC 27; *Naeem v Secretary of State for Justice* [2016] ICR 289 (CA), overruled [2017] UKSC 27; *Lewisham LBC v Malcolm* [2008] 1 AC 1399 (HL), reversed, EA 2010, ss 15 and 19; *Perera v Civil Service Commission (no. 2)* [1983] ICR 428 (CA) and *Meer v London Borough of Tower Hamlets* [1988] IRLR 399 (CA), reversed, RRA 1976, s 1(1A); *Mandla v Dowell Lee* [1983] QB 1 (CA), reversed, [1983] 2 AC 548 (HL).
41 *Rutherford v Secretary of State for Trade and Industry (No. 2)* [2006] ICR 785 (HL); *Lewisham LBC v Malcolm* [2008] 1 AC 1399 (HL).
42 [2000] 1 AC 501.
43 [2003] ICR 337.
44 See Chapter 4, especially 'The importunate dissenters', p 99.
45 [1982] ICR 618 (CA).
46 *Simon v Brinham Associates* [1987] ICR 596 (CA) (where – on behalf of a Middle East client who would not employ Jews – asking all candidates if they were Jewish was held not to be less favourable treatment).
47 See EA 2010, Explanatory Note (63) and Case C-54/07 *Feryn* [2008] ECR I-5187 (announcing 'I will not employ immigrants' could amount to direct discrimination).
48 [1996] ICR 868.
49 Of the little precedent that existed, see *Schmidt v Austicks Bookshops Ltd* [1978] ICR 85 (EAT) and *Cootes v John Lewis plc* (EAT, 27 February 2001) EAT/1414/00.
50 [2005] IRLR 46 (CA), especially [84]–[91].

Gill v El Vino[51] established the standard required for the treatment to be 'less' favourable, and has been widely accepted. And although the House of Lords in *R (European Roma Rights Centre) v Immigration Officer at Prague Airport*[52] reversed the Court of Appeal below on the matter of stereotyping (Roma air passengers), the case was particularly fact sensitive and the decision did not upset the orthodoxy that stereotyping could amount to less favourable treatment.[53]

In relatively recent times, the issue of motive and victimisation arose in the Court of Appeal. In *Bird v Sylvester*,[54] the Court merely applied either of two arguably contradictory House of Lords precedents, coming to the same result. Controversial it may be, but its roots lay in those House of Lords' judgments, which are included for review,[55] leaving no reason to include this case.

Problems with indirect discrimination

In *Coker v Lord Chancellor*, the Court of Appeal ruled that selecting from a group of friends (or family) would not necessarily amount to (prima facie) indirect discrimination. Whatever the merits of that ruling, it did not upset any precedent nor has the matter been addressed by the Supreme Court or Parliament.[56] The Court of Appeal in *R (Elias) v Secretary of State for Defence*[57] explained that direct and indirect discrimination were mutually exclusive. Whatever the integrity of that analysis, it upset no orthodoxy and has been well received in the Supreme Court[58] and left untouched by Parliament.

Requiring a referral to the Court of Justice of the European Union (CJEU), *R v Secretary of State for Employment, ex p Seymour-Smith*[59] provided an important House of Lords' judgment (with dissents) on statistical proof required for a prima facie case. The eventual majority decision has not been expressly overruled, although the assumption made for the *pool* for the comparison may stand as an orthodoxy subsequently upset. As such, the case is subsumed into the discussion on the required comparison.[60]

The justification defence to indirect discrimination, originating in the Court of Appeal[61] and arguably out of step with EU law, has had its formula approved

51 [1983] QB 425 (CA).
52 [2005] 2 AC 1 (HL).
53 See e.g. *Alexander v Home Office* [1988] ICR 685 (CA).
54 [2007] EWCA Civ 1052, especially [8]–[13].
55 *Chief Constable of West Yorkshire v Khan* [2001] UKHL 48 and *St Helens MBC v Derbyshire* [2007] ICR 841 (HL). See Chapter 6, p 134 et al.
56 [2002] ICR 321 (CA). The Court's wider comment regarding word-of-mouth hiring amounting to indirect discrimination was relied on in *Jivraj v Hashwani* [2010] EWCA Civ 712 [24] (selection from the Ismaili community) but reversed on other grounds: [2011] IRLR 827 (SC).
57 [2006] 1 WLR 3213 (CA) [114] and [119] (Mummery LJ, giving the leading judgment).
58 See e.g. *JFS* [2010] 2 AC 728 (SC) [56]–[57] (Baroness Hale), [214] (Lord Hope), [236] (Lord Walker); *Patmalniece v Secretary of State for Work and Pensions* [2011] UKSC 11, [69] (Lord Walker).
59 Case C-167/97 *Seymour-Smith* [1999] ICR 447 (on referral from [1997] ICR 371 (HL)), and applied *(No. 2)* [2000] ICR 244 (HL).
60 See Chapter 8, 'The comparison required', p 174.
61 See e.g. *Hampson v Department of Education* [1989] ICR 179 (CA).

by the House of Lords/Supreme Court,[62] and has been left untouched by subsequent domestic legislation. The matter is noted in Chapter 2.[63]

There have been several cases in the senior courts on the matter of indirect discrimination and group identity. In *CRE v Dutton*,[64] the Court of Appeal confirmed (what has now become) the orthodoxy that protected status identity (such as race) is not based on immutability, and so there was no warrant to include it for specific review. In *Orphanos v QMC*,[65] the House of Lords identified claimants by who they were not, a point overlooked by the Supreme Court in *JFS*,[66] and by the Court of Appeal in *Tejani v Superintendent Registrar for the District of Peterborough*.[67] *Orphanos* and *Tejani* are subsumed into the analysis of *JFS*.[68]

The definitions not specifically considered include: equal pay; some aspects of disability discrimination; and sexual harassment, sexual orientation, and pregnancy discrimination. Each is taken in turn.

Equal pay

It is arguable that the key definitions of discrimination do not include the equal pay provisions, which nowadays do not appear as key concepts in the Equality Act 2010,[69] although the equal pay provisions allude to them.[70] The case law provides a history of courts struggling to manage scenarios of direct and indirect discrimination with legislation that did not expressly recognise either. It may well be that this body of case law is worthy of a dedicated thesis in itself, but given the parameters for this work, notably on key concepts, save where they are subsumed into the key concepts,[71] the interpretations of the equal pay provisions per se have been excluded.

Disability discrimination

The case law on direct disability discrimination is relatively new and uncontroversial,[72] while the senior courts have entertained no cases on the meaning of indirect disability

62 See e.g. *Webb v EMO Cargo* [1993] 1 WLR 49 (HL) 56; *Ministry of Justice v O'Brien* [2013] UKSC 6; *Homer v Chief Constable of West Yorkshire* [2012] UKSC 15 [23] (Baroness Hale).
63 See Chapter 2, 'Proportionality', p 39.
64 [1989] QB 783 (CA), 803.
65 [1985] AC 761 (HL).
66 [2010] 2 AC 728 (SC).
67 [1986] IRLR 502 (CA). See also *Dhatt v McDonalds Hamburgers Ltd* [1991] 1 WLR 527 (CA), taking a similar approach.
68 See Chapter 6 respectively, p 107, n 96 and p 105, n 91.
69 The 'key concepts' are set out in EA 2010, Part 1, while Equal Pay is provided for in Part 5, Chapter 3.
70 See EA 2010, ss 69 and 71.
71 See e.g. the consideration of *Enderby v Frenchay Health Authority* [1991] ICR 382 (EAT), effectively reversed Case C-127/92, [1994] ICR 112, discussed, Chapter 2, p 40 et al. and the lengthy appraisal of equal pay cases in Chapter 8, 'The equal pay precedents', p 196.
72 In Case C-303/06 *Coleman v Attridge Law* [1998] 3 CMLR 27 the CJEU ruled that domestic legislation (DDA 1995, ss 3A and 3B), which read literally would exclude associative discrimination, should be read to cover it. The reference was made by the Employment Appeal Tribunal (EAT) and neither the Court of Appeal nor House of Lords were involved.

discrimination.[73] The leading House of Lords case on the reasonable adjustments duty, *Archibald v Fife Council*,[74] reversed plurality opinions below, with one of its own. But the decision has fared well, with no revisits or legislative reversals. Given this, and that the case originated in Scotland, so not involving the (English) Court of Appeal, this case was not included.

Sexual harassment, sexual orientation, and pregnancy discrimination

There is a group of cases which could be loosely tagged 'piggy-back claims', where the claim stumbles upon the symmetrical definition of direct sex discrimination.[75] These relate to sexual harassment,[76] sexual orientation,[77] and pregnancy discrimination.[78] They pre-dated respective dedicated legislation, hence the 'piggy back' description. Legislation *resolved* (rather than reversed) the first two of these issues with additional dedicated causes of action,[79] leaving the key concepts (and their interpretation) undisturbed. As such, these cases do not qualify for inclusion in this book. The resolution of the pregnancy discrimination cases was more complex. The CJEU effectively overruled the EAT[80] (the matter had gone no higher domestically) on the issue of pregnancy discrimination, although the Court of Appeal and the House of Lords did come to the matter somewhat later to rule (wrongly under EU law) that firing a maternity-cover replacement for pregnancy was not sex discrimination.[81] Even here, the House of Lords was content to defer to the CJEU, making a referral it subsequently implemented.[82] The interpretive dispute here was between the domestic and EU courts. There was no disagreement among domestic courts over the symmetrical formula not encompassing pregnancy discrimination per se. In fact, the legislation was readily readable that way,[83] and the matter was *resolved* in domestic law, again, with a new statutory dedicated cause of action for pregnancy and maternity discrimination,[84] again leaving the key concepts undisturbed. Thus, no orthodoxy was upset here. And given the single effective reversal, and Parliament's response in respecting

73 For direct discrimination, see *Stockton on Tees BC v Aylott* [2010] ICR 1278 (CA).

74 [2004] UKHL 32, reversing [2004] IRLR 197 (CSIH) and (EAT Scotland, 12 December 2002).

75 See Chapter 3, '1 Formal equality', p 59.

76 *Macdonald v Advocate General for Scotland*; *Pearce v Governing Body of Mayfield Secondary School* [2003] UKHL 34.

77 ibid.

78 E.g. *Hayes v Malleable Working Men's Club and Institute* [1985] ICR 703 (EAT).

79 See now respectively EA 2010, s 27 and s 4.

80 *Hayes v Malleable Working Men's Club and Institute* [1985] ICR 703; Case C-177/88 *Dekker v Stichting Vormingscentrum voor Jonge Volwassen (VJV-Centrum) Plus* [1990] ECR I-3941.

81 Case C-32/93 *Webb v EMO Cargo Ltd* [1992] ICR 445 (CA), [1993] ICR 175 (HL), effectively reversed, [1994] ECR I-3567.

82 ibid [1995] ICR 1021 (HL).

83 As found by the US Supreme Court, *General Electric v Gilbert* 429 US 125 (1976), 134–135), remedied by the (non-symmetrical) Pregnancy Discrimination Act 1978 (codified, USC s 2000e(k)).

84 Originally, Sex Discrimination Act (hereafter SDA in notes) 1975, s 3A. See now EA 2010, ss 4, 13(6), 17, 18.

the symmetrical logic of the domestic decisions, these cases are not the most compelling of those considered to warrant inclusion for a technical appraisal.

Boundaries of this book's approach

This book does not seek to question, challenge, or advance the key concepts as they are set out by the legislation or generally understood. Thus, it does not promote a new or particular theory or concept of discrimination law. It takes the legislative definitions and widely received concepts as fixed points of reference. By coincidence, the textual analysis of the judgments may identify shortcomings in the statutory drafting. But this methodology can only test whether the judgment identifies the drafting error, and, if so, how well the judgment handles it.

In line with this, the book makes no attempt to personalise the matter by endowing any particular judge with a particular trait, be it for instance, political, ideological, technical, or even ascribing to one a particular interpretive characteristic. In this regard, it does no more than treat each judgment as a free-standing speech by *a* member of the court in question. This does not prevent the analysis detecting, say, personal predilections in any particular speech, notably when this appears at the expense of an orthodox approach to statutory interpretation or an understanding of the legislation's technical aspects. Neither does it exclude the identification of inconsistencies by the same judge in different cases, but only for the purpose of analysing the speech, and not the judge.

A further limitation is that the mini-history embraced here is not held out as a definitive representation of any evolutionary characteristics of the judiciary and the key definitions of equality law, or more generally. Any conclusions here are supplementary to the main thesis. That said, this history can provide some insight into the thought processes behind a particular judgment. For instance, a judgment disregarding a progressive precedent to regress the law suggests that it may be driven more by some external ideological predilection, rather than an appreciation of the law's purpose. Also, depending on the results, it can present an additional useful observation on the law's progress (or otherwise), and perhaps a starting point for a more quantitative study.

Similarly, there is no express attempt in this work to project the findings onto other areas of the discrimination legislation, or indeed further afield (although, given the results here, testing any case that the reader finds troublesome by this methodology may well prove enlightening). But, as noted above, these cases are central to the law's commitment to challenge deep-seated assumptions, attitudes, and patterns of inequality. It also cannot be denied that a measure of the ability of the senior judiciary to interpret the key definitions can serve as a suggestion, at the least, that any shortcomings in the understanding of these definitions may well indicate a lack of necessary expertise in discrimination law more generally. In any case, the reforms proposed (equality law education and a statutory command on interpretation),[85] can only have a beneficial (or at its lowest, neutral) effect more generally.

2 The layout

The work sets the scene in Chapter 2 with an overview of the developed rules of statutory interpretation, by the common law and relevant European institutions. This shows the fluidity of the process, its vulnerability to ideological predilections, and hints at the relationship with the political climate and arrangements of the day. All the same, it remains possible to map out a framework of interpretative rules, to which the judiciary owes some fidelity.

Chapter 3 offers a brief overview of the commonly held theories, concepts, and aims of discrimination law. From this, a (broadly received) statutory purpose is distilled, providing another reference by which the decisions may be analysed and tested. Chapter 4 provides an illuminating history tracking the common law's negative and sometimes hostile attitude to matters of equality, pervading well into the 20th century. This provides further dimension to the judiciary's approach to the modern equality legislation.

The main body of the work draws on these chapters with a detailed study of the speeches in cases covering some principal definitions of discrimination law; these are direct and indirect discrimination, victimisation, and disability discrimination. The purpose of these chapters is to expose the judgments as technically flawed, prolix, and more easily resolved using standard methods of statutory interpretation.

The first of these is Chapter 5, exploring the to and fro of judicial attitudes, notably in the House of Lords and the Supreme Court, to notions of a benign motive 'defence' to direct discrimination, a concept appearing nowhere in the legislation. The main scrutiny in this chapter falls upon *James v Eastleigh BC*[86] and *JFS*.[87] Chapter 6 highlights the problems caused by the House of Lords' decision in the victimisation case, *Chief Constable of West Yorkshire v Khan*[88] (again, suggesting without foundation a benign motive 'defence'), and details the Lords' excruciating attempts to escape from this just five years later in *St Helens MBC v Derbyshire*.[89] But many of the controversies with the victimisation provisions are discussed in Chapter 7, where it is argued that the decisions have an unexpressed relationship with the law of contempt of court.

Chapter 8 explores numerous problems with the more complicated and challenging indirect discrimination provisions. It raises perhaps the most serious issues of expertise, in relation to establishing group and individual

85 See Chapter 10, 'Proposals', p 238.
86 [1990] 2 AC 751 (HL).
87 *R (E) v Governing Body of JFS* [2010] 2 AC 728 (SC).
88 [2001] UKHL 48.
89 [2007] ICR 841 (HL).

disadvantage, with the cases of *Rutherford v Secretary of State for Trade and Industry (No. 2)*[90] in the House of Lords, and a pair of Court of Appeal decisions, *Essop v Home Office* and *Naeem v Secretary of State for Justice*.[91] It also scrutinises the unduly narrow interpretation given in *Perera v Civil Service Commission*,[92] eventually resolved by legislation. Finally, Chapter 9 explores the text of the controversial case of *Lewisham LBC v Malcolm*,[93] which effectively reduced the statutory definition of disability-related discrimination to something less than direct discrimination, rendering the provision largely otiose. Again, this was effectively (and predictably) reversed by legislation.

Having established that these leading judgments were technically flawed and prolix, the Conclusion in Chapter 10 identifies some prevalent themes underlying this slippage. The most obvious was the absence of the basic tools of statutory interpretation, notably the purposive and literal rules. There was also a gravitation towards a fault-based binary approach (at odds with the societal and group-based purpose of equality legislation), and some judicial ideological predilections (in lieu of established definitions). These two features have the flavour of the historical negativity towards matters of equality. As such, the Conclusion considers these themes in its Proposals.

On 23 June 2016, by a referendum, the United Kingdom voted to leave the EU. At the time of writing, Britain's secession was due by 28 March 2019,[94] with a transition period negotiated until 31 December 2020.[95] The British Government vowed to 'convert the "acquis" – the body of existing EU law – into domestic law', thus protecting workers' rights, and, at the same time, 'end the jurisdiction' of the Court of Justice.[96] At the time of writing, this policy was expressed in the European Union (Withdrawal) Bill 2017, with the *acquis* now classified as 'retained EU law'.[97] To supplement this, clause 6(2) provided: 'A court or tribunal need not have regard to anything done on or after exit day by the European Court, another EU entity or the EU but may do so if it considers it appropriate to do so.'

90 [2006] ICR 785 (HL).
91 Respectively [2015] ICR 1063 (CA); [2016] ICR 289 (CA), respectively reversed and overruled, [2017] UKSCT 27.
92 [1983] ICR 428 (CA).
93 [2008] 1 AC 1399 (HL).
94 The secession process was triggered on 29 March 2017. Treaty of the European Union (TEU), Article 50(3) dictates that this should take no more than 2 years.
95 'Draft agreement on the withdrawal of the United Kingdom of Great Britain and Northern Ireland from the European Union and the European Atomic Energy Community', Article 121, < https://www.gov.uk/government/uploads/system/uploads/attachment_data/file/691366/20180319_DRAFT_WITHDRAWAL_AGREEMENT.pdf > accessed 26 March 2018.
96 See e.g. 'The Lancaster House speech', < www.gov.uk/government/speeches/the-governments-negotiating-objectives-for-exiting-the-eu-pm-speech > accessed 10 April 2018; HC Deb, 29 March 2017, vol 624, cols 252–253; HM Government, *The United Kingdom's Exit from and New Partnership with the European Union* (White Paper, Cm 9417, 2017) pp 9 ('acquis'), 31–33 (workers' rights), 13 (jurisdiction).
97 Clauses 2–6.

The findings of this book demonstrate that this mechanism would not be sufficient fully to maintain equality rights on a par with those of the EU. There are two principal reasons for this. First, clause 6(2) allows too much discretion as *when* to 'have regard' to the European Court,[98] as well as providing no mandate to follow a particular approach to statutory interpretation. Second, in any case, the respective courts would be obligated ultimately to comply with their differing constitutional strictures. The Proposals in the Conclusion would have the benefit of lessening this divergence. In the meantime, the United Kingdom continues to be a member of the EU (or somewhat effectively so during the transition), and so subject to its laws as interpreted by the Court of Justice. The cases under review in this work were decided before the referendum.[99] Consequently, the analysis of those cases is made on the basis of continuing membership, although where appropriate, post-referendum, -secession and -transition comment will be made. The law is stated as correct on 1 May 2018.

98 See e.g. the concerns of Lord Neuberger, calling for 'greater clarity': (see e.g. < www.bbc.co.uk/news/uk-40855526 > accessed 4 June 2018; *The Independent*, 8 August 2017).

99 Two connected cases were overruled since the referendum: see *Essop v Home Office* [2017] UKSC 27.

2 Common tools of statutory interpretation

Introduction

This book is premised, in part at least, on the notion that indeed there *are* rules of statutory interpretation. The notion is supported by the basic truths that a judge must read, understand, and apply the text of a statute. Even if legislation were unambiguous and uncontroversial, this task, like all reading, requires some rules of language, otherwise all text would be meaningless. Once a text is ambiguous or controversial, the task of interpretation is elevated to an art, if only for the sake of consistency. Thus, it is inevitable that practices, or rules, will be developed, either by the legislature, or, as is largely the case in England and Wales, by the judges. This chapter is an attempt to map out a code, or points of reference, required by English law, by which any interpretation should be made, and thus by which the cases can be scrutinised.

Finding the rules

One might assume that the Interpretation Act 1978 would be the starting point for any discourse on statutory interpretation. However, the Act contains no general principles, just some very specific rules, such as that 'words importing the masculine gender include the feminine' and vice versa,[1] and a 'glossary of terms', providing a fixed meaning for, say, 'Secretary of State', 'Court of Appeal', 'month', and so on.[2]

Thus, the starting point is case law, and the rules it has developed, espoused, or inadvertently engaged when interpreting and applying legislation. Generally, although there is precedent on the meaning of a particular enactment, provision, clause, or just one word, there is a less formal structure of precedent on the rules of interpretation. There have been two growing erosions into this statement. These stem from the obligations to follow the case law and interpretive approaches of the European Court of Human Rights (ECtHR) and Court of Justice of the European Union ('CJEU', which may fall away following secession/the transitional period). These, and their influence on English law, are considered presently.

The next point to make is that just as divining the ratio decidendi of a judgment can be an inexact science, or even an art form, so is understanding any particular rule employed in a decision on the meaning of a piece of legislation.

1 Interpretation Act 1978, s 6 (unless the contrary intention appears).
2 ibid, Sch 1, s 5 (unless the contrary intention appears).

Judges are rarely explicit in their reasoning or terminology to explain their decisions, especially for the benefit of the academic observer, let alone a layperson. Further, once the observer *can* decide on a rule or approach employed in a particular decision, it is just as difficult to discern the reason for that choice. The high-minded suggest that a particular rule is chosen as the best means to identify the intention of Parliament,[3] while others suggest it is to arrive at a 'balanced conclusion',[4] or do justice in the particular case,[5] or, more basically, 'to ensure that the meritorious triumph and the dirty dogs lick their wounds'.[6] Student textbooks in common law jurisdictions tend to expound three basic 'rules of statutory interpretation': the literal, golden, and mischief (or purposive) rules. Francis Bennion asserts that statutory interpretation is vastly more complicated than that:

> The court does not 'select' any one of the many guides, and then apply it to the exclusion of the others. What the court does (or should do) is to take an overall view, weigh all the relative interpretative factors.[7]

Some are not merely suspicious of reducing interpretation to just three rules; they are cynical about the whole process as a subject for study. Lord Wilberforce once dubbed statutory interpretation 'a non-subject'.[8] Rupert Cross was only slightly less cynical when observing that the principles of statutory interpretation are 'incapable of arrangement',[9] and while there is no hierarchy of rules, 'some are, in general, less compelling than others'.[10]

Thus, the art, science, or 'non-subject' of statutory interpretation is seen by a body of scholarship as a rather ethereal matter. Nonetheless, there exist numerous ways of classifying and organising the 'rules'. Some scholars have dedicated much time and thought to this, with Bennion rejecting the habitual 'literal/golden/mischief' approach as a 'mistake'.[11] Instead, at one time, he alluded to 'six common law rules, a varying number of *rules* laid down by statute, eight *principles* derived from legal policy, ten presumptions as to legislative intention, and a collection of linguistic *canons* of construction . . .'.[12] Meanwhile, Cross, also discontented with the habitual approach, provides three 'basic rules'

3 *Cusack v London Borough of Harrow* [2013] UKSC 40, [58] (Lord Neuberger JSC, with whom Lords Sumption and Hughes JJSC agreed).

4 O Jones, *Bennion on Statutory Interpretation* (6th edn, LexisNexis 2013) Div 3, Pt XI, s 193.

5 See e.g. *Maunsell v Olins* [1975] AC 373 (HL) 391 (Lord Simon) espousing the golden rule.

6 Lord Browne-Wilkinson, in B Markesinis (ed) *The Impact of the Human Rights Act on English Law* (OUP, 1998) 22.

7 O Jones, *Bennion on Statutory Interpretation* (6th edn, LexisNexis 2013) Div 3, Pt XI, s 193.

8 HL Deb, 16 November 1966, vol 277, col 1294.

9 J Bell, G Engle, and R Cross, *Statutory Interpretation* (3rd edn, LexisNexis 2005) 39.

10 ibid, 41.

11 O Jones, *Bennion on Statutory Interpretation* (6th edn, LexisNexis 2013) Div 3, Pt XI, s 193, tracing this 'mistake' to a 1938 article by J Willis. 'Statutory interpretation in a nutshell' (1938) 16 *Canadian Bar Review* 1, 16.

12 F Bennion, *Statutory Interpretation* (3rd edn, Longman 1997) 104–105. See now O Jones, ibid, Introduction to Pt XI.

(context, evidence, different kinds of meaning), a number of internal and external aids, and a number of presumptions.[13] That said, the habitual three-rule approach still prevails in more general textbooks, learned articles, many judgments, and indeed the last Law Commission to consider the matter (led by a Law Lord).[14] Moreover, in cases within the purview of EU law (as most equality cases are), there is an obligation to adopt a purposive approach, whilst a looser set of obligatory interpretive practices apply under the Human Rights Act 1998. Thus, the habitual rules, including the European influences, will be the point of reference in the outline that follows, and indeed throughout this work.

An outline of the habitual rules

1 The literal rule[15]

The distinction between the literal and other rules is easily made. The literal rule will take the primary meaning of the words, whereas the others will allocate to them a secondary meaning (where possible), or modify them, add to them, or, at times, 'disapply' them. The starting point is that the literal rule supposes that the intention of Parliament is expressed by the words it employs in its statutes. This places Parliament's actual intention one step back from the process. As Lord Reid once observed: 'We often say that we are looking for the intention of Parliament, but that is not quite accurate. We are seeking the meaning of the words which Parliament used.'[16]

Although its roots lay in the Bill of Rights 1688,[17] the literal rule emerged to its full prominence during 1800s. The reference point for most aficionados today is *The Sussex Peerage* claim of 1844,[18] which coincided with the rise of parliamentary sovereignty.[19] The literal approach assumes that statutes are drafted with perfect precision and foresight, which, of course, is not always the case; thus, the literal rule can produce unforeseen and perhaps undesirable results. There are numerous reported examples; two prominent ones illustrate the difficulties. *Whiteley v*

13 J Bell, G Engle, and R Cross, *Statutory Interpretation* (3rd edn, LexisNexis 2005) 50.

14 *The Interpretation of Statutes* (Law Com No. 21, Scot Law Com No. 11, 1969) chaired by Lord Scarman. The Law Commission has since advised the purposive approach should be preferred the literal one where words in different language versions are inconsistent. 'Form and accessibility of the law applicable to Wales' (Law Com No. 366, 30 June 2015), < www.lawcom.gov.uk/project/the-form-and-accessibility-of-the-law-applicable-in-wales > accessed 10 April 2018.

15 Confusingly, sometimes the literal rule is referred to as the golden rule: e.g. 'Hence the so-called canons of construction, some of which are of relatively general application, such as the so-called golden rule (that words are prima facie to be given their ordinary meaning) . . .' (Lord Neuberger in *Cusack v Harrow* LBC [2013] UKSC 40, [60].

16 *Black-Clawson International Ltd v Papierwerke Waldhof-Aschaffenberg AG* [1975] AC 591 (HL) 613.

17 Article 9 of which provided 'the freedom of speech and debates or proceedings in Parlyament ought not to be impeached or questioned in any court or place out of Parlyament'.

18 (1844) XI Clark & Finnelly 85, 143; 8 ER 1034, 1057.

19 AV Dicey, *Introduction to the Study of the Law of the Constitution* (9th edn, Macmillan 1939) 39–40.

Chappell[20] concerned the offence, to 'impersonate a person entitled to vote' at an election.[21] The defendant was acquitted because, although he impersonated an elector, at the time of the election that elector had died, and thus no longer a 'person entitled to vote'. In *Fisher v Bell*,[22] a shopkeeper who displayed a flick knife with a price tag attached was found *not* guilty of 'offering for sale' an offensive weapon, contrary to the Restriction of Offensive Weapons Act 1959. At first, Lord Parker CJ admitted that such a decision was 'just nonsense'[23] but he went on to hold that Parliament must be taken to know the law of the land, and that that the phrase 'offer for sale' is a term of art confined (in contract law) to an offer that can be accepted to form a contract. Merely *exposing* goods for sale invites offers, but does not constitute an offer.

Casus omissus and the rule in Inco Europe

A particular consequence of the literal approach was the *casus omissus* rule.[24] The practical effect of this historical rule was that even where the omission is patently the result of a drafting error, the court will nonetheless persist in the fiction that it was intended. It took until the year 2000 for the House of Lords to address the matter, by effectively providing a new rule of interpretation, which in turn detached the *casus omissus* doctrine from the literal rule. The case was *Inco Europe Ltd v First Choice Distribution*.[25] Giving judgment for the House, Lord Nicholls said: '[T]he role of the courts in construing legislation is not confined to resolving ambiguities in statutory language. The court must be able to correct obvious drafting errors.'[26] Mindful of the constitutional aspect of this pronouncement, he added:

> This power is confined to plain cases of drafting mistakes. The courts are ever mindful that their constitutional role in this field is interpretative. They must abstain from any course which might have the appearance of judicial legislation. A statute is expressed in language approved and enacted by the legislature. So the courts exercise considerable caution before adding or omitting or substituting words.[27]

Lord Nicholls thus produced the following formula to be followed. Before exercising this power, a court had to be 'abundantly sure' of three matters:

20 (1868–1869) LR 4 QB 147.
21 Poor Law Amendment Act 1851 (14 & 15 Vict c 105) s 3.
22 [1961] 1 QB 394 (DC).
23 ibid, 399.
24 *Jones v Smart* (1785) 1 Term Reports 44, 52; 99 ER 963, 967 (Buller J); *Gladstone v Bower* [1960] 2 QB 384 (CA) 395–396 (Devlin LJ).
25 [2000] 1 WLR 586 (HL).
26 ibid, 592.
27 ibid.

(i) The intended purpose of the relevant provision;
(ii) through inadvertence, the draftsman had failed to give effect to the intended purpose of that provision; and
(iii) the substance of the provision Parliament would have made, although not necessarily the precise words Parliament would have used, had the error in the Bill been noticed.'[28]

The third requirement, he stressed was 'of crucial importance' because here lies the danger of judicial legislating. And even if these pre-requisites were met: 'Sometimes, . . . the court may find itself inhibited . . . The alteration in language may be too far-reaching. . . . Or the subject matter may call for a strict interpretation of the statutory language, as in penal legislation.'[29]

An example in the context of equality law arose in *Rowstock Ltd v Jessemey*.[30] The provision in question was section 108 of the Equality Act 2010, headed 'Relationships that have ended'. Sub-section (1) expressly outlaws discrimination that 'arises out of and is closely connected to a relationship that used to exist between them . . .' Sub-section (2) repeats this formula for harassment. The section concludes with sub-section (7): 'But conduct is not a contravention of this section in so far as it also amounts to victimisation . . . '. On the face of the Act, the matter is quite plain. The Act covers post-employment discrimination and harassment, but *not* post-employment victimisation. But put into context, it becomes obvious this is a drafting error.

The context begins with the 'first generation' of discrimination statutes,[31] which provided that an employer must not discriminate against a person 'employed by him'.[32] This appeared to exclude ex-employees from protection, until the CJEU, in *Coote v Granada*, ruled that such a position was incompatible with EU law.[33] The House of Lords responded by holding that 'employed by him' was less about an existing employment status, and more about an employment *connection*.[34] This purposive approach extended the legislation to cover post-employment victimisation (at the time, a species of discrimination), and reconciled domestic law with *Granada*.

As a result of *Granada*, the equality Directives specified that judicial and/or administrative procedures should be available to those complaining of discrimination even after the relationship in which the alleged discrimination occurred

28 ibid.
29 ibid.
30 [2014] 1 WLR 3615 (CA).
31 SDA 1975 and RRA 1976.
32 See SDA 1975, s 6(2) RRA 1976, s 4(2).
33 Case C-185/97 *Coote v Granada Hospitality* [1999] ICR 100, discussed further on pp 128 and 146.
34 *Rhys-Harper v Relaxion* [2003] 2 CMLR 44. See e.g. [37] ('benefits arising from' the employment relationship) and [44] (Lord Nicholls); [137]–[140], [162] (Lord Hobhouse). Lord Scott dissented [196], holding that it not being possible to ascertain the precise intention of Parliament, a purposive approach was inappropriate.

has ended.[35] Strictly speaking, this did not cover victimisation, which although outlawed by the Directives, is not expressed as a form of discrimination (unlike the domestic law at the time). Nonetheless, *Granada* remains good law (until UK secession, at least). Gradually, the domestic statutes were amended to comply with *Granada*. But when they were consolidated into the Equality Act 2010, victimisation was no longer defined as a form of discrimination, ***and*** there was no longer a provision for the ***victimisation*** of former employees, nor indeed for any 'post-relationship' victimisation, such as that of former (housing) tenants, (school) pupils, service users, and so on.

The context convinced the Court of Appeal that this was the result of a drafting error. Several explanations were advanced. First, until the Equality Act 2010, victimisation was designated as a form of discrimination, and would not need a dedicated sub-section; on this basis, section 108(1) would suffice. It might be that the drafter overlooked the redefining of victimisation, which uncoupled it from discrimination. But this does not explain the inclusion of section 108(7). The Explanatory Note to this stated that victimisation 'will be dealt with under the victimisation provisions and not under this section',[36] which suggests the drafter contemplated providing for post-relationship victimisation elsewhere. (This more accurately reflects the structure of the equality Directives.) But no reason could be fathomed in support of this theory.

Undeterred by the absence of a definite explanation for the error ('this beats me', bemoaned Underhill LJ[37]), the Court of Appeal added a 'section 108A', replicating the section 108(1) formula, but for victimisation. This bold step was taken under the cover of complying with EU law, and the *Ghaidan* approach.[38] As an alternative, the Court was able to achieve the same result using the *Inco Europe* guidelines. Given the context, the Court could be sure of the parliamentary intent, its error, and the solution should the drafter have become aware of the error.[39]

2 The golden rule

The golden rule was heavily promoted in the Victorian era, most notably by Lord Wensleydale.[40] Well into the 20th century, Lords Simon and Scarman, in *Stock v Frank Jones (Tipton)*,[41] offered a refined version. In combination, they suggested a departure from the literal approach was legitimate where the primary meaning produces some absurdity or anomaly not envisaged by the drafter and/or the result of a drafting error. But there is no definitive golden rule. At best, it is an

35 Race Directive 2000/43/EC, art 7; Framework Directive 2000/78/EC, art 9; Recast Directive 2006/54/EC, art 17 (first appearing in Equal Treatment (Amendment) Directive 2002/73/EC, art 1(5) and Recital 17, in force October 2005).
36 Explanatory Notes to the EA 2010, para 353.
37 [2014] 1 WLR 3615 [45(5)].
38 ibid [41]–[45], invoking *Godin-Mendoza v Ghaidan* [2004] 2 AC 557. See p 44.
39 ibid [50]–[53].
40 *Grey v Pearson* (1857) VI HL Cas (Clark's) 61, 106; 10 ER 1216, 1234.
41 [1978] 1 WLR 231 (HL) 237 (Lord Simon) 238–239 (Lord Scarman).

umbrella term encompassing a variety of anomalies and absurdities.[42] Bennion observed that 'the courts give a wide meaning to the concept of "absurdity", using to it to include virtually any result which is unworkable or impracticable, inconvenient, anomalous or illogical, futile or pointless, artificial, or productive of a disproportionate counter-mischief'.[43]

If an absurdity has been identified, the next step is the remedy. Lord Simon cautioned that the language must be 'susceptible' to any modification.[44] But this is no definitive rule, nor part of a pattern of development. Older cases can be found espousing an even more limited view,[45] whilst some modern ones respect Lord Simon's caution,[46] others ignore it, cite more convenient cases, and, 'if driven to it', would omit statutory words.[47]

3 The mischief rule

The mischief rule was set out in 1584 in *Heydon's Case*.[48] A more up-to-date rehearsal of the necessary conditions was provided by Lord Diplock in *Jones v Wrotham Park Settled Estates*:[49]

> First, it was possible to determine from . . . the Act . . . what the mischief was . . . to remedy; secondly, it was apparent that the draftsman and Parliament had by inadvertence overlooked . . . an eventuality that required to be dealt with if the purpose of the Act was to be achieved; and thirdly, it was possible to state with certainty what were the additional words that would have been inserted by the draftsman and approved by Parliament had their attention been drawn to the omission before the Bill passed into law.[50]

This third condition also governs the bounds of the court's power to rectify the statute:

> Unless this third condition is fulfilled any attempt by a court of justice to repair the omission in the Act cannot be justified as an exercise of its jurisdiction . . . .

42 O Jones, *Bennion on Statutory Interpretation* (6th edn, LexisNexis 2013) Div 5, Introduction to Pt XXI.
43 ibid, Pt XXI, s 312. These are Bennion's 'six types of absurdity'.
44 [1978] 1 WLR 231 (HL) 237.
45 E.g. *River Wear Commissioners v Adamson* (1877) 2 App Cas 743, 764–765 (Lord Blackburn): '[T]to justify the court in putting on them some other signification, which, though less proper, is one which the court thinks the words will bear.'
46 E.g. *Yarl's Wood Immigration Ltd v Bedfordshire Police Authority* [2010] QB 698 (CA); *Greenweb Ltd v Wandsworth LBC* [2009] 1 WLR 612 (CA).
47 *Dingmar v Dingmar* [2007] Ch 109 (CA) [70] (Jacob LJ) citing *Stone v Yeovil* (1876) 1 CPD 691, 701.
48 (1584) 3 Co Rep 7, 7b; 76 ER 637, 638.
49 [1980] AC 74 (HL).
50 ibid, 105.

> Such an attempt crosses the boundary between construction and legislation. It becomes a usurpation of a function which under the constitution of this country is vested in the legislature to the exclusion of the courts.[51]

The flavour contrasts with *Heydon's Case*, which was expressed more as a mandatory duty to cure the problem, and with no 20th century deference to parliamentary sovereignty, offered a seemingly limitless power to 'modify' the statute.[52] Another aspect of the old formula was updated for modern times. The common law is much less prevalent than in 1584, and so often there is little to be learnt by asking 'what was the common law before Act?', as required by the original formula.[53] Judges nowadays may well trace the previous state of affairs through a succession of statutes (be they codifying or not),[54] or consider the 'mischief' in wider terms than those merely governed by the common law.[55]

4 The purposive approach

The purposive approach resembles the mischief rule,[56] and at times overlaps with the golden rule. Indeed, the language of both often is used interchangeably.[57] The purposive rule arguably is wider in scope, for, as Lord Renton put it: '[I]n modern times many statutes are intended to do much more than merely correct defects in the common law as in Coke's day. Parliament now legislates for us from the cradle to the grave.'[58] Nowadays, much of legislation is not necessarily restricted to resolving a 'mischief', but enacted for the *advancement* of matters, such as providing for public services, the improvement of workers' rights, providing confidence in the consumer market, or (until succession, and perhaps beyond) harmonising the law across the EU. Hence, this approach

51 ibid, 105–106.

52 (1584) 3 Co Rep 7, 7b; 76 ER 637, 638.

53 ibid. See *The Interpretation of Statutes* (Law Com No. 21, Scot Law Com No. 11, 1969) 20.

54 See e.g. *Stevenson v Rogers* [1999] 2 QB 1028 (CA) tracing the phrase 'sale in the course of a business' in the Sale of Goods Act 1979 through various (amending) statutes back to the Sale of Goods Act 1893; *National Employers v Jones* [1990] 1 AC 24 (HL) by tracing the Sales of Goods Act 1979 back to the Factors Act 1823, the statutory word 'seller' was read to mean 'original owner' to prevent title to stolen goods passing through a thief.

55 See *Royal College of Nursing of the United Kingdom v Department of Health and Social Security* [1981] AC 800 (HL) (permitting a new, much longer, abortion procedure to be supervised by a nurse when the Abortion Act 1967 required 'a registered medical practitioner', because of the mischief of avoiding back-street abortions).

56 See e.g. *Manchester CC v McCann* [1999] QB 1214 (CA) 1222–1223, where the Court identified the mischief and applied the purposive approach.

57 See e.g. *Royal College of Nursing of the United Kingdom v Department of Health and Social Security* [1981] AC 800 (HL); *Yarl's Wood Immigration Ltd v Bedfordshire Police Authority* [2010] QB 698 (CA); *Stock v Frank Jones* [1978] 1 WLR 231 (HL) 236 (Lord Simon, who also conflates all three). See also *The Interpretation of Statutes* (Law Com No. 21, Scot Law Com No. 11, 1969) n 177.

58 Lord Renton, 'The interpretation of statutes' (1982) 9 J Legis 252, 258.

may be called upon more frequently than the mischief rule. In these cases, the starting point was generally tolerated, and any mischief addressed was less relevant than the goal to be achieved. Discrimination law may stand out as exceptional, straddling both ends of the spectrum. It assumes the status quo was intolerable, but sees its goal, which could be loosely put as equality of opportunity,[59] as something aspirational, rather than achievable overnight.

There are no precise limits to the rule. It is often expressed more in spirit than with a precise formula. In *R (Quintavalle) v Secretary of State for Health*, Lord Steyn adopted a famous American exposition of the purposive approach:

> Of course it is true that the words used, even in their literal sense, are the primary, and ordinarily the most reliable, source of interpreting the meaning of any writing: be it a statute, a contract, or anything else. But it is one of the surest indexes of a mature and developed jurisprudence not to make a fortress out of the dictionary; but to remember that statutes always have some purpose or object to accomplish, whose sympathetic and imaginative discovery is the surest guide to their meaning.[60]

Lord Steyn concluded: 'The qualification is that the degree of liberality permitted is influenced by the context, e.g. social welfare legislation and tax statutes may have to be approached somewhat differently.'[61]

This suggests that judges have a freer hand to realise a societal ambition. One reason for this may be because societal ambitions are more difficult to express in legalistic language than 'black letter' legislation, such as a tax statute. That may be so, but in modern times judges have also been encouraged, if not compelled, to take a purposive approach by EU membership and the Human Rights Act 1998.[62] The Law Commission once proposed[63] that the rule become universal by statutory command. This has not occurred, but, as will be seen in the cases under review, its use is far from universal, even in the 'social welfare' category of discrimination law.

5 Context

Whatever approach is taken, the words in question must be considered in context. This is the case even for the literal rule: the progenitor of which, *The Sussex Peerage*, involved the court using other parts of the statute to confirm its opinion.[64] House of Lords authority has for a long time considered context

59 A common theme for decades. See e.g. *Griggs v Duke Power* (US Sup Ct, 1971) 401 US 424, 431, and nowadays the Long Title to EA 2010. See further pp 65–68 and 77.
60 [2003] 2 AC 687 (HL) [21], citing *Cabell v Markham* 148 F 2d 737 (2nd Cir 1945), 739 (Learned Hand J).
61 ibid.
62 See, respectively, pp 31 and 45.
63 *The Interpretation of Statutes* (Law Com No. 21, Scot Law Com No. 11, 1969) para 81.
64 (1844) XI Clark & Finnelly 85, 143; 8 ER 1034, 1057.

in a broad sense. In *Attorney General v Prince Ernest Augustus of Hanover*,[65] Viscount Simonds said:

> [W]ords, and particularly general words, cannot be read in isolation: their colour and content are derived from their context. So it is that I conceive it to be my right and duty to examine every word of a statute in its context, and I use 'context' in its widest sense, . . . as including not only other enacting provisions of the same statute, but its preamble, the existing state of the law, other statutes *in pari materia*,[66] and the mischief which I can, by those and other legitimate means, discern the statute was intended to remedy.[67]

This points to a number sources as aids to interpretation. These can be categorised for convenience as *intrinsic* and *extrinsic* aids.

6 *Intrinsic aids to construction*

Preamble and long title

Although enacting parts of the statute, these serve different purposes and have, it seems, a varying status. The long title describes the Act. Preambles are rare in British legislation (in contrast to EU Directives), but when used, they set out the facts and assumptions on which the Act is based,[68] but cannot necessarily alter the meaning of plain enacted words.[69]

Other words and sections of the instrument

It is a 'cardinal rule'[70] that a statute ought not to be interpreted in a way that renders otiose any of its words.[71] As Viscount Simon said, in *Hill v William Hill (Park Lane) Ltd*:[72]

> When the legislature enacts a particular phrase in a statute the presumption is that it is saying something which has not been said immediately before. The rule that a meaning should, if possible, be given to every word in the

65 [1957] AC 436 (HL).
66 See 'In the same matter', p 28.
67 [1957] AC 436 (HL) 461.
68 J Bell, G Engle, and R Cross, *Statutory Interpretation* (3rd edn, LexisNexis 2005) 126.
69 *Attorney General v Prince Ernest Augustus of Hanover* [1957] AC 436 (HL). (Plaintiff granted British citizenship under an historical statute (Princess Sophia Naturalization Act 1705 (4 & 5 Anne c 16)) despite the preamble limiting its effect to those born within the lifetime of Queen Anne.)
70 *Re Florence Land Co* (1878) 10 Ch D 530 (CA), 544 (James LJ).
71 The Latin maxim sometimes used is *ut res magis valeat quam pereat*, meaning 'words are to be understood such that the subject matter may be more effective than wasted'.
72 [1949] AC 530 (HL).

> statute implies that, unless there is good reason to the contrary, the words add something which would not be there if the words were left out.[73]

More generally, there is a presumption, it seems, not to construe a word inconsistently with other parts of the statute.[74]

Marginal notes and headings

Unlike the long title, marginal notes (sometimes referred to as 'sidenotes') and headings are not debated in Parliament, but added by the government department processing the bill. All the same, they are fixed before royal assent and 'can be fairly regarded as representing the intention of Parliament'.[75]

There have been some highly conflicting authorities over the status of marginal notes, probably explainable by the policy adopted in individual cases. In *Chandler v DPP*,[76] on the one hand, the House of Lords held that they could not be used to aid construction, and in doing so confirmed the conviction of anti-nuclear weapon protesters for the statutory offence of being in or near a 'prohibited place', which was accompanied by the sidenote, 'Penalties for spying'.[77] On the other hand, just seven years later, the House of Lords took a different view. Here, a sidenote entitled, 'Offences antecedent to or in course of Winding Up' saved a company director from a conviction for fraud,[78] simply because, at the time, his company had not been wound up.[79] Thus, the presumption is somewhat selective, or at least subservient to policy.

More recently, the House of Lords took a more pragmatic view, which probably represents the current position:

> Account must, of course, be taken of the fact that these components were included in the Bill not for debate but for ease of reference. This indicates that less weight can be attached to them . . . . But it is another matter to be required by a rule of law to disregard them altogether . . . . Subject, of course, to the fact that they are unamendable, they ought to be open to consideration as part of the enactment when it reaches the statute book.[80]

73 ibid, 546–547.
74 *Clarke v Kato; Cutter v Eagle Star Insurance* [1998] 1 WLR 1647 (HL).
75 J Bell, G Engle, and R Cross, *Statutory Interpretation* (3rd edn, LexisNexis 2005) 124 (a view not expressed in Cross's own 1976 first edition).
76 [1964] AC 763.
77 Under the Official Secrets Act 1911, s 1(1) anyone who 'approaches or is in the neighbourhood of, or enters any prohibited place' commits an offence.
78 Companies Act 1948 332(3).
79 *DPP v Schildkamp* [1971] AC 1. See also *Adekeye v Post Office (No. 2)* [1997] ICR 110 (CA), 118–119 (discussed in Chapter 7, p 146).
80 *R v Montila (Steven William)* [2005] 1 All ER 113, [34] (Lord Hope, for the House).

Explanatory Notes

In 2007, the Office of Public Sector Information described Explanatory Notes thus:

> The text of the Explanatory Notes is produced by the Government Department responsible for the subject matter of the Act. The purpose of these Explanatory Notes is to make the Act of Parliament accessible to readers who are not legally qualified and who have no specialised knowledge of the matters dealt with. They are intended to allow the reader to grasp what the Act sets out to achieve and place its effect in context.[81]

In *R (Westminster City Council) v National Asylum Support Service*,[82] Lord Steyn provided guidance as to their use. First, the text of an Act did not have to be ambiguous before a court could take into account Explanatory Notes in order to understand its 'contextual scene'. Second, they are *always* admissible in so far as they 'can cast light on the objective setting or contextual scene of the statute, and the mischief at which it is aimed'. Third, having a closer connection to the 'shape of the proposed legislation', they will be sometimes be 'more informative and valuable' than pre-parliamentary texts, such as Law Commission reports, Green and White Papers. Fourth, constitutional reservations on the use of *Hansard*[83] are not engaged. And finally, any meaning put forward by the executive in an Explanatory Note may be used against it, should it place a contrary meaning before a court. But, the aims of the Government revealed by Explanatory Notes cannot be attributed to Parliament: 'The object is to see what is the intention expressed by the words enacted.' This last point endows Explanatory Notes with a subtle dual identity. On the one hand, they are the expressed will of the Government of the day, and *not* of Parliament. On the other, they can provide meaning to words enacted *by Parliament.*

All this suggests that resort to Explanatory Notes will be common, which indeed it is, especially when establishing the meanings in recent statutes, or hitherto uncontested provisions. The Supreme Court went further in *X v Mid Sussex Citizens Advice Bureau*,[84] and relied on a Government Explanatory *Booklet*, which accompanied a statutory instrument, to find that the instrument was not intended to apply to volunteer workers.

81 It states also that notes are 'optional' for Private Members Bills, < webarchive.nationalarchives.gov.uk/20070701085532/opsi.gov.uk/acts.htm > accessed 10 April 2018.

82 [2002] UKHL 38, [2]–[6].

83 See p 30.

84 [2013] ICR 249, [56] (Lord Mance, speaking for a unanimous Court). (SI 2003/1673, amending the Disability Discrimination Act 1995.)

7 Extrinsic aids to construction

A general caution about the use of extraneous sources to interpret a statute was expressed by Lord Diplock:

> The acceptance of the rule of law as a constitutional principle requires that a citizen, before committing himself to any course of action, should be able to know in advance what are the legal consequences that will flow from it. Where those consequences are regulated by a statute the source of that knowledge is what the statute says. In construing it the court must give effect to what the words of the statute would be reasonably understood to mean by those whose conduct it regulates.[85]

Given that few areas of law are consolidated, and even fewer codified, and the complexity of the drafting of some statutes, Lord Diplock's caution is based on rather idealistic grounds. Nonetheless, there are good reasons to stay within the instrument itself, not least because one should be able to trust the drafting of Parliament, which is well resourced nowadays. Further, if not the commoner, his or her lawyer at least would have a better chance of understanding a particular statute, rather having to trawl through a raft of extrinsic materials. That said, extrinsic aids are used occasionally. Three of the most prominent practices are highlighted below.

Statutes in pari materia *('in the same matter')*

The phrase *in pari materia* is used when courts give statutes on the same matter the same interpretation. The phrase has a loose meaning. It can relate to a statutes expressly stated to be read together, enabling the export of a qualification in one statute to a provision of another.[86] It can also be relevant to statutes forming part of a scheme, even if not expressed as such. The Sex Discrimination Act 1975 and the Race Relations Act 1976 had many obviously parallel provisions, which at times were similarly interpreted.[87] Likewise, the Equal Pay Act 1970 and the Sex Discrimination Act 1975 have been treated at times as a 'single comprehensive code'.[88] This harmony can break down where only one of the statutes, or parallel provisions, falls under EU law inviting a different interpretation.[89]

85 *Black-Clawson International Ltd v Papierwerke Waldhof-Aschaffenberg AG* [1975] AC 591 (HL) 638.

86 See *Phillips v Parnaby* [1934] 2 KB 299 (DC) where the Sale of Food (Weights and Measures) Act 1926, s 15(1) stated that the Act was to be construed as one with the Weights and Measures Acts 1878 to 1926.

87 For instance, the phrase 'on the grounds of' (sex or race) have been given parallel interpretations, e.g. to prevent 'benign motive defences': see *Grieg v Community Industry* [1979] ICR 356 (EAT); *R v Commission for Racial Equality ex p Westminster City Council* [1985] ICR 827 (CA).

88 *Shields v Coomes* [1978] 1 WLR 1408 (CA), 1425 (Bridge LJ) 1422–1423 (Orr LJ). Cited with approval by Wood J, *Enderby v Frenchay Health Authority* [1991] ICR 382 (EAT) 402H. See also *Rainey v Greater Glasgow Health Board* [1987] AC 224, 240B (Lord Keith).

89 See e.g. *Perera v Civil Service Commission* [1983] ICR 428 (CA), a case under the RRA 1976, not followed for the SDA 1975 by the EAT in deference to the Equal Treatment Directive 76/207/EEC: *Falkirk Council v Whyte* [1997] IRLR 560 (EAT).

When it comes to consolidating statutes, the courts have been more tentative. A consolidating Act's predecessors should not be used to aid construction unless there is an ambiguity. As Lord Simon once observed: 'The docked tail must not be allowed to wag the dog.'[90] This would suggest that reviewing previous enactments would be unhelpful, if not misleading, especially in the case of the Equality Act 2010, which is an example of consolidation, modification, refinement, codification,[91] and reversal.[92] But it would be an unduly obstinate judge who ignored a body of case law built up around a provision that has simply been re-enacted. The Explanatory Notes to the Equality Act 2010 expressly refer to the meaning afforded to terms used in its predecessors.[93] And, as noted above, in *Rowstock v Jessemey*,[94] a trawl through the legislative history was required to confirm a drafting error.

Official reports, White Papers, etc.

The history of the admissibility of official reports, such as Government-commissioned reports, Law Commission reports and White Papers is not one of certainty. In *Pepper v Hart*, Lord Browne-Wilkinson traced a bar to their use back to 1848.[95] By 1898, a commission report was relied upon, citing the mischief rule and *Heydon's Case*[96] as justification.[97] By the 1970s (if not earlier), it seems the practice was commonplace, and made without any discussion of the principle or any precedent for justification.[98] In *Shields v Coomes (Holdings) Ltd*, for instance, Bridge LJ cited the White Paper *Equality for Women*[99] as an aid to interpreting the Equal Pay Act 1970 to exclude hypothetical job responsibilities when making comparisons for an equal-pay claim.[100]

The use of such reports must be heavily distinguished from the use parliamentary debates, reported in *Hansard*, which is a more carefully controlled matter.

90 *Maunsell v Olins* [1975] AC 373 (HL) 392-393 (on behalf of Lord Diplock and himself). See also Lord Wilberforce in *Farrell v Alexander* [1977] AC 59, 72–73 (HL) 72–73.
91 E.g. s 15(2) codifying one part of *Lewisham LBC v Malcolm* [2008] 1 AC 1399 (HL).
92 E.g. s 15(1) reversing the main part of *Lewisham LBC v Malcolm* [2008] 1 AC 1399 (HL).
93 See e.g. (Revised Edition, August 2010) para 219: 'Section 64(2) is a new provision which is intended to ensure that the effect of pre-existing case law *Macarthys Ltd v Smith* (Case 129/79. . .) is maintained: that a comparator need not be someone who is employed at the same time as the person making a claim under these provisions, but could be a predecessor in the job.'
94 [2014] 1 WLR 3615 (CA). See p 20.
95 [1993] AC 593 (HL) 630, citing *Salkeld v Johnson* (1848) 2 Exch 256, 273; 154 ER 487, 495.
96 (1584) 3 Coke 7a, 7 b; 76 ER 637, 638.
97 *Eastman Photographic Materials Company v The Comptroller-General of Patents, Designs, and Trade-Marks* [1898] AC 571 (HL) 573–574.
98 See e.g. *Black-Clawson International v Papierwerke Waldhof-Aschaffenburg AG* [1975] AC 591, 638 (Lord Diplock) 622 (Viscount Dilhorne) and more cautiously 646–647 (Lord Simon). See also *Pepper v Hart* [1993] AC 593 (HL), 630, 633, 635, 640 (Lord Browne-Wilkinson) *Wilson v First County Trust Ltd (No. 2)* [2004] 1 AC 816 (HL) [56], [64] (Lord Nicholls).
99 Home Office (Cmnd 5724, 1974).
100 [1978] 1 WLR 1408 (CA) 1425.

Using Hansard

The reasons given for excluding extraneous materials[101] apply with all the more force towards parliamentary materials. At the root of this is the settlement of 1688. Save for the occasional indulgence,[102] the exclusionary rule was been applied rigidly until 1993, when the House of Lords broke this abstinence. In *Pepper v Hart*,[103] Lord Browne-Wilkinson's majority speech set the parameters for resort to parliamentary materials, which have since been both qualified and embellished. As things stand now, if the legislation (1) was ambiguous or obscure, or led to an absurdity, or (2) did not appear compatible with, or properly to implement, EU law[104] or rights under the European Convention on Human Rights (ECHR),[105] then (3) resort may be made to one or more statements by a minister or other promoter of the Bill together, if necessary, with such other parliamentary material as might be necessary to understand such statements and their effect, if (4) the effect of such statements was clear. In addition, no materials subsequent to the introduction of the legislation to Parliament may be relied upon,[106] unless (it seems) it is a matter of EU law and the matter in question arose during the passage of the Bill.[107]

Several Law Lords subsequently have sounded warnings against an overly liberal use of *Hansard*, stating that the conditions should be complied with strictly.[108] Indeed, writing extra-judicially, Lord Steyn considered that the doctrine raised conceptual and constitutional difficulties, in that it assumes the

101 Set out by Lord Diplock, *Black-Clawson International Ltd v Papierwerke Waldhof-Aschaffenberg AG* [1975] AC 591 (HL) 638. See p 28, text to n 85.

102 Notably, Lord Upjohn in *Beswick v Beswick* [1968] AC 58 (HL) 105, referring to a report by the Joint Committee on Consolidation Bills, and Lord Denning in *Sagnata Investments v Norwich Corporation* [1971] 2 QB 614 (CA) 623–625, using *Hansard* in support of his dissent.

103 [1993] AC 593 (HL).

104 *U v W (Attorney General Intervening) (No. 1)* [1997] Fam Law 403 (Fam).

105 *Wilson v First County Trust (No. 2)* [2004] 1 AC 816 (HL) [65] (Lord Nicholls), [116] (Lord Hope), [173] (Lord Scott), [178] (Lord Rodger).

106 [1993] AC 593 (HL) 617B (Lord Bridge), 620D (Lord Oliver), 635A and 640C (Lord Browne-Wilkinson). See also *Melluish (Inspector of Taxes) Appellant v BMI (No. 3)* [1996] AC 454 (HL) 481–482. In *R v Secretary of State for the Environment, Transport and the Regions, ex p Spath Holme Ltd* [2001] 2 AC 349 (HL), Lord Bingham said (393): 'It is one thing to rely on a statement by a responsible minister or promoter as to the meaning or effect of a provision in a bill thereafter accepted without amendment. It is quite another to rely on a statement made by anyone else, or even by a minister or promoter in the course of what may be lengthy and contentious parliamentary exchanges . . . .'

107 *U v W (No.1)* [1997] Fam Law 403 (Fam) following *Three Rivers DC v Bank of England (No. 2)* [1996] 2 All ER 363 (QB) 366 (Clarke J). See also *Wilson v First County Trust Ltd (No. 2)* [2004] 1 AC 816 (HL) [118] (Lord Hope).

108 See e.g. *Melluish (Inspector of Taxes) Appellant v BMI (No. 3)* [1996] AC 454 (HL), 481–482 (Lord Browne-Wilkinson, for the House); *R v Secretary of State for the Environment, Transport and the Regions, ex p Spath Holme Ltd* [2001] 2 AC 349 (HL), 393 (Lord Bingham) 399–400 (Lord Nicholls) 408 (Lord Hope) and 414–415 (Lord Hutton); *R v A (No. 2)* [2002] 1 AC 45 (HL) 79 (Lord Hope).

fiction of group (parliamentary) intention,[109] and that the Government and not Parliament makes the law.[110] This was in addition to the practical problems and expense of legal advisors having to study *Hansard* for every case, per chance something indicative could be found. In this sense *Pepper v Hart* was an 'expensive luxury'.[111] Maxwell adds that there is a danger that during debates, members might try to influence a statute's interpretation by expressing particular views on its purpose, even though they remain unexpressed in the Bill itself.[112] Lord Steyn's conclusion was that the ratio of *Pepper v Hart* could be confined 'to be used only against the executive when it seems to go back on an assurance given to Parliament'.[113]

But this was not supported by the evidence. Not long after *Pepper v Hart*, the House of Lords (including Lord Browne-Wilkinson) invoked *Hansard* in *support* of the Government's case (and *against* a vulnerable individual vis-à-vis the state).[114] It was also used by the Court of Appeal in a discrimination case when not strictly necessary.[115] Even after Lord Steyn's caution, examples can be found of the use of parliamentary materials when Lord Browne-Wilkinson's conditions are met.[116] In one instance, the EAT readily referred to *Hansard* without even reference to *Pepper v Hart* or its criteria.[117]

These are the tools traditionally invoked by the common law, although the influence of the European institutions is already apparent. So it is now necessary to consider their principles and role in the interpretative process.

The influence of the European courts

Any vulnerability to ideological predilections noted in Chapter 1 may be checked somewhat by the two external influences on interpretation, the Court of Justice of the European Union (CJEU), and the European Court of Human Rights ('Strasbourg'). The effect of the European Communities Act 1972 (hereafter EC Act 1972) is that domestic law falling within EU jurisdiction *must* be interpreted according to the approach taken by the Court of Justice. Under the Human Rights

109 '*Pepper v Hart;* A Re-examination' (2001) 21 OJLS 59, 64.
110 ibid, 68.
111 ibid, 63. See also Lord MacKay's dissent, *Pepper v Hart* [1993] AC 593 (HL) 614–615, and *Beswick v Beswick* [1968] AC 58 (HL) 73–74 (Lord Reid).
112 P Maxwell, *On the Interpretation of Statutes* (12th edn, Sweet & Maxwell 1969) 51.
113 (2001) 21 OJLS 59, 70.
114 *Chief Adjudication Officer v Foster* [1993] AC 754 (HL). (Regulations (SI 1987/1967) redefining 'severe disability' by factoring in 'non-dependant' cohabitants were intra virus, even though this did not relate to the claimant's disability.)
115 See *Clark v Novacold* [1999] ICR 951, 964, discussed on p 210 et al.
116 See e.g. *Lewisham LBC v Malcolm* [2008] 1 AC 1399 (HL) (discussed in Chapter 9); *Morgan v Fletcher* [2009] UKUT 186 (LC); *R (Oxfordshire and Buckinghamshire Mental Health NHS Foundation Trust) v Oxfordshire CC* [2010] EWHC 530 (Admin).
117 *Usdaw v Ethel Austin* [2013] ICR 1300 (EAT), effectively reversed Case C-80/14, [2015] ICR 675.

Act 1998, domestic courts have a less well defined (and more debated) obligation to follow the approach of the Strasbourg Court on matters falling within the European Convention on Human Rights. The approaches to interpretation by these European Courts are markedly different to their English counterparts.

The Court of Justice has concrete goals, notably an 'ever closer union among the peoples of Europe', and with it a collection of complementary and relatively harmonious principles and rules; chief among these is the teleological approach. Strasbourg does not have a singular constitutional target, but rather an approach centred on the singular theme of human rights. In doing so, it uses the teleological, 'living instrument', and proportionality, principles of interpretation, offset by the more pragmatic 'margin of appreciation' afforded to state defendants. Each court will be taken in turn.

The approach of the EU Court of Justice

Most of Britain's discrimination law derives from, or is subservient to, EU law. Thus, the interpretation afforded to this legislation by the Court of Justice is vital to the meaning of domestic law. Of course, it is not enough to know the meaning attributed to this or that directive. In order to interpret domestic legislation falling within the ambit of EU legislation, domestic tribunals must understand the Court of Justice's approach to statutory interpretation, which is quite different from the traditional English methods. The approach of the Court of Justice encompasses three principal canons of interpretation: literal, schematic, and teleological. However, there is more to it than just a different arrangement of canons. The Court is under the influence of the continental civil-law system, and tasked to oversee a unique project set out by the Treaties of the Union. The rules must be appreciated in this context to be understood.

1 Context

From the inception of the European Economic Community (EEC) in 1957, the Court has taken upon itself a mission to play its part in fulfilling the objectives of the Treaty of Rome and its successors. These objectives are an increase in integration, an 'ever closer union among the peoples of Europe'[118] and economic and social progress, by the elimination of barriers to the movement of capital, workers, goods, and the right to establish and receive services.[119] These political and economic objectives inform many legal principles upon which the Court relies when interpreting EU legislation. Thus, it is necessary to consider some of the relevant principles before mapping out the basic rules of interpretation.

118 See preambles to the (founding) Treaty of Rome 1957, and the most recent the TEU and the Treaty of the Functioning of the European Union (TFEU).

119 Respectively, art 67 EEC (see now TFEU, art 63); art 48 EEC (45); arts 23–31 EEC (28–37); arts 52 and 59 (49 and 56).

The principles considered below are: supremacy of EU law; direct effect of EU law; and the 'general principles' of equality, proportionality, and subsidiarity.

Supremacy

From the earliest days of the EEC, the Court, in *Van Gend en Loos*,[120] asserted that the EEC was not merely an international treaty between nation states but it has a constitutional nature, with member states ceding sovereignty to the Union. The Court is an integral part of this constitution. This means that general rules of interpretation associated with public international law do not necessarily hold here. Most notably, the Court has no hesitation in encroaching upon the sovereignty of a member state, should it be necessary in deference to the Treaties. In the extreme, the Court will declare domestic legislation invalid as far as it offends EU law.[121]

This principle of supremacy also applies to judgments of the Court of Justice, and, in particular, its approach to statutory interpretation. In *R v Henn and Darby*,[122] the House of Lords reminded domestic courts that:

> Section 3(1) of the European Communities Act 1972 expressly provides that the meaning or effect of any of the Treaties 'shall be treated as a question of law' (and, if not referred to the European Court, be for determination as such in accordance with the principles laid down by and any relevant decision of the European Court).[123]

Section 3 has since been modified to include all EU instruments, including directives.[124] This calls for a brief account of the relevant principles laid down by the Court of Justice.

2 Enforcement in member states

Principles of direct applicability, direct effect, and indirect effect, relate to the enforceability of EU law. Directly applicable laws are ones that become part of the internal domestic legal system. Section 2(1) of the EC Act 1972 confirms that all Community law is directly applicable in the United Kingdom. This does not necessarily make it enforceable *by* individuals (direct effect), or *against* private parties (horizontal direct effect). At this stage, a member state can only be

120 Case 26/62 NV *Algemene Transport- en Expeditie Onderneming van Gend en Loos v Nederlandse Administratie der Belastingen* [1963] ECR 1, paras 12–13.

121 Case C-213/89 *Factortame v Secretary of State for Transport* [1990] ECR I-2433. The offending provision does not necessarily become non-existent: Joined cases C-10/97 to C-22/97 *IN. CO.GE '90* [1998] E.C.R. I-6307, para 21.

122 [1981] 1 AC 850. See pp 42.

123 ibid, 905 (Lord Diplock, giving judgment for the House).

124 European Union (Amendment) Act 2008, Sch 1(1) para 1.

called to account by the Commission or other member states.[125] Thus, the precise 'effect' within domestic law of any particular EU provision can be critical to individual enforceability.

In addition to supremacy, *Van Gend en Loos* established a pillar of enforceability: that individuals should be able – as a far as possible – to enforce EU law. The Court's enthusiasm for individual enforcement is based on two notions. First, '[t]he vigilance of individuals interested in protecting their rights creates an effective control additional to that entrusted . . . to the diligence of the Commission and the member-States.'[126] Second, as noted above, the EU is more than an international treaty between states – it is expressed to be for the benefit of its citizens: 'The Union's aim is to promote peace, its values, and the well-being of its peoples.'[127] As will be seen, this enthusiasm has led to a number of enforcement methods, which, ironically perhaps, are not particularly easy for the individual to comprehend.

The direct effect of treaties

To be directly effective, a treaty provision must be clear, unconditional, non-discretionary, and final. Mere enabling provisions of the treaties are not directly effective. Thus, Article 19, TFEU, is not directly effective under this test. It provides that

> the Council, acting unanimously in accordance with a special legislative procedure and after obtaining the consent of the European Parliament, may take appropriate action to combat discrimination based on sex, racial or ethnic origin, religion or belief, disability, age or sexual orientation.

Clearly, this is neither unconditional nor final. By contrast, the two principal forms of discrimination addressed in the treaties – nationality[128] and equal pay[129] – have been held to be directly effective, and thus enforceable by individuals against either private or state parties.[130]

The direct effect of directives

Directives are quite different in nature from treaty articles and other secondary legislation, such as Regulations (directly applicable) and Decisions (binding on

125 Under TFEU, arts 258 and 259, respectively.
126 Case 26/62, [1963] ECR 1, para 13.
127 Art 3(1) TEU (ex 2 TEU).
128 Art 18 TFEU (ex 12 TEC).
129 Art 157 TFEU (ex 141 TEC).
130 See e.g. (nationality) Case C-281/98 *Roman Angonese v Cassa di Risparmio di Bolzano SpA* [2000] ECR I-4139, Case C-415/9 *Royal Club Liegois SA v Bosman* [1995] ECR I-4921; and (equal pay) Case 43/75 *Defrenne v SABENA (No 2)* [1976] ECR 455, para 39 ('since Article 119 is mandatory in nature, the prohibition on discrimination between men and women applies not only to the action of public authorities, but also extends to all agreements which are intended to regulate paid labour collectively, as well as to contracts between individuals'.).

the addressee):[131] 'A directive shall be binding, as to the result to be achieved, upon each member state to which it is addressed, but shall leave to the national authorities the choice of form and methods.'[132] On the face of it, directives bind only member states, 'as to the result to be achieved' and provide individuals with no cause of action. However, in line with its 'vigilance' philosophy, the Court has extended somewhat their enforceability. The opportunity arises when a member state fails to implement a directive within its time limit, or fails to implement it properly. Here, the Court reasons, the culpable member state cannot rely on such a failure to evade its obligation to implement the directive and the broader treaty objectives. Hence, in such a case, the Court strives to permit individuals to enforce their rights under the directive in question, at the least against the culpable member state.[133] It thus operates as a form of estoppel. The principle holds even where the enabling treaty article is not directly effective.[134] This is relevant to domestic equality law, as some dedicated discrimination directives have been made under (what is now) Article 19, TFEU (not itself directly effective). It means that conflicting domestic law must defer even to these directives.[135]

There are some limits to this doctrine, however. First, the directive provision must impose an obligation on the member state that is 'unconditional and sufficiently precise'.[136] Second, the estoppel nature of this reasoning means that it is only the state that can be sued. Private parties, not being culpable for the failure to implement, cannot be 'estopped' from relying on any non-compliance. In legal parlance, this limit means that directives have 'vertical', but not 'horizontal', direct effect. In the context of discrimination law, the most common situation affected by this arises where a worker is calling on directive rights. Here, the identity of the employer becomes crucial. If it is an emanation of the state, such as a local authority or the National Health Service, the employer is bound by the directive. Otherwise, it is not.[137]

3 Circumventing direct effect

These logical limits to the direct-effect doctrine have not prevented the Court devising ways of circumventing this limit on horizontal direct effect. There are

131 TFEU, art 228.

132 ibid.

133 Case 148/78 *Pubblico Ministero v Ratti* [1979] ECR 1629, para 22. See also Case 41/74 *Van Duyn v Home Office* [1974] ECR 1337, paras 9–15, where the Court rejected an argument that the choice of a directive over a regulation meant that it was never intended to be directly applicable.

134 Case 51/76 *Verbond van Nederlandse Ondernemingen v Inspecteur der Invoerrechten en Accijnzen* [1977] ECR 113.

135 ibid.

136 Case 8/81 *Becker v Finanzamt Münster-Innenstadt* [1982] ECR 53. See also Case 148/78 *Pubblico Ministero v Ratti* [1979] ECR 1629, para 23.

137 Case 152/84 *Marshall v Southampton and SW Hants AHA* [1986] ECR 723. See also Case C-91/92 *Faccini Dori v Recreb Srl* [1994] ECR I-3325.

three principal devices: incidental direct effect; indirect effect; and the *Francovich* principle. In addition, the Court has, on occasion, bypassed the whole issue by adopting a 'general principle' of equality, discussed in the next section.

The first, commonly referred to as *incidental direct effect*, arises where domestic legislation conflicts with a directive. If the private defendant is relying on the domestic measure, then a court is obliged to disregard the measure in favour of the directive.[138] The second method of circumvention is *indirect effect*. This doctrine requires domestic courts to interpret domestic legislation as far as possible to accord with a directive; this applies whether or not the domestic law in question was enacted *before or after* the directive.[139] The third method of circumventing the limit to direct effect has become known as the *Francovich* principle, named after the case,[140] which held it possible for a private individual to sue its government in circumstances where the government's failure to implement a directive caused that individual loss.

4 Some general principles of interpretation

The Court also has adopted a number of *general principles* of law, which it will use to interpret legislation. The most relevant to this book are equality, proportionality, subsidiarity, and uniformity.

The principle of equality

The equality principle applies, it seems, to all activities within EU competence, and to all legislation within the Court's domain, embracing activities well beyond the traditional human-rights areas commonly associated with equality law.[141] But for a successful justification defence, the Court was prepared to strike down two directives for indirectly discriminating on the ground of sex, contrary to a 'fundamental right' forming a general principle of EU law.[142] This right was expressed in a treaty.[143] It cannot be assumed from this that the Court would address discrimination on *any* personal characteristics in a vacuum, that is in a scenario absent of any dedicated discrimination legislation,[144] although the general principle *can* be used

138 Case C-129/94 *Criminal Proceedings against Bernaldez* [1996] ECR I-1829. Spanish legislation absolving motor insurers for damage caused by drink-driving contradicted the Motor Insurance Directive 72/166/EEC; see now Directive 2009/103/EC. See also Case C-194/94 *CIA Security International SA v Signalson SA* [1996] ECR I-2201.

139 Case C-106/89 *Marleasing SA v La Comercial Internacional de Alimentación* [1990] ECR I-4135. See e.g. *Litster v Forth Dry Dock & Engineering* [1990] 1 AC 546 (HL).

140 Case C-6/90 *Francovich v Italy* [1991] ECR I-5357.

141 E.g. Case 103/77 *Royal Scholten-Honig (Holdings) v Board for Agricultural Produce* [1978] ECR 2037, paras 26–27 on equality in agricultural markets.

142 Case C-25/02 *Rinke v Ärztekammer Hamburg* [2003] ECR I-8349.

143 Art 141 EC (see now Art 157 TFEU); noted by the Opinion of AG Geelhoed, ibid, paras 76 and 80.

144 See Case C-249/96 *Grant v SW Trains* [1998] ECR I-621.

to extend existing equality legislation beyond its defined procedural boundaries. In *Mangold v Helm*, citing the general principal of equality, the Court held that the Framework Directive applied before its date for implementation was due.[145]

This suggests that in the field of discrimination and personal characteristics, the general principle of equality extends no further than those characteristics already expressed in dedicated EU legislation.[146] It may be that the introduction of the Charter of Fundamental Rights leads the Court, at least when reviewing EU or domestic law, to incorporate a broader range of personal characteristics into its general principle of equality. The Charter became binding with the Lisbon Treaty in December 2009, and Article 21 extends the grounds of discrimination to those 'such as sex, race, colour, ethnic or social origin, genetic features, language, religion or belief, political or any other opinion, membership of a national minority, property, birth disability, age or sexual orientation'.

The jurisprudence on the Charter is developing in a slow, piecemeal, fashion. What we do know is that it has the same legal status as the treaties,[147] expresses existing rights and principles, making them 'more visible', but does not create new ones,[148] and cannot be relied upon on matters beyond EU law.[149] It is worth noting in this context, contrary to the Advocate General's Opinion that the Court refused to recognise 'combined discrimination' (sexual orientation and age) as this the Framework Directive did not expressly provide for this.[150] No reference was made to the Charter, but this could be read to mean that the Court assumed the Charter could not supplement the Directive to broaden its definition of discrimination. The Court has invoked the Charter when building on Mangold to extend the procedural reach of existing legislation. In *Kücükdeveci v Swedex*, the Court cited Article 21 when disapplying conflicting domestic law and giving the Framework Directive 'horizontal effect' in an age discrimination case between private parties.[151] And in *CHEZ v Komisia*, the Court cited the Charter 'in support' of its holding that a non-Roma person affected by the challenged measure could sue for discrimination against a Roma community.[152]

Some grounds (e.g. social origin, property, birth) included in Article 21 are beyond those expressed in the dedicated discrimination Directives, while the

145 Case C-144/04 *Mangold v Helm* [2005] ECR I-9981, paras 74–75.

146 See e.g. Council Directives 2004/113/EC and 2006/54/EC (sex) 2000/43/EC (race) and 2000/78/EC (religion or belief, disability, age or sexual orientation); Art 45 TFEU (ex 39 TEC) (nationality of workers of member states).

147 Case C-476/11 *HK Danmark v Experian A/S* [2014] 1 CMLR 42, para 19.

148 Joined Cases C-411/10 and C-493/10 *NS v Secretary of State for the Home Department* [2013] QB 102, para 119.

149 Art 51(1). See e.g. Case C-122/15 *'C' (Finland)* [2017] CMLR 2 (taxation of pensions falls outside of Framework Directive and so Charter not applicable) paras 28–29.

150 Case C-443/15 *Parris v Trinity College Dublin* [2016] ICR 313 (judgment); [2016] Pens L R 249 (AG), para 155.

151 Case C-555/07 *Kücükdeveci v Swedex GmbH & Co KG* [2010] ECR I-365, para 21. See also Case C-441/14 *Dansk Industri (DI) v Rasmussen's Estate* [2016] IRLR 552.

152 Case C-83/14 *CHEZ Razpredelenie Bulgaria AD v Komisia za zashtita ot diskriminatsias* [2016] 1 CMLR 14 [58]. See also [AG53]. See further p 206.

introductory phrase 'such as' suggests that Article 21 is not confined even to its broad list of grounds. Indeed, the Court has held that Article 21 was engaged against a state employer in a case of discrimination on the ground of employment status (civil service).[153] The case was unusual. Employees with a disability, save for civil servants, were afforded extra protection against dismissal. As the extra protection amounted to positive action, it came within the Framework Directive,[154] enabling the Court, apparently, to invoke the Charter 'within the implementation of EU law'.[155]

Article 47 of the Charter could prove equally important to discrimination issues. It provides a right to a fair trial and effective remedy (in the same terms as ECHR, Article 6). The general principle of effective remedy underpinned the CJEU decision in *Coote v Granada*, extending the reach of the victimisation provisions in sex discrimination legislation to protect former employees.[156] Moreover, it has been used to provide access to race discrimination legislation. In *Benkharbouche v Embassy of Sudan*,[157] the English Court of Appeal (via the EC Act 1972) gave Article 47 horizontal effect to disapply the State Immunity Act 1978, allowing workers to sue their otherwise immune employers under the Working Time and Race Directives.[158] In some cases, it may be that where offending domestic legislation cannot be read down to comply with the European Convention on Human Rights (via the Human Rights Act 1998), the Charter may prove a more effective vehicle of enforcement.

Thus far, it seems that the general principle of equality can be used to inform the interpretation of any dedicated equality legislation and, especially in the light of the Charter, extend the procedural reach of such legislation beyond any defined boundaries. It remains to be seen how the case law progresses in the Court of Justice, and of course, how the UK's secession affects the status in the UK of the general principle of equality and the Charter.[159]

153 Case C-406/15 *Milkova v Izpalnitelen director na Agentsiata za privatizatsia i sledprivatizatsionen control* [2017] IRLR 566.
154 Framework Directive 2000/78/EC, art 7(2).
155 Case C-406/15 *Milkova*, para 54.
156 Case C-185/97 *Coote v Granada Hospitality* [1999] ICR 100, paras 21–22. See further pp 128 and 146.
157 [2016] QB 347. Affirmed [2017] UKSC 62 [78].
158 Respectively, Directive 2003/88/EC and Directive 2000/43/EC. Domestic law rights, such as the national minimum wage, and unfair dismissal, remained non-justiciable.
159 On 30 March 2017, the UK Government announced that the Charter was not part of *acquis* of EU law to be 'converted' into domestic law upon secession: Department for Exiting the European Union, *Legislating for the United Kingdom's Withdrawal from the European Union* (White Paper, Cm 9446, 30 March 2017) paras 2.21–2.25. (Expressed, European Union (Withdrawal) Bill 2017, cl 5(4).) The UK had 'opted out' of the Charter (TEU, Protocol 30) although the efficacy of this was questionable because it merely stated that the Charter could not create new rights within the UK, a principle it was claimed applied to all member states. See e.g. House of Lords European Union Committee, *Tenth Report* (HL 2007–2008 62-I) Ch 3, [5.84]–[5.111].

Proportionality

Proportionality is the principle by which derogations from EU law are scrutinised by the Court of Justice.[160] It is the rough equivalent to '*Wednesbury* reasonableness'[161] used traditionally by English courts in cases of judicial review, although proportionality tends to be a stricter test.

Its importance to discrimination law cannot be overstated. It is the touchstone for any justification defence to a prima facie case of discrimination. In *Bilka*,[162] the Court provided a systematic objective justification defence, tailored for *indirect* (sex) discrimination. Fusing the defence with the principle of proportionality, it produced the three part '*Bilka* test'. Any challenged practice may be justified only if 'the means chosen to attain this objective meet a genuine need of the enterprise, are suitable for attaining the objective in question and are necessary for that purpose'.[163] In *Johnston v RUC* the Court went on the hold that the proportionality principle applies to any derogation, including from *direct* discrimination.[164]

Where a defence is based on social policy, the *Bilka* test is modified. Defendants must still show that the practice reflects a necessary aim of its social policy and is suitable and necessary for achieving that aim, but at the same time, they are afforded a broad margin of discretion in choosing the appropriate means to achieve that policy. But the margin of discretion is not so broad to have the effect of frustrating the implementation of the fundamental principle of equal treatment. Mere generalisations will not suffice.[165]

The difference between the *Bilka* test and the traditional English 'reasonableness' scrutiny became starkly apparent in the field of discrimination law. The original defence to indirect discrimination in the British legislation provided that it must be 'justifiable irrespective of sex [or race]'.[166] The English courts' interpretation of this was heavily laden with the concept of reasonableness. In 1982, the Court of Appeal in *Ojutiku v Manpower Services Commission*[167] *contrasted* 'necessity' with the statutory word 'justifiable'. Kerr LJ stated that 'justifiable . . . clearly applies a lower standard than . . . necessary'.[168] Eveleigh LJ considered it to mean 'something . . . acceptable to right-thinking

160 Now codified, art 5(4) TEU.
161 *Associated Provincial Picture Houses Ltd v Wednesbury Corporation* [1948] 1 KB 223 (CA).
162 Case 170/84 *Bilka-Kaufhaus GmbH v Weber von Hartz* [1986] ECR 1607.
163 ibid, para 37.
164 Case 222/84 *Johnston v Chief Constable of the Royal Ulster Constabulary* [1986] ECR 1651, para 38.
165 Case C-167/97 *Seymour-Smith* [1999] ICR 447, paras 69–77 (Sex discrimination/equal pay); Case C-208/05 *ITC Innovative Technology Center GmbH v Bundesagentur für Arbeit* [2007] ECR I-181, paras 40–41 (Nationality discrimination).
166 SDA 1975, s 1(1)(b); RRA 1976, s 1(1)(b).
167 [1982] ICR 661 (CA).
168 ibid, 670.

people as sound and tolerable'.[169] Following this, Balcombe LJ, in *Hampson v Department of Education*,[170] created the '*Hampson* (balancing) test', which weighs the discriminatory effect of the challenged practice against the reasonable needs of the defendant.[171]

The difference was illustrated in *Enderby v Frenchay Health Authority*,[172] which also provides a foretaste of the cases to come in this book. Here, the defendant health authority was trying to justify a 40 per cent difference in pay between speech therapists (98 per cent female) and pharmacists (63 per cent female). As women were over-represented in the lower-paid group, the health authority was obliged to justify the difference. It argued that market forces caused the difference. But the evidence was that only an extra 10 per cent pay was needed to recruit a sufficient number of pharmacists. Thus, there existed a less discriminatory alternative of paying the pharmacists a 10 per cent premium. In the UK, the EAT[173] applied the *Hampson* test and weighed the 40 per cent difference in pay against the need for sufficient pharmacists. Given that stark choice, the EAT held that the difference in pay was justified. In other words, the leeway provided by the less strict *Hampson* approach meant that employers were not bound to use the least discriminatory practice available. The CJEU held that the pay difference could only be justified to the proportion that market forces required (10 per cent). The existence of the less discriminatory alternative meant that the practice (a 40 per cent pay difference) could not be justified. For the CJEU, proportionality meant *no more than* necessary. *Bilka* had been in the books for some six years when the EAT came to decide *Enderby*. Yet, not only did it fail to implement the statutory purpose of equal pay legislation, but also it failed to appreciate its obligation to do so, a theme that will become increasingly apparent during the scrutiny of the cases later in this book (beginning with Chapter 5).

Subsidiarity

In a formal sense, this doctrine defines the boundary between EU and member state competence to legislate. It operates as a companion to proportionality, to control EU competence. Subsidiarity is now enshrined in TEU, Article 5. Less formally though, the Court operates the principle regularly. One of

169 ibid, 668.

170 [1989] ICR 179 (CA).

171 ibid, 196. In Parliament, the Government resisted amendments to the Sex Discrimination Bill (which became the SDA 1975) that would have replaced 'justifiable' with 'necessary'. Lord Harris stated that where a body offered reduced fares for pensioners, the policy might be justifiable, but not necessary (HL Deb 14 July 1975, vol 362, cols 1016–17). Of course, the *Bilka* test is different: it requires the *need* to be *genuine* (reduced fares for pensioners) with only the means to achieve it to be necessary. Unlike *Hampson*, this opinion was made long before *Bilka* was decided.

172 Case C-127/92, [1994] ICR 112.

173 [1991] ICR 382.

the most common phrases to found in European Court reports is: 'It is for the national court to decide . . .'. It may, for instance, defer to a national court in the interpretation and/or application of national legislation, within the bounds of EU law, of course. In *Feryn*,[174] an employer announced he would not employ immigrants. On the assumption (under the Race Directive 2000/43/EC) that this could amount to direct discrimination where there was no identifiable complainant, a secondary issue was whether an interested third party could bring proceedings against this employer. It was held that although the Directive did not demand this, it did not prohibit national legislation establishing such bodies. And then the boundary is drawn: 'It is, however, solely for the national court to assess whether national legislation allows such a possibility.'[175]

Uniformity

Under the principle of uniformity, EU law must apply to all member states uniformly. This is necessary if the treaties' objectives are to be fulfilled, and is a particular aim of Article 267 TFEU,[176] which provides the Court jurisdiction to make preliminary rulings on the interpretation of EU legislation.[177]

5 The rules of interpretation

It is clear from the 'context'[178] that the ultimate goal for the Court is to fulfil the objectives of the Treaties. It will become apparent from the rules themselves that the literal, schematic, and teleological rules are in ascending order of importance, and used to identify the purpose of a provision, which itself must fulfil the Treaties' objectives.

The literal approach is of limited value in a system of many languages, where any instrument may contain nuanced, but important, differences in wording. Nonetheless, in rare cases, where a common meaning can be divined without contradicting other principles, the Court has adopted a literal approach.[179] As all secondary legislation must be made under the authority of the Treaties, recourse to the 'parent' treaty provision is often made. Indeed, all directives will refer in the preamble to the enabling treaty provision. However, this does no more than refer up the legislative hierarchy for guidance. The schematic approach operates in multi-layered and multi-dimensional ways, looking at, for instance, other

174 Case C-54/07 *Centrum voor Gelijkheid van Kansen en voor Racismebestrijding v Firma Feryn NV* [2008] ECR I-5187.
175 ibid, para 27.
176 Ex 177 EEC, 234 TEC.
177 Case 26/62 *Van Gend en Loos* [1963] ECR 1, para 12. See also Case 30/77 *R v Bouchereau* [1977] ECR 1999, para 14.
178 See p 32.
179 Case 19/83 *Wendelboe v LJ Music* [1985] ECR 457.

provisions in the act under question, parallel (perhaps complimentary) legislation, as well as treaty provisions.[180]

The word teleological is little different from *purposive*, 'teleo' deriving from the Greek for design or purpose. That said, the Court's mission reflects its somewhat grander dictionary definition: 'relating to ends or final causes; dealing with design or purpose, esp. in natural phenomena'.[181] This chimes with the Court's schematic practice and frequent references to Treaty objectives.

The classic example of the difference between this and the traditional English approach arose in the early days of Britain's membership of the Community. In *R v Henn and Darby*,[182] the Court of Appeal was asked to hold that a statutory prohibition of importing obscene materials could not be enforced because Article 30 of the Treaty of Rome barred 'quantitative restrictions' on imports from other member states. Providing a classic specimen of blinkered literal interpretation, Lord Widgery LJ (for the Court) held:

> [Article 30] is a provision striking at restrictions on imports of the kind which warrant the adjective 'quantitative'. Here . . . the prohibition is total; the prohibition is on all obscene goods, not merely measured by quantity. At first blush, and subject to the authorities which follow, we would, I think, be inclined to say that Article 30 did not apply to this case because the restriction was not related to a quantitative measure.[183]

The case progressed to the Court of Justice, where the Commission argued: 'If quantitative restrictions do not include total prohibitions this would seriously undermine the principle of free movement of goods which is one of the foundations of the Community.'[184] The Court endorsed this deference to a Treaty objective, with the simple logic that a ban 'is the most extreme form of restriction'.[185] Upon return to the House of Lords, Lord Diplock warned that Lord Widgery's interpretation 'shows the danger of an English court applying English canons of statutory construction to the interpretation of the Treaty or, for that matter, of Regulations or Directives'.[186] More generally, he observed:

> The European court, in contrast to English courts, applies teleological rather than historical methods to the interpretation of the Treaties and other Community legislation. It seeks to give effect to what it conceives to be the spirit rather than the letter of the Treaties; sometimes, indeed, to an English

180 E.g. Case 135/83 *Abels v Administrative Board of the Bedrijfsvereniging Voor de Metaal-Industrie en de Electrotechnische Industrie* [1985] ECR 469.
181 *OED*, 2016, < http://oed.com > accessed 10 April 2018.
182 Case 34/79 *R v Henn and Darby* [1978] 1 WLR 1031 (CA).
183 ibid, 1036.
184 Case 34/79 [1979] ECR 3795, 3807.
185 ibid, 3812, para 12.
186 [1981] 1 AC 850, 904.

> judge, it may seem to the exclusion of the letter. It views the Communities as living and expanding organisms and the interpretation of the provisions of the Treaties as changing to match their growth. For these reasons the European Court does not apply the doctrine of precedent to its own decisions as rigidly as does an English court.[187]

This exposes in more mechanical terms how even the English *purposive* approach cannot duplicate the European teleological one. Treaty objectives, by their nature, are aspirational, typified by the ambition for an 'ever closer union' between member states. In the context of discrimination law, a more detailed set of goals is provided by the Race and Framework Directives. These aspired to a wide range of objectives, comprising: a 'high level' of employment and social protection; the raising of the standard of living and quality of life; economic and social cohesion and solidarity; developing the EU as an area of freedom, security, and justice, with democratic and tolerant societies that allow the participation of all persons; and the free movement of persons.[188] For the Court of Justice these objectives are likely to precede legislative history and precedent.

6 Summary

Even with deference to any literal/schematic/teleological 'hierarchy', sub-dividing these principles and canons of interpretation over-simplifies the process, as the principles and canons overlap and intertwine. Thus, for instance, where the Court affords a member state a margin of discretion, it is also deferring to the principle of subsidiarity. It is notable as well that they are complementary. Principles of equality, proportionality, and subsidiarity tend not to jar against each other. They are all tools to achieve the objectives of the Treaties.

7 EU law in the English courts

This brief account shows that where domestic legislation falls under the purview of EU law, courts feel obliged to give it a purposive interpretation.[189] A more concrete rule is that where it is directly applicable, or has direct effect, EU law must prevail over any conflicting domestic legislation, which must be 'disapplied'.[190] Where the EU law does not have direct effect, the doctrine of *indirect effect* requires domestic courts to interpret domestic legislation as far as possible to accord with a directive whether the domestic law in question was enacted *before or after* the

187 ibid, 905.
188 Race Directive 2000/43/EC, Recitals 9, 12, and 13; Framework Directive 2000/78/EC, Recitals 8, 9, and 11. See also Case C-83/14 *CHEZ Razpredelenie Bulgaria AD v Komisia za zashtita ot diskriminatsias* [2016] 1 CMLR 14, para 74.
189 See e.g. *Litster v Forth Dry Dock & Engineering* [1990] 1 AC 546 (HL).
190 *R v Secretary of State for Transport, ex p Factortame (No. 2)* [1991] 1 AC 603 (HL).

directive.[191] In recent times, domestic courts have achieved this by adopting the '*Ghaidan* approach'.[192] This assimilation of the domestic approaches to both ECHR and EU law was encapsulated by Sir Andrew Morritt C in a Chancery tax case, *Vodafone 2 v Revenue and Customs Commissioners*.[193] It has met with little resistance,[194] and, without much ado, found its way into the vocabulary of many a judicial speech.[195]

The 'obligation' was 'broad and far-reaching', and the judge summarised it thus:

(a) It is not constrained by conventional rules of construction.
(b) It does not require ambiguity in the legislative language.
(c) It is not an exercise in semantics or linguistics.
(d) It permits departure from the strict and literal application of the words which the legislature has elected to use.
(e) It permits the implication of words necessary to comply with Community law obligations.
(f) The precise form of the words to be implied does not matter.

The only constraints on the broad and far-reaching nature of the interpretative obligation were that:

(a) the meaning should 'go with the grain of the legislation' and be 'compatible with the underlying thrust of the legislation being construed'; and
(b) the exercise of the interpretative obligation cannot require the courts to make decisions for which they are not equipped or give rise to important practical repercussions which the court is not equipped to evaluate.[196]

This is an ambitious move, notably because it is not mandated by the Court of Justice's requirements under *indirect effect*, which are to interpret legislation only *as far as is possible* to comply with EU law. As such, this principle is likely

191 Case C-106/89 *Marleasing SA v La Comercial Internacional de Alimentación* [1990] ECR I-4135, [8]. See also *Litster v Forth Dry Dock & Engineering* [1990] 1 AC 546 (HL).
192 After *Godin-Mendoza v Ghaidan* [2004] 2 AC 557 (HL). See further p 49.
193 [2010] Ch 77 (CA) [38]. Its authority was enhanced when permission to appeal was refused by the Supreme Court: UKSC 2009/0162 (16 December 2009), < https://www.supremecourt.uk/docs/pta-0910-1002.pdf > accessed 3 April 2018.
194 See exceptionally *Bear Scotland Ltd v Fulton* [2015] 1 CMLR 40 (EAT), [48]–[54], where Dinah Rose QC argued that they were distinguishable, with the EU principle of indirect effect being narrower. Langstaff J did not to resolve the point to decide the case.
195 See e.g. *Swift v Robertson* [2014] 1 WLR 3438 (SC) [21]; *Cartier International AG v British Sky Broadcasting* [2015] Bus LR 298 (Ch), [89]; *Sub One Limited (t/a Subway) v The Commissioners for Her Majesty's Revenue and Customs* [2014] EWCA Civ 773 [49], *Kennedy v Charity Commission* [2015] AC 455 (SC) [224] (Lord Carnworth); *Football Association Premier League Ltd v QC Leisure* [2013] Bus LR 866 (CA), [46]; *Assange v Swedish Prosecution Authority (Nos 1 and 2)* [2012] 2 AC 471 (SC) [203] (Lord Mance); *Lock v British Gas Trading Ltd* [2016] ICR 503 (EAT).
196 [2010] Ch 77 (CA) [38].

to be more vulnerable than most under the UK's secession negotiations. That said, as will be seen in the following chapters, for discrimination cases, with the notable exception of *Rowstock v Jessemey*,[197] the '*Ghaidan* approach' largely has been ignored.

The European Convention on Human Rights and the Strasbourg Court

The European Court of Human Rights ('Strasbourg') employs several principles when interpreting and applying the Convention. In the main, these comprise, teleological, 'living instrument', proportionality, and the margin of appreciation. The scope for a teleological approach can be seen in the non-exhaustive range of grounds recognised in discrimination claims. Article 14 of the Convention provides:

> The enjoyment of the rights and freedoms set forth in the Convention shall be secured without discrimination on any ground such as sex, race, colour, language, religion, political or other opinion, national or social origin, association with a national minority, property, birth or other status.

Not only are the specific examples far wider than current dedicated domestic legislation or EU directives, the use of the phrases *such as* and *or other status* (a fortiori the French version *toute autre situation*[198]) opens Article 14 to more grounds than those listed. A similar formula was adopted of course by the EU's Charter of Fundamental Rights, Article 21, as mentioned earlier.[199] The difference is that the longer history of the Convention has afforded the Strasbourg Court time to develop the potential of this formula. Its teleological approach has enabled the Court to entertain discrimination cases on grounds wide and varied, preferring to control the outcome under the objective justification defence and the margin of appreciation, discussed later.[200] Hence, the Court has entertained Article 14 claims from groups as wide-ranging as owners of non-residential buildings (distinct from residential), owners of pit bull terriers (distinct from other breeds of dog), small landowners (distinct from large landowners), coastal (distinct from open sea) fishermen, foreign residence, and previous employment by the KGB.[201] More conventionally,

197 *Rowstock Ltd v Jessemey* [2014] 1 WLR 3615 (CA). See p 20.

198 'Or any other situation'. Noted in *Carson v UK* (App No. 42184/05) (2010) 51 EHRR 13, [70]; see also *R (RJM) v Secretary of State for Work and Pensions* [2009] 1 AC 311 (HL) [39].

199 See pp 36–38.

200 See p 48.

201 Respectively, *Spadea v Italy* (1996) 21 EHRR 482, [42]–[46]; *Bullock v UK* (1996) 21 EHRR CD 85, para 5; *Chassagnou v France* (2000) 29 EHRR 615, [86]–[95]; *Posti and Rahko v Finland* (2002) 37 EHRR 158, [79]–[87]; *Darby v Sweden* (App No. 11581/85) (1990) EHRR 774; *Sidabras v Lithuania* (App No. 55480/2000) (2006) 42 EHRR 6.

the Court has recognised sexual orientation, marital status, illegitimacy, trade union status, military rank, and conscientious objection,[202] as falling within this residual category.

In order to establish discrimination under Article 14, the applicant has to show treatment different to another person in an analogous situation, or a failure 'to treat differently persons whose situations are significantly different'.[203] These two phrases correspond to direct and indirect discrimination. Although the Court was slow to recognise indirect discrimination,[204] once it did so, it rapidly adopted a widely established model, which recognised a prima facie case based upon statistics.[205] In doing so, it cited numerous EU sources,[206] as well as UK and US case law.[207]

The 'living instrument', or 'living tree',[208] school of interpretation holds that legislation of a constitutional nature should be read according to the values of the present day, as opposed to the time it was enacted, or the 'framer's intent'. The modern approach has become entrenched in the Strasbourg Court's reasoning:

> The Court reiterates that the Convention is a living instrument which must be interpreted in the light of present-day conditions and that the increasingly high standard being required in the area of the protection of human rights and fundamental liberties correspondingly and inevitably requires greater firmness in assessing breaches of the fundamental values of democratic societies.[209]

A marked example of this is apparent in the Court's evolving approach to transsexualism. As late as 1998, it found a state's failure to recognise gender reassignment was objectively justified and within the margin of appreciation.[210] But by 2002, it reversed this view, noting 'an increase in the social acceptance of the phenomenon of transsexualism and a growing recognition of the problems with

202 Respectively, *Salgueiro v Portugal* (2001) 31 EHRR 47; *Wessels-Bergervoet v The Netherlands* (2004) 38 EHRR 793 (incl. *unmarried: PM v UK* (App No. 6638/03) (2006) 42 EHRR 45, [27]); *Sahin v Germany* [2003] 2 FLR 671, [94] (incl. different treatment of *parents* of children born out of wedlock: *Zaunegger v Germany* (App No. 22028/04) (2010) 50 EHRR 38, [51]); *Swedish Engine Drivers Union v Sweden* (1976) 1 EHRR 617; *Engel v NL* (1979–80) 1 EHRR 647, [72] ('house arrest' for commissioned officers, jail for other servicemen); *De Jong, Baljet and Van den Brink v The Netherlands (No. 1)* (1986) 8 EHRR 20.

203 *Thlimmenos v Greece* (2001) 31 EHRR 14, [44].

204 Starting with ibid.

205 *DH v Czech Republic* (App No. 57325/00) (2008) 47 EHRR 3. Cf *Jordan v UK* (App No. 24746/94) (2001) 37 EHRR 2 [154]: '[T]he Court does not consider that statistics can in themselves disclose a practice which could be classified as discriminatory within the meaning of Article 14.'

206 ibid, paras 81–91.

207 ibid, respectively, *R (European Roma Rights Centre) v Immigration Officer at Prague Airport* [2005] 2 AC 1, [73]–[91]; *Griggs v Duke Power* 401 US 424, 429–432 (Sup Ct, 1971).

208 *Edwards v Attorney General of Canada* [1930] AC 124 (PC), 136 (Lord Sankey LC); see B Wilson, 'The making of a constitution' [1988] PL 370.

209 *Öcalan v Turkey* (App No. 46221/99) (2005) 41 EHRR 45, [163].

210 *Sheffield & Horsham v UK* (1999) 27 EHRR 163.

which transsexuals are confronted'.[211] Accordingly, '[the] Court must have regard to the changing conditions within the respondent State and within Contracting States generally and respond, for example, to any evolving convergence as to the standards to be achieved'.[212]

As noted above, the non-exhaustive range of recognisable grounds of discrimination means that most cases are decided under the element of justification. In line with indirect discrimination jurisprudence,[213] the Court directs that under Article 14, the (state) defendant has the burden to justify the challenged discriminatory measure. But then there are some notable differences. The contrast with most conventional discrimination theories is that direct discrimination is potentially justifiable. The justification process divides, loosely, into two stages. First, the general policy must pursue a legitimate aim, and second, it must have reasonable relationship of proportionality between the means employed and the aim sought to be realised.[214] It is on this principle of proportionality that the Court gives itself room for manoeuvre with the interpretation and application of Convention rights.

In some cases, the Court subjects the defence to 'intensive' scrutiny, demanding 'very weighty reasons' to justify discrimination. There is no hard and fast rule as to when this should occur, but one emerging theme is that these cases can be distinguished by the *ground* of the discrimination. The Court has demanded 'very weighty reasons' in cases of discrimination on grounds of sex, sexual orientation, birth out of wedlock (including different treatment of unmarried parents), marital status, and nationality.[215] Without saying as much, the Court appears to be dividing cases into 'suspect' and 'non-suspect' classes, loosely corresponding to the classifications made by the US Supreme Court.[216] This certainly is the view of some senior British judges.[217] The 'living instrument' principle can inhabit and inform the Court's proportionality debate. For instance, in *Zaunegger v*

211 *Goodwin v UK* (2002) 35 EHRR 18, [92].

212 ibid [74]. See also [75] & [90].

213 Notably *Griggs v Duke Power* 401 US 424 (Sup Ct, 1971), cited in *DH v Czech Republic* (2008) 47 EHRR 3 [107].

214 *Belgian Linguistic Case* (A/6) (1979–1980) 1 EHRR 252, [I B 10]; *Karner v Austria* (2003) 2 FLR 623, [37].

215 Respectively *Ünal Tekeli v Turkey* [2005] 1 FCR 663, [53]; *Karner v Austria* (2003) 2 FLR 623, [37]; *Sahin v Germany* [2003] 2 FLR 671, [94] (*Zaunegger v Germany* (App No. 22028/04) (2010) 50 EHRR 38, [51]); *Wessels-Bergervoet v The Netherlands* (2004) 38 EHRR 793, [49]; and *Koua Poirrez v France* (2005) 40 EHRR 34, [46].

216 See e.g. *City of Cleburne, Texas v Cleburne Living Center* 473 US 432, 446 (Sup Ct, 1985). See also O de Schutter, 'The prohibition of discrimination under European human rights law: Relevance for the EU' (2005, European Commission). ISBN 92-894-9171-X (EN) 14–15, < www.migpolgroup.com/public/docs/41.ProhibitionofDiscriminationunderHumanRtsLaw_EN_02.05.pdf > accessed 10 April 2018.

217 E.g. *AL (Serbia) v Secretary of State for the Home Department* [2008] UKHL 42, [30]–[31] (Baroness Hale) [53] (Lord Brown); *R (Carson) v Secretary of State for Work and Pensions* [2005] UKHL 37, [15]–[17] (Lord Hoffman), [55]–[57] (Lord Walker); *R (RJM) v Secretary of State for Work and Pensions* [2009] 1 AC 311 (HL) [5] (Lord Walker), [14] (Lord Mance).

Germany,[218] a father challenged the inferior parental rights afforded to unmarried parents (among others). In finding a violation of Article 14, the Court took into consideration the 'evolving European context in this sphere and the growing number of unmarried parents'.[219]

The 'margin of appreciation' varies according to the circumstances, the subject matter and its background.[220] It cuts through any suspect/non-suspect dichotomy, and so, for instance, a wide margin may be afforded even in a case of sex discrimination, a so-called suspect ground.[221] As such, any certainty created by the suspect/non-suspect dichotomy is somewhat undermined by this doctrine. But the case law provides some guiding principles. A wide margin may be given to general measures of social and economic policy.[222] And it seems that where there is no common value or practice across Contracting States, it is more likely that the Court will afford a defendant state a wide margin of appreciation. For instance, in *Petrovic v Austria*,[223] the Austrian Government was afforded a wide margin of appreciation when paying only women parental leave allowances, because, at the time, there was no common standard in this field: the majority of the Contracting States did not provide parental leave allowances. Likewise, in *Schalk v Austria*,[224] the Court noted the absence of a consensus among Contracting States towards legal recognition of same-sex couples (another 'suspect' category), and so 'States must also enjoy a margin of appreciation in the timing of the introduction of legislative changes'.[225] On the other hand, the Court has observed,

> an emerging international consensus amongst the contracting states . . . recognising the special needs of minorities and an obligation to protect their security, identity and lifestyle, not only for the purpose of safeguarding the interests of the minorities themselves but to preserve a cultural diversity of value to the whole community.[226]

The recognition of these common values meant a state could not justify practices that resulted in the majority of Roma children being placed in special schools for those with learning disabilities.[227]

This sketch of the definitions and principles reveals a good deal of flexibility, which is driven by the Court's willingness to incorporate changing external

218 (App No. 22028/04) (2010) 50 EHRR 38.
219 ibid [60].
220 *Ünal Tekeli v Turkey* [2005] 1 FCR 663, [52]; *Handyside v UK* (1979–80) 1 EHRR 737, [48]. For a thorough discussion, see Y Arai-Takahashi, *The Margin of Appreciation Doctrine and the Principle of Proportionality in the Jurisprudence of the ECHR* (Intersentia 2001).
221 *Petrovic v Austria* (1998) 33 EHRR 307. See further I Radacic, 'Gender equality jurisprudence of the European Court of Human Rights' (2008) 19(4) EJIL 841.
222 *Stec v UK* (App No. 65731/01) (2006) 43 EHRR 47, [52].
223 (1998) 33 EHRR 307, [38]–[39].
224 (App No. 30141/04) (24 June 2010).
225 ibid [105].
226 *DH v Czech Republic* (2008) 47 EHRR 3 [181], citing *Chapman v UK* (App No. 27238/94) (2001) 33 EHRR 18, [93].
227 ibid.

'conditions' and its equally dynamic aspiration to an 'increasingly high standard' of protection. This, of course, presents a particular challenge for a common law court steeped in the doctrine of precedent. As can be seen next, the English courts have a less than solid record when interpreting the Convention, or human rights more broadly, which does not bode well for their treatment of the domestic discrimination law.

1 The Convention in the English courts

The Human Rights Act 1998 (HRA 1998) incorporated the European Convention on Human Rights into domestic law, coming into force on 2 October 2000.[228] Section 3(1) of the Act provides: 'So far as it is possible to do so, primary legislation and subordinate legislation must be read and given effect in a way which is compatible with the Convention rights.' Failing this, by section 4, a court must issue a declaration of incompatibility.[229]

This makes it possible for parties to call upon Convention rights in a private dispute that is governed by legislation. It also raises the question of how far a court should distort statutory language to comply with the Convention. An early indicator came in 2004 with *Godin-Mendoza v Ghaidan*.[230] Here, Mr Mendoza and Mr Walwyn-Jones lived together in a same-sex relationship in Mr Walwyn-Jones' rented flat. When Mr Walwyn-Jones died, Mr Mendoza claimed from the landlord a right to succeed the statutory tenancy under the Rent Act 1977, which provided that the surviving spouse of the original tenant shall succeed the tenancy.[231] It defined 'spouse' as 'a person who was living with the original tenant as his or her wife or husband'. The Court of Appeal held that 'as his or her wife or husband' should read to mean 'as if they were his wife or husband'.[232] The House of Lords upheld that decision, but it is notable that Lord Nicholls reasoned: 'The precise form of words read in for this purpose is of no significance. It is their substantive effect which matters.'[233] This tells us that courts should not be fettered by an impossibility of a grammatical solution and that section 3 goes further merely than resolving ambiguities in legislation. However, the interpretation should 'go with the grain of the legislation'[234] and not be against a fundamental feature of it or amount to a decision better suited for Parliament, for instance, where recognising a male-to-female transsexual as female under the Matrimonial Causes Act 1973 'would have had exceedingly wide ramifications'.[235] As seen above, this '*Ghaidan* approach' now has a life of its own in the sphere of EU law.[236]

228 SI 2000/1851.

229 The Act provides a fast-track procedure enabling the relevant minister to amend the legislation appropriately either before Parliament or (because of 'urgency') without parliamentary approval. See HRA 1998, s 10 and Sch 2, para 2.

230 [2004] 2 AC 557 (HL).

231 Rent Act 1977, Sch 1, para 2.

232 [2003] 1 FLR 468, [35].

233 [2004] 2 AC 557, [35].

234 ibid [121] (Lord Rodger).

235 ibid [33] (Lord Nicholls) citing *Bellinger v Bellinger* [2003] UKHL 21.

236 See p 44.

Meanwhile, HRA 1998, section 2(1) declares that courts and tribunals 'must take into account' any judgment, decision, declaration, or advisory opinion of the European Court of Human Rights, or opinions and decisions of the Commission (of Human Rights). This suggests that domestic courts should not only follow existing Strasbourg decisions, but also adopt Strasbourg's somewhat different approach to interpretation, which, most notably, treats the Convention as a 'living instrument', rather than something confined to the intent of the original drafters.[237] Indeed, without saying as much, the House of Lords in *Ghaidan* adopted this approach to a statute whose drafters, just 16 years previously,[238] did not envisage that it would encompass a same-sex relationship.

The White Paper introducing the Human Rights Bill took this view:

> The Convention is often described as a 'living instrument' because it is interpreted by the European court in the light of present day conditions and therefore reflects changing social attitudes and the changes in the circumstances of society. In future our judges will be able to contribute to this dynamic and evolving interpretation of the Convention.[239]

Accordingly, Judicial Studies Board instituted a programme of training on the Hunan Rights Act 1998 for every judge in the country from the House of Lords to District Judges, although how far that went beyond the basic mechanics of the Act into interpretive training remains unclear.[240]

As it happened, some of England's judges already had experience of interpreting human-rights documents. In the Privy Council, for several decades preceding the 1998 Act, senior British judges presided over cases from the Commonwealth, some of which concerned the interpretation a country's particular human-rights legislation. As long ago as 1930, in *Edwards v Attorney General of Canada*, Lord Sankey, speaking for the Board, held that the British Constitutional Act 1867, which granted Canada a constitution, had 'planted in Canada a living tree capable of growth and expansion within its natural limits'.[241] In a rare, if not unique, departure from the English common law presumption that women were not entitled to hold public office,[242] the Board held that the word 'persons' in the Act applied to both men and women, thus entitling women to sit in the Senate. This prototype for the living-instrument approach received only occasional

237 See p 46.
238 The provision originates from 1988, a result of an amendment by the Housing Act 1988.
239 Home Office, *Rights Brought Home: the Human Rights Bill* (Cm 3782, 1997) para 2.5.
240 The Judicial Studies Board (now the Judicial College) has no record of the training. Sedley LJ said of the training seminars for 'the new legal culture': 'You cannot teach anyone, even a judge, very much in a day.' (M. Hill (ed) *Religious Liberty and Human Rights* (University of Wales Press, 2002) Preface, ix–x).
241 [1930] AC 124 (PC), 136.
242 See p 81 et al.

endorsements, with Lord Bingham cautioning that 'those limits will often call for very careful consideration'.[243]

On the matter of the literal/purposive dichotomy, three Privy Council cases present a similarly mixed picture. In *Attorney General for Gambia v Momodou Jobe*,[244] Lord Diplock said: 'A constitution . . . which protects fundamental human rights . . . is to be given a generous and purposive interpretation.'[245] However, in *Robinson v The Queen*,[246] the defendant's trial for murder – a capital offence – was adjourned nineteen times. On the twentieth, his lawyer resigned, apparently because his fees were unpaid. The trial judge was keen not to lose a key witness and so persisted with the trial; the unrepresented defendant was convicted and sentenced to death. He appealed to the Privy Council under the Jamaican Bill of Rights which provided that every person on trial for a capital offence shall be *permitted* to be represented by a lawyer. Lord Roskill examined the statutory word *permitted* and concluded that it did not give an *absolute right* to a defence lawyer. He held that the trial accorded with the Bill of Rights and sent Mr Robinson to his death following a trial without legal representation.[247] Lords Keith and Templeman concurred. Lords Scarman and Edmund-Davies dissented, preferring a 'generous and purposive' construction of the Bill of Rights.[248] And as late February 1998, with the Human Rights Act on the horizon, the Privy Council cautioned:

> What the interpretation of commercial documents and constitutions have in common is that in each case the court is concerned with the meaning of the language which has been used: . . . 'If the language used by the lawgiver is ignored in favour of a general resort to "values" the result is not interpretation but divination.'[249]

Ghaidan signalled that post-Human Rights Act cases can take a liberal approach to statutory language to protect a Convention right. But there remains caution around the 'living instrument' notion when it comes to *advancing* human rights. In general, domestic courts have not acted on the prompt given by the White Paper, instead adopting a more limited role of taking account of Strasbourg

243 *Brown v Stott* [2003] 1 AC 681 (HL) 703.
244 [1984] 3 WLR 174.
245 ibid, 183*b*.
246 [1985] AC 956.
247 Robinson was eventually reprieved following a hearing by the UN Human Rights Committee: *Frank Robinson v Jamaica*, UN Doc CCPR/C/35/D/223/1987 (1989). See < www.ohchr.org/_layouts/15/WopiFrame.aspx?sourcedoc=/Documents/Publications/SDecisionsVol3en.pdf&action=default&DefaultItemOpen=1 > accessed 10 April 2018. See also 'UN attacks breach of rights by Law Lords' *The Independent* (London, 1 May 1989) 3.
248 [1985] AC 956, 974.
249 *Matadeen v Pointu* [1999] 1 AC 98, 108, citing, *State v Zuma* (1995) (4) BCLR 401 (South Africa Constitutional Court), 412 (Kentridge AJ).

decisions.[250] The general rubric was set out by Lord Bingham, in *R (Ullah) v Special Adjudicator*: 'The duty of national courts is to keep pace with the Strasbourg jurisprudence as it evolves over time: no more, but certainly no less.'[251] The reason for this, it seemed, was that 'the meaning of the Convention should be uniform throughout the states party to it'.[252] In short, courts should *follow* the Convention, but not *develop* it. There have been substantial variations on this theme.[253] In *Clift v Secretary of State for the Home Department*,[254] the House of Lords adopted the narrowest interpretation of the grounds of discrimination covered by Article 14,[255] ignoring more recent case law suggesting a broader approach. Predictably, the decision was upset by the Strasbourg Court.[256] On the other hand, in *Re G*, a majority of the House seemed content to extend Strasbourg jurisprudence beyond a homosexual *individual's* right to adopt,[257] to afford that right to same-sex couples,[258] with two judges citing the White Paper's enunciation to that effect.[259] More recently, the interpretive duties under the Human Rights Act 1998 have come under increasing scrutiny, with an array of extra-judicial[260] and political pronouncements[261] that Parliament should be sovereign and the Supreme Court the ultimate decision-maker on Convention rights in the UK.

250 Although see the advancement on the law of privacy, see e.g. *Campbell v MGN Ltd* [2004] 2 AC 457 (HL).

251 [2004] 2 AC 323, [20].

252 ibid.

253 See R Masterman, 'The mirror crack'd', UK Const L Blog (13 February 2013), < https://ukconstitutionallaw.org/2013/02/13/roger-masterman-the-mirror-crackd/ > accessed 10 April 2018.

254 [2007] 1 AC 484.

255 Holding that bracketing prisoners by length of sentence did not invoke Article 14 because 'the distinction is not a personal characteristic of the offender but what the offender has done' (ibid [62] (Baroness Hale)).

256 *Clift v UK* (App No. 7205/07) (ECtHR, 13 July 2010).

257 *EB v France* (2008) 47 EHRR 509. Cf the earlier decision, *Fretté v France* (2002) 38 EHRR 438.

258 [2009] 1 AC 173 (HL), see especially [119] (Baroness Hale), [52] (Lord Hope), [21]–[29] (Lord Hoffman).

259 ibid [119] (Baroness Hale), [52] (Lord Hope).

260 See e.g. Lord Sumption, 'The limits of law' 27th Sultan Azlan Shah Lecture, Kuala Lumpur 20 November 2013, < https://www.supremecourt.uk/docs/speech-131120.pdf > ; Laws LJ, 'Lecture III: the common law and Europe', Hamlyn Lectures 2013, 27 November 2013, < https://www.judiciary.gov.uk/announcements/speech-lj-laws-hamlyn-lecture-2013/ > ; Lord Hoffmann, 'The universality of human rights', Judicial Studies Board Annual Lecture, 19 March 2009, < https://www.judiciary.gov.uk/announcements/speech-by-lord-hoffmann-the-universality-of-human-rights/ > all accessed 10 April 2018.

261 The 2015 Conservative Party Manifesto promised (p 60) to 'scrap the Human Rights Act' and 'break the formal link between British courts and the European Court of Human Rights'. See also David Cameron, HC Deb 27 May 2015, vol 596, col 52: 'Be in no doubt: we will be introducing legislation and legislating on this issue because I want these decisions made by British judges in British courts, not in Strasbourg.' His successor, Theresa May, as Home Secretary, often called for its repeal. See e.g. Party Conference Speech, 4 October 2001, < www.politics.co.uk/comment-analysis/2011/10/04/theresa-may-speech-in-full > accessed 10 April 2018. (No longer available at the Conservative Party website.) The 2017 manifesto reneged on this, to some extent anyway (p 37): 'We . . . will consider our human rights legal framework when the process of leaving the EU concludes. We will remain signatories to the European Convention on Human Rights for the duration of the next parliament', < https://www.conservatives.com/manifesto > accessed 29 March 2018.

Conclusion

From this collection of seemingly unrelated practices, some principles and rules can be found. The starting point is the literal approach. The words employed by the legislature must be taken at face value, unless there is a reason to depart from them. Reasons have included avoiding an absurdity, correcting a drafting error, addressing the mischief at which the provision was aimed, achieving the purpose of the provision (this is more likely if it is a societal purpose), or complying with EU or ECHR law.

The courts' willingness to interfere with statutory wording ranges from only where the language would bear it, to omitting words, reading words in, or even adding (or disregarding) whole sections. Some explanation for the extent of this willingness can be drawn from the broad theme of the political arrangements or climate of the day, ranging from Coke's CJ famous defiance of Parliament in *Dr Bonham's Case*,[262] through to the Bill of Rights 1688 and the Diceyan deference to Parliament rising in the Victorian age, and the increasing disrespect for statutory wording in recent years, commonly under the cover of the EC Act 1972 or the HRA 1998. Otherwise, the choice of approach may appear more capricious. It could be the mischief, or purpose of a provision, or perhaps, a mere slap on the wrist for the drafter.[263] Where there is no evidence underpinning the chosen approach, the matter can appear subjective, which can bring even further uncertainty. For instance, it appeared that the courts took it on themselves to depart from the literal rule to presume against anti-nuclear weapon protesters (ignoring contrary sidenotes and headings) and in favour of a fraudulent company director (encompassing favourable sidenotes and headings).[264] Such 'pick and mix' inconsistencies expose the vulnerability of the rules of English statutory interpretation to unevidenced and unannounced policy decisions; and as will become apparent in the cases under review later in this book, it is the same vulnerability that is exploited by personal predilections in the field of equality law.

But these criticisms could only be made by reference to a set of rules and principles, which, as this chapter shows, clearly exists. And if a decision is to accord with the rule of law and be 'reasonably understood . . . by those whose conduct it regulates',[265] or by lawyers and non-lawyers alike,[266] then it is not being particularly fanciful to assume some form of framework exists with an expectation that judgments refer to it. Moreover, such capriciousness ought not to apply to

262 (1609) 8 Co Rep 113, 118a; 77 ER 646; 652: 'when an Act of Parliament is against common right and reason, or repugnant, or impossible to be performed, the common law will controul it, and adjudge such Act to be void'.

263 *Fisher v Bell* [1961] 1 QB 394 (DC). See p 19.

264 See respectively *Chandler v DPP* [1964] AC 763 and *DPP v Schildkamp* [1971] AC 1 (HL). See p 26.

265 *Black-Clawson International Ltd v Papierwerke Waldhof-Aschaffenberg AG* [1975] AC 591 (HL) 638 (Lord Diplock).

266 Lord Neuberger, 'Open justice unbound?' Judicial Studies Board annual lecture 2011, 16 March 2011, para 5, < webarchive.nationalarchives.gov.uk/20131202164909/http://judiciary.gov.uk/media/speeches/2011 > accessed 10 April 2018.

equality law, for which more obligatory approaches have emerged, most notably under EU law. There are also duties under the HRA 1998, and even Lord Steyn's 'purposive' direction for social welfare legislation and the like.[267] Given this, it would not be overly ambitious or onerous to summarise the process of the interpretation of equality law as follows:

1 The primary goal is to give effect to the intention of Parliament, although in certain cases this may be found from external European instruments and cases via the EC Act 1972 (until EU secession, at least) or HRA 1998. In the case of equality law, given that most definitions have their roots in the generally more experienced US jurisprudence, where relevant, this source may inform the intention as well.
2 Given this primary goal, the purpose should always be considered. To this end, given that discrimination legislation resembles social welfare legislation (unlike a tax statute), courts should observe the advice adopted by the House of Lords that this may require a 'sympathetic and imaginative discovery'.[268]
3 The statutory words should be given their literal meaning unless there is a reason for not doing so.
4 A reason would be that it would not fulfil the purpose. Other reasons could be that the words are ambiguous, there is an obvious drafting error, or the interpretation would cause an absurdity.
5 In such cases, courts have a number of 'alternative' tools to resolve the problem. The main ones are context, the golden, mischief, purposive, and *Inco Europe* 'rules', and the 'constitutional' deference to the HRA 1998 and (until secession, at least) the EC Act 1972 (which may provide more latitude to distort, interfere with, or ignore statutory language). Irrespective of secession, bearing in mind the greater 'degree of liberality permitted' with this 'social welfare' legislation,[269] in any of these cases, the courts will sometimes attempt to assign statutory words a secondary meaning, or render them subservient to other words, or redraft the provision accordingly. But in others, notably (but not exclusively) under the '*Ghaidan* approach', they will simply make a decision without attempting a redraft.
6 In all cases, the judgment should state which rule is being deployed, and why. If no recognised rule is being used, the judgment again should state why. In particular, any deviation from the statutory language should be explained to show at least *some* respect for Lord Diplock's plea that interested parties ought to be able to take a statute at face value.[270]

267 *R (Quintavalle) v Secretary of State for Health* [2003] 2 AC 687 (HL) [21]. See p 24.
268 ibid, citing *Cabell v Markham* 148 F 2d 737 (2nd Cir 1945), 739 (Learned Hand J).
269 ibid [21] (Lord Steyn).
270 *Black-Clawson International Ltd v Papierwerke Waldhof-Aschaffenberg AG* [1975] AC 591 (HL) 638 (Lord Diplock). See p 28, text to n 85.

This should help to produce a technically correct judgment. In itself, this approach should aid certainty and understanding of the decisions; it should help reduce prolixity and vulnerability to personal predilections. Of course, these virtues are intertwined and interdependent. A judge committed to a clear, concise decision is more likely to reference that decision to a method of interpretation. Similarly, a judge committed to an interpretation consistent with the statutory purpose will do so with an appreciation of the basic principles and goals of anti-discrimination law. This strand is sketched out in the next chapter.

Further reading

O Jones, *Bennion on Statutory Interpretation* (6th edn, LexisNexis 2013).
J Bell, G Engle, and R Cross, *Statutory Interpretation* (3rd edn, LexisNexis 2005).
P Maxwell, *On the Interpretation of Statutes* (12th edn, Sweet & Maxwell 1969).
J Willis, 'Statutory interpretation in a nutshell' (1938) 16 Canadian Bar Review 1.
The Interpretation of Statutes (Law Com No. 21, Scot Law Com No. 11, 1969, especially paras 22–33 & 79–81).
Lord Steyn, '*Pepper v Hart*; A Re-examination' (2001) 21 OJLS 59.
Robinson v The Queen [1985] AC 956 (PC).
R (Quintavalle) v Secretary of State for Health [2003] 2 AC 687 (HL).
R Masterman, 'The mirror crack'd', UK Const L Blog (13th February 2013), < https://ukconstitutionallaw.org/2013/02/13/roger-masterman-the-mirror-crackd/ > accessed 10 April 2018.
B Wilson, 'The making of a constitution' [1988] PL 370.
Lord Sumption, 'The limits of law' 27th Sultan Azlan Shah Lecture, Kuala Lumpur 20 November 2013, < https://www.supremecourt.uk/docs/speech-131120.pdf > accessed 10 April 2018.
Laws LJ, 'Lecture III: The Common Law and Europe', Hamlyn Lectures 2013, 27 November 2013, < https://www.judiciary.gov.uk/announcements/speech-lj-laws-hamlyn-lecture-2013/ > accessed 10 April 2018.
Lord Hoffmann, 'The universality of human rights', Judicial Studies Board Annual Lecture, 19 March 2009, < https://www.judiciary.gov.uk/announcements/speech-by-lord-hoffmann-the-universality-of-human-rights/ > accessed 10 April 2018.
Lord Neuberger, 'Open justice unbound?' Judicial Studies Board annual lecture 2011, 16 March 2011, para 5, < webarchive.nationalarchives.gov.uk/20131202164909/http://judiciary.gov.uk/media/speeches/2011 > accessed 10 April 2018.
O de Schutter, 'The prohibition of discrimination under European human rights law: relevance for the EU' (2005, European Commission). ISBN 92-894-9171-X (EN) 14–15, < www.migpolgroup.com/public/docs/41.ProhibitionofDiscriminationunderHumanRtsLaw_EN_02.05.pdf > accessed 10 April 2018.
Y Arai-Takahashi, *The Margin of Appreciation Doctrine and the Principle of Proportionality in the Jurisprudence of the ECHR* (Intersentia 2001).

3 An introduction to theories and aims of discrimination law

Introduction

As noted in Chapter 2, an appreciation of the basic principles and aims underpinning the statutory definitions will aid a sound understanding of the statutory purpose, which in turn will inform the statutory interpretation. These can be gleaned from the antecedent case law and preparatory materials, as well as the wider (largely academic) literature exploring the theories of discrimination law. Of course, the theoretical views will vary widely, which is of little use when trying to divine *a* statutory purpose. But often these are more exploratory than advisory, while other more advocatory or critical views call for a *change* in the legislative definitions to implement a preferred theory or aim. As such, this recognises the characteristics of the existing provision in question. Thus, despite the variety of theories available, there is a general consensus as to the underlying theory, policy, and aims of the existing definitions. This ought to prevent the danger of random theories entering the law at the interpretive stage, via a judge's personal predilection, by-passing the legislative process altogether. That would be quite different from an *understanding* of the theories and aims as an aid to appreciate the statutory purpose.

The meaning of discrimination

For the general public, an easily received legal definition of discrimination is different treatment motivated by prejudice or hostility.[1] For practitioners of discrimination law, this is too simplistic. The specialist lawyer, familiar with practices and patterns, as well as principles gleaned from the case law, knows that discrimination must include, at the least, behaviour that has an unintended adverse effect on a protected group, say, a customary length of residence requirement to work in local services, or an uninterrupted employment record to attain certain work benefits. Meanwhile the judiciary, aware of this professional opinion, is conscious of the public's perception when defining discrimination. Lord Woolf MR once opined that liability for

1 Alexander argues strongly that not all discrimination should be unlawful, even where it is immoral. 'For example, a person who, in choosing a spouse . . . excludes members of a particular race solely because of a bias, may be acting within her moral rights even if she is acting immorally.' L Alexander, 'What makes wrongful discrimination wrong? Biases, preferences, stereotypes and proxies' (1992) 141 Penn UL Rev 149, 201.

unintended discrimination (either consciously or unconsciously) 'is hardly likely to assist the objective of promoting harmonious racial relations.'[2] Similarly, a dissenting Lord Browne-Wilkinson asserted that finding liability for 'unconscious' racial discrimination 'is unlikely to recommend the legislation to the public as being fair and proper protection for the minorities that they are seeking to protect'.[3] The use of public understanding as an interpretive tool is clearly controversial, but for some, public understanding is 'crucial in a democracy . . . and necessary for the enactment and enforcement of civil rights law'.[4] This, of course, is somewhat different from Lord Diplock's plea for a public understanding of statutes;[5] here, the onus is on the interpreter not to deviate from the plain words of a statute, save it mislead and disadvantage those laypersons who had gone to the trouble of locating and reading a statutory provision. All the same, these judicial comments mean that the public's opinion cannot be ignored in the following discussion.

Even as a simplistic notion of prejudice, discrimination can be attributed with several meanings. Sunstein considers that it encompasses three types of mistake.[6] The first is an incorrect view that people in certain groups possess certain characteristics.[7] The second is a belief that many members of a group have certain characteristics when in fact only a few of them do. Here the error is an extremely over-broad generalisation. The third mistake is a reliance on fairly accurate group-based generalisations when more accurate (and not especially costly) classifying devices are available. Thus, even where a group predominantly possesses a particular characteristic, it is possible to identify the relevant individuals, rather than treat the group as a whole. An example arose in *Bohon-Mitchell v Common Professional Examination Board*,[8] where those with degrees from outside the British Isles were presumed to be unfamiliar with the British way of life.

A new more subtle and challenging definition of *racial* discrimination was brought into the public's consciousness in 1999 by the Macpherson Report (the inquiry into the police response to the murder of the black teenager, Stephen Lawrence). The Report drew together many explanations of the phrase *institutional racism* to produce a widely received definition, which ought to inform the legal definition of discrimination. After making the point that overt racism was not at issue in the inquiry, it identified 'unwitting', and 'unconscious', racism.

2 *Khan v Chief Constable of West Yorkshire* [2000] ICR 1169 (CA) [14]. See further pp 71 and 122–129.

3 *Nagarajan v London Regional Transport* [2000] 1 AC 501 (HL) 510.

4 G Rutherglen, 'Discrimination and its discontents' (1995) 81 Virginia L Rev 117, 127–128.

5 *Black-Clawson International Ltd v Papierwerke Waldhof-Aschaffenberg AG* [1975] AC 591 (HL) 638. See Chapter 2, p 28, text to n 85.

6 C Sunstein, 'Three civil rights fallacies' (1991) 79 California L Rev 751, 752–753.

7 MO McGowan, 'Engendered differences' SSRN Library 1361196 (2009) suggests that for gender: 'We have created difference and inequality despite our sameness, partly because of our irresistible cognitive urge to categorize people on the basis of sex and the systematic errors in judgments that result from that categorization', < https://papers.ssrn.com/sol3/papers.cfm?abstract_id=1361196 > accessed 10 April 2018.

8 [1978] IRLR 525 (IT). 'Foreign' graduates were hence required to take a longer course, which in this case was not justified: the claimant was married to an Englishman and had lived in England for many years.

The Report then noted the *effect* of actions and police culture as areas for attention: the problem lies not with individual officers, but with the organisation. The Macpherson Report defined institutional racism as:

> The collective failure of an organisation to provide an appropriate and professional service to people because of their colour, culture or ethnic origin. It can be seen or detected in processes, attitudes and behaviour which amount to discrimination through unwitting prejudice, ignorance, thoughtlessness and racist stereotyping which disadvantage minority ethnic people.[9]

Discrimination can also be characterised under principles of either *harm* or *unfairness*.[10] The harm principle rests on a strong connection between the stigma that leads to different treatment and denied group opportunity, and social historical factors, such as the forms of second-class citizenship experienced typically (but not exclusively) by some racial groups and by women. The stigma, degradation, and humiliation of slavery (and the more recent racial segregation) is revived with every modern-day act of racial discrimination. Well into the 20th century, women were legal second-class citizens. They were inferior in marriage, where their legal existence was suspended, domestic violence was condoned, and rape lawful. They were denied the vote, and suffered inferior job opportunities, prospects, and pay.[11] Consequently, every act of sex discrimination may be seen and felt as an act championing the old arrangements.

The fairness principle relies on a much weaker link between social history and discriminatory practices. History informs us that decision-making based on irrational factors such as race and sex is inherently *unfair*. This view is easier to reconcile with the law of indirect discrimination, as less, or no, blame need be attached to the discriminator. It also makes it easier to explain the inclusion of other grounds (such as age) within the anti-discrimination legal framework. Its weakness is that it risks treating 'all non-meritocratic preferences as being on all fours with slavery'[12] and 'opens up the possibility of white male legal actions which exploit the vulnerability of any legal recognition of race or gender difference'.[13]

The fairness principle is also harder to reconcile with positive-action programmes, which inherently discriminate against a dominant but protected group, typically white males. Preferences for women or minority racial groups repeat the same wrong that caused their subjugation in the first place. Positive action is easier to reconcile with the harm principle because here the 'wrongs' are not comparable. One is to subjugate a class of persons, while the other is to redress

9 The Stephen Lawrence Inquiry, Report of an Inquiry by Sir William Macpherson, advised by Tom Cook, the Right Reverend Dr John Sentamu, and Dr Richard Stone. Presented to Parliament by the Home Secretary (Cm 4262-I, 1999) at paras 6.1–6.34.

10 See J Gardner, 'Liberals and unlawful discrimination' (1989) 9 OJLS 1, 2–8.

11 See S Fredman, *Women and the Law* (Clarendon Press 1997) ch 2. On the common law's 'disability' of women, see pp 81–83.

12 J Gardner, 'Liberals and unlawful discrimination' (1989) 9 OJLS 1, 8.

13 N Lacey, 'From individual to group', in B Hepple and E Szyszczak (eds), *Discrimination: The Limits of Law* (Mansell 1992) 104.

subjugation. Assuming that various forms of discrimination can be characterised as harmful or unfair (or both), institutional or solely hostile, or a form of 'mistake', the next question is what should be the aim of legal intervention.

The aims of the law

The single aspiration upon which all interested parties appear to agree is the achievement of 'equality'. This word appears in discrimination legislation and human-rights instruments (as well as political discourses) the world over. But it is not free of debate. First, after examination, one learns that its most distinctive feature is its 'shifting meaning'.[14] Rather like a politician seeking a broad mandate, it reflects whatever meaning the observer wishes it to have. The second problem is that although equality is a 'virtue word'[15] and as such difficult to criticise, once it is given a firm meaning it becomes clear that equality is not necessarily a good thing. There are various models and ideals of equality within discrimination law, ranging from formal to substantive equality, and including human dignity, pluralism, and compassion.

1 Formal equality

Equality has been the underpinning principle of modern anti-discrimination law, beginning in the United States with the Civil Rights Act 1964. The primary goal of that Act was redressing the historic inequalities suffered by the United States' African-American population. The Act made it unlawful to 'discriminate' because of such individual's race, colour, religion, sex, or national origin.[16] From this, the US Supreme Court developed the disparate treatment (or direct discrimination) model.[17] The logical consequence is that those obligated by the Act must practice same – or *equal* – treatment. Britain adopted this model, with, for example, the Race Relations Act 1976, providing that direct discrimination was treating someone 'less favourably' on racial grounds, with the obvious and intended meaning that, on racial grounds, persons should be treated equally.

This model of equality is symmetrical, meaning that the law protects whites as well as blacks, men as well as women, and so on and so forth. In its simplest form, this model represents *formal* equality, that like should be treated as like.[18] (The notable exceptions here are disability and pregnancy/maternity discrimination laws, which commonly insist upon *different* treatment.[19]) There are a number of problems associated with formal equality.

14 P Westen, *Speaking of Equality* (Princeton University Press 1990) xviii.

15 ibid.

16 E.g. Title VII, s 703(a) codified as 42 USC s 2000e-2.

17 See e.g. *McDonnell Douglas Corp v Green* 411 US 792 (Sup Ct, 1973).

18 This can be traced back to Aristotle in *Nicomachean Ethics*, V.3.

19 Hugh Collins identified three 'deviations' from a simple equal treatment principle. First, different treatment is required in some cases, e.g. pregnancy and disability. Second, equal treatment is not permitted where it causes unjustifiable indirect discrimination. Third, affirmative action. See H Collins, 'Discrimination, equality and social inclusion' (2003) 66 MLR 16, 16–17.

The first problem is that equal treatment is not necessarily virtuous. At its most general, equal treatment is a consequence of the rule of law, by which laws must be enforced equally. But this does not prevent discriminatory laws, such as apartheid, being enacted and enforced equally.[20] A law of equal treatment is a step removed from unequal laws, but its enforcement can have counter-productive or unequal results. In his comment on the French law of vagrancy and theft, Anatole France mocked: 'The law, in its majestic equality, forbids the rich as well as the poor to sleep under bridges, to beg in the streets, and to steal bread.'[21] On this theme, Westen notes the equal treatment handed out in Hitler's concentration camps.[22]

Thus, equal treatment can amount to equally *bad* treatment. In one infamous US case, after a court ordered the city of Jackson, Mississippi, to abandon its racial segregation policy for its swimming pools (four white-only, one black-only), the city administration responded by closing down *all* its pools. *This* act did not offend the US constitutional right to equality.[23] In the context of sex-discrimination law, employers have defended claims by arguing (successfully) that they treated the claimant and her comparator equally *badly*. This has arisen in the field of sexual harassment, where homophobic abuse of a lesbian was not actionable because a male homosexual would have been equally abused.[24] Similarly, men and women in a factory were held to have been treated equally by the display of pornographic pictures of women.[25] In the field of pregnancy, British courts have compared the pregnant woman with a 'sick man', allowing employers to prevail if they can show that they would dismiss any worker who took a certain amount of time off work for illness.[26] The irony here is that the worse that the comparator is treated, the more likely it is that the employer would be believed. Some industries employing predominantly female or minority workers may pay poverty wages. In all these cases, the solution has been asymmetrical law, requiring no comparator, such as free-standing laws against sexual harassment and pregnancy discrimination, or even laws outside of the discrimination sphere, such as the National Minimum Wage Act 1998.

20 See J Jowell, 'Is equality a constitutional principle?' (1994) 47 CLP (Part 2, Collected Papers) 1, 4–91.

21 Anatole France, *Le Lys Rouge* (*The Red Lily*) [1894], quoted in John Bartlett, *Familiar Quotations* (14th rev edn, Little Brown 1968) 802a.

22 P Westen, *Speaking of Equality* (Princeton University Press 1990) xvii.

23 *Palmer v Thompson* 403 US 217 (Sup Ct, 1971).

24 *Pearce v Governing Body of Mayfield Secondary School* [2003] UKHL 34. The case predated the introduction of the Employment Equality (Sexual Orientation) Regulations 2003, SI 2003/1661 (nowadays EA 2010, s 4).

25 *Stewart v Cleveland Guest Ltd* [1996] ICR 535 (EAT). Sexual, and sex, harassment is now specifically outlawed: EA 2010, s 26.

26 *Hayes v Malleable Working Men's Club and Institute* [1985] ICR 703 (EAT). This approach was effectively overruled by the CJEU in Case C-177/88 *Dekker v Stichting Vormingscentrum voor Jonge Volwassen (VJV-Centrum) Plus* [1990] ECR I-3941. 'Pregnancy and maternity' are now protected characteristics: EA 2010, s 4.

Workers also may be 'equally' victimised for bringing discrimination claims, so long as all workers are treated that way, whatever the nature of their claim. Under this meaning of equality, such workers can be denied a reference,[27] a transfer, or a grievance hearing.[28]

The second problem of the equal treatment model is the need for a comparator. For instance, a woman cannot insist that she has been treated unequally until she produces a man who was, or would have been, treated more favourably. There are technical and philosophical problems associated with the comparator-driven approach. Technical problems arise because this model does not allow for differences between the protected characteristics. This most notable case here is pregnancy discrimination. A claimant cannot produce a pregnant male comparator. Similarly, in cases involving religion, claimants will often be seeking *different*, rather than equal treatment. For instance, there is no obviously suitable comparator for a Muslim worker requesting Friday afternoons off work to attend a mosque. This problem has been recognised overtly in the United States. In *EEOC v Ithaca Industries*[29] the employer was obliged to accommodate a worker's refusal to work on a Sunday for a religious reason, by enquiring if fellow workers would cover that shift. This was because, for cases of religious discrimination, the legislation's equality theory is not disparate treatment or disparate impact, but 'reasonable accommodation'.[30] This theory was reconciled with a notion of equality: 'We are convinced that [the legislation] . . . has the primary secular effect of preserving the *equal* employment opportunities of those employees whose moral scruples conflict with work rules'.[31]

The philosophical objection to the need for a comparator is that the comparator, when found, 'is clothed with the attributes of the dominant gender, culture, religion, ethnicity or sexuality'.[32] In the context of sex discrimination, this approach provides only '*equality in terms of a norm set by men*' leaving women with the right only to aspire to be the same as men.[33] Similarly, Townsend-Smith feared that the law could be used to reinforce male-based values, such as an ability to work longer hours, have unbroken and long service, aggression, or dynamism:

27 *Chief Constable of West Yorkshire v Khan* [2001] UKHL 48. See further pp 71 and 122–129.

28 *Cornelius v University College Swansea* [1987] IRLR 141 (CA). See further pp 127–128.

29 849 F 2d 116 (4th Cir 1988) certiorari denied, 488 US 924 (1988).

30 In 1972, an amendment to Title VII, s 701(j) (codified in 42 USC s 2000e(j)) was enacted with the stated purpose to protect Sabbath observers whose employers fail to adjust work schedules to fit their needs. 'The Act thus requires that an employer, short of undue hardship, make reasonable accommodations to the religious needs of its employees.' ibid, 118 (Judge Hall). In the UK, the matter has been litigated as indirect discrimination: *Walker v Hussain* [1996] ICR 291 (EAT) (Eid); *Cherfi v G4S Security Services Ltd* [2011] Eq LR 825 (EAT) (Friday prayers).

31 849 F 2d 116 (4th Cir 1988) 119 (Judge Hall). Emphasis supplied. Certiorari denied, 488 US 924 (1988)

32 S Fredman, *Discrimination Law* (2nd edn, Oxford University Press 2011) 11.

33 See T Ward, 'Beyond sex equality: the limits of sex equality in the new Europe', in T Hervey and D O'Keeffe (eds), *Sex Equality Law in the European Union* (Wiley 1996) 370.

> [I]t is important to see how deep-rooted is the notion of merit in our society, and that merit has historically been determined in male terms. The danger is that the law will accept male definitions of what is meritorious in employment, and that this will not correspond with the desires or best interests of many or most women.[34]

Likewise, equipment and machinery in the workplace can have gender connotations: 'In a training workshop . . . it is impossible to get a teenage lad to wipe the floor with a mop, though he may be persuaded to sweep it with a broom.'[35]

Lacey argues that, for women, formal equality does not go far enough as 'it has little bite in view of the disadvantages which women suffer in private areas such as family life, untouched by the sex discrimination legislation'.[36] The problem, she argues, is formal equality conceptualises the problem as *sex discrimination* rather than *discrimination against women*, rendering 'invisible the real social problem'. This objection applies to other characteristics as well as gender. A benign quality, such as being socially reserved, can be used as a reason not to hire, even though this quality is characteristic of Indian Hindus of the Brahmin caste.[37]

The third issue with the equal treatment model is that, in principle, equal treatment prevents *more* favourable treatment, and so prevents positive action. It is naive to believe that positive action is not necessary to redress the effects of past discrimination, which is a major reason for the legislation in the first place. Yet it clashes with the basic notion of equal treatment, especially in the mind of the public. Positive-action plans are only permissible as an exception to the equal treatment model.

The fourth feature of the equal treatment model is that it suggests that *everyone* is entitled to it, rather than just those groups specified in dedicated legislation. On the face of it, this should not be a problem. But dedicated legislation confining *equal* treatment to just *some* groups can ferment discontent and resentment by those not formally protected. And many other groups, whose political power is not so strong, are as likely to be in need of equal treatment as many of those covered by the legislation. Further, it is difficult to construct arguments to deny equal treatment to any individual, whether idiosyncratic or conventional. There is ample evidence that anyone feeling aggrieved will feel entitled to equal treatment. Men,[38]

34 R Townshend-Smith, *Sex Discrimination in Employment: Law, Practice and Policy* (Sweet & Maxwell 1989) 25–26. See *Price Waterhouse v Hopkins* 490 US 228 (Sup Ct, 1989) where the job required aggressiveness.

35 C Cockburn, *In The Way of Women: Men's Resistance to Sex Equality in Organisations* (Macmillan 1991) 38.

36 N Lacey, 'Legislation against sex discrimination: questions from a feminist perspective' (1986) 14 JLS 411, 413–417.

37 See *Kapoor v Monash University* (2001) VSCA 0247, 4 VR 483 (Supreme Court of Victoria, Australia).

38 *Jepson and Dyas-Elliott v The Labour Party* [1996] IRLR 116 (IT). Cases brought by male claimants under equal-pay legislation have been instrumental in the restructuring of pension plans. See e.g. Case C-262/88 *Barber v Guardian Royal Exchange* [1990] IRLR 240.

atheists,[39] whites,[40] and racists[41] readily have used the symmetry of the equal treatment model to redress their own grievances. In Britain, before the introduction of dedicated religious discrimination legislation, religious groups argued that they, by coincidence, were also racial groups, and so fell within the protection of the Race Relations Act 1976.[42] Many disgruntled with their pay have tried obtaining a 'fair' wage using equal pay law.[43]

In a relatively short time, the world has progressed from a 'norm' of identifying race and sex as grounds for anti-discrimination law, to specifying religion, disability, sexual orientation, gender reassignment, and age, as deserving of equal treatment. People generally may feel entitled to equal treatment because there is little evidence of any single fundamental principle dictating which groups should be singled out for particular protection. And although each of these grounds may be defensible on its own terms, the roots of their inclusion appear to be as capricious as they were principled.

One explanation is that these groups operated successful political campaigns. President Kennedy was moved by Martin Luther King's 'I have a dream' speech to promote the Civil Rights Act 1964.[44] In Britain, the daughter of the Minister for Disabled People drew huge public support by leading a campaign that embarrassed a reluctant government to introduce the Disability Discrimination Act 1995.[45] But not all groups obtained protection principally through their own political campaigns. The EU's Race Directive was partly, at least, the result of the politicians' fear of Europe's far-right exploiting the enlargement from 15 to 25 nations.[46] The EU's equal pay law was enshrined in the original Treaty of Rome at the insistence of French *business*: as France was the only country with an equal pay law at the time, French *employers* (not workers or feminist groups) campaigned for its inclusion

39 *EEOC v Townley Engineering* 859 F 2d 610 (9th Cir 1988). The employer made 'a covenant with God' that the company would be a 'would be a Christian, faith-operated business' and insisted that employees attend a weekly devotional service. It was held that this was religious discrimination against an atheist.

40 See e.g. *McDonald v Santa Fe Trail Transportation Co.* 427 US 273 (Sup Ct, 1976); *Carter v Gallagher* 452 F 2d 315 (8th Cir 1971) cert denied 406 US 950 (1972).

41 *Redfearn v Serco* [2006] EWCA 659. There are numerous examples in the US of the Ku Klux Klan invoking (unsuccessfully) equality law. See e.g. *New York ex rel Bryant v Zimmerman (No. 2)* 278 US 63 (Sup Ct, 1928).

42 *Mandla v Dowell Lee* [1983] 2 AC 548 (HL) (Sikhs recognised as racial group); *Crown Suppliers v Dawkins* [1993] ICR 517 (CA) (Rastafarians denied recognition).

43 See e.g. *Strathclyde Regional Council v Wallace* [1998] ICR 205 (HL); *Glasgow CC v Marshall* [2000] ICR 196 (HL). Discussed p 199 et al.

44 See e.g. C Whalen and B Whalen, *The Longest Debate: a Legislative History of the Civil Rights Act* (Seven Locks Press 1985).

45 Respectively, Victoria and Nicholas Scott. See *The Times* (London, 12 May 1994 and 21 May 1994); *The Independent* (London, 12 May 1994).

46 In its proposal, the European Commission stated: '[T]he [Race] Directive will provide a solid basis for the enlargement of the EU, which must be founded on the full and effective respect of human rights. The process of enlargement will bring into the EU new and different cultures and ethnic minorities. To avoid social strains in both existing and new Member States and to create a common Community of respect and tolerance for racial and ethnic diversity, it is essential to put in place a common European framework for the fight against racism.' COM/99/0566 final – CNS 99/0253, at p 4, para [6].

in the Treaty to avoid unfair competition from other member states.[47] Gender was introduced into the US Civil Rights Act 1964 as a wrecking amendment, the proposer believing that Congress would never vote for it.[48]

Thus, the reasons why particular groups have been singled out for dedicated anti-discrimination legislation are many and varied. By contrast, a sense of a principle can be detected from attempts to apply the 'equality' rubric contained in human-rights or constitutional instruments. The Supreme Court of Canada once centred its approach on 'human dignity.'[49] The US Supreme Court identifies 'suspect', 'quasi-suspect', and 'residual' classes of persons.[50] The jurisprudence of the European Court of Human Rights is less developed, with tentative notions of discrimination on *some* grounds requiring 'very weighty reasons' for justification, but offering little theory to explain this.[51]

A fifth objection to the equal treatment model is its characteristic of 'equality as consistency'. Its like-for-like nature is too rigid to address to all forms of inequality.[52] The equal treatment model starts from the position that the claimant and comparator are in the same position, say a woman and man doing work of equal value. Of course, they are not like-for-like when the woman is doing work of less value. Yet, theoretically at least, the formal equality model dictates that she may be paid 30 per cent less even though her work is only 20 per cent less value. Conversely, a woman doing work of *more* value is only entitled to the same pay. She cannot claim proportionally more money than him.[53] But this problem is less to do with principle and more to do with the restriction in the equal pay legislation that allows only a real (i.e. not hypothetical) comparator. Once this restriction is disregarded, claims like this can succeed under the equal treatment principle.[54]

The last objection is that formal equality can be used as a facade for bigotry. In 1896, in *Plessy v Ferguson*,[55] the US Supreme Court held that 'separate but equal' segregation in streetcars did not breach the constitutional right to equal protection of the laws. Its brutal opinion was that once formal equality had been achieved, how people felt about the result was their problem:

47 'What is particularly striking about what we know of the debates and manoeuvres which produced Article 119 is the level of abstraction at which they took place. At no time are the interests of women considered even obliquely or the issues of social justice raised. The distance from the reality of work or any real struggle seems complete. However, the potential for a stronger implementation of equal pay was embedded in the history of the article and, paradoxically, in the history of the EC itself. It took activist women to realise these possibilities – and switch the debate from one of economic rationality to a demand for rights.' C Hoskyns, *Integrating Gender* (Verso 1996) 57.

48 110 Cong Rec 2577–2584 (1964). The initiator was the 80-year-old segregationist Democrat Howard Smith of Virginia.

49 See p 67 et al.

50 See p 67 et al.

51 See the discussion on the levels of scrutiny, pp 47–48.

52 See S Fredman, *Discrimination Law* (2nd edn, Clarendon Law 2011) 13.

53 *Evesham v North Hertfordshire Health Authority* [2000] ICR 612 (CA).

54 See *County of Washington v Gunther* 452 US 161 (Sup Ct, 1981).

55 163 US 537 (1896).

> We consider the underlying fallacy of the plaintiff's argument to consist in the assumption that the enforced separation of the two races stamps the colored race with a badge of inferiority. If this be so, it is not by reason of anything found in the act, but solely because the colored race chooses to put that construction upon it.[56]

2 Substantive equality[57]

These limitations of formal equality have led to moves towards substantive equality. Perhaps the most dramatic shift occurred with the US Supreme Court's change of heart towards the racial segregation policies of the southern states. Some 60 years after *Plessy v Ferguson*, the US Supreme Court in *Brown v Board of Education*[58] ruled that segregation in education was inherently unequal and unconstitutional.[59] And so substantive equality demands that social justice and equality is meaningful and real to disadvantaged groups. The shift has been recognised expressly by the Canadian Supreme Court Justice, Beverly McLachlin:

> It is the belief that if equality is to be realized, we must move beyond formal legalism to measures that will make a practical difference in the lives of members of groups that have been traditionally subject to the tactics of subordination . . .. The use of the law to promote substantive equality, the phase we presently find ourselves in, takes two forms. The first is legislated programs whereby government, social and economic institutions are encouraged or, in some cases, required, to include people of under-represented groups. The second is the judicial concept of substantive equality, developed by the courts.[60]

Substantive equality suggests that responsibility for discrimination rests not just with the wrongdoer in court, but the dominant group as a whole that has benefited from society's structuring on racial, gender, and other grounds. This means that the dominant group should bear the cost of change.[61] It arises, for example, when 'innocent' whites and males lose out to apparently lesser-qualified minorities or women in positive-action programmes in employment,

56 ibid, 551.

57 See C Barnard and B Hepple, 'Substantive equality' (2000) 59(3) CLJ 562. For a discussion of EU discrimination law as a substantive rights, or anti-discrimination, model, see M Barbera, 'Not the same? The judicial role in the new community anti-discrimination law context' (2002) 31 ILJ 82. For a Canadian perspective, see CD Bavis, '*Vriend v Alberta*, *Law v Canada*, *Ontario v M and H*: the latest steps on the winding path to substantive equality' 37 Alberta L Rev 683.

58 347 US 483 (1954).

59 Under the Fourteenth Amendment's guarantee of equal protection of the laws.

60 B McLachlin, 'The evolution of equality' (1996) 54 Advocate 563, citing *Andrews v Law Society of British Columbia* (1989) 56 DLR (4th) 1.

61 See S Fredman, *Discrimination Law* (Oxford University Press 2001) 129.

education, or housing. Substantive equality also suggests that the state has a role. If it does nothing, it is condoning discrimination, which will perpetuate. Thus, it has a positive duty to intervene.[62]

Two particular theories are aligned with substantive equality: ***equality of opportunity*** and ***equality of results***. Lustgarten described these two notions in this way:

> In its purest or most extreme form the first accepts that discrimination has been abolished when all formal and deliberate barriers against blacks have been dismantled. Its concern stops with determining whether the factor of race has caused an individual to suffer adverse treatment. At the furthest point at the other end of the spectrum the unalloyed fair-share approach is concerned only with equality of result, measured in terms of proportionality. Its inherent logic leads to the adoption of quotas as a remedy once a finding of discrimination is made.[63]

The shift from formal equality to equality of opportunity was articulated by Wasserstrom, who suggested that that in a sea of inequalities, it seems pointless, philosophically and practically, to redress just one. As formal equality seeks to reward individual merit (rather than group status), it is the most qualified who deserve the most benefits. Yet, the distribution of these qualifications is dictated by factors beyond the control of the individual, such as the home environment, socio-economic class of parents, and the quality of the schools attended:

> Since individuals do not deserve having had any of these things vis-à-vis other individuals, they do not, for the most part, deserve their qualifications. And since they do not deserve their abilities they do not in any strong sense deserve to be admitted because of their abilities.[64]

Thus, there can only be true equality if the competitors in a race begin from the same starting point.[65] Lacey's criticism of formal equality[66] can be just as relevant here. If the race is one designed by white men, and is one in which they naturally prevail, even an equality of opportunity model fails to address the true problem.[67] Regardless of the merits of that opinion, it is undeniable that equality of opportunity

62 ibid. The Canadian Charter of Rights and Freedoms, s 15(2) provides a general green light to positive action, as the equality rights do not 'preclude any law, program or activity that has as its object the amelioration of conditions of disadvantaged individuals or groups'.

63 L Lustgarten, *Legal Control of Racial Discrimination* (Macmillan 1980) 6–7; see also L Mayhew, *Law and Equal Opportunity* (Harvard University Press 1968) 59–74.

64 R Wasserstrom, 'Racism, sexism and preferential treatment: an approach to the topics' (1977) 24 UCLA L Rev 581, 619–620.

65 K O'Donovan and E Szyszczak, *Equality and Sex Discrimination Law* (Blackwell 1988) 4–5; S Fredman, *Discrimination Law* (Oxford University Press 2011) 18.

66 See p 62.

67 S Fredman, *Discrimination Law* (Oxford University Press 2001) 128–129.

cannot guarantee that society's benefits will be evenly distributed. The *equality of results* approach rests on the patent injustice of unevenly distributed benefits. At the least, this a measure by which the equality of opportunity model can be tested.

Some recognition of these broader inequalities can be detected in a practice of the US Supreme Court, pointing to another theory, which centres on identifying the 'underdog', or those in a state of inferiority or subjection. The Equal Protection Clause of the Fourteenth or Fifth Amendments of the US Constitution provides a constitutional guarantee of equal protection of the laws.[68] The Court has identified three classes of protected groups under the Clause: suspect class; quasi-suspect class; and a residual, 'normal', class. Measures discriminating against these classes are given, respectively, strict scrutiny, 'heightened' scrutiny, or 'normal' or 'rational' scrutiny.[69]

In deciding if a group qualifies as a suspect class, a court will normally consider three factors. The first is a history of purposeful discrimination.[70] Second, is whether the discrimination embodies such a gross unfairness to be 'invidious'. Considerations here could be a class trait that bears no relation to ability to perform or contribute to society, or that the class has been saddled with unique disabilities because of prejudice or inaccurate stereotypes, or that the trait defining the class is immutable. Third, whether the group lacks the political power necessary to obtain redress from the political branches of government.[71]

This third factor points to a degree of social inclusion in the reckoning. Hence, the range of legislation on disability discrimination helped to disqualify 'disability' from the suspect class.[72] Similarly, it was once noted in this context that 'homosexuals are not without political power; they have the ability to and do "attract the attention of the lawmakers"'.[73]

Hugh Collins considers a notion of social inclusion that goes beyond perhaps mere political power, and sees it as a unifying explanation of discrimination law.[74] The difficulty with this as a comprehensive explanation is that it does not

68 The equal protection component of the Fifth Amendment imposes precisely the same constitutional requirements on the federal government as the equal protection clause of the Fourteenth Amendment imposes on state governments: *Weinberger v Wiesenfeld* 420 US 636, 638 n2 (Sup Ct, 1975).

69 Respectively, *McLaughlin v Florida* 379 US 184, 192 (Sup Ct, 1964); *Graham v Richardson* 403 US 365 (Sup Ct, 1971); *Mills v Hahluetzel* 456 US 91, 99 (Sup Ct, 1982); *City of Cleburne, Texas v Cleburne Living Center* 473 US 432, 446 (Sup Ct, 1985).

70 See e.g. *City of Cleburne, Texas v Cleburne Living Center* 473 US 432, 441 (Sup Ct, 1985); *Massachusetts Board of Retirement v Murgia* 427 US 307, 313 (Sup Ct, 1976).

71 See also *Andres v Law Society* [1989] 1 SCR 143 (Supreme Court of Canada) 152 (Wilson J) 195 (La Forest J).

72 *City of Cleburne, Texas v Cleburne Living Center* 473 US 432 (Sup Ct, 1985) 442–446.

73 *High Tech Gays v Defense Indus. Sec. Clearance Office* 895 F 2d 563, 573–574 (9th Cir 1990) citing *City of Cleburne, Texas v Cleburne Living Center* 473 US 432, 446 (Sup Ct, 1985). Cf *Witt v Department of the Air Force*, 527 F 3d 806 (9th Cir 2008) subjecting to heightened scrutiny the military's 'Don't Ask Don't Tell' policy towards homosexuality. The policy was repealed soon afterwards.

74 H Collins, 'Discrimination, equality and social inclusion' (2003) 66 MLR 16.

account for all equality claims, despite them being considered meritorious by most discrimination lawyers and, indeed, the public as a whole. Notable here would be six-figure equal pay claims by female City workers.[75]

The conspicuous shortfall of all of these theories is that they do not directly address social economic inequalities:

> [A]s one might have suspected from its American antecedents the fair-share approach is in no way compatible with great inequalities of income, wealth and social resources: it merely requires that blacks fit into the existing patterns of inequality in the same proportions as whites.[76]

The pragmatic view of this is that the undefined slogan ***equal opportunities*** was able to unite diverse political groups to support anti-discrimination legislation. They were unlikely to support substantive inroads into social-economic inequality, or more radical steps: 'How many liberal supporters of the current legislation, for example, would have been content to reflect on the implications of a thorough-going commitment to equality of opportunity in terms of socialisation of childrearing or even genetic engineering?'[77]

3 Human dignity and equality

A different, apparently more restrictive, approach is to centre recognition of equality rights on the principle of human dignity.[78] This principle can be detected in most human-rights discourses and is expressed in the dedicated discrimination legislation.[79]

In South Africa, dignity is a cornerstone of the (Final) Constitution and a principal right,[80] although rarely used as such.[81] However, the ***notion*** of dignity is used more commonly to decide if there has been unlawful discrimination.[82]

75 See e.g. *Barton v Investec* [2003] ICR 1205 (EAT).

76 L Lustgarten, *Legal Control of Racial Discrimination* (Macmillan 1980) 6–7.

77 N Lacey, 'Legislation against sex discrimination: questions from a feminist perspective' (1986) 14 JLS 411, 414.

78 See e.g. *Law v Canada* [1999] 1 SCR 497 (SCC). For a discussion of dignity in English law, see D Feldman, 'Human dignity as a legal value', Part I [1999] PL 682, Part II [2000] PL 61.

79 By Equality Act 2006, s 3(c). The Commission for Equality and Human Rights is charged to carry out its duties, *inter alia*, 'with a view to encouraging and supporting the development of a society in which there is respect for the dignity and worth of each individual'. By the Equality Directives (2006/54/EC, 2000/78/EC, 2000/43/EC) and the EA 2010, s 26(1)(b) harassment can occur when conduct has the purpose or effect of 'violating' the victim's 'dignity'. See also *English v Thomas Sanderson Blinds* [2009] ICR 543 (CA), especially [37].

80 Constitution of the Republic of South Africa 1996, s 10, < www.gov.za/documents/constitution-republic-south-africa-1996 > accessed 10 April 2018.

81 *Dawood v Minister of Home Affairs* (2000) (3) SA 936 (CC) [35].

82 Constitution of the Republic of South Africa 1996, s 9.

For instance, under the Black Administration Act 1927 (and regulations made under it), the estate of an intestate person would be administered by a Master of the High Court, or if the person was black, by a magistrate. Despite magistrates being more conveniently located and inexpensive, this law was struck down as unconstitutional because 'even if there are practical advantages for many people in the system, it is rooted in racial discrimination which severely assails the dignity of those concerned and undermines attempts to establish a fair and equitable system of public administration'.[83]

Similarly, 'separate but equal' segregated education was ruled constitutionally *un*equal by the US Supreme Court, because *inter alia*, it generated 'a feeling of inferiority as to their status in the community that may affect their hearts and minds in a way unlikely ever to be undone',[84] a sentiment rooted in human dignity, although not expressed as such. As these examples show, dignity can resolve issues in discrimination law.[85] But as a unifying theory underpinning all discrimination law, the notion of dignity is problematic.

Its utility in resolving apparently symmetrical separate-but-equal scenarios also betrays an uneasy relationship with the symmetrical nature of the equal treatment model, the first problem. In one sense, the notion of *dignity* is inadequate to explain the groups covered by the dedicated legislation. This is because the symmetrical nature of equal treatment model is available to *men* as well as women, *whites* as well as blacks, and so on. *These* groups, of course, are not the intended principal beneficiaries of the legislation, and are hardly – as *groups* – suffering a lack of dignity. On the contrary, in historical terms these groups are the respective *oppressors* of the intended beneficiaries. In a broader sense though, the strict *equal* treatment model has the benefit of not patronising the principal protected beneficiaries, and thus preserving some dignity. As such, it is difficult even for the most conservative critic of discrimination law to argue that equal treatment is *special* treatment undermining the dignity of the principal beneficiaries. This neutralises their criticism somewhat, but, at best, merely shows that the equal treatment model could be consistent with dignity. It does not show it is dependent upon it.

The second problem, which has been examined by Rory O'Connell, is that dignity is too vague a concept to underpin a legal principle. He illustrates this by reference to South African and Canadian Constitutional judgments centred on dignity, with a common feature that the courts were fiercely divided. Hence: 'The competing interpretations of dignity, in particular, allow for unarticulated value judgments to

83 *Moseneke v Master of the High Court* (2001) (2) SA 18 (CC), [22]–[23].

84 *Brown v Board of Education* 347 US 483 (1954) 494.

85 Eight specific issues are considered by G Moon and R Allen, 'Dignity discourse in discrimination law: a better route to equality?' (2006) 6 EHRLR 610, none of which relate to identifying a protected group.

determine their decisions.'[86] But strong dissents and divided courts are not confined to cases involving dignity. If a concept under discussion were abandoned simply because of a divided court, most of Britain's anti-discrimination legislation would have been repealed by now.[87] That said, dignity as a basis for equality law is particularly capricious. Take, for example, Britain's approach to dignity and justifying compulsory retirement. In 2009, the High Court rejected the notion that compulsory retirement preserved a worker's dignity.[88] A year later, in a different case, the Court of Appeal thought that compulsory retirement allowed workers 'to retire with dignity'.[89] In 2011, the Government suggested that compulsory retirement (in the absence of performance management) could cause a 'loss of dignity'.[90] The uncertainty surrounding its definition prompted the Canadian Supreme Court to abandon it as a mainstay of applying its Charter of Rights, because it was 'an abstract and subjective notion that [can be] confusing and difficult to apply . . . [and] an *additional* burden on equality claimants, rather than the philosophical enhancement it was intended to be'.[91] This confusing picture is better understood perhaps by subdividing some various notions of 'dignity'. Its meaning may turn on whether we consider the dignity of an individual, a group, or the human race.

Individual dignity itself has been afforded three aspects (at least). It starts with personal autonomy. In general, the autonomy begins with the notion that as humans can make moral choices, they have 'unconditioned and incomparable worth', or dignity.[92] As such, humans ought to be treated as ends in themselves, never merely as means to an end.[93] This lends itself to a notion of human autonomy: equality law protects an individual's freedom of choice (e.g. choosing to practise a

86 R O'Connell, 'The role of dignity in equality law: lessons from Canada and South Africa' (2008) 6(2) IJCL 267–286. He could have added *McKinney v University of Guelph* [1990] 3 SCR 229, where both sides of a divided Canadian Supreme Court cited 'dignity' in coming to their respective decisions on compulsory retirement as age discrimination: [295], [297], [303], [314], [319], [391], [393], [410], [413], [424], [431], & [447].

87 Consider the judgments at all levels in the following cases: *Mandla v Dowell Lee* [1983] 2 AC 548 (HL); (4 dissenters against 5); *R (E) v Governing Body of JFS* [2010] 2 AC 278 (SC) (5 against 8); *James v Eastleigh BC* [1990] 2 AC 751 (HL) (6 against 3); *Archibald v Fife Council* [2004] UKHL 32 (4 against 5); *Matthews v Kent & Medway Towns Fire Authority* [2006] ICR 365 (HL) (11 against 3!).

88 *R (Age UK) v Secretary of State for Business, Innovation and Skills* [2009] IRLR 1017, [108], [122].

89 *Seldon v Clarkson, Wright & Jakes* [2010] EWCA Civ 899, [22]–[24] affirmed with caution [2012] UKSC 16, [61].

90 'Age positive: workforce management without a fixed retirement age' (2011) page 12, < webarchive.nationalarchives.gov.uk/20130703133823/http://www.dwp.gov.uk/docs/workforce-mgt-without-fixed-retirement-age.pdf > accessed 10 April 2018. Contrast the CJEU, which accepted that compulsory retirement of public prosecutors could 'improve personnel management and thereby to prevent possible disputes concerning employees' fitness to work beyond a certain age': Case C-159/10 *Fuchs v Land Hessen* [2011] Pens. LR 335, [5], [53].

91 *R v Kapp* [2008] 2 SCR 483 (SCC) [19]–[24].

92 Immanuel Kant, *The Moral Law: Groundwork of the Metaphysics of Morals* [1785] (Hutchinson 1948) 434–440, especially 436.

93 See this ideal cited to hold that sentencing should not be based solely on a deterrent principle, bearing no proportion to the defendant's culpability in *R v Dodo* (2001) (5) BCLR 423; (2001) (3) SA 382 (South African Constitutional Ct) [38].

certain religion).[94] Of course, excessive deference to individual autonomy tolerating excessive behaviour – such as bigamy, unrestricted abortion, and incitement to racial hatred – would necessitate the repeal of laws that restrict behaviour, including anti-discrimination laws. So, personal autonomy, in itself, cannot be a goal of equality law, as it could permit all manner of discriminatory conduct.

Personal autonomy can be connected to a notion of how an individual *feels* within a society: a person's self-respect.[95] Objections to this subjective approach are twofold. First, the practical problem would be placing in the hands of judges an evaluation of a claimant's feelings, leading to wildly different decisions depending on the judge's empathy with the claimant. At a domestic level, judges have overcome this problem, but only by introducing an objective dimension. To the slightly different question of whether a claimant has suffered less favourable treatment for the purposes of direct discrimination, British judges ask if the claimant perceived the treatment as less favourable and was not unreasonable in doing so. In other words, it is not necessary that *every* reasonable person in the shoes of the claimant would have perceived that the treatment was unfavourable. Thus, in *Gill v El Vino*,[96] it was reasonable for *a* woman to consider that bar service for men and waited table-service for women to be less favourable, because she was denied a choice, even though some women may have preferred that arrangement. In *Chief Constable of West Yorkshire v Khan*[97] it was reasonable for a job candidate to expect his current employer to provide a reference, even though it would have been negative and *reduced* his chances, even though that most people in his position would have preferred that the reference was not provided.

Similarly, in the United States, courts have understood that even 'an inadvertent racial slight unnoticed either by its white speaker or white bystanders will reverberate in the memory of its black victim'. Accordingly, the trier of fact must 'walk a mile in the victim's shoes' to understand the effects.[98] This subjective/objective

94 See J Gardner, 'On the grounds of her sex(uality)' (1998) 18 OJLS 167, 169–174, who argues that Wintemute's dual explanation for protected grounds, especially sexual orientation – immutability and fundamental choices (equating to sexual attraction and sexual activity) – has a common foundation of autonomy: 'the ideal of a life substantially lived through the successive valuable choices of the person who lives it, where valuable choices are choices from among an adequate range of valuable options' (170). Wintemute's theory can be found in R Wintemute, *Sexual Orientation and Human Rights: The United States Constitution, the European Convention, and the Canadian Charter* (Clarendon Press 1997).

95 J Rawls, *A Theory of Justice* (Oxford University Press 1972) 62, 178, 440. See also *Law v Canada* [1999] 1 SCR 497 (SCC) [53].

96 [1983] QB 425 (CA).

97 [2001] UKHL 48 (a case on victimisation under the RRA 1976). See pp 71 and 122–129.

98 *Harris v International Paper* 765 F Supp 1509, 1515–1516 (vacated on other grounds 765 F Supp 1529) (1991), citing in support: CR Lawrence, 'The id, the ego, and equal protection: reckoning with unconscious racism' (1987) 39 Stan L Rev 317; MJ Matsuda, 'Public response to racist speech: considering the victim's story' (1989) 87 Mich L Rev 2320, 2326–2335; PJ Williams, 'Alchemical notes: reconstructing ideals from deconstructed rights' (1987) 22 Harv CR-CL L Rev 401, 406–413 (explaining why black and white apartment-seekers assume different perspectives on the formalities of renting an apartment).

approach was incorporated into Britain's statutory definition of harassment,[99] which applies to the question of whether or not the defendant's conduct had the purpose or effect of 'violating' the claimant's 'dignity'.[100]

Even if the first objection can be met, albeit with a compromise, there remains a second objection, which is less easily overcome. Much of equality law is about *ambition*. It seeks to challenge and alter ingrained, outdated, and/or pernicious values. The Civil Rights Act 1964 sought to address the de facto racial segregation and discrimination in many walks of life in the United States. Britain's Equal Pay Act 1970 was an expression of changing values: women were no longer to be regarded as secondary earners in a nuclear family. More recently, legislation enacts the notion that childbirth and child-rearing is no longer sole responsibility of the mother; employers, fathers, and the state all have a role to play.[101] These statutes challenged the status quo, which was accepted by many of those they were passed to protect, or liberate. At the time, and in diminishing numbers since, some women would have no expectation to anything better, and thus had not perceived their dignity as undermined by inferior pay or the one-sided parental responsibilities. There are countless examples of members of groups who suffer discrimination actually resisting a change to their circumstances: women campaigned against having the vote,[102] and led anti-abortion campaigns,[103] whilst South Africa's Black Consciousness movement had black dignity as its principal goal, above the abolition of apartheid.[104] If dignity is the basis of equality law, it follows that these dissenters (and perhaps the apathetic) were incapable of holding a sense of self-worth.[105] Of course, quite the opposite is true. The dissenters saw the equality law as paternalistic, and something diminishing, or threatening, or secondary to, their personal sense of dignity.

99 EA 2010, s 26(4) although there is leeway here over the precise meaning afforded to the objective element. See M Connolly, *Discrimination Law* (Sweet & Maxwell 2011) 134–138.

100 See e.g. *Richmond Pharmacology v Dhaliwal* (2009) ICR 724 (EAT) [15]. Decided under RRA 1976, s 3A.

101 See e.g. Recast Directive 2006/54/EC, Recitals 11, 26, and art 16; Additional Paternity Leave Regulations 2010, SI 2010/1055.

102 See e.g. Helen Kendrick Johnson, *Women and the Republic* [1897] (Bibliobazaar 2006). A referendum, held in 1895 in Massachusetts asking women to vote for suffrage, polled only 22,204 (under 4 per cent) out of an estimated 575,000 women in the state: Molly Elliot Seawell, 'Two suffrage mistakes' (1914) 199(700) March *North American Review* 366–382, 380.

103 For instance, Minnesota Congresswoman and presidential nominee, Michele Bachmann, is a leading 'pro-life' campaigner and denigrates *Roe v Wade* 410 US 113 (1973) the seminal Supreme Court 'pro-choice' decision on abortion. See < http://history.house.gov/People/Detail/10411#biography > accessed 10 April 2018; Bachmann has since left Congress, see now M Bachmann, *Core of Conviction* (Senitel 2011) 2–4, 47, 58, 127.

104 S Biko, *I Write What I Like* (Heinemann 1987) 22, urging (metaphorically) blacks to reject invitations by white liberals to 'come round for tea at home'. See also JL Gibson, *Overcoming Apartheid* (Russell Sage Foundation Publications 2006) 79–82, considering a survey where one-half of whites and one-third of blacks considered that *in principle* apartheid was a good idea. Of course, most disfavoured its *implementation* in South Africa, and notions of racial hierarchy.

105 Feldman envisages only a narrow class unable to cultivate their sense of dignity, such as very young children and people in a persistent vegetative state: D Feldman, 'Human dignity as a legal value' Part I [1999] PL 682, 686.

Thus, a subjective notion of dignity does not account for the ambition of equality law to challenge and change existing values, no matter how ingrained in some they may be. How any particular individual *feels* about this ambition is less important than a societal goal to achieve a change in values and liberate people from their own expectations.

This leads to a consideration of *group* dignity, or even the dignity of the human race, which in the examples above appears to trump a (dissenting) individual's dignity, even though the individual belongs to the group. More extreme, paternalistic examples would be banning a willing, well-paid, and well-protected, dwarf from participating in 'dwarf-throwing',[106] or forcing a blood transfusion upon a Jehovah's Witness.[107] Here dignity of the human race would appear to trump individual or even group dignity.

Once placed in the legal arena, the notions of dignity of the individual, the group, and the human race, to some degree, are in conflict. Hence, although notions of dignity have a part to play in understanding discrimination law, they cannot operate as a unifying theory for equality law. Of course, individual or group *in*dignity can trigger society's *compassion* to address the matter as one of inequality, which is discussed next.

4 Equality, pluralism, and compassion

Wasserstrom[108] has presented three alternative goals of 'equality' law. The first is the *assimilationist* model. Here, in a non-racist society, a person's race is the 'functional equivalent' of their eye colour. This is less easy to present in respect to sex, disability, and religion, where there are accepted differences that characterise these groups. The second is diversity. Here genuine differences, say between religions, are a 'positive good'. It would be a worse society if everyone were a member of one religion. The third is tolerance. Here, there is nothing intrinsically positive about diversity, but tolerance outweighs the evils of achieving homogeneity.

The second and third of these goals align with current policy in North America and the EU, with a celebration and tolerance of multiculturalism. It is true that, in recent years, some European leaders have criticised 'state

106 Ban upheld by the *Conseil d'Eta*: CE, ass, 27 October 1995, *Cne de Morsang-sur-Orge*, Dalloz Jur., 1995, p 257; CE, ass, 27 October 1995, *Ville d'Aix-en-Provence, Rec.* CE, p 372; Dalloz Jur., 1996, p 177, with annotation by G Leberton. Cited by Feldman, ibid, 701.

107 The case of *Mme X* in *Cour administrative d'appel de Paris*, where it was argued that the dignity of humanity prevailed over the autonomy of the individual, although dignity was not mentioned in the judgment upholding the transfusion: CAA Paris, form. plén., 9 juin 1998 (*Mme X* . . .) Dalloz Jur., 1999, p 277, note by Dr Gilles Pellissier at p 281, citing, *inter alios*, B Edelman, 'La dignité humaine, un concept nouveau', Dalloz Chron., 1997, p 185. Cited by Feldman, [1999] PL 682, 701.

108 R Wasserstrom, 'Racism, sexism and preferential treatment: an approach to the topics' (1977) 24 UCLA L Rev 581, 585–589.

multiculturalism',[109] but there is yet to be a formalised alternative. Moreover, at the same time, the discrimination legislation has extended its reach to the recognition of more mutable characteristics, such as religion or belief, and manifestations related to religion, as well as transsexualism and sexual orientation,[110] thus celebrating and tolerating an individual's choice of culture, and with it, even more diversity.

But slogans commonly used by governments in search of these goals, such as *different but equal* and *equality and diversity*[111] appear paradoxical, giving the law the delicate task of achieving both equality and diversity. Wasserstrom suggests that this may be achieved with celebration or tolerance. Of course, in reality a dose of both is required. It suggests that the key is psychological, or emotional, rather than formal. Human rights law – including anti-discrimination rubrics – originates, partly at least, from human compassion, or the milk of human kindness. People generally have a sense of compassion, especially for the underdog. This appears at odds with the resistance by ordinary (so presumably decent) people to much discrimination law, especially positive-action programmes[112] and the truism that anti-discrimination laws are enacted to combat prejudices in mainstream society. The comments by Lords Woolf and Browne-Wilkinson at the beginning of this chapter reveal that the general public's perception is important in defining the law. But in complex societies where so much disadvantage is invisible to an uninformed public, this is no more useful than asking for a jury's opinion after providing it with newspapers instead of the evidence. The notion falls well short of an ideal. This implies that there is a duty on politicians and the judiciary to educate the public in the real disadvantages that exist in their society, so triggering their innate human compassion. The neglect of this duty is perhaps most sadly apparent with immigration and asylum. Mainstream politicians commonly and quite comfortably inform the public of problems associated with

109 See e.g. David Cameron's Munich Speech, < webarchive.nationalarchives.gov.uk/20130109092234/http://number10.gov.uk/news/pms-speech-at-munich-security-conference/ >; M Weaver, 'Angela Merkel: German multiculturalism has "utterly failed"' *Guardian* (London, 17 October 2010), < www.youtube.com/watch?v=UKG76HF24_k&feature=related > each accessed 10 May 2018.

110 Respectively, e.g. wearing of religious symbols, 'presenting', and same-sex relationships.

111 Government consultation documents on discrimination law have employed this phrase, e.g. DTI, *Equality and Diversity: Coming of Age* (July 2005, DTI/Pub 7851/3k/07/05/NP. URN 05/1171); Women and Equality Unit, DTI, *Equality and Diversity: Updating the Sex Discrimination Act 1975* (March 2005); Office of the Deputy Prime Minister, *Towards Equality and Diversity: Implementing the Employment and Race Directives* (December 2001); Government Equalities Office, 'Closing the Gender pay gap. Government consultation' (February 2016) 43 ('diversity and equality'), < https://www.gov.uk/government/consultations/closing-the-gender-pay-gap> accessed 10 April 2018.

112 In the 2004 general election, in a core Labour constituency, Peter Law resigned from the Labour Party in protest at the selection of a candidate from an all-women short list. He stood as an independent and overturned the Labour majority of 19,000 votes, winning with a majority of 9,000: *The Times* (London, 6 April 2004). In 2006 the Labour Party issued an apology to the electorate 'for getting it wrong' (*The Independent* (London, 8 May 2006).

asylum seekers[113] but rarely explain a traumatic story behind any plea for sanctuary. Similarly, politicians shamelessly express 'populist' but pernicious opinions on minority groups such as Romanies and travellers.[114] This breeds cynicism rather than compassion, which in turn feeds into the legal interpretations, as Lords Woolf and Browne-Wilkinson have confirmed.

The judiciary can take a lead as well. For the law to be structured around human compassion is not as fanciful as it first seems. As noted above, the Canadian Supreme Court at one time developed its human-rights jurisprudence around the theme of 'human dignity', as does the South African Constitution. Also noted above is the US Supreme Court's practice of identifying the 'underdog' for constitutional protection against discrimination. These observations about the state of groups in society are as loaded with compassion as they are with intellectual rigour. This attempt at defining legally the underdog shows that positive human emotions can be identified and realised in law.

5 Statutory purpose

If anything from this rather broad range of theories is to inform judiciary seeking sound ***and*** consistent judgments, it must be sieved and sorted, or even funnelled, to produce some relatively simplistic political and intellectual consensus on the statutory purpose to be understood in the interpretive process. As noted above, the political consensus centres on a celebration of multiculturalism, along with a tolerance of the consequent differences. For these aims to be realised in law, something more detailed is required.

Britain's dedicated anti-discrimination legislation, now consolidated by the Equality Act 2010, covers a number of grounds, such as race, sex, transsexualism, sexual orientation, religion or belief, age, and disability. The background, and consequent ambition and purpose of the legislation, may vary depending on the protected characteristic and particular problem involved. But they have in common patterns of disadvantage, represented, say, by under-achievement or poor participation in certain civil activities and environments, such as education, employment, and housing. There is a political consensus that these patterns are signs of failure, and so should be addressed with ideals of formal and substantive

113 There are countless examples. In 2002, the Home Secretary, David Blunkett, observed that the children of asylum seekers were 'swamping' some schools: *The Times* (London, 25 April 2002). In 1972 it was observed that the Government's 'ambivalent' policy was to proclaim racism wrong whilst declaring that Britain was too small to absorb any more immigrants: 'Understandably, few people have grasped the distinction. The more obvious conclusion that has generally been drawn is that if coloured immigration presents a threat to Britain's well-being, so does the coloured minority living in Britain.' A Lester and G Bindman, *Race and Law* (Penguin 1972) 13.

114 See Royce Turner, 'Gypsies and British parliamentary language: an analysis' (2002) 12 *Romani Studies*, 1–34, who summarises that they are portrayed in Parliament as: 'dishonest, criminal, dirty'. For an account of the Coalition's 'offensive' on Gypsies and travellers, see J Grayson, 'Playing the Gypsy "race card"' (2010) Institute of Race Relations, 4 June 2010, < www.irr.org.uk/news/playing-the-gypsy-race-card/ > accessed 10 April 2018.

equality. There are multiple tools to do this, such as economic and social policy, strategic enforcement, and, of course, providing causes of action for discrimination, the subject of this study.

The notions of formal and substantive equality are loosely represented by the principal causes of action, direct and indirect discrimination, respectively. These legal tools of addressing patterns of disadvantage must be understood within the confines of binary litigation. This is a challenging, if not unique, proposition, given the Act's societal ambitions. This law must extend beyond the common law's traditional mind-set of an at-fault tortfeasor causing harm to an individual victim, but not beyond the outer boundaries of the basic notion of *a* defendant, *a* cause, and *a* victim.

The 1975 White Paper, *Racial Discrimination* noted, 'it is insufficient for the law to deal only with overt discrimination. It should also prohibit practices which are fair in a formal sense but discriminatory in their operation and *effect*'.[115] This, of course, has roots in the notion of indirect discrimination and *Griggs v Duke Power*[116] (where a requirement for a high-school diploma adversely affected African-Americans). But it tells us a number of more general things. First, that a *precise* cause is not necessary, as many patterns have multiple causes, many of which may not be known, or not within the control of the defendant. For instance, Duke Power qua employer could not be held responsible for the inferior segregated education. And second, although the claimant may need standing to sue, this need not be so for every member of the disadvantaged group,[117] even though they may benefit from the remedy. Moreover, the preoccupation with the patterns of disadvantage enables interested non-group members to sue for discrimination (direct or indirect). This can include victims of the same disadvantage,[118] or targeted 'associates' of a protected group,[119] or even those otherwise harmed by the discrimination.[120] As the US Supreme Court once stated: 'The [African American] on the landlord's blacklist is not the only victim of discriminatory housing practices; it is . . ."the whole community"'.[121]

115 Home Office, *Racial Discrimination* (Cmnd 6234, 1975) para 35. This explained the inclusion of indirect discrimination in the then forthcoming RRA 1976, now consolidated in the EA 2010. Emphasis supplied.

116 (1971) 401 US 424 (US Sup Ct). See further pp 153, 177 and 187.

117 *Essop v Home Office* [2017] UKSC 27 [27].

118 Case C-83/14 *CHEZ Razpredelenie Bulgaria AD v Komisia za zashtita ot diskriminatsias* [2016] 1 CMLR 14 (non-Roma inconvenienced by raised electricity meters). See further p 206.

119 Case C-303/06 *Coleman v Attridge Law* [1998] 3 CMLR 27 (discriminating against disabled child's mother). See Explanatory Notes to the EA 2010, para 63.

120 Case C-54/07 *Centrum voor Gelijkheid van Kansen en voor Racismebestrijding v Firma Feryn NV* [2008] ECR I-5187 (employer announced he would not employ immigrants). See Explanatory Notes to the EA 2010, para 63.

121 *Trafficante v Metropolitan Life* 409 US 205, 211 (Sup Ct, 1972) (white tenant had standing to sue landlord for discriminating against prospective black tenants under the Fair Housing Act 1968) citing Senator Jacob Javits speaking in support of the Bill: 114 Cong Rec 2706.

This liberal approach to causation and identifying a victim is also necessary when considering the required 'culpability' of the defendant. In fact, no culpability is required. The patterns of disadvantage can be caused by conduct ranging from openly hostile to completely benign. And so, for the law to address these patterns, the *effect* of conduct should be able to trump its apparent neutrality. Indeed, *Griggs* also tells us any sort of discriminatory intent is not required for indirect discrimination liability. This places even the notion of 'institutional racism'[122] some way up the culpability scale, as tacit approval of apparently benign conduct, such as word-of-mouth hiring ('help a friend'),[123] or even well-intentioned conduct (most obviously, positive action), can have discriminatory effects.[124]

If *mere* conduct (including acquiescence) is all that is required, then defendants in such cases should not fear being stamped as racist or the like. In turn, judges should not fear finding liability out of a misplaced, or artificial, sympathy for the defendant, nor should they formulate their judgments in terms of blame or exculpation. In all, the established liberal approach to all three aspects (victim–cause–defendant) requires the courts not to be unduly constrained by the traditional common law tortfeasor and victim mind-set.

The propositions in this section, rooted themselves in the various theories and aims, are embedded in the domestic equality legislation, either expressly, or by the (presently) obligatory EU legislation and case law, or by its (commonly US) antecedents. Moreover, the societal ambition of the legislation is express nowadays, with the Equality Act 2010 announcing its ambition 'to increase equality of opportunity' and to 'strengthen the law to support progress on equality'.[125] Thus, it is the judge's obligation to use the Act as a progressive tool to reduce inequality within its bounds (most notably of protected characteristics and activities). As such, the judiciary should not fear taking a purposive approach to equality law; indeed, it is an obligation. As noted near the start of this section (on statutory purpose), the background, and consequent ambition and purpose of the legislation, may vary depending on the particular circumstances. Some broader principles, flowing from the law's effect-based ambition, are advocated here. More specific statutory purposes may be required according to the issue arising. These will be explored on a case-by-case basis after a consideration of the common law and equality in the next chapter.

122 The Stephen Lawrence Inquiry, Report of an Inquiry by Sir William Macpherson, advised by Tom Cook, the Right Reverend Dr John Sentamu, and Dr Richard Stone, February 1999. Presented to Parliament by the Home Secretary (Cm 4262-I, 1999) at paras 6.1–6.34. See p 58.

123 Suggested in *Coker v Lord Chancellor* [2002] ICR 321 (CA), [57]. Cf *Pel Ltd v Modgill* [1980] IRLR 142 (EAT). See generally, 'subjective hiring practices', pp 165–167 et al.

124 See also *James v Eastleigh BC* [1990] 2 AC 751 (HL), discussed p 92 et al; *Amnesty International v Ahmed* [2009] ICR 1450 (EAT).

125 Respectively the Long Title and Explanatory Notes to the EA 2010, para 10.

Further reading

L Alexander, 'What makes wrongful discrimination wrong? Biases, preferences, stereotypes and proxies' (1992) 141 Penn UL Rev 149.
G Rutherglen, 'Discrimination and its discontents' (1995) 81 Virginia L Rev 117.
C Sunstein, 'Three civil rights fallacies' (1991) 79 California L Rev 751.
J Gardner, 'Liberals and unlawful discrimination' (1989) 9 OJLS 1.
S Fredman, *Women and the Law* (Clarendon Press 1997).
N Lacey, 'From individual to group', in B Hepple and E Szyszczak (eds), *Discrimination: The Limits of Law* (Mansell 1992) 104.
P Westen, *Speaking of Equality* (Princeton University Press 1990) xviii.
H Collins, 'Discrimination, equality and social inclusion' (2003) 66 MLR 16, 16–17.
J Jowell, 'Is equality a constitutional principle?' (1994) 47 CLP (Part 2, Collected Papers) 1.
C Whalen and B Whalen, *The Longest Debate: a Legislative History of the Civil Rights Act* (Seven Locks Press 1985).
S Fredman, *Discrimination Law* (2nd edn, Clarendon Law 2011).
L Lustgarten, *Legal Control of Racial Discrimination* (Macmillan 1980).
Brown v Board of Education 347 US 483 (1954) 494.
G Moon and R Allen, 'Dignity discourse in discrimination law: a better route to equality?' (2006) 6 EHRLR 610.
R O'Connell, 'The role of dignity in equality law: lessons from Canada and South Africa' (2008) 6(2) IJCL 267.
J Gardner, 'On the grounds of her sex(uality)' (1998) 18 OJLS 167.
R Turner, 'Gypsies and British parliamentary language: an analysis' (2002) 12 *Romani Studies* 1.

4 The common law and equality

Introduction

A central argument of this book is that many interpretations of the discrimination legislation are technically flawed. The preceding chapters have accumulated some principles by which equality legislation ought to be interpreted. In particular, Chapter 2 showed the judiciary to be perfectly familiar with the task of statutory interpretation per se. Less was expressed about the judiciary's aptitude for this task with discrimination legislation. So, this chapter scrutinises the common law's predisposition to address matters of equality.

Chapter 2 also noted the rise and fall of deference to Parliament and statutory wording, along with the corresponding inverted relationship to the judicial willingness to challenge the text of legislation. But the history of the common law and equality presents a different profile, which is detached from any patterns of deference. It is also detached from the espoused common law principles of morality. It shows the common law failing to engage with matters of equality, or, when doing so, being overtly hostile, and that problems with statutory interpretation and equality predate the modern (post-1970) era of dedicated legislation. As such, it presents the judiciary as ill-disposed to the task presented by the wholesale legislative impositions presented in the 1970s, and offers some insights to the modern-day technical flaws.

1 The common law and morality

From its earliest days, the common law has enshrined a moral dimension. In 1609 Coke CJ pronounced that law must be consistent with 'common right and reason'.[1] In 1774, Lord Mansfield declared: '[W]hatsoever is contrary, *bonos mores et decorum* [good morals and propriety], the principles of our law prohibit, and the King's court, as the general censor and guardian of the public manners, is bound to restrain and punish.'[2] These opinions are not antique

1 *Dr Bonham's Case* (1609) 8 Co Rep 113, 118 a; 77 ER 646, 652. See Chapter 2, p 53, n 262.
2 *Jones v Randall* (1774) Lofft 383, 385; 98 ER 706, 707. See also *Rex v Delaval* (1763) 3 Burr 1434, 1438–1439; 97 ER 913, 915 (Lord Mansfield).

curiosities. Lord Mansfield's sentiments were cited by the House of Lords in 1961. In *Shaw v DPP*,[3] Viscount Simonds asserted that the court has 'a residual power, where no statute has yet intervened to supersede the common law, to superintend those offences which are prejudicial to the public welfare'.[4] Similarly, Lord Morris proclaimed:

> There are certain manifestations of conduct which are an affront to and an attack upon recognised public standards of morals and decency, and which all well-disposed persons would stigmatise and condemn as deserving of punishment. The cases afford examples of the conduct of individuals which has been punished because it outraged public decency or because its tendency was to corrupt the public morals.[5]

In *Shaw*, the House of Lords used this residual power to bypass the Obscene Publications Act 1959 and convict a person of a conspiracy to corrupt public morals for publishing a directory of prostitutes shortly after 'street soliciting' was outlawed (by the Street Offences Act 1959). One might suppose that these sentiments, appearing in the *criminal* law, would inform the civil law.[6] And, further, one might suppose that they would have been invoked by the common law to address, at least, the worst scenarios of discrimination, being rather obviously 'prejudicial to the public welfare' or tending to 'corrupt the public morals'.[7] But a brief history of the English common law shows a laissez-faire approach (at best) to racial and religious discrimination, the active disabling of women from participation in civil affairs, and manifest hostility towards homosexuality.

2 Racial discrimination

At common law, it seems, racism is permissible save where it coincides with some other recognisable wrong. In *Scala Ballroom v Ratcliffe*[8] the Court of Appeal observed that a 'colour bar' was a policy that the owners of a ballroom 'were entitled to adopt in their own business interests'.[9] There are some duties from medieval times placed by the common law upon the likes of innkeepers, common carriers, and some monopoly enterprises such as ports and harbours to accept all travellers and others who are 'in a fit and reasonable condition to be received'.[10] A rare (if not only) example of one of these duties coinciding

3 [1962] AC 220 (HL).
4 ibid, 268.
5 ibid, 292.
6 In *Mohamud v WM Morrison Supermarkets* [2016] UKSC 11 [45], the Supreme Court engaged 'principles of social justice' for deciding on the scope of common-law vicarious liability.
7 In *Rhys-Harper v Relaxion* [2003] 2 CMLR 44 (HL) [78], Lord Hope commented that discrimination was 'morally unacceptable'. See further p 87.
8 [1958] 3 All ER 220.
9 ibid, 221, although, in the same laissez-faire spirit, the Court refused an injunction to prevent the musician's union from boycotting the ballroom.
10 See J Jowell, 'Is equality a constitutional principle?' (1994) 47 CLP (Part 2, Collected Papers) 1, 91. See also Lord Diplock, *Dockers Labour Club and Institute Ltd v Race Relations Board* [1976] AC 285 (HL) 295–296.

with racial discrimination arose in *Constantine v Imperial Hotels*.[11] Here, a black West Indian cricketer (and later a member of the Race Relations Board) was refused accommodation for fear of upsetting resident white American soldiers. The Kings Bench Division awarded Constantine nominal damages for the breach of the innkeepers' duty to receive all travellers.

The common law attitude to slavery was less certain. It approached slavery with ambivalence and pragmatism, preferring to leave its legal status to Parliament. Towards the end of the 18th century, it had inched from treating slaves as chattels,[12] to the excruciating position of refusing to recognise several rights asserted by slave owners, but not outlawing slavery itself. Even in the case heralded as signalling the end of slavery, *Somerset v Stewart*,[13] Lord Mansfield's judgment was carefully confined to habeas corpus, ***and*** the jurisdiction of England, leaving alone the British slave owners (and the wealth they produced) in the colonies. This pragmatism was demonstrated most shamelessly in *The Zong*,[14] where around 133 slaves were 'jettisoned' to preserve the remainder, as the ship was short of drinking water. The only legal proceedings that followed concerned the ship-owner's insurance claim, based on the notion that the drowned slaves were insurable chattels. The claim succeeded and a retrial was ordered, but solely on the basis of new evidence that rain had fallen before all of the slaves were thrown overboard, and so there was no 'necessity', as required by insurance law. All the common law could manage in this notorious case of the slave trade was to preserve the commercial legal principle that it was lawful to jettison some of the cargo to save the remainder. The ***abolition*** of the slave trade and, subsequently, of slavery itself, was implemented by Parliament, not the courts.[15]

3 Gender discrimination

In the meantime, the common law was more brazen with the rights of women, dictating that women were under a disability to perform public functions, even in the face of apparently contradictory legislation. Older cases provide plenty of examples. Women were not entitled to sit in the House of Lords,[16] vote in Parliamentary elections,[17] serve as a town, or county, councillor,[18] or as a judge or juror,[19] or practise law.[20]

11 [1944] 1 KB 693. For a (failed) claim under the Scottish equivalent, see *Rothfield v North British Railway Co* [1920] SC 805 (2nd Div).

12 *Pearne v Lisle* (1749) Amb 75; 27 ER 47. Cf *Smith v Gould* (1706) 2 Lord Raymond 1274; 92 ER 338.

13 (1772) Lofft 1, 98 ER 499.

14 Reported as *Gregson v Gilbert* (1783) 3 Dougl 232, 99 ER 629.

15 Respectively, Slave Trade Act 1807, Slavery Abolition Act 1833.

16 *Viscountess Rhondda's Claim* [1922] 2 AC 339 (HL).

17 *Chorlton v Lings* (1868) LR 4 C P 374.

18 Respectively, *R v Harrald* (1871–72) LR 7 QB 361 (QB), *Beresford-Hope v Sandhurst* (1889) 23 QBD 79 (CA).

19 Coke, 2 Inst. 119, 3 Bl. Comm. 362. See *Edwards v Attorney General of Canada* [1930] AC 124, 129 (Lord Sankey LC).

20 *Bebb v Law Society* [1914] 1 Ch 286 (CA).

Moreover, *this* common law, it seems, trumped statute. The Interpretation Act 1850,[21] section 4, stated: '[I]n all Acts, words importing the masculine gender shall be deemed and taken to include females, and the singular to include the plural, and the plural the singular, unless the contrary as to gender or number is expressly provided.' The subsequent Representation of the People Act 1867, by section 3, provided that every 'man' shall be entitled to vote in Parliamentary elections. One would imagine the result was straightforward. But in *Chorlton v Lings*,[22] the Court of Common Pleas thought otherwise. The technical reason centred on section 57 of the Representation of the People Act, which stated that 'this Act, so far as is consistent with the tenor thereof, shall be construed as one with the enactments for the time being in force relating to the representation of the people'. Accordingly, it was held, as the older election statutes expressly excluded women, it would be 'consistent' to interpret this one accordingly.[23] The court was keen to avoid the situation where some constituencies (created by the new Act) would have female electors while others would not. This is a rather one-eyed approach. The court could just as easily be reasoned that where previous statutes (e.g. Reform Act 1832) expressly excluded women, the absence of such an expression in a later Act indicated that women were included. After all, the later statute was passed in the full light of the Interpretation Act 1850. The court's trump card was the common law disability of women to vote, which was a 'very strong presumption',[24] for no better reason than it had been the practice for several centuries.[25] Without a hint of irony, Keating J proclaimed that 'the injustice of excluding females from the exercise of the franchise . . . is not a matter within our province. It is for the legislature to consider whether the existing incapacity ought to be removed.'[26] Thus, it was within the province of the common law to ban women from voting, but not to permit it.

The presumption of disability was the sole reason for the decision in *Nairn v University of St Andrews*,[27] where the House of Lords held that even the word *person* in section 27 of the Representation of the People (Scotland) Act 1868 did not include women, this time elevating the presumption to a 'constitutional principle'.[28] Accordingly: 'If it was intended to make a vast constitutional change in favour of women graduates, one would expect to find plain language and express statement.'[29] Using similar logic, the Court of Appeal, in *Bebb v Law Society*,[30] held that the Solicitors Act 1843 did not rebut the 'inveterate'[31] common law presumption

21 Lord Brougham's Act, 13 & 14 Vict c 21.
22 (1868) LR 4 C P 374.
23 ibid, 386 (Bovill CJ).
24 ibid, 383 (Bovill CJ).
25 ibid, 383 ('this alone is sufficient'). See also 385 (Bovill CJ), 394 (Byles J), & 395 (Keating J).
26 Ibid, 397.
27 [1909] AC 147 (HL).
28 ibid, 161 (Lord Loreburn LC) 162–164 (Lord Ashbourne) 166 (Lord Robertson). Lord Collins concurred (166).
29 ibid, 163 (Lord Ashbourne).
30 [1914] 1 Ch 286 (CA).
31 ibid, 298, 297 (Phillimore LJ) 297 (Swinfen Eady LJ).

that women were disabled from practising law, despite section 43 (of the *same* Act) stating 'every word importing the masculine gender only shall extend and be applied to a female', unless 'there be something in the subject or context repugnant to such construction'.

4 Sexual orientation discrimination

Until the very late (post-Thatcher) 20th century, attitudes to homosexuality were particularly hostile, as these two successful prosecutions demonstrate. In 1973, in *Knuller v DPP*,[32] the publisher of a magazine carrying advertisements placed by homosexuals for the purpose of meeting possible sexual partners was convicted at common law of a conspiracy to 'corrupt public morals', despite the legality at the time of such sexual relations in private. Matters of equality and discrimination did not even arise in any of the House of Lords or Court of Appeal speeches. As in *Shaw*,[33] the existence of otherwise exonerating legislation in this area,[34] and even a subsequent undertaking to Parliament that such a common law offence would not be used to bypass the Act,[35] did nothing to persuade the courts that the common law should step back.

In the meantime, public-order law was being used to prosecute overt homosexual conduct without any resistance from the courts. In *Masterson v Holden*,[36] in the early hours in Oxford Street, London, two men were seen embraced in a kiss at a bus stop. The witnesses were a pair of heterosexual couples, one of whom approached the men and shouted: 'You filthy sods. How dare you in front of our girls?' This outburst in the early hours attracted the attention of the police, who proceeded to arrest the *gay* couple. Their convictions for 'insulting . . . behaviour . . . whereby a breach of the peace may be occasioned',[37] were upheld by a two-judge panel of the Queen's Bench. The only nod to equality was buried in this rather lame comment from Glidewell LJ: 'Overt homosexual conduct in a public street, indeed overt heterosexual conduct in a public street, may well be considered by many persons to be objectionable.' Any gravitas of the equality element in this comment evaporated with his next sentence,

32 [1973] AC 435 (HL) affirming in part [1972] 2 QB 179 (CA).
33 [1962] AC 220 (HL). See p 80.
34 The Obscene Publications Act 1959, s 2(4) provided: 'A person publishing an article shall not be proceeded against for an offence at common law consisting of the publication of any matter contained or embodied in the article where it is of the essence of the offence that the matter is obscene.' It seems a charge under the Act would have failed because any publication would have to 'deprave or corrupt' those likely to read it. (See e.g. [1973] AC 435, 462, Lord Morris.)
35 See e.g. [1973] AC 435, 480 (Lord Diplock, dissenting). The undertaking was made by the Solicitor-General with the passing of the amending Obscene Publications Act 1964: HC Deb 3 June 1964, vol 695, col 1212.
36 [1986] 1 WLR 1017 (Glidewell LJ and Schiemann J).
37 Metropolitan Police Act 1839, s 54(13) now repealed, Public Order Act 1986, s 40 (3) Sch 3.

> [T]he display of such objectionable conduct in a public street may well be regarded by another person, particularly by a young woman, as conduct which insults her by suggesting that she is somebody who would find such conduct in public acceptable herself.[38]

Nowhere in the speeches was it suggested that the police had arrested the wrong persons for insulting behaviour causing a breach of the peace, which, of course, described perfectly the act of the (heterosexual) witness, who had insulted the defendants at the top of his voice in the street at two o'clock in the morning. Even into the 21st century, an attitude of indifference to *state* hostility persisted, when the House of Lords refused to interfere with the policy of debasing, humiliating, and then discharging homosexuals in military.[39]

5 Religious discrimination

In *Miller v Salomons*,[40] the Court of Exchequer upheld steep fines imposed upon a Jewish MP for refusing to complete the statutory 'oath of abjuration', ending 'on the true faith of a Christian'.[41] The majority accepted that the oath was so framed in earlier, more volatile times, purposely to secure the allegiance of Roman Catholics, yet upheld the fines upon a literal interpretation. A second argument put by Salomons was that the statute itself was void for being obsolete. The oath required a recognition that King George was the rightful King. By the time the facts of this case arose, George III was long dead and Queen Victoria was the rightful monarch. Upon this point, the deference to statutory wording vanished, and the whole court found no trouble substituting 'George' for 'Victoria' and 'him' for 'her', in order to resurrect the crime.

Such indifference to religious discrimination persisted into the 20th century, with the Chancery Court holding that a legacy excluding Jews and Roman Catholics was not contrary to public policy,[42] and as late as 1976, the House of Lords did not consider a testamentary condition excluding Roman Catholics to offend public policy.[43]

6 A common law principle of equality?

The common law fared no better when required to engage more directly with principles of equality. In *Roberts v Hopwood*,[44] Poplar Borough Council embarked

38 [1986] 1 WLR 1017, 1024.

39 *Macdonald v Advocate General for Scotland* [2003] UKHL 34.

40 (1852) 7 Exchequer Reports (Welsby, Hurlstone, and Gordon) 475; 155 ER 1036, affirmed, *Salomons v Miller* (1853) 8 Exchequer Reports (Welsby, Hurlstone, and Gordon) 778. For an exhaustive account of this issue, cumulating in the Parliamentary Oaths Act of 1866 (29 & 30 Vict c 19), see HSQ Henriques, 'The political rights of English Jews' (1907) 19 (4) *Jewish Quarterly Review* 751, especially 761 et al.

41 Treason Act 1766 (6 Geo 3, c 53).

42 *Re Lysaght* [1966] Ch 191, 206 (Buckley J).

43 *Blathwayt v Baron Cawley* [1976] AC 397.

44 [1925] AC 578 (HL).

upon an equal pay policy for its lowest-paid workers. The policy was struck down by the House of Lords on the ground that the Council had been misguided 'by some eccentric principles of socialistic philanthropy, or by a feminist ambition to secure the equality of the sexes in the matter of wages in the world of labour'.[45]

The introduction of discrimination legislation paradoxically reinforced this attitude, allowing the common law, apparently in deference to Parliament, to wash its hands of discrimination issues whenever the facts fell outside of an activity prescribed by the legislation. This is in stark contrast to its usual approach to matters of 'morality', where it readily would venture where even dedicated statutes would not tread.[46] So even where there was patent[47] or indirect[48] sex discrimination by the immigration authorities the courts considered themselves powerless to act: 'sex discrimination of itself is not unlawful. It is unlawful only in circumstances prescribed by the Act [Sex Discrimination Act 1975]'.[49] Similarly, the House of Lords rejected overt and extreme homophobic and sexual harassment *by the state* as causes of action, while noting that dedicated legislation outlawing such conduct came 'too late to assist'[50] and that this 'area of law' was 'entirely a creature of statute'.[51] In the post-war years of the 20th century, while the common law exercised itself with 'outraging public decency',[52] 'corrupting public morals',[53] and 'insulting behaviour',[54] notices such as 'No Blacks, No Irish, and No Dogs' were displayed with apparent impunity.[55] Coming on the back of the Holocaust and the defeat of Hitler, this blind spot on the common law 'moral radar' is perhaps all the more surprising.

45 ibid, 599 (Lord Atkinson).

46 See '1 The common law and morality', p 79. Cf the CJEU's adoption of the principle of equality. See p 36.

47 *R v Entry Clearance Officer Bombay ex p Amin* [1983] 2 AC 818 (HL). (Married women, not being 'head of the household', could not apply for UK settlement, but held (3–2) that immigration officers were not providing a facility or service within SDA 1975, s 29.)

48 *Bernstein v Immigration Appeal Tribunal and Department of Employment* [1988] 3 CMLR 445 (CA). (Refusal of work permits for low paid – predominantly female – jobs.)

49 ibid [41] (Mann LJ).

50 *Macdonald v Advocate General for Scotland; Pearce v Governing Body of Mayfield Secondary School* [2003] UKHL 34, [20] (Lord Nicholls). See also [182] (Lord Rodger).

51 ibid [53] (Lord Hope).

52 *Shaw v DPP* [1962] AC 220 (HL); see p 80. See also *R v Gibson* [1990] 2 QB 619 (CA) (display in gallery of earrings made from aborted foetuses 'outraged public decency').

53 *Knuller v DPP* [1973] AC 435 (HL) reversing only the 'public decency' conviction, [1972] 2 QB 179 (CA). See p 83.

54 *Masterson v Holden* [1986] 1 WLR 1017 (Glidewell LJ and Schiemann J). See p 83.

55 'In those days before equality regulation, bigotry . . . was allowed to roam free and unashamed.' M McCleod, 'Theresa May's immigration bill is a valuable tool for racist landlords' *Guardian* (London, October 15 2013). See < https://www.theguardian.com/commentisfree/2013/oct/15/theresa-may-immigration-bill-racist-landlords > accessed 10 April 2018. For colour bars, see *Scala Ballroom v Ratcliffe* [1958] 3 All ER 220 (CA) (see p 80); *Dockers Labour Club and Institute Ltd v Race Relations Board* [1976] AC 285 (HL); in *Charter v Race Relations Board* [1973] AC 885 (HL) a Conservative Party social club voted against the membership of an Indian applicant. The latter two cases were held to be outside the scope of 'public' services under the RRA 1968.

As if this record of failure did not exist, from time to time, judges have suggested that the common law carries some form of equality principle. In *Short v Poole Corporation*,[56] the Court of Appeal suggested that the courts could strike down as *ultra vires* any decision made by a public body made on 'alien and irrelevant grounds', such as a teacher being dismissed 'because she had red hair, or for some equally frivolous or foolish reason'.[57] Any hope inferred from this pronouncement was immediately crushed when the Court upheld a policy to dismiss married women teachers. Likewise, in *Cumings v Birkenhead Corporation*[58] Lord Denning MR uttered a similar piety (including skin colour), only to disappoint when upholding a policy of confining Roman Catholic primary-school children to Roman Catholic secondary schools.

More recently, Lord Hoffman hinted that there exists an equality principle in the common law of a more substantive nature. In *Matadeen v Pointu*[59] he said 'that treating like cases alike and unlike cases differently is a general axiom of rational behaviour', and thus irrational discrimination was subject to judicial review.[60] In *Hall v Simons*,[61] he invoked a 'fundamental principle of justice which requires that people should be treated equally and like cases treated alike', as one of his reasons for holding that advocates, like any other professional, should enjoy no immunity from professional negligence claims, a private-law matter. Lord Steyn has written that there is a 'constitutional principle of equality developed domestically by English courts', which is wider than the 'relatively weak' Article 14 of the ECHR.[62] However, arguments (based on these comments) that there exists at common law a general tenet against discrimination have so far found little favour in the courts' decision-making, either being rejected or sidelined. Lord Hoffman's comments do no more than pronounce that irrational discrimination (like any irrational behaviour) could be subject to judicial review in public law,[63] and any principle of equality does not add much, if anything, to a claimant's Convention Rights under the HRA 1998.[64] Indeed, Lord Steyn's assertion must appear a little hollow to those who, having lost their discrimination claims in the

56 [1926] Ch 66 (CA).

57 ibid, 91 (Warrington LJ).

58 [1972] Ch 12 (CA) 37.

59 [1999] 1 AC 98, delivering the opinion of the Privy Council. Cited in *R (Rotherham MBC) v Secretary of State for Business, Innovation and Skills* [2015] UKSC 6, [26] Lord Sumption (with whom Lord Hodge agreed).

60 ibid, 109, but Lord Hoffman also highlighted the difficulties of a general principle of non-discrimination, in contrast to specified enumerated grounds, such as sex and race. See also *Godin-Mendoza v Ghaidan* [2004] 2 AC 557 (HL) [132], where Baroness Hale equated discrimination with (public-law) irrational conduct.

61 [2000] 3 All ER 673 (HL) 689.

62 Lord Steyn, 'Democracy through law' [2002] (6) EHRLR 723, 731–732.

63 Under the *Wednesbury* ([1948] 1 KB 223) principle; see *R (Association of British Civilian Internees: Far East Region) v Secretary of State for Defence* [2003] EWCA Civ 473, [83]–[86] (also effectively overruling *Gurung v Ministry of Defence* [2002] EWHC 2463 (Admin) so far as it suggested (at [29]) that discrimination on the ground of birthplace was irrational).

64 *R (Montana) v Secretary of State for the Home Department* [2001] 1 WLR 552 (CA) [15].

English courts, found success at Strasbourg, either under Article 14,[65] or without even the need to resort to it.[66]

A similarly unfulfilled ambition was once suggested by Lord Woolf:

> Suppose Parliament enacts a statute depriving Jews of their British nationality, prohibits marriages between Christians and non-Christians, dissolving marriages between blacks and whites or vesting the property of all red haired women in the State. Is it really suggested that English judges would have to apply such a law?[67]

All this came to nothing when a year later the Court of Appeal upheld a ban, partly entrenched in legislation, on homosexuals serving in the armed forces.[68]

As this brief history shows, notions that the common law would ever develop substantial anti-discrimination principles are far from the reality, seen in the case-law reasoning and decisions. Some insight into this negativity, especially in the private-law field, was provided by Lord Diplock.[69] Commenting on the Race Relations Act 1968, he lamented: 'This is a statute which, however admirable its motives, restricts the liberty which the citizen has previously enjoyed at common law to differentiate between one person and another in entering or declining to enter into transactions with them.'[70] More recently, in *Rhys-Harper v Relaxion*,[71] Lord Hope provided a more palatable explanation:

> It is a remarkable fact that, although discrimination on whatever grounds is widely regarded as morally unacceptable, the common law was unable to provide a sound basis for removing it from situations where those who were vulnerable to discrimination were at risk and ensuring that all people were treated equally. Experience has taught us that this is a matter which can only be dealt with by legislation, and that it requires careful regulation by Parliament. . . . The fact is that the principle of equal treatment is easy to state but difficult to apply in practice.[72]

65 See e.g. *Clift v UK* (App No. 7205/07) (ECtHR, 13 July 2010), disagreeing with [2007] 1 AC 484 (HL) (classifying prisoners according to sentence imposed not objectively justifiable).

66 *Eweida v UK* (2013) 57 EHRR 8, reversing [2010] ICR 890 (CA) (ban on display of crucifix violated Art 9); *Smith & Grady v UK* (2000) 29 EHRR 493 (ban on homosexuals in the armed forces violated Art 8).

67 Lord Woolf, 'Droit public – English style' [1995] PL 57, 67–68.

68 *R v Ministry of Defence ex p Smith* [1996] QB 517 (complaint upheld, (2000) 29 EHRR 493). Criminal Justice and Public Order Act 1994, s 146(4) was intended as 'an expression of Parliamentary approval for the existing policy and an indication that the change in the criminal law should not be seen as signalling any Parliamentary desire for a change also in the practice of administratively discharging homosexuals' (Simon Brown LJ, 527). The complaint was upheld by the Strasbourg court: *Smith & Grady v UK* (2000) 29 EHRR 493.

69 *Dockers Labour Club and Institute Ltd v Race Relations Board* [1976] AC 285 (HL).

70 ibid, 295–296.

71 [2003] 2 CMLR 44 (HL).

72 ibid [78].

Lord Diplock's comment hints that notions of equality interfere with the common law's moral touchstone of individual liberty to choose with whom to deal. This might explain why the common law seemed all too willing to step into what it considered to be moral vacuums in other areas of public and private life and even promote *inequality* as a 'constitutional principle'.[73] Lord Hope's slightly more up-to-date observation at least brings discrimination into the moral sphere of the common law. But excusing the common law for being just as useless because addressing discrimination was 'too difficult' renders his comment vacuous, as well as somewhat disingenuous. The 'experience' of which he speaks (but does not cite) has taught us that the common law was indifferent or positively hostile to matters of equality, as shown above. In none of those cases would applying a principle of equality have been too difficult. In some, in fact, it would have amounted to a simpler interpretation of the legislation.[74] Moreover, the Court of Justice of the European Union, the European Court of Human Rights, and the US Supreme Court each managed to produce a sophisticated jurisprudence from a rudimentary 'equality' rubric.[75] Equality law was not 'too difficult' for these judges. We must then either accept that Lord Hope believed the English judiciary to be inferior to its overseas counterparts, or muse that there is some other excuse for the law's detachment.

From this brief account, despite the declarations of concern for the public welfare and morals, it is clear that the common law was indifferent – and in some cases, hostile – to matters of equality. And this persisted despite dedicated legislation exemplifying a markedly different attitude towards discrimination. When Parliament in the 1970s signalled that discrimination fell within the sphere of morality, the courts used the legislation as cover for refusing to extend its anti-discrimination principles into other areas. This is in stark contrast to the blanket effect given to the principles lying within the Obscene Publications Act 1959, seemingly *against* the express instruction within that Act.[76] The only expressed reason for this reticence is that discrimination law is 'too difficult'. As we shall see in the following chapters, leaving the matter to Parliament did not unburden the judiciary entirely of their apparent difficulties with the principle of equality.

73 *Nairn v University of St Andrews* [1909] AC 147 (HL). See p 82.

74 E.g. *Nairn*; *Miller v Salomons* (1852) 7 Exchequer Reports (Welsby, Hurlstone, and Gordon) 475; 155 ER 1036 (see p 84); *Chorlton v Lings* (1868) LR 4 C P 374 (see p 82).

75 From Art 119 EEC (now Art 157 TFEU) and the 'principle that men and women should receive equal pay for equal work' the CJEU produced the notions of indirect discrimination (Case 96/80 *Jenkins v Kingsgate* [1981] 1 WLR 972), objective justification (Case 170/84 *Bilka-Kaufhaus* [1986] ECR 1607), and predecessor comparators (Case 129/79 *Macarthys v Smith* [1980] ECR 1275). See similarly, ECHR, Art 14: rights to be 'secured without discrimination on any ground'; Civil Rights Act 1964, s 703(a)(2): it is unlawful 'to limit, segregate, or classify . . . because of such individual's race, color, religion, sex, or national origin'.

76 See p 83 and n 34.

Further reading

Lord Steyn, 'Democracy through law' [2002] (6) EHRLR 723.
J Jowell, 'Is equality a constitutional principle?' (1994) 47 CLP (Part 2, Collected Papers) 1.
Dr Bonham's Case (1609) 8 Co Rep 113; 77 ER 646.
Chorlton v Lings (1868) LR 4 C P 374.
Bebb v Law Society [1914] 1 Ch 286 (CA).
Re Lysaght [1966] Ch 191, 206 (Buckley J)
R v Entry Clearance Officer Bombay ex p Amin [1983] 2 AC 818 (HL).
Macdonald v Advocate General for Scotland; *Pearce v Governing Body of Mayfield Secondary School* [2003] UKHL 34.
Shaw v DPP [1962] AC 220 (HL).
Knuller v DPP [1973] AC 435 (HL).
Masterson v Holden [1986] 1 WLR 1017.
Nairn v University of St Andrews [1909] AC 147 (HL).
Miller v Salomons (1852) 7 Exchequer Reports (Welsby, Hurlstone, and Gordon) 475; 155 ER 1036.

5 The benign motive 'defence' and direct discrimination

Introduction

The preceding chapters have set a context, albeit somewhat pessimistic, for the main body of this book, which begins here. This is the first chapter (of the remaining six) to explore particular cases on key definitions of the modern discrimination legislation in this context of the common law, history, theories, and concepts, and, most notably, the principles and rules of statutory interpretation. The purpose of these chapters is to explain the relative simplicity of the cases, and expose the technical flaws and apparent lack of expertise in the judgments.

The focus of this chapter is on the legislative definition of direct discrimination, and, in particular, an importunate insistence by some judges that a discriminatory motive is a necessary ingredient for liability. This is notable in cases where defendants have argued that there existed a benign, benevolent, or alternative motive for their action. This chapter explores how these arguments have been addressed, and concludes that the notion of discriminatory motive in this sense is based on a flawed statutory interpretation and an ignorance of the basic tenets of the symmetrical model of direct discrimination employed by the legislation. It also finds that judgments rejecting such an approach are themselves flawed. It is not surprising, then, that many relatively simple cases have become a muddle of dissents, uncertainty, and prolixity.

1 Direct discrimination and motive

The legislation

In its simplest form, direct discrimination arises when a defendant expressly links the victim's protected characteristic (say, sex) with his less favourable treatment of her. For instance, a job advertisement may read: 'Librarians wanted, no women need apply.' In reality, most cases, being multifaceted, are not as straightforward as that, as we shall see. There is no general (objective justification) defence to direct discrimination (except for age),[1] only specific exceptions for a particular

1 EA 2010, s 3(2).

field, such as employment,[2] the provision of goods, facilities, services,[3] premises,[4] or education.[5] These are very limited defences, and so a finding of direct discrimination can be an all-or-nothing affair.

The EU equality directives adopted this formula for direct discrimination, which is 'where one person is treated less favourably on grounds of sex than another is, has been or would be treated in a comparable situation'.[6] The formulas for other grounds are substantially the same, as is the domestic version given by section 13(1) of the Equality Act 2010, which (save for pregnancy cases) uses this single definition: 'A person (A) discriminates against another (B) if, because of a protected characteristic, A treats B less favourably than A treats or would treat others.' This replaced the previous formula, which was expressed thus: 'A person discriminates against a woman if: (a) on the ground of her sex he treats her less favourably than he treats or would treat a man.'[7] A similar formula was used for race: 'on racial grounds he treats that other less favourably than he treats or would treat other persons.'[8]

These formulas have in common two broad elements: (1) 'treats less favourably' and (2) '*because of* a protected characteristic'. The phrase 'because of' replaced the one used in previous legislation, e.g. 'on the ground of'. The Explanatory Note (61) to the Equality Act 2010 stated that this 'does not change the legal meaning of the definition'. It was merely 'designed to make it more accessible to the ordinary user of the Act'. Thus, there should be no difference between the older and newer cases on this basis. It is under this element that some judgments have pursued the notion that direct discrimination requires a hostile or discriminatory motive on the part of the defendant; this narrowing of the definition thus makes space for a benign motive 'defence'. The main scrutiny in this chapter falls upon the *JFS* case,[9] and first, *James v Eastleigh BC*,[10] which is set in the context of the rise and fall of the *but for* test, beginning with its emergence.

The emergence of the but for *test*

The matter of discriminatory motive and the definition of direct discrimination came to the House of Lords for the first time in 1989. In *R v Birmingham City Council, ex p Equal Opportunities Commission*,[11] there was a general trend over a number of years to move away from (selective) grammar schools

2 ibid, Sch 9.
3 ibid, Sch 3.
4 ibid, Sch 5.
5 ibid, Sch 11.
6 Recast Directive 2006/54/EC, art 2(2)(a). See also Framework Directive 2000/78/EC, art 2(2)(a); Race Directive 2000/43/EC, art 2(2)(a).
7 SDA 1975, 1(1)*(a)*.
8 RRA 1976, s 1(1)*(a)*. The substantial difference is the absence of the possessive adjective *her* or *his*, which is not relevant to this discussion.
9 *R (E) v Governing Body of JFS* [2010] 2 AC 728 (SC).
10 [1990] 2 AC 751 (HL).
11 [1989] AC 1155 (HL).

towards (non-selective) comprehensive schools. Small pockets of resistance ensured that a few remained, the majority of which were exclusive for boys. The Council found itself in the position of having more grammar-school places for boys than for girls. The Equal Opportunities Commission argued that the Council's consequent allocation of places directly discriminated against girls. So the question became whether the allocation of grammar-school places was 'on the ground of' sex. The Council argued that, for liability, there had to be an *intention* or *motive* to discriminate on the ground of sex, which was absent here. A unanimous House of Lords concurred with Lord Goff's speech rejecting that argument: a *but for* test showed that the council offered fewer places to girls on *the ground of* their sex. It was couched in this way: 'would the complainant have received the same treatment from the defendant but for his or her sex?'[12] The point of this 'objective and not subjective'[13] approach was to avoid questions of defendants' discriminatory intent, or 'benign motive'. Otherwise it would be a good defence for a defendant to show that he discriminated not because of a hostile intent, but (for example) because of customer preference, or to save money, or avoid controversy.[14]

A year or so after the *Birmingham City Council* case, in *James v Eastleigh BC*,[15] only a bare majority held this line. This is where the *but for* test began to unravel, albeit for spurious reasons. These relate to three themes in the speeches. First, the *but for* test was poorly expressed. Second, Lord Lowry's dissent took this at face value, and used it to debunk the test, leaving the way clear to introduce a requirement of discriminatory motive. Third, Lord Griffiths' dissent promoted an inappropriate 'benevolence defence'. Moreover, the whole House largely ignored the foundation matter of whether such case should be analysed as direct or indirect discrimination.

In *James*, the Council's municipal swimming baths admitted persons 'of pensionable age' free-of-charge. In the United Kingdom at the time, the state pension age was 65 for men and 60 for women.[16] So when Mr and Mrs James, each aged 61, visited the baths, Mrs James was admitted free whilst Mr James was required to pay. Mr James complained that he had been treated less favourably on the ground of his sex. The Council argued that the policy was motivated not by sex, but by a wish to help pensioners. The County Court found for the Council. The Court of Appeal upheld the decision, expressly agreeing with the Council's reasoning, but a bare majority of the House of Lords reversed, seemingly adhering

12 [1989] AC 1155 (HL) 1194; *James v Eastleigh BC* [1990] 2 AC 751 (HL) 765 (Lord Goff).

13 *Nagarajan v London Regional Transport* [2000] 1 AC 501 (HL) 511 (Lord Nicholls).

14 *R v Birmingham City Council, ex p Equal Opportunities Commission* [1989] AC 1155 (HL) 1194 (Lord Goff) citing *R v Commission for Racial Equality ex p Westminster City Council* [1985] ICR 827 (CA).

15 [1990] 2 AC 751 (HL).

16 Under the Pensions Act 2011, women's state pension age will increase to 65 between April 2016 and November 2018. From December 2018, the state pension age for both men and women will start to increase and reach 66 by October 2020. But note that the Pensions Act 2014 provides for a regular review of the state pension age.

to the *but for* test.[17] Before considering other aspects of the majority decision, it is worth considering the speech that dedicated the most attention to the *but for* test, which was Lord Lowry's dissent.

Lord Lowry offered a meticulous grammatical interpretation of the statutory formula (Sex Discrimination Act 1975, section 1(1)*(a)* above), and pointed out that 'ground' was attached to the treatment, which was the act of the discriminator:

> On reading section 1(1)*(a)*, it can be seen that the discriminator does something to the victim, that is, he treats him in a certain fashion, to wit, less favourably than he treats or would treat a woman and he treats him in that fashion on a certain *ground*, namely, on the ground of his sex. These words, it is scarcely necessary for me to point out, constitute an adverbial phrase modifying the transitive verb 'treats' in a clause of which the discriminator is the subject and the victim is the object. . . . the point I wish to make is that the *ground* on which the alleged discriminator treats the victim less favourably is inescapably linked to the subject and the verb; it is the reason which has caused him to act.[18]

Lord Lowry then turned to the dictionary for the meaning of 'ground', which read:

> A circumstance on which an opinion, inference, argument, statement or claim is founded, or which has given rise to an action, procedure or mental feeling; a reason, motive. Often with additional implication: a valid reason, justifying motive, or what is alleged as such.[19]

Consequently, Lord Lowry endorsed Lord Browne-Wilkinson's opinion in the Court of Appeal: 'In my judgment section 1(1)*(a)* is looking to the case where, subjectively, the defendant has treated the plaintiff less favourably because of his or her sex.'[20] The inevitable conclusion was that direct discrimination carries a subjective element. But Lord Lowry was minded to endorse the *Birmingham City Council* case, and the rejected benign motive 'defences' alluded to above. In other words, his interpretation would provide the same result. For instance:

> If a men's hairdresser dismisses the only woman on his staff because the customers prefer to have their hair cut by a man, he may regret losing her but he treats her less favourably because she is a woman, that is, on the ground of her sex, having made a deliberate decision to do so.[21]

17 [1990] 2 AC 751, 774 (Lord Goff) 765 (Lord Bridge). Lord Ackner agreed with both Lord Goff and Lord Bridge (769).
18 ibid, 775.
19 ibid citing *Oxford English Dictionary*, 2nd edn (1989) vol VI, p 876.
20 ibid, 776 citing [1990] 1 QB 61 (CA) 74.
21 ibid, 779.

This prompts the question of why provide an alternative test if the result would be the same? The answer lies, of course, in the facts of *James*. Moreover, it is rooted in what Lord Lowry feared. The *but for* test was wrong because

> [it] relieves the complainant of the need to prove anything except that A has done an act which results in less favourable treatment for B by reason of B's sex, which reduces to insignificance the words 'on the ground of'.[22]

In other words, instead of asking 'What was the ground of the treatment?' the *but for* test would encourage tribunals to ask: 'Did the treatment disfavour her because she has a protected characteristic?' The difference between these questions is illustrated by considering the two principal types of discrimination: direct and indirect. *Indirect* discrimination was developed to catch cases where an apparently neutral practice causes an adverse effect upon a protected group. Take the classic case of indirect discrimination from the United States, *Griggs v Duke Power*: an employer's requirement that its workers have a high-school diploma adversely affected African-Americans, who had a history inferior schooling.[23] A black applicant, without a diploma, was disfavoured by the requirement because, *inter alia*, he was black; had he been white, he would have had a better chance of meeting the requirement. Now compare a case of *direct* discrimination: an employer states simply: 'No blacks need apply.' In *either* case it could be said that that *but for* his race the African-American applicant would have been recruited. But something more is needed for liability in the latter (direct discrimination) case, otherwise it cannot be distinguished from the high-school diploma case of *indirect* discrimination. As Lord Lowry interprets it, the *but for* test cannot distinguish between direct and indirect discrimination. Its chief proponent, Lord Goff, seemed to appreciate this and 'stressed' that the test should be confined to cases of direct discrimination.[24] With respect, if one has to identify direct discrimination before applying a test designed to identify the very same thing, the test is flawed. In terms of statutory interpretation, Lord Goff grasped the purpose of avoiding benign motive defences, but then implemented it with an unnecessary and flawed gloss on the statutory language that would have no lasting credibility.[25]

But Lord Lowry's criticism is a somewhat overreaction. A slight variation on Lord Goff's formula would resolve Lord Lowry's particular difficulty. Instead of asking whether the claimant would have *received* the treatment but for a protected characteristic, one should ask would the defendant *have treated* the claimant so, but for a protected characteristic? This shifts the focus from the *effect*

22 ibid, 780.

23 401 US 424 (Sup Ct, 1971). The employer here will have the opportunity to 'justify' the requirement, by showing that the diploma was necessary for the job.

24 *James v Eastleigh BC* [1990] 2 AC 751, 774.

25 In fact both the purpose and flawed 'test' were presented to Lord Goff by counsel in *R v Birmingham City Council, ex p Equal Opportunities Commission* [1989] AC 1155 (HL) 1194 (Lord Goff); 1184–1185 (Anthony Lester QC).

of the treatment to the cause, and, without much ado, resolves Lord Lowry's difficulty, which was not with the test per se, but with the imprecision with which it was expressed. The first question cannot distinguish between direct and indirect discrimination. The second question can.

On this basis, Lord Lowry's interpretation was no different from the *but for* test, more properly expressed. That he came to a different result to the majority is down to an additional requirement. It will be recalled that Lord Lowry illustrated his endorsement of Browne-Wilkinson's LJ 'subjective' approach,[26] with his 'hairdresser' example mentioned previously, which ended with these words: 'he treats her less favourably because she is a woman, that is, on the ground of her sex, ***having made a deliberate decision to do so***'.[27] Without this final phrase, Lord Lowry's example should be harmless enough. *This* was Lord Lowry's reason to reject Mr James' claim, as the council's *intention* was to treat him less favourably because of his (pensionable) age, and not his sex.[28] Thus, for Lord Lowry's speech, the demolition of the *but for* test was less about its ability to distinguish direct from indirect discrimination, and more about removing the obstacle to consideration of the defendant's subjective intent.

Demanding *deliberate* treatment on the ground of sex narrows the scope of direct discrimination and would exclude, *inter alia*, subconscious discrimination and stereotyping. This unnecessary additional requirement would significantly reduce the efficacy of the statutory definition. As Lord Browne-Wilkinson later observed in *Glasgow CC v Zafar*, 'those who discriminate on the grounds of race or gender do not in general advertise their prejudices: indeed, they may not even be aware of them'.[29] That is to say, most instances of direct discrimination are not 'deliberate'. As such, Lord Lowry's interpretation read words into the section (which are not even required by the dictionary definition he cited), and cannot fully address the mischief nor serve the purpose of the legislation (which applies irrespective of motive). In other words, it fails on all mainstream canons of statutory interpretation.

Also dissenting, Lord Griffiths simply agreed with Lord Lowry's speech and presumably with his disapproval of the *but for* test. But Lord Griffiths added for his own part a less technical approach. He reasoned that the disparate state pension age resulted in women being less well off than men at 60. On that basis,

> [W]hat I do not accept is that an attempt to redress the result of that unfair act of discrimination by offering free facilities to those disadvantaged by the earlier act of discrimination is, itself, necessarily discriminatory 'on grounds of sex'.[30]

26 [1990] 1 QB 61 (CA) 74. See p 93.
27 [1990] 2 AC 751, 779. Emphasis supplied.
28 ibid, 780, excluding objective notions for foreseeability or even inevitability.
29 [1998] ICR 120 (HL) 126.
30 [1990] 2 AC 751, 768.

The conclusion is built on a half-truth (that retired women are less well off). The disparate retirement ages may well be discriminatory, but not necessarily in favour of men. In terms of disadvantage, compulsory retirement is double edged, and something resisted by some workers, but positively embraced by others. Although these issues were not within the UK (legal) domain at the time of *James*, they were well-developed in both Canada and the United States.[31] And as recent experience shows, women have resisted the raising (and concurrent equalising) of their retirement age.[32] For Lord Griffiths, the benign motive to redress discrimination caused by the disparate state pension ages was the key. As a matter of statutory interpretation, he observed that Parliament must have been aware of concessions given to pensioners when passing the Sex Discrimination Act 1975, and so concluded: 'I cannot believe that it was the intention of Parliament that this benevolent practice should be declared to be unlawful.'[33]

That the courts ought to be able to sanction any scheme designed to redress past or existing disadvantage drives the proverbial coach and horses through the conventional notion that the direct discrimination formula provides a formal equality model, symmetrical in nature, available not only to the principal target groups (e.g. racial minorities and women) but also to their generally advantaged counterparts (whites and men).[34] The logical consequence of measures addressing disadvantage is they would disfavour the generally advantaged groups, and are thus prima facie unlawful as direct discrimination. That is why otherwise directly discriminatory measures used to redress past discrimination or underrepresentation were catered for on a strictly limited basis elsewhere in the Act.[35] Given the presumption that sections within the same statute should be construed consistently,[36] it would take more than a generalised assumption of parliamentary intent to rebut the presumption

31 See respectively, *McKinney v University of Guelph* [1990] 3 SCR 229 (Sup Ct, Canada); Age Discrimination in Employment Act 1967 29 USC s 626(f)(1) providing (from 1990) a waiver scheme for those workers opting for compulsory retirement. Extensive details and examples are provided by EEOC 29 CFR s 1625.22, < https://www.gpo.gov/fdsys/pkg/CFR-2017-title29-vol4/xml/CFR-2017-title29-vol4-part1625.xml > accessed 10 April 2018.

32 See e.g. 'Pension age madness hurts millions of women' *The Sunday Times* (London, 21 February 2016); 'Retirement rate rise: millions of women born in 1950s say they weren't given enough notice' *Independent* (London, 1 February 2016); 'All the plans I had for my retirement have been shattered' *Independent* (London, 30 January 2016).

33 [1990] 2 AC 751, 767.

34 This observation was made by Baroness Hale, *JFS* [2010] 2 AC 728 (SC) [60]. On formal equality, see Chapter 3, p 59.

35 See SDA 1975, ss 47–49; RRA 1976, ss 35–38. See also *Hughes v Hackney LB* (1986) unreported, London Central Industrial Tribunal, digested 7 EOR 27. Discussed by C. McCrudden, 'Rethinking positive action' (1986) 15 ILJ 219, 233–234. In *Hughes*, a positive discrimination policy was struck down because, *inter alia*, the employer had compared its ethnic minority (under) representation with that of the borough, and not its recruitment area. See now, EA 2010, ss 104, 158, and 159, which may permit less exact comparisons.

36 *Clarke v Kato*; *Cutter v Eagle Star Insurance* [1998] 1 WLR 1647 (HL).

that Sex Discrimination Act 1975, section 1, did not permit a range of positive actions where these were expressly catered for elsewhere in the statute, and, moreover, expressed within very strict boundaries. Lord Griffiths' speech showed no awareness of this context.

Thus, his conclusion was based on a half-truth, ignored other parts of the statute, and displayed a lack of understanding of a basic tenet of the legislation before him. It also attributed an intention to Parliament, that, had he recourse to *Hansard*, he would have seen did not exist, or at least not in the context of direct discrimination: during the passage of the Sex Discrimination Bill, the Government informed Parliament that such concessions should be objectively justified on the basis that they were indirectly, rather than directly, discriminatory.[37]

Direct or indirect discrimination?

This Government presumption (that this was *indirect* discrimination) hints at the real issue in *James*, which was marginalised as both sides debated the *but for* test. The case was brought principally to test if concessions for pensioners (which disfavoured those men aged 60–65) were permissible without specific statutory authority.[38] The plaintiff, supported by the Equal Opportunities Commission, argued the point solely on direct discrimination, not pleading indirect discrimination in the alternative. This assumes that (apart from the benign motive issue) such concessions would amount to direct discrimination. Thus, where, say, an organisation introduced such a policy purely for tax purposes, or some other non-altruistic motive, it would amount to direct discrimination.

The complication in this case was that a concession for those of pensionable age is not a mainstream example of direct discrimination. It differs as it is a facially neutral policy incorporating a facially discriminatory factor from an independent source. More conventional 'benign motive' cases of direct discrimination present themselves as facially discriminatory conduct implemented to fulfil a 'benign' motive, such as customer preference,[39] chivalry,[40] appearing neutral,[41] or protecting women from workplace harassment[42] or workers from violence.[43]

37 HL Deb 14 July 1975, vol 362, cols 1016–1017 (Lord Harris).

38 [1990] 2 AC 751, 760–761 (Lord Bridge).

39 See the US case, *Diaz v Pan Am* 442 F 2d 385 (5th Cir 1971), certiorari denied, 404 US 950 (1971) (preference for (female) cabin crew) and *Chaney v Plainfield Healthcare* 612 F 3d 908 (7th Cir 2010) (where a care home acceded to patient's preference for a white nurse).

40 *Ministry of Defence v Jeremiah* [1980] QB 87 (CA) (women not required to work in dirty part of factory).

41 *Amnesty International v Ahmed* [2009] ICR 1450 (EAT) (preference for case-workers *not* to be a national of the country under investigation).

42 *Grieg v Community Industry* [1979] ICR 356 (EAT) (woman denied work with all-male decorating team).

43 *Amnesty International v Ahmed* [2009] ICR 1450 (EAT) (Northern Sudanese case-worker would have been in danger in the South, and vice versa).

Thus, the real issue in *James* was whether a facially neutral policy incorporating a facially discriminatory factor should be classified as direct or indirect discrimination. In the context of the facts of *James*, this meant whether the policy could amount to direct discrimination *irrespective* of the benign motive, and. if not, whether it could amount to indirect discrimination, which would afford the Council the opportunity to justify its policy.

Much less was said about this. As an afterthought, Lord Lowry suggested that the policy could be analysed as indirect discrimination because the legislative formula required that it was *applied* equally to all, and not that it 'applies equally' to all (in the sense that men and women are equally affected). As such, for Lord Lowry, this was no different to height or strength requirements, which would have equally predictable results.[44]

Of the majority, only Lords Bridge and Ackner gave the matter some (relatively brief) attention. Lord Bridge dismissed any notion of the policy amounting to indirect discrimination because (in contrast to Lord Lowry's view) it was *not* applied equally to all.[45] This, of course, touches on the heart of the issue: does the incorporated factor convert a facially neutral policy into a directly discriminatory one? But this was as close as the House came to the matter. Instead, Lord Bridge addressed it as one of semantics:

> The expression 'pensionable age' is no more than a convenient shorthand expression which refers to the age of 60 in a woman and to the age of 65 in a man. In considering whether there has been discrimination against a man 'on the ground of his sex' it cannot possibly make any difference whether the alleged discriminator uses the shorthand expression or spells out its full meaning.[46]

Thus, for Lord Bridge, the language used disguised the actual policy. And if the policy could similarly be described with facially discriminatory language, it must be directly discriminatory.

Lord Ackner incorporated the discriminatory factor *before* analysing the policy, rather than its wording, and so concluded:

> The policy itself was crystal clear – if you were a male you had, vis-à-vis a female, a five-year handicap. You had to achieve the age of 65 before you were allowed to swim free of payment, but if you were a female you qualified for free swimming five years earlier.[47]

44 [1990] 2 AC 751, 781. Responding to James' argument that if this discrimination were not indirect, it must be direct. Hence, Lord Lowry suggests that it could be indirect.

45 ibid, 766.

46 ibid, 764.

47 ibid, 769.

Despite their differences, these two extracts go some way to recognising the particular facts in *James*. The reasoning within both is deceptively powerful, short-circuiting the heart of the matter as well as any need to consider a benign motive and the *but for* test: Mr James was asked to pay because he was a man; Mrs James was admitted free because she was a woman.

The importunate dissenters

This means that only Lord Goff's speech in *James* actually resolved the issue using the *but for* test, making this in fact a pluralist rather than majority decision.[48] It may have been that this began the decline of the test.[49] But there were other factors as well. There was the technical problem, that (improperly expressed) it could not distinguish direct from indirect discrimination. There was also the spectacle of a council, in trying to benefit old-age pensioners, being found 'guilty' of discrimination, which for many was a counter-intuitive outcome.

Given this spectacle and the polarised debate over the test, it was predictable that several judicial statements sympathetic to Lord Lowry's dissent followed, suggesting a more subjective approach. First, comments arose in two cases on the parallel phrase *by reason that* in the victimisation provisions of the discrimination legislation.[50] In *Nagarajan v London Regional Transport*,[51] Lord Nicholls suggested: 'Save in obvious cases, answering the crucial question will call for some consideration of the mental processes of the alleged discriminator.'[52] In his dissent, Lord Browne-Wilkinson went further and considered that the courts should not introduce 'something akin to strict liability . . . which will lead to individuals being stamped as racially discriminatory . . . where these matters were not consciously in their minds'.[53] And as we saw in Chapter 3, in *Khan v Chief Constable of West Yorkshire*, Lord Woolf MR commented: 'To regard a person as acting unlawfully when he had not been motivated either consciously or unconsciously by any discriminatory motive is hardly likely to assist the objective of promoting harmonious racial relations.'[54]

On appeal, the House of Lords appeared to agree by holding that the question was 'subjective' and found the employer was not liable for victimisation because

48 Indeed, a reading of Lord Phillip's speech in *JFS* shows he actually endorsed the *James* 'majority' of just Lords Bridge and Ackner (*JFS* [2010] 2 AC 728 (SC) [16]–[20]).

49 In his dissent in *JFS*, Lord Brown distinguished *James*, and noted: 'Even then, the case was decided only by the narrowest majority of the House overturning a unanimous Court of Appeal' (ibid [246].)

50 See now, EA 2010, s 27, which, in line with the change to the definition of direct discrimination, replaced this phrase with 'because'.

51 [2000] 1 AC 501 (HL).

52 ibid, 511.

53 ibid, 510.

54 [2000] ICR 1169 (CA) [14]. In spite of this opinion, Lord Woolf felt bound by *James* and the *Birmingham* grammar-school case to apply the *but for* test and decide for the claimant. But this dictum was vindicated by the reversal of his decision: [2001] UKHL 48. The case is discussed at p 122 et al.

he had acted 'honestly and reasonably',[55] a classic example of a benign motive defence. A year or so later, in *Shamoon v Chief Constable of the RUC*,[56] neither the *but for* test, *James v Eastleigh*, nor the *Birmingham City Council* case were mentioned during five lengthy speeches over a claim of direct sex discrimination. Instead, the Law Lords asked *why* the claimant was treated so. What few other comments were made on the issue suggested that tribunals should look for a discriminatory motive,[57] and that the relevant circumstances for the comparison[58] should be those that the *defendant* took into account,[59] again pointing to a subjective approach. The sentiment reaches into more recent times, with the Court of Appeal rejecting the 'Cat's Paw' theory in one case,[60] and presuming that direct discrimination required motive or intent (conscious or unconscious) in support of its doomed *reason why* theory for indirect discrimination.[61]

Conclusion on James

The case at least settled the pleaded matter: that concessions for those of state pension age amounted to direct sex discrimination and were unlawful as such.[62] Aside from this, *James* produced five judgments rich in opinion and good intention, but wanting in mastery. The speeches failed in a number of ways. First, they did not identify and address the fundamental matter of whether this type of policy (facially neutral, incorporating a facially discriminatory factor from an independent source) should be analysed as direct or indirect discrimination. Second, Lord Lowry's eventual demand for discriminatory intent, along with Lord Griffiths' flirtation with positive action shared the characteristics of having no basis in the legislative language or purpose. Third, although the *but for* test was conceived

55 [2001] UKHL 48, [29] (Lord Nicholls), and requiring 'motive' [77] (Lord Scott). Discussed at pp 122–129.
56 [2003] ICR 337 (HL).
57 ibid [55] (Lord Hope), [116] (Lord Scott). See also *Azmi v Kirklees MBC* [2007] IRLR 484 (EAT) [75] (Wilkie J): '[T]here was in any event no evidence of any motivation to discriminate on the grounds of religious belief.'
58 A statutory requirement. See now EA 2010, s 23: 'On a comparison of cases for the purposes of [direct or indirect discrimination] there must be no material difference between the circumstances relating to each case.'
59 [2003] ICR 337, [134] (Lord Rodger).
60 *Reynolds v CLFIS* [2015] ICR 1010 (CA) [34]–[36]. The theory finds liability against an 'innocent' decision-maker influenced by a prejudiced colleague. The Court of Appeal held that the decision-maker must have a discriminatory motive for liability: 'It would be quite unjust for X to be liable to C where he personally was innocent of any discriminatory motivation.' See further Chapter 9, p 219.
61 *Essop v Home Office* [2015] ICR 1063, [58]–[59]. Reversed [2017] UKSC 27. See p 183 et al.
62 Although it took an unrelated petition to Strasbourg to invoke a legislative response. In response to a challenge in the European Court of Human Rights (*Matthews v UK* (App No. 40302/98)), Parliament legislated that travel concession for the elderly should apply all those aged 60 or over: Travel Concessions (Eligibility) Act 2002. This settled the petition, which did not progress to the Court. This has since been modified in line with the equalising of the state pension age: SI 2010/459, reg 2(1).

with a statutory purpose in mind (to exclude benign motive defences), it was improperly expressed and thus vulnerable to the dissenters, starting with Lord Lowry, and continuing with those sympathetic to his dissent, or at least its sentiment. It is unsurprising, then, that *James* also marked the beginning of the end for the *but for* test in direct discrimination law.

R (E) v Governing Body of JFS

Given the continuing judicial uncertainty, it is no surprise that the matter of a benign motive returned to the Supreme Court, despite having been discussed by the House of Lords a further five occasions following *James*.[63] In *R (E) v Governing Body of JFS*,[64] eight speeches and a 5–4 split on this issue continued the division, although the majority speeches delivered *some* coherent guidance on the matter.

The case centred on the admissions policy of an Orthodox Jewish school. In addition to the 'benign motive' issue, the Supreme Court addressed the meaning of racial group where several sub-groups are involved. For many of the speeches, the two issues were intertwined: for these Justices, it was not possible to identify the *ground* of the treatment without first identifying the protected characteristic of the claimant. And so this discussion of benign motives and the *but for* test inevitably is conflated with the meaning of race and ethnic origins.

The Jewish Free School (JFS) admissions policy gave preference to children recognised as Orthodox Jewish by the Office of the Chief Rabbi (OCR), which required that the child's mother be Jewish either by matrilineal descent or by conversion under the OCR doctrine. The child, 'M', was refused admission because he did not meet these requirements. His Italian (previously Roman Catholic) mother was a Masorti Jew convert, a denomination not recognised by the OCR. His father brought claims of direct and indirect *racial* discrimination under the education provisions of the Race Relations Act 1976, as 'faith schools' enjoyed an exemption from *religious* discrimination in their admissions.[65]

The High Court rejected his claim. The Court of Appeal reversed, holding that the admissions policy amounted to direct discrimination. The Supreme Court, by 5–4 majority (Lord Phillips PSC, Baroness Hale, Lords Kerr, Clarke, and Mance, JJSC) affirmed, although of the minority (Lord Hope DPSC, Lords Rodger, Walker, and Brown JJSC), two (Lords Hope and Walker) found the policy indirectly discriminated, and so a 7–2 majority found in favour of M. (Lords Rodger and Brown found that any prima facie indirect discrimination was objectively justified.) Eight of the Justices gave reasoned speeches, with Lord Walker agreeing with Lord Hope.

63 *Nagarajan v London Regional Transport* [2000] 1 AC 501; *Chief Constable of West Yorkshire v Khan* [2001] UKHL 48; *Shamoon v Chief Constable of the RUC* [2003] ICR 337; *R (European Roma Rights Centre) v Immigration Officer at Prague Airport* [2005] 2 AC 1; *St Helens MBC v Derbyshire* [2007] ICR 841.

64 [2010] 2 AC 728 (SC).

65 At the time, EA 2006, s 50. See now EA 2010, Sch 11, para 5, exempting liability from s 85(1) and (2) (a)–(d) (discrimination in school admissions and provision of education).

The principal difficulty in this case is that being Jewish is both a religious and a racial matter. The principal issues were whether the admissions policy was religious and/or racial; and even if it were facially racial, whether the religious motive behind it rendered the ground of the treatment solely religious. Unlike *James*, the default position seemed to be that if it were not directly discriminatory, the policy would be analysed as indirect discrimination.

1 Identifying the 'racial group'

Section 3(1) of the Race Relations Act 1976 defined 'racial grounds' to mean 'colour, race nationality or ethnic or national origins'.[66] In *Mandla v Dowell Lee*, Lord Fraser provided guidance on the meaning of 'ethnic origins'.[67] It contained two 'essential' and five further 'relevant' characteristics. The essential characteristics were: (1) a long shared history, of which the group is conscious as distinguishing it from other groups, and the memory of which it keeps alive; and (2) a cultural tradition of its own, including family and social customs and manners, often but not necessarily associated with religious observance. The 'relevant' characteristics were: (1) a common geographical origin or descent from a small number of common ancestors; (2) a common language, not necessarily peculiar to the group; (3) a common literature peculiar to the group; (4) a common religion differing from that of neighbouring groups or from the general community surrounding it; and (5) being a minority, or being an oppressed or a dominant group within a larger community. Lord Fraser noted that this definition could include converts.

It is not in dispute that Jews form a racial group by ethnic origins.[68] The *JFS* case was argued over the ethnic status of Jewish sub-groups. The JFS's defence rested on identifying two Jewish groups: first, the OCR group; and second, the *Mandla* group, which is all practising Jews, or those recognisable by 'the man in the street'.[69] The *Mandla* ethnic group would exclude some 'racially Jewish'[70] who have long since abandoned the Jewish faith and may even be unaware of the genetic link. This is because they do not satisfy Lord Fraser's two essential characteristics. Of course, these persons fell *within* the OCR group. The JFS's argument ran that as the OCR definition includes persons *not* within the (*Mandla*) Jewish group, it cannot be based on ethnic origins, or race. It must be solely religious.[71]

Lord Phillips accepted the first part of this proposition but rejected its conclusion, noting: 'The fallacy lies in treating current membership of a *Mandla* ethnic group as the exclusive ground of racial discrimination.' The requirement for matrilineal

66 See now EA 2010, s 9.
67 [1983] 2 AC 548 (HL) 562.
68 ibid, 563, citing *King-Ansell v Police* [1979] 2 NZLR 531 (NZCA).
69 *JFS* [2010] 2 AC 728, [30] (Lord Phillips).
70 That is the Jewish people whose ancestor was the patriarch Jacob (Israel) and with whom the covenant of Mount Sinai was made through Moses upon the Exodus from Egypt. See e.g. ibid [86] (Lord Mance).
71 ibid [30]–[31].

descent (cases of conversion to one side) was 'racial, and in any event, ethnic'.[72] Hence, he concluded: 'Discrimination against a person on the grounds that he or she is, or is not, a member of either group is racial discrimination.'[73]

Lord Kerr explained that although the claimant could be defined as Jewish according to the *Mandla* criteria, 'belonging to that group is not comprehensive of his ethnicity'.[74] There can be 'mixed ethnic origins that do not fall neatly into one group or category' and so the claimant also could define his ethnic origins as a half-Italian Masorti Jew;[75] that was the ground of discrimination in this case. Similarly, Lord Clarke found that identifying the ground of treatment was not an either/or question (either religious *or* ethnic). The definition of ethnic origins was more flexible. So it was possible to discriminate on both religious and ethnic grounds.[76] Lord Mance suggested that the Orthodox Judaism could be regarded as a separate *Mandla* ethnic group,[77] but in any case, M was at a disadvantage because of his descent.[78] Baroness Hale held that 'M was rejected because of his mother's ethnic origins, which were Italian and Roman Catholic'.[79]

At its heart, the decision means this: the JFS's criteria included a racial element: those 'racially Jewish'. This included those who had long since abandoned the Jewish religion, and could even be practising Roman Catholics, Buddhists, atheists, or, indeed, Masorti Jews. No matter what other compensating elements were provided, this element was racial. If the claimant were racially Jewish, he would have been preferred no matter what his faith. If not, he would have to satisfy the (purely religious) 'convert test'. The wider comments call for some consideration.

The consideration begins with the notion of sub-groups and overlaps. Section 3(2) of the Race Relations Act 1976 provided: 'The fact that a racial group comprises two or more distinct racial groups does not prevent it from constituting a particular racial group for the purposes of this Act.'[80] On the face of it, this prevents reducing each racial group to its smallest possible number. Thus, discrimination against 'the Spanish' would be actionable, even though that group comprises Basques and Catalans, among others. It is implicit in section 3(2) that this logic can be inverted. In *Ealing LBC v Race Relations Board*,[81] Lord Simon suggested that within Great Britain, Scots, Welsh, and English could each

72 ibid [42].
73 ibid [46].
74 ibid [121].
75 ibid [108]–[109].
76 ibid [127]–[129].
77 ibid [86].
78 ibid [89].
79 ibid [66].
80 See now EA 2010, s 9(4).
81 [1972] AC 342 (HL).

be defined by national origins.[82] On this basis, 'sub-groups' such as Catalans, Basques, Walloons (Belgians of French origin), Sicilians, Bretons, and the Cornish are definable by ethnic or national origins, and discrimination against one of these sub-groups would be actionable.

Lord Simon's example also suggests that sub-groups can still exist even if they overlap. After all, the English, Welsh, and Scottish certainly overlap. This should also be the case with further sub-groups, such as the Cornish. But, when the *JFS* case was in the High Court, Munby J found 'there is no evidence . . . to suggest that, for example, either Orthodox Jews or Masorti Jews (as opposed to Jews generally) have distinct ethnic origins'.[83] The key word here is 'distinct'. It means that to qualify under the Act, a racial group must have no (or very little) overlap with any other group. While this *accorded* with section 3(2), the sub-section could not be the basis of such a statement. Section 3(2) could only apply where there *are* distinct groups, which was not the finding of Munby J. It is also in no way exclusionary. It merely offers the courts an option of recognising a group as a whole, despite being made up of distinctive sub-groups.

In any case, Munby's J view was not shared by the Supreme Court, where Lord Mance in particular disagreed: 'That may be said to focus purely on ethnic origins in a way which the *Mandla* test was intended to discourage.'[84] Presumably, he means that the *Mandla* definition of *ethnic origins* is more fluid than that. In any case, the majority speeches confirm that a sub-group exists even if it overlaps with other sub-groups.

The fluidity of identifying sub-groups was illustrated in the United States case *Walker v Secretary of the Treasury*,[85] where a predominantly dark-skinned black workforce discriminated against a light-skinned black colleague. The Federal District Court found that Ms Walker could succeed under the Civil Rights Act 1964 in her claim for direct discrimination claim based solely on her colour ('light-skinned black' being a sub-group of, and overlapping with, 'black'). The Court cited *Felix v Marquez*,[86] where it was noted that 'colour' may be the 'most practical' claim where the victim has mixed heritage.

The logical extension of this approach is that there can be liability even where a racial group discriminates against a person from the same racial group. This was confirmed by Lord Clarke:

> I do not see that the identity of the discriminator is of any real relevance . . . . There is certainly nothing in the language or the context of section 1 of the Act or in its statutory purpose to limit the section in that way.[87]

82 ibid, 363–364, applied in *Northern Joint Police Board v Power* [1997] IRLR 610 (EAT) (English). See also *BBC Scotland v Souster* [2001] IRLR 150 (CS) (English); and *Griffiths v Reading University Students Union* (EAT 24 October 1996) see 31 DCLD 3 (Welsh).
83 [2008] EWHC 1535 (Admin) [166].
84 [2010] 2 AC 728 [86].
85 713 F Supp 403 (ND Ga 1989) and 742 F Supp 670 (ND Ga 1990).
86 24 Empl Prac Dec (CCH) 279 (DDC 1980) [31].
87 [2010] 2 AC 728, [152i].

Again, this follows the practice in the United States.[88] It is also correct under the British legislation. There is nothing in the statutory definition restricting its scope in such a way. It points in the other direction, in fact, stating that there should be no less favourable treatment 'because' of race. It says nothing about the characteristic of the discriminator, save that he must be acting within one of the specified activities, such as employment, education, housing, etc. Moreover, the logical consequence of barring such claims would be extraordinary. A man could not claim sex discrimination at work if his employer were male, neither, in a corresponding scenario, could a woman. An Asian worker could make a claim against a black employer, but not an Asian one. On this basis, a victim of sexual-orientation discrimination would have to discover the orientation of the defendant before making a claim.[89]

So far, so good. On the matter of distinguishing ethnic and religious groups, the majority speeches were quite right to emphasise the flexibility permitted in identifying a racial group. However, in the context of this religion/ethnic debate, they overlooked one important point. The legislation only demanded that the treatment is on *racial grounds*, or nowadays, *because of* race. Thus, it is not necessary for the victim to *belong* to a racial group, although that will often be the case. It is enough for liability that the victim does not belong to a particular racial group.[90] And, here, M could not meet the racial element. The complicating factor in this case is that M's essential complaint was that as a Masorti Jew he could not gain access to a Jewish school. But this cause of action could have been brought by *anyone* not 'racially Jewish', which is all M needed to argue, and all that the Court needed to identify to resolve the case.[91] Some recognition of this can be found in Lord Mance's speech:

> A test of membership of a religion that focuses on descent from a particular people is a test based on ethnic origins. This case cannot therefore be viewed as a mere disagreement between different Jewish denominations . . . . It turns, more fundamentally, on whether it is permissible for any school to treat one child less favourably than another because the child does not have whatever ancestry is required, in the school's view, to make the child Jewish.[92]

88 See *Ross v Douglas County, Nebraska* 234 F 3d 391 (8th Cir 2000), finding liability where a black supervisor racially abused a black subordinate.

89 See *English v Thomas Sanderson Blinds* [2009] ICR 543 (CA) where even the orientation of the claimant was held to be irrelevant in claim of homophobic harassment.

90 For instance, 'whites only', or 'men only'. Such 'positively' expressed criteria can arise also in (failed) positive-action cases: e.g. women-only shortlists: *Jepson and Dyas-Elliott v The Labour Party* [1996] IRLR 116 (IT) (now legitimised, EA 2010, s 104); Afro-Caribbean required for Housing Department to correspond to its housing population: *London Borough of Lambeth v Commission for Racial Equality* [1990] ICR 768 (CA) (see now EA 2010, s 158).

91 In *Tejani v Superintendent Registrar for the District of Peterborough* [1986] IRLR 502, the Court of Appeal made the same error, this time fatal to the claim. It held that a practice disfavouring anyone from overseas was lawful, because no specific nationally was specified.

92 [2010] 2 AC 728, [86]. Baroness Hale noted: 'As Lord Kerr JSC explains, there can be no logical distinction between treating a person less favourably because he does have a particular ethnic origin and treating him less favourably because he does not' [68]. In context though, this seems to be another way of identifying M's ethnic identity; Lord Kerr had said: 'Logically, therefore, the absence of such a feature [the matrilineal link] from M's heritage cannot be denied, and must be accepted, as a defining characteristic of his ethnicity' [110].

Thus, elaborate discussions on the meaning of 'ethnic origins', and the ethnic identity of the claimant (such as a 'half-Italian Masorti Jew' or 'Italian Roman Catholic') were irrelevant. As such, even entertaining the JFS's elaborate argument was unnecessary.

Less favourable treatment and the comparison

Identifying the relevant racial group inevitably affects the identity of any comparator for the purpose of establishing less favourable treatment. To this end, section 3(4) of the Race Relations Act 1976 provided:

> A comparison of the case of a person of a particular racial group with that of a person not of that group . . . must be such that the relevant circumstances in the one case are the same, or not materially different, in the other.[93]

Upon this, if the favoured group is identified as those 'racially Jewish', then the comparator would be anyone not racially Jewish. On the way the case was presented (on the claimant's status as a Masorti Jew), the comparison could be refined by using more 'relevant circumstances'. Bearing in mind this was a claim of *racial* discrimination, the racial factor should be the only difference. As such, while the claimant is a Masorti Jew who had not descended from Jacob[94] through the matrilineal line, the comparator is a Masorti Jew who had. This comparator would have qualified without more, while the claimant would not have done.

For most, the comparison was not a major issue, their focus being on the claimant's racial identity and issues flowing from the benign motive 'defence'. But for Lord Rodger's dissent, it was central. It began by noting (correctly) that the claimant's *particular* racial identity was irrelevant (all that mattered is that he was not Orthodox). But this led Lord Roger to bypass the racial question and jump to the 'conversion' stage of the admissions policy when making the comparison:

> [M's] mother's Jewish status as a result of her conversion was accordingly the only issue which the governors were asked to consider or did consider . . . . Therefore . . . the appropriate comparator could only be a boy whose mother had converted under Orthodox auspices.[95]

This comparison tests the defendant's argument by its own (religious) terms, rather than by the (race) legislation invoked by the claimant. Given that the defence rests on the proposition that the whole matter is purely religious, the result was inevitable.

93 See now EA 2010, s 23: 'On a comparison of cases for the purposes of [direct or indirect discrimination] there must be no material difference between the circumstances relating to each case.'
94 See e.g. [2010] 2 AC 728, [86] (Lord Mance) noted above, p 102, n 70.
95 ibid [228–229]. Cf Lord Hope (pp 108–110), who arrived at a similar comparison, but this time via the OCR's 'benign motive'.

Rather than test the claimant's *racial* discrimination claim, Lord Rodger bypassed it, treating the *defence* as the 'only' issue. This was most odd, and ignores completely the 'descent' element of the challenged policy. The 'conversion' criterion only came into play because M was not racially Jewish, a point overlooked in Lord Rodger's speech. The technical, or 'mechanical', failure here is the illogical progression from the racial identity question to a religious comparison, which – for this case at least – deprived the definition of direct racial discrimination of any efficacy at all.

Conclusion on groups

Overall, the majority speeches confirmed four principles of racial identity under the legislation. First, there can be sub-groups of a racial group. Second, groups or sub-groups may overlap. Third, a sub-group may include persons *not* included in the parent group, rather like Basques and Catalans (each group straddles the Spanish-French border). Fourth, it makes no difference to liability if the discriminator belongs to the same racial group as the victim. Given the statutory wording, its purpose, and the existing UK and US case law at the time, none of this broke new ground. Moreover, what the majority speeches failed to do was to grasp the simplicity of the case: M was subjected to the 'conversion test' because of who he was *not*. This reveals a technical misunderstanding of the definition of direct discrimination, which does not require that the claimant belongs to a specific (racial) group, only that the treatment was because of race (or another protected characteristic). Otherwise, practices such as 'whites only', or 'British only', would be lawful. It also shows a lack of appreciation of precedent, where the House of Lords recognised 'non-British' and 'non-ECC' as racial groups.[96] Thus, discussions as to whether or not M belonged to an ethnic group, occupying some 65 paragraphs,[97] were irrelevant.

2 Direct discrimination, the **but for** *test, and the benign motive 'defence'*

Once they had established that the descent requirement was racial, the majority turned their attention to whether the 'benign' religious motive behind it rendered the ground of the treatment solely religious, and so not 'on racial grounds'. They dealt with this by invoking Lord Nicholls' suggestion from *Nagarajan v London Regional Transport*: 'Save in obvious cases, answering the crucial question will call for some consideration of the mental processes of the alleged discriminator.'[98]

This envisages two types of direct discrimination.[99] There were 'obvious' (or 'inherent') cases, where the reason for the treatment is patently racial

96 *Orphanos v QMC* [1985] AC 761 (HL), 771.

97 ibid [28]–[46] (Lord Phillips); [66]–[71] (Baroness Hale); [75]–[77] & [79]–[89] (Lord Mance); [108]–[110] & [119]–[122] (Lord Kerr); [127]–[132] (Lord Clarke); [157]–[162] & [183]–[186] (Lord Hope); [228]–[230] (Lord Rodger); [238]–[245] (Lord Brown).

98 [2000] 1 AC 501 (HL) 511. Lords Rodger ([228]) and Brown ([248]–[249]) appeared to grasp the point, but only to embark upon a misconceived 'religious' comparison (Lord Rodger, see p 106, text to n 95) or as a reason to avoid stigmatising Judaism as a directly racially discriminating religion (Lord Brown, see pp 110, text to n 119).

99 [2010] 2 AC 728, [21]–[23] (Lord Phillips), [62]–[64] (Baroness Hale), [78] (Lord Mance), [114]–[117] (Lord Kerr), [132] (Lord Clarke).

(or patently because of another protected characteristic). Presumably, an example would be 'No Blacks need apply'. In these cases, there is no need to enquire into the defendant's motive, no matter how worthy it might be. Second, there are 'less obvious' (or 'subjective') cases. Lord Phillips provided a vivid example: A shopkeeper says to a fat black man, 'I do not serve people like you.'[100] A more subtle example was given by Baroness Hale, where in job applications, the patent criterion is 'that elusive quality known as "merit"'.[101] In such cases, it is necessary to assess the motive of the defendant to ascertain the ground of the treatment: respectively, whether it was obesity or colour, or merit or race. The racial bias may even be subconscious, to be discovered by proper inferences from the evidence.[102]

Although little was said about the actual application of the *but for* test, it was not expressly overruled. Of the majority, only Lord Phillips expressed an opinion, and that was in the mildest of terms, saying that he did not find the test 'helpful'.[103] Baroness Hale cited the *Birmingham City Council* and *James* cases, and expressly approved the *decisions*, rather than the *but for* test itself.[104] Lords Mance and Kerr stuck to Lord Nicholls' formula, and only Lord Clarke stated that the *but for* test was reconcilable with Lord Nicholls' formula, stating that 'it is inherently unlikely that there is any distinction between the principles established by those cases [*Birmingham City Council* and *James*] and the reasoning in the *Nagarajan* case'.[105] This was because *Nagarajan* provided 'a separate basis on which direct discrimination can be established'.[106]

The dissenters and the benign motive 'defence'

As all agreed this was an 'obvious' case, it was not strictly necessary to address the *but for* test. Not so for Lord Hope (with whom Lord Walker agreed entirely), who had to sideline the test in order to embark upon a tortuous route to a benign motive 'defence', which went via Lord Nicholls' 'mental processes' test, the mind of the Chief Rabbi, and the comparison. Thus, of the minority (on direct discrimination), Lord Hope was the only Justice to criticise the *but for* test, stating that it was 'expressed too broadly'.[107] Upon this, he read Lord Nicholls' 'mental processes' formula to be applicable to obvious, as well as less obvious, cases:

100 ibid [21].
101 ibid [64].
102 ibid.
103 ibid [16].
104 ibid [78].
105 ibid [139].
106 ibid [137].
107 ibid [197].

> It may be that the tribunal will not *need* to look at the alleged discriminator's mental processes in 'obvious cases', as his mental state is indeed obvious. But he does not say that the tribunal is precluded from doing so.[108]

This enabled Lord Hope to distinguish cases of anti-Semitic abuse[109] (racial in nature), from the present case, where '[t]hose who are said to have been responsible for the discrimination, whether at the level of the school authorities, the OCR or the Chief Rabbi himself, are thoughtful, well-intentioned and articulate'.[110]

The difficulty here is that there is nothing in Lord Nicholls' 'mental processes' speech from *Nagarajan* to support this interpretation. Lord Nicholls said, it will be recalled, that some consideration of the mental processes of the defendant will be called for, *save* in obvious cases.[111] Furthermore, where it was appropriate to consider the defendant's mental processes, this was not for the purpose of establishing a benign motive. In the following paragraph Lord Nicholls stated that this question must be 'distinguished sharply' from the reason why the defendant acted so. 'In particular,' he continued, 'if the reason why the alleged discriminator rejected the complainant's job application was racial, it matters not that his intention may have been benign'.[112] Lord Nicholls could not have been clearer. Lord Hope did not misinterpret or distort Lord Nicholls' speech. He re-wrote it.

Regardless of this, having aligned the 'mental processes test' with the 'obvious' ground of the treatment, Lord Hope turned to the mind of the Chief Rabbi, and found that his motive was purely religious. In doing so, he compared how the OCR treated (1) a secular descendant of an orthodox convert, and (2) a practising descendant of a non-orthodox convert, in order to show that the OCR motive was purely religious, on the basis that the secular descendant would be admitted.[113] Thus, the reasoning goes, the OCR requirement is rooted in the historical 'religious' event of conversion. Rather like Lord Rodger's comparison,[114] the example bypasses the claim and the racial discrimination legislation. In Lord Hope's comparison, the claimant has no racial identity and *two* religious ones, as does his comparator (if one accepts secularism as a religious identity). Thus, it is not even clear what Lord Hope considers to be the basis of the claim. It could be 'secularism' or 'conversion'. Whichever it is, his comparison introduces secondary non-relevant circumstances.

Presumably, in conceding that this is an 'obvious' case, Lord Hope acknowledged that those not 'racially Jewish' were at a disadvantage. To combine the 'mental processes' test with a comparison using the non-racial factors

108 ibid [198]. Emphasis original.
109 Citing *Seide v Gillette Industries* [1980] IRLR 427 (EAT), discussed, p 118.
110 [2010] 2 AC 728, [201].
111 [2000] 1 AC 501 (HL) 511. Emphasis supplied.
112 ibid.
113 [2010] 2 AC 728 [203].
114 See above, p 106, text to n 95.

was incoherent, and, of course, technically flawed. It seems that Lord Hope's manoeuvre was to load the comparison with benign (solely religious) factors and reflect them back to the mental processes of the Chief Rabbi.

Lord Brown's dissent (with which Lord Rodger agreed[115]) went further, arguing that benign preferential treatment should be defendable, this time, using the vehicle of *indirect* discrimination: 'It therefore seems to me of the greatest importance not to expand the scope of direct discrimination and thereby place preferential treatment which could well be regarded as no more than indirectly discriminatory beyond the reach of possible justification.'[116] This is of a similar flavour to the dissents in *James*. As Lord Griffiths endorsed the 'benign' preferential treatment of women,[117] Lord Lowry flirted with indirect discrimination.[118] In any case, Lord Brown appeared to rely on two similar bases for his view. First was the good faith behind the policy. He continued:

> This is especially so where, as here, no one doubts the Chief Rabbi's utmost good faith and that the manifest purpose of his policy is to give effect to the principles of Orthodox Judaism as universally recognised for millennia past.[119]

In other words, 'utmost good faith' transforms a case of direct discrimination into one of indirect discrimination, permitting preferential treatment, should it be 'justifiable'.

Second, Lord Brown had to dispose of the seemingly incompatible *but for* test. He dealt with this by distinguishing *James:* 'There is not the same exact correlation between membership of the Jewish religion and membership of the group regarded on the Mandla approach as being of Jewish ethnicity as there was between retirement age and sex in *James.*'[120]

With respect, it is difficult to see how *James* could be distinguished on this basis. In both cases the defendant has adopted a policy which incorporates a facially discriminatory factor. And, if anything, a correlation between pensionable age and sex is somewhat looser, as the recent enactments equalising the ages demonstrate,[121] thus making it somewhat more mutable than a religious law 'recognised for millennia past'. The particular feature common to *James* and *JFS* (facially neutral factor incorporating a facially discriminatory factor from another source) may be the basis of arguments that they should be analysed as indirect discrimination.[122] But none of the arguments could depend on something as

115 [2010] 2 AC 728 [232].
116 ibid [247].
117 [1990] 2 AC 751 768. See p 96.
118 ibid, 781. See above, 'Direct or indirect discrimination?' p 97.
119 [2010] 2 AC 728, [247].
120 ibid.
121 Under the Pensions Act 2011, women's state pension age will increase to 65 between April 2016 and November 2018. From December 2018, the state pension age for both men and women will start to increase and reach 66 by October 2020.
122 See above, 'Direct or indirect discrimination?' p 97.

hollow as 'utmost good faith'. More generally, by casting the school policy as 'preferential treatment', at the same time, Lord Brown acknowledges it is facially discriminatory, and so, presumably, directly discriminatory. The arguments of principle and statutory interpretation attacking Lord Griffiths' speech in *James*[123] apply with all the more force here, because Lord Brown had at his disposal an additional 20 years in which neither the courts, nor Parliament, saw a reason to upset the basic tenet of *James*, that aside from specific legislative exceptions, a benign motive is no defence to facially discriminatory conduct.[124]

Save for Lord Brown's misplaced understanding of the purpose of the legislative structure, the judgments of Lords Hope and Brown failed to engage with the text of the legislation or employ any rules of statutory interpretation, and, notably, as they were departing from the strict wording, expressed no allusions to the intention of Parliament or statutory purpose. This was in addition to their questionable treatment of precedent. They would have done better to have explored whether cases such as *James* and *JFS* could be analysed as indirect discrimination, given their particular nature (discussed in more detail later),[125] or at least have adopted one of Counsel's secondary arguments, that when providing a faith-school exception for religious discrimination, Parliament could not have intended that it applied to all religious schools bar Jewish ones.[126]

Policy and purposive considerations

Those were the technical solutions of the Court. The benign motive issue also gave the case a public policy dimension. Many of the Justices expressed 'sympathy'[127] for the predicament of the JFS, having a definition of religion that included a racial element. For them, the Chief Rabbi had expressed a Jewish law that had stood for thousands of years;[128] he had given an 'honest and sincere' opinion,[129] with an 'unimpeachable' motive,[130] and (as already noted) had acted in 'utmost good faith'.[131] Of course, none of this mattered to the majority decision. Jews were free to practise their longstanding law, so far as this did not encroach into certain defined activities. As Lord Kerr put it, although it was 'logical' to describe

123 E.g. ignoring the symmetrical model of direct discrimination and that positive action is catered for elsewhere in the statute. See pp 95–97.
124 See e.g. *Jepson and Dyas-Elliott v The Labour Party* [1996] IRLR 116 (IT) (all-women shortlists); *London Borough of Lambeth v Commission for Racial Equality* [1990] ICR 768 (CA) (Afro-Caribbean required for Housing Department to correspond to its housing population); *Amnesty International v Ahmed* [2009] ICR 1450 (EAT) (requirement that applicant is not Sudanese for her own safety).
125 See p 114.
126 [2010] 2 AC 728, 734 (SC) (Lord Pannick QC).
127 ibid [124] (Lord Kerr).
128 See e.g. ibid [201] (Lord Hope), [247] (Lord Brown) and [2008] EWHC 1535 (Admin) [15] (Munby J).
129 ibid [65] (Baroness Hale).
130 ibid [122] (Lord Kerr).
131 ibid [182] (Lord Hope), [247] (Lord Brown).

the OCR definition as religious, 'when the answer to that religious question has consequences in the civil law sphere, its legality falls to be examined'.[132] Lord Clarke used an extreme, albeit real, case to make the same point:

> [A] person who honestly believed, as the Dutch Reformed Church of South Africa until recently believed, that God had made black people inferior and had destined them to live separately from whites, would be able to discriminate openly against them without breaking the law.[133]

Lord Clarke went on to cite *Bob Jones University v United States*,[134] where the US Supreme Court upheld the IRS decision to revoke the University's tax-exempt status because it denied admission to anyone engaged in interracial marriage, despite this policy being based on a sincerely held religious belief. He also cited *Campbell and Cosans v UK*, where the European Court of Human Rights stated that beliefs 'must be worthy of respect in a democratic society' and not 'incompatible with human dignity'.[135]

Given this, and the result, the majority's aforementioned expressions of sympathy may ring a little hollow. But the sympathies of the minority drove them to some extraordinary thinking. For two of these Justices, the consequences of lifting the policy was a reason to find that it was not discriminatory. Lord Brown, for instance, reasoned:

> This policy could as well have been struck down at the suit of anyone desiring admission to the school. If the argument succeeds it follows that Jewish religious law as to who is a Jew . . . must henceforth be treated as irrelevant. Jewish schools in future, if oversubscribed, must decide on preference by reference only to outward manifestations of religious practice . . . . To hold the contrary would be to stigmatise Judaism as a directly racially discriminating religion.[136]

Here, Lord Brown observes that the majority decision meant that the policy not only excluded Masorti Jews, but also *anyone* not 'racially Jewish', and concludes that the accompanying stigmatism *of the school* was a basis for holding that it did not directly discriminate. While this observation inadvertently acknowledged the true nature of the case, the conclusion is reminiscent of the comments in the wake of *James*, suggesting that the well-meaning should not be 'stamped' as culpable, or even racist,[137] which, of course, have no basis in the statutory wording, purpose,[138] or precedent.

132 ibid [119].
133 ibid [150]. See also in the Court of Appeal [2009] PTSR 1442, [30] (Sedley LJ).
134 461 US 574 (1983).
135 (1982) 4 EHRR 293, [36] (recognising parents' belief against corporal punishment of their child at school).
136 [2010] 2 AC 728, [248]–[249].
137 E.g. *Nagarajan v London Regional Transport* [2000] 1 AC 501 (HL) 510 (Lord Browne-Wilkinson, dissenting). See also, *Khan v Chief Constable of West Yorkshire* [2000] ICR 1169 (CA) (Lord Woolf MR) [14], reversed on different grounds, [2001] UKHL 48. See p 122 et al.
138 See p 75.

Lord Rodger's reasoning was similarly sensationalist: 'The majority's decision leads to such extraordinary results, and produces such manifest discrimination against Jewish schools in comparison with other faith schools, that one can't help feeling that something has gone wrong.'[139] Once again, Lord Rodger provides no basis in the statutory wording. This dictum appears in ignorance of the school's racially-based preference, which distinguished it from most other faith schools. This 'feeling' also evokes an ideological predilection voiced by Lord Diplock back in 1974[140] of the individual's freedom to define his or her business, enterprise, or religion (and correspondingly whom is suitable for admission), a liberty not to be trumped by meddlesome equality law. But rather than 'feeling that something has gone wrong', he would have better made the point by bringing the matter back to the process of statutory interpretation, and embracing and examining Counsel's more, sober, articulate, and concrete reflection (noted earlier) that Parliament could not have intended that the religious exemption applied to all faith schools bar Jewish ones.[141] Moreover, these comments of Lords Brown and Rodger can only serve to encourage further indulgencies in a benign motive defence, and maintain an argument that should have been put to bed decades ago.

Treating some of the group less favourably

In their dissents (on the direct discrimination claim), Lord Hope found the Dutch Reformed Church analogy 'quite different' as it was 'overtly racist',[142] whilst Lord Brown did not consider the examples to be 'parallel', as the Church rule was 'self-evidently . . . on the ground of race and irredeemable by reference to the church's underlying religious motive'.[143]

The Dutch Reformed Church example *is* different, because in racial terms it is binary in nature, excluding 100 per cent of blacks, unlike the JFS policy, which, with its convert rule, does not exclude all those not (racially) Jewish. But should that make a difference? What if the Church admitted all whites and only black converts? This issue thus becomes quasi-technical: can there be direct discrimination if only some of the claimant's group are treated less favourably? This matter was barely addressed by the majority.

The clearest answer was provided by Counsel for the claimant, and adopted by Lord Mance: '[A]n organisation which admitted all men but only women graduates would be engaged in direct discrimination on the grounds of sex.'[144] This makes the point succinctly and effectively, but none of the speeches explained how the statutory wording supported this conclusion.

139 [2010] 2 AC 728, [226].
140 *Dockers Labour Club and Institute Ltd v Race Relations Board* [1976] AC 285 (HL), 295–296. See p 87, text to n 70.
141 ibid, 734 (Lord Pannick QC). A similar criticism is made of Lords Hope and Brown. See p 111, text to n 126.
142 ibid [202].
143 ibid [245].
144 ibid [89], 738, citing Counsel Dinah Rose QC.

The legislative formula(s), set out at the start of this chapter, describes the victim as an individual. This suggests that there can be direct discrimination against just one of a racial group, which in turn suggests that there can be direct discrimination against just *some* members of a group. This makes sense when realised in two corresponding examples. An employer of several black persons says to just one, 'I am dismissing you because you are a typical lazy black.' This is undoubtedly direct discrimination, even though the employer does not mistreat any other black workers. Second, in addition to Counsel's example, a nightclub admitting all women, and only 'good looking' men would be treating men less favourably because they are men, even though some would be admitted. Thus, the conclusion that direct discrimination covers less favourable treatment of just some of the group appears a logical extension of the assumption it covers less favourable treatment against just one of the group.

The 'incorporated' issue

But that, combined with identifying the racial or ethnic element in the admissions policy, was as far as the majority went in explaining why this was a case of direct discrimination. What they missed was that 'structurally' the JFS policy resembled *James*: a facially neutral ('religious') policy incorporating a facially discriminatory factor ('racially Jewish') from an independent source (Jewish Law). This distinguishes these two cases from the 'some-of-the-group' examples, and the vast majority of direct discrimination cases. It suggests that there are arguments that such cases should be analysed as *indirect* discrimination.[145] Indeed, the matter was not entirely without authority. In *Schnorbus v Land Hessen*,[146] the issue was considered by Advocate General Jacobs in the context of sex discrimination, who advised that unless the incorporated measure was 'indissociable' from sex (e.g. pregnancy) the case should be addressed as indirect discrimination.[147] The Court of Justice agreed.[148] Thus, not only was the issue ignored in *JFS*, but also there existed an authoritative basis on which to discuss it.[149] Given the simplicity of the case in terms of identifying racial groups, this was in fact the only issue of substance, which went unrecognised and unaddressed.

145 As noted earlier (p 97, n 37 and accompanying text) in the discussion of *James*, during the passage of the Sex Discrimination Bill, the Government considered that concessions for pensioners would amount to (justifiable) indirect discrimination: HL Deb 14 July 1975, vol 362, cols 1016–1017 (Lord Harris).

146 Case C-79/99 [2000] ECR I-10997 (vocational training priority for those completing military service where military service was only available to men).

147 ibid [AG33] & [AG36]–[AG41].

148 ibid, paras 30–34.

149 The matter was addressed eventually by the Supreme Court in 2011, but only because it was expressly raised in the wake of a (subsequent) CJEU decision on nationality discrimination. See *Patmalniece v Secretary of State for Work and Pensions* [2011] UKSC 11, following Case C-73/08 *Bressol v Gouvernement de la Communauté Française* [2010] 3 CMLR 20 ruling that for (EU) nationality discrimination, a 'residency' requirement for certain benefits incorporating an automatic right to residence for Belgian nationals, amounted to *indirect* discrimination (despite the contrary Opinion of AG Sharpston ([AG43]–[AG58])).

3 Conclusion on JFS

The decision confirmed that (1) group definition could be fluid, multiple, and overlapping; (2) there is no benign motive defence to direct discrimination; (3) the defendant's motive is relevant only in 'less obvious' cases; (4) the only purpose of identifying the motive is to discover the ground (protected characteristic) of the treatment; (5) it is possible for one member of a protected group to directly discriminate against a member of the same group; and (6) it is possible to directly discriminate against just some members of a protected group.

Whilst it may be helpful to have these points reaffirmed, they say nothing new to anyone familiar with discrimination law. The obvious difficulty in this case was that the OCR's definition straddled religious and racial factors. However, it was not difficult to unravel the two and identify the racial strand, and then grasp the point that the claimant's particular racial identity was unimportant: what mattered is that he was not 'racially Jewish'. Instead, the Justices were drawn into an irrelevant debate over JFS's over-elaborate submission, which in essence argued that the definition of a racial group was fixed, exclusive, and static. Addressing a party's misplaced argument is one thing, but defining a judgment by it is quite another.

Technical shortcomings aside, the failure of the minority to reject the benign motive defence, and the majority's attempts to reconcile its previous seven cases on the matter, still leaves some doubt. Most notably, the majority failed to overrule, refine, or even distinguish, the 'honest and reasonable defence' advanced in *Chief Constable of West Yorkshire Police v Khan*.[150] Treating it as good law can only fuel the advocates of a benign motive defence. Indeed, in his dissent on this issue, Lord Hope (with whom Lord Walker agreed) used *Khan* to support the JFS defence of religious motivation.[151] More generally, the speeches appeared to prefer the 'mental processes' formula to the *but for* test. This follows the general drift, but the preference was neither expressed nor explained, leaving many interested parties, and the layperson, with little chance of understanding what the test should be, and why it has changed. After all, the *but for* test was the basis, or ratio decidendi, of the unanimous decision in *Birmingham City Council* and played a part, at least, in *James*, cases that have never been overruled.

There was also a complete failure to address the distinguishing and, in substance, central issue in this case: whether a facially neutral policy incorporating a facially discriminatory factor amounted to direct or indirect discrimination. Given that cases raising matters of public importance go to the Supreme Court, this was a serious omission.

150 [2001] UKHL 48. See e.g. *JFS* [2010] 2 AC 728, [21]–[23] (Lord Phillips), [78] (Lord Mance), [144] (Lord Clarke). Two attempts have been made. In *St Helens MBC v Derbyshire* [2007] ICR 841 (SC) [36] Baroness Hale alone and dissenting wrote that the 'honest and reasonable' aspect of *Khan* should be 'laid to rest'. In *Pothecary Witham Weld v Bullimore* [2010] ICR 1008 (EAT) [18] Underhill J suggested that the defence was confined to victimisation cases where the parties were opponents in litigation. See further p 128, n 56 and p 130, n 63.

151 [2010] 2 AC 728, [199], noting that in *Khan* Lord Nicholls advocated a 'subjective' approach (see [2001] UKHL 48 [29]). Lord Hope did not mention the 'honest and reasonable defence' by name. *Khan* is discussed at pp 71 and 122–129.

The minority speeches fared worse, with Lords Hope and Rodger simply bypassing the racial identity question and Lord Hope re-writing Lord Nicholls' 'mental processes' test. All gave undue weight to the 'good faith' behind the policy, encouraging, once again, the arguments for a benign motive 'defence' made in the wake of the dissents in *James*, and the continuing validity of *Khan*'s 'honest and reasonable defence'. That this was a 5–4 split on the benign motive issue, and came on top of seven previous House of Lords cases on that question, undermines any confidence that the *JFS* case, for all its judicial input, will stand as a seminal one.

At this point, it is worth repeating the caution made by Lord Diplock:

> The acceptance of the rule of law as a constitutional principle requires that a citizen, before committing himself to any course of action, should be able to know in advance what are the legal consequences that will flow from it. . . . [T]he court must give effect to what the words of the statute would be reasonably understood to mean by those whose conduct it regulates.[152]

Little of the reasoning in *JFS* (or indeed *James*) was rooted in any recognisable notions of statutory interpretation. For nine Justices of the Supreme Court to entertain this case seemed excessive, and was likely to cause more uncertainty than understanding. This was exacerbated with the abundance of eight divisive and over-elaborate speeches, which left the best of lawyers debating their meaning, let alone the wider audience with equality-law interests.

Finally, one must be concerned why this case attracted the attention not only of the Supreme Court, but also the unusually large panel of nine Justices. Given the rare nature of Jewish identity – straddling religious and racial factors – the decision is unlikely to affect many other faith schools, if any.[153] Further, on the assumption that parents would have to engage their children in outward manifestations of Jewish religious practice, and that successful entrants would be taught the Orthodox Jewish faith 'in the hope and expectation that they will come to practise it',[154] the majority decision is unlikely to encourage hordes of non-Jewish 'pushy parents' to sign up, no matter how high the academic standards. Indeed, the JFS maintained that dropping the policy would endanger the school's survival: 'we are going to need to supply children out of thin air'.[155] And although using the dramatic potential of the case as a reason to dismiss the claim, the minority was more obviously concerned with the relatively *narrow,* but *serious* consequences for just 27 out of many thousands of the nation's schools.[156]

152 *Black-Clawson International Ltd v Papierwerke Waldhof-Aschaffenberg AG* [1975] AC 591 (HL) 638.
153 The Secretary of State for Children, Schools, and Families (Intervening) observed that it might affect some Sikh schools as well: [2010] 2 AC 728, 736.
154 United Synagogue (intervening) [2010] 2 AC 728, 735.
155 [2010] 2 AC 728, cited at [87] (Lord Mance).

The point is that, save for the unaddressed 'incorporated' point, the case was of little interest beyond a tiny fraction of the nation's schools. The racial group question was straightforward and the benign motive defence question had been (apparently) well settled for some 20 years. Given all this, it is baffling that it has taken 610 paragraphs, 10 judicial speeches, and 13 judges to settle the matter. And even then, given the range and number of opinions, the case must be a candidate for one of the worst examples of prolixity in the law reports.

4 The status of the **but for** *test*

Unlike the House of Lords in the *Birmingham City Council* case (and perhaps some counterparts in *James*), the majority in *JFS* rejected the benign motive defence without expressly relying on the *but for* test, displaying a similar indifference to it as displayed in the House of Lords cases following *James.*[157] They merely found that its apparent antithesis, the 'mental processes test', was suitable for 'less obvious' cases. Although the *Birmingham* and *James* decisions were not overruled, or at all criticised, the implication is that the *but for* test itself is defunct. A short time before the *JFS* judgment was handed down, a thoughtful judgment from Underhill J afforded the test more credibility, but, inadvertently perhaps, provided another reason for its demise. In *Amnesty International v Ahmed*,[158] he stated that the *but for* test was appropriate for both 'obvious' and 'less obvious' cases, although its 'real value' was in the *latter*. In this context, he explained its purpose thus:

> [I]f the discriminator would not have done the act complained of but for the claimant's sex (or race), it does not matter whether you describe the mental process involved as his intention, his motive, his reason, his purpose or anything else – all that matters is that the proscribed factor operated on his mind. This is therefore a useful gloss on the statutory test.[159]

This, of course, is the *but for* test, properly expressed, and would have produced the same outcome in *JFS*. Underhill J went further however, and identified a third category of direct discrimination where the *but for* test would be 'misleading'.[160]

156 See evidence of Secretary of State (intervening) [2008] EWHC 1535 (Admin) [102]. For England alone, January 2012, there were 24,372 schools (including nursery schools, state-funded primary schools, state-funded secondary schools, special schools, pupil referral units, and independent schools). See Department of Education, < https://www.gov.uk/government/publications/number-of-schools-teachers-and-students-in-england/number-of-schools-teachers-and-students-in-england > accessed 10 April 2018.

157 *Nagarajan v London Regional Transport* [2000] 1 AC 501; *Chief Constable of West Yorkshire v Khan* [2001] UKHL 48; *Shamoon v Chief Constable of the RUC* [2003] ICR 337.

158 [2009] ICR 1450 (EAT).

159 ibid [37].

160 ibid.

This could be conveniently labelled 'background cases'. He gave an example of the case of *Seide v Gillette Industries*,[161] where a worker was moved to a different department to escape anti-Semitic harassment. In his new department, he fell out (for non-racial reasons) with his colleagues and was disciplined. The claimant argued that *but for* the prior anti-Semitic harassment, he would not have been in the situation where he was disciplined. It was held, however, that he had not been disciplined on racial grounds.

Underhill's J analysis that the *but for* test would have led to the wrong decision was based upon a reversion to the improper expression of the test. Properly expressed, it would have provided the identical result for Mr Seide: it could not be said that the employer would not have disciplined Mr Seide *but for* Mr Seide being Jewish, or indeed because of the harassment he had once suffered. If the test were properly expressed, the 'background' in this case has nothing to do with the question. Once again, it seems, a judge (who has presided over numerous discrimination cases, and now sits in the Court of Appeal[162]) has neither grasped the technicalities of the test nor the significance of expressing it precisely.

Aside from this misplaced loyalty, and the more fashionable cold-shoulder for the *but for* test, there exists a concrete reason to doubt its correctness. It loses its efficacy when applied to mixed ground cases. Take *Owen and Briggs v James*,[163] for instance, where an applicant was rejected because of her poor employment record, her 'unsatisfactory demeanour', ***and*** her race. Here, where there were both discriminatory and non-discriminatory reasons for the treatment, the test becomes problematic. The theoretical objection was explained by the US Supreme Court in *Price Waterhouse v Hopkins*:[164]

> Suppose two physical forces act upon and move an object, and suppose that either force acting alone would have moved the object. As the [*but for* test] would have it, *neither* physical force was a 'cause' of the motion unless we can show that but for one or both of them, the object would not have moved; apparently both forces were simply 'in the air' unless we can identify at least one of them as a but-for cause of the object's movement. . . . Events that are causally overdetermined, in other words, may not have any 'cause' at all. This cannot be so.[165]

161 [1980] IRLR 427 (EAT). Less helpfully (in *Ahmed*), Underhill J also cited the controversial decision in *Martin v Lancehawk* (EAT, 22 March 2004), where a (female) worker was dismissed following the breakdown of her relationship with her (male) managing director. The *but for* test was not used and so the worker lost her sex discrimination claim. See also *B v A* [2007] IRLR 576 (EAT); S. Middlemiss, 'A licence to discard? Failed sexual relationships in the workplace and sex discrimination' (2007) 78 Emp LB 2 (Westlaw).

162 In the EAT 2000–2003 (part-time) and 2006–2013. See < https://www.judiciary.gov.uk/you-and-the-judiciary/going-to-court/court-of-appeal-home/coa-biogs/ > accessed 30 March 2018. A Westlaw search up to the date of *Amnesty International v Ahmed* (12 August 2009), indicated he presided in 31 discrimination cases.

163 [1982] ICR 618 (CA).

164 490 US 228 (1989).

165 ibid, 241 (Brennan J). This was a criticism of the conservative minority's dissent, which was using the *but for* test to *restrict* the application of the legislation so as not to apply to sex stereotyping.

Its practical weakness is that it could lead a tribunal into far too much speculation as to the proportion, or weight, of the various factors that led to the treatment, as well as what might have been, *but for* the protected ground. If it were applied in the *Owen and Briggs v James* case (which predated the *but for* test), the tribunal would have been drawn into the position of deciding – or speculating – whether Ms James still would have been rejected simply because of her employment record and/or her 'unsatisfactory demeanour'. Being inappropriate for mixed ground cases, the *but for* test is flawed as a universal test for direct discrimination.

Thus, the test has two problems, one superficial, and one fundamental. The superficial problem is that, constantly it seems, it has been improperly expressed. The second, fundamental problem is that it is unsuitable for mixed ground cases. That it has caused so much judicial debate is largely down to the first problem, which was entirely judge-made. Nonetheless, if a statutory definition should have a consistent interpretation, the second problem indicates that the *but for* test is not the vehicle to deliver this.

Underhill's J cheer for the *but for* test could not disguise its general fall from grace in favour of the 'mental processes' formula, a fall barely acknowledged, let alone explained, in the *JFS* speeches, or indeed in any cases. Yet good reasons existed to abandon the test, and had been expressed in the United States Supreme Court as early as 1989. That these were not apparent to the (UK) Supreme Court in *JFS* is not only ironic, given the almost invisible rejection of a test so prominent in the House of Lords some years before, but also it displays once again an apparent lack of mastery of the subject.

We shall see in the next chapter how the benign motive 'defence' also occupied the judiciary in cases of victimisation.

Further reading

G Mead, 'The role of intention in direct discrimination' (1990) 19(4) ILJ 250
B Watt, 'Goodbye "but-for", hello "but-why?"?' (1998) 27 ILJ 121.
JM Finnis, 'Directly discriminatory decisions: a missed opportunity' (2010) 126 LQR 491.
James v Eastleigh BC [1990] 2 AC 751 (HL).
Nagarajan v London Regional Transport [2000] 1 AC 501 (HL).
Patmalniece v Secretary of State for Work and Pensions [2011] UKSC 11.

6 The benign motive 'defence' and victimisation

Introduction

The importunate dissenters[1] did not confine their desire for a benign motive 'defence' to direct discrimination. They were equally exercised about its need in cases of victimisation, even though, once again, the legislative text afforded no scope for this. There is one difference though: in these cases, the defence seems to have prevailed, albeit in a coded form. The focus in this chapter falls on the emergence of the defence in two House of Lords cases decided under the Sex Discrimination Act 1975 (SDA 1975) and the similarly worded Race Relations Act 1976 (RRA 1976).

Victimisation provides a separate course of action for persons treated unfavourably because they had complained of discrimination, or supported a complaint, or did something else by reference to the legislation. The appeal in *St Helens MBC v Derbyshire*[2] turned on whether placing public pressure on equal pay claimants to compromise their claim amounted to victimisation. The House of Lords took this opportunity to attempt a clarification of the meaning of an apparent benign motive defence afforded to employers by the House previously in *Chief Constable of West Yorkshire Police v Khan*,[3] where it was expressed as 'honest and reasonable' conduct.

1 The legislation

At the time,[4] victimisation was defined in the SDA 1975, section 4:

> (1) A person ('the discriminator') discriminates against another person ('the person victimised') in any circumstances relevant for the purposes of any provision of this Act if he treats the person victimised less favourably than in those circumstances he treats or would treat other persons, and does so by reason that the person victimised has—
> (a) brought proceedings against the discriminator or any other person under this Act or the Equal Pay Act 1970 . . . or

1 See p 99.
2 [2007] ICR 841 (HL).
3 [2001] UKHL 48.
4 This has been reformulated by EA 2010, s 27. See below, p 131.

(b) given evidence or information in connection with proceedings brought by any person . . . under this Act or the Equal Pay Act 1970 . . . or
(c) otherwise done anything under or by reference to this Act or the Equal Pay Act 1970 . . ., or
(d) alleged that the discriminator or any other person has committed an act which (whether or not the allegation so states) would amount to a contravention of this Act or . . . the Equal Pay Act 1970 . . .

Paragraphs (a) to (d) are known generally as 'protected acts'. Along with discrimination and harassment, victimisation was outlawed only for certain activities, in this case employment. Section 6 of the SDA 1975 outlawed discrimination by employers in recruitment, access to opportunities for promotion, transfer or training, or any other benefits, facilities, or services; dismissal; or by subjecting her to any other detriment. So the elements appear to be: (1) the victim does a protected act; (2) the employer treats the victim less favourably in recruitment, or access to benefits etc., or by dismissal, or any other detriment; and (3) it did so 'by reason that' the victim did the protected act. The RRA 1976 provided substantially the same definitions for both victimisation and employment.[5]

The phrase 'by reason that' was parallel to 'on the ground of' used for direct discrimination, and it has been accepted that it should share the same meaning,[6] an approach endorsed by the Equality Act 2010, which replaced both terms with the common phrase, *because of*.[7] This element was the initial vehicle for the benign motive 'defence', although, as we shall see, it was subsequently switched to the 'catch-all' employment requirement that the employer subjected the claimant to 'any other detriment'.

2 The cases

In *St Helens MBC v Derbyshire*,[8] 510 catering staff brought an equal pay claim. Most compromised, but 39 persisted. The employer then wrote directly to all 510 members of staff (bypassing their trade union and the claimants' solicitor) stating that should the claim succeed, the resulting cost was likely to cause redundancies. The employment tribunal found that the letter was 'effectively a threat', 'intimidating', and 'directed against people who were in no position to debate the accuracy of the . . . pessimistic prognostications'. Reasonable reactions could include 'surrender induced by fear, fear of public odium or the reproaches of colleagues'.[9]

5 RRA 1976, ss 2 & 4 respectively.
6 *Nagarajan v London Regional Transport* [2000] 1 AC 501 (HL) 521 (Lord Steyn).
7 See EA 2010, ss 13 & 27. The change was not intended to the change the meaning of either element: Explanatory Note 61.
8 [2007] ICR 841 (HL).
9 Para 4(d) of the ET Reasons, cited, [2007] ICR 841 (HL) [38].

Consequently, the 39 claimants brought a separate claim of victimisation. They succeeded in the employment tribunal and the EAT. The Court of Appeal reversed, only for the House of Lords to restore the employment tribunal's decision. (In the event, the 39 persisted and won six times the compromise offer. The price of a school meal increased by a third, and job losses were approximately 10 per cent, with no redundancies.[10])

At first sight, this attempt to bully litigants into abandoning their equal pay claim appears to be a rather obvious example of victimisation. That the case progressed to House of Lords can be explained by its complex legal backdrop, comprising a number of cases, from the Court of Appeal, the House of Lords, and the CJEU, one of which requires particular attention.

In the House of Lords case, *Chief Constable of West Yorkshire Police v Khan*,[11] Sergeant Khan brought proceedings for racial discrimination against his employer. Whilst his claim was pending, he applied for a job with the Norfolk Police. His employer, the Chief Constable, acting on legal advice, refused to provide a job reference to 'protect his position in the discrimination claim'. It seems that the Chief Constable was minded to provide a negative reference and his lawyers feared that this could be used against him in the discrimination trial. As a consequence, Khan brought a separate claim of victimisation. The House of Lords unanimously rejected this claim, holding that the Chief Constable had not acted 'by reason that' Khan had brought proceedings, because he had acted 'honestly and reasonably' in accordance with 'perfectly understandable advice'.[12] In coming to this conclusion, the House relied on the distinction, made by the Court of Appeal in *Cornelius v University College Swansea*,[13] between a reaction to the *bringing* of proceedings (unlawful) and their *existence* (lawful).

It was no surprise that the employer in *Derbyshire* relied on this analysis. However, the employment tribunal distinguished *Khan*, noting that the employer wanted the applicants to abandon their claims. It was reacting, 'if not to the commencement of proceedings, certainly to their continuance'.[14] A majority of the Court of Appeal reversed.[15] Lloyd and Parker LJJ, applied *Khan*, and after noting the distinction between the *bringing* and the *existence* of the proceedings, held that the 'honest and reasonable' test applied equally to attempts to compromise proceedings. Thus, the tribunal's distinguishing of *Khan* was an error of law.[16]

A unanimous House of Lords restored the decision of the employment tribunal, holding that the tribunal was entitled to come to its decision. Lord Bingham held that the tribunal was entitled to distinguish *Khan*: 'The contrast with the

10 See [2004] IRLR 851 (EAT) [16].
11 [2001] UKHL 48.
12 ibid [31], [44], [59], & [80].
13 [1987] IRLR 141 (CA), 145–146. See further pp 127–128.
14 Para 4(e) cited [2007] ICR 841 (HL) [55].
15 [2006] ICR 90. Mummery LJ dissented: while endorsing *Khan*, he agreed with the ET's finding that the council had not acted reasonably. See especially [30]–[39].
16 ibid [49], [55], & [75].

present case is striking and obvious, for the object of sending the letters was to put pressure on the appellants to drop their claims.'[17] Lord Hope interpreted the tribunal's reasoning as a finding that the employer's conduct 'while no doubt honest, could not be said to have been reasonable'; in other words, the tribunal had properly distinguished *Khan* on its finding of fact.[18] Baroness Hale held that the correct test was whether the employer's conduct caused the claimant a 'detriment'. As the tribunal had addressed that question,[19] its decision could not be disturbed.[20] Lord Neuberger came to much the same conclusion,[21] but added, in line with Lord Hope's reasoning, that the tribunal had found the employer's conduct did not satisfy the 'honest and reasonable' test.[22] Lord Carswell agreed with Lord Neuberger.

It is apparent from this that although the House was unanimous in the decision, the reasoning varied. Four Law Lords gave speeches, with Lord Bingham agreeing with them all,[23] Baroness Hale[24] and Lord Carswell[25] agreeing with Lord Neuberger, Lord Hope agreeing with Lord Neuberger on the Court of Appeal's decision,[26] but not on the meaning of *Khan* (or *Cornelius*). However, Lord Neuberger agreed with Lord Hope's entire opinion.[27] From this, it can be deduced that Lord Neuberger's was the leading judgment.

The 'honest and reasonable defence'

In *Khan* Lord Nicholls had said:

> Employers, acting honestly and reasonably, ought to be able to take steps to preserve their position in pending discrimination proceedings without laying themselves open to a charge of victimisation. . . . An employer who conducts himself in this way is not doing so because of the fact that the complainant has brought discrimination proceedings. He is doing so because, currently and temporarily, he needs to take steps to preserve his position in the outstanding proceedings.[28]

Lord Neuberger stated that whilst this conclusion was correct, its judicial analysis and subsequent interpretation were 'not entirely satisfactory'.[29] He gave four

17 [2007] ICR 841, [9].
18 ibid [17] & [28].
19 Para 4(d) of the ET Reasons, cited ibid [38].
20 ibid [36] & [39].
21 ibid [68] & [75].
22 ibid [74].
23 ibid [9].
24 ibid [42].
25 ibid [43].
26 ibid [16].
27 ibid [71].
28 [2001] UKHL 48, [31].
29 [2007] ICR 841, [65].

reasons. First, no such defence is provided by the legislation. Second, it placed a 'somewhat uncomfortable and unclear meaning on the words "by reason that"'.[30] Third, it suggested that the matter should be judged from the point of view of the employer, when it should be 'primarily from the perspective of the alleged victim'.[31]

From this, Lord Neuberger reasoned, when considering the employer's defence or reaction to proceedings, 'a more satisfactory conclusion' was to focus on the element 'any other detriment' rather than 'by reason that'.[32] Citing *Ministry of Defence v Jeremiah*, he said this test was objective: 'a detriment exists if a reasonable worker would or might take the view that the [treatment] was in all the circumstances to his detriment'.[33] Lord Neuberger speculated:

> If . . . the employer's solicitor were to write to the employee's solicitor setting out, in appropriately measured and accurate terms, the financial or employment consequences of the claim succeeding, or the risks to the employee if the claim fails, or terms of settlement which are unattractive to the employee, I do not see how any distress thereby induced in the employee could be said to constitute 'detriment' . . . The bringing of an equal pay claim, however strong the claim may be, carries with it, like any other litigation inevitable distress and worry. Distress and worry which may be induced by the employer's honest and reasonable conduct in the course of his defence or in the conduct of any settlement negotiations, cannot (save, possibly, in the most unusual circumstances) constitute 'detriment' for the purposes of sections 4 and 6 of the 1975 Act.[34]

Thus, the employer's attempts to settle became unlawful by 'going public'. Otherwise, it seems normal private responses in discrimination litigation will not amount to victimisation.

Lord Neuberger's fourth reason for this change of approach was EU law, which applied in this case, but not in *Khan*, and which predated the Race Directive.[35] In the victimisation case, *Coote v Granada*, the CJEU focused on the deterrent effect of the employer's act on workers.[36] In other words, the consideration was from the perspective of the worker, rather the employer.

Lord Hope took a similar line,[37] but Baroness Hale alone was more trenchant, succinctly stating: 'It would be better if the [honest and reasonable] "defence" were laid to rest and the language of the legislation, construed in the light of the

30 ibid [65].
31 ibid [66].
32 ibid [68].
33 [1980] QB 87 (CA) 104 (Brightman LJ).
34 [2007] ICR 841, [68].
35 Directive 2000/43/EC of 29 June 2000 implementing the principle of equal treatment between persons irrespective of racial or ethnic origin. See [2007] ICR 841 [70].
36 Case C-185/97, [1999] ICR 100 [24]. See further p 128 et al.
37 [2007] ICR 841, [24]–[27].

requirements of the Directives, applied.' Baroness Hale reduced her analysis to the statutory elements.[38]

By contrast, Lord Neuberger attempted the seemingly impossible task of finding a just result without upsetting *Khan*. The trick was switching the 'honest and reasonable defence' to the element of 'any other detriment'. His logic was that honest and reasonable conduct by the employer equates to causing the worker no detriment: 'In my judgment, a more satisfactory conclusion, which in practice would almost always involve identical considerations, and produce a result identical, to that in *Khan*, involves focusing on the word 'detriment' rather than on the words "by reason that".'[39] The obvious difficulty with this is that overlooks the holding in *Khan* that the claimant *had* suffered a detriment. The only fact which Lord Neuberger might have raised in support (he did not) was that Sergeant Khan's reference would have been negative. So it was arguable he suffered no detriment. But as Lord Hoffman observed in *Khan*, the employment tribunal has jurisdiction to award compensation for injury to feelings, and so 'the courts have given the term "detriment" a wide meaning'.[40] Hence, in *Khan*, Lord Hoffman adopted the interpretation of 'detriment' from *Jeremiah* (mentioned earlier) and held:

> Mr Khan plainly did take the view, . . . that not having his assessment forwarded was to his detriment and I do not think that, in his state of knowledge at the time, he can be said to have been unreasonable.[41]

Similarly, in *Khan*, Lord Nicholls had reasoned: 'I accept Sergeant Khan's claim that the refusal to provide a reference for him constituted a detriment . . . even though . . . this did not cause him any financial loss. Provision of a reference is a normal feature of employment.'[42] Not only is Lord Neuberger's opinion in *Derbyshire* effectively overruling *Khan* on this point, it is ignoring the two reasons underpinning the decision on the element of 'detriment': that the legislation envisages liability purely for injury to feelings, and the (apparently approved) dictum from *Jeremiah*.

It also overlooks that the Chief Constable did more than merely refuse to provide a reference. He wrote to the Norfolk Police explaining the reason, that Khan had brought industrial tribunal proceedings. That alone would be enough to dissuade many employers from selecting a candidate, and even if that did not happen in Khan's case, a reasonable worker would be entitled to fear so. This alone would cause a detriment.[43] Further, in many cases, withholding a negative

38 ibid [36].
39 ibid [68].
40 [2001] UKHL 48, [53].
41 ibid.
42 ibid [14]. See also ibid [37], [38] (Lord Mackay).
43 See the US case *Rutherford v American Bank of Commerce* 565 F 2d 1162, 1164 (10th Cir 1977) (informing prospective employer of current discrimination action amounted to victimisation).

reference will cause the claimants a detriment simply because they will present an incomplete application, excluding them from any selection process.

Finally, even if Lord Neuberger's opinion could be reconciled with *Khan*, his opinion remains exposed. Where, more commonly, a reference would be positive (or neutral), its withholding is even more likely to cause a detriment and, notably, a tangible loss. Of course, the employer may be withholding the reference for the same ('honest and reasonable') motive as Khan's employer: a positive reference could be used against the employer in the principal proceedings.[44] Thus, the technical flaw in Lord Neuberger's reasoning is the holding that honest and reasonable conduct can be equated to causing no detriment.

Moreover, there was any number of reasons why an 'honest and reasonable defence' should have been purged from *any* element of victimisation. First and most obvious, the reasons given by Lord Neuberger for ruling out an 'honest and reasonable defence' for the element of 'by reason that' apply as cogently to the element of detriment (it does not appear in the legislation, and the matter should be viewed from the worker's perspective). This chimes with a literal reading of the statutory phrase 'subjecting him to any other detriment', which suggests merely that the employer causes the worker to suffer a detriment. Thus, there are two considerations of relevance: first, the suffering of the claimant; and second, whether this was caused by the employer. As relatively innocuous conduct, such as standard reactions in defence to litigation, can cause considerable detriment (e.g. a frozen career or prolonged unemployment), the reasonableness and honesty of the defendant's conduct are relatively minor, if not irrelevant, considerations.

Second, many employer responses could be characterised, not as 'any other detriment', but as discrimination in relation to 'access to benefits, facilities or services' under, say, what was SDA 1975, section 6(2)(a).[45] This would include the suspension of a grievance procedure, transfer rights, or indeed the withholding of a reference.[46] In these scenarios, the honest and reasonable defence, logically tied (as Lord Neuberger would have it) to the element of detriment, becomes redundant. The error of interpretation and application here is the assumption that the phrase 'any other detriment' applies exclusively to a number of scenarios more specifically covered by other parts of the provision.

Third, as noted in Chapter 5, in spite of the importunate dissenters, such a benign motive 'defence' has been ruled out of the similarly formulated definition of direct discrimination. The flawed equation between honest and reasonable conduct on the employer's side, and 'detriment' on the claimant's, in substance disregards the claimant's perspective in favour to that of the employer: if the employer acts honestly and reasonably, then, according to the equation, the claimant could not have suffered a detriment. Yet, as noted above, in such cases a worker can suffer a frozen career, or even lengthy unemployment, for several

44 See the US case, *Sparrow v Piedmont* 593 F Supp 1107, 1112 (MDNC 1984).
45 See above, p 121. See now, EA 2010, s 39(2)(b).
46 As Lord MacKay alone found in *Khan* [2001] UKHL 48, [38].

years if the matter goes to appeal, no matter how honestly and reasonably the employer behaved. Given that the House of Lords had ruled that the elements of direct discrimination and victimisation should be given parallel meanings, and that 'victimisation was as serious a mischief as direct discrimination',[47] this was a major, and unacknowledged, departure from precedent. As such, all bar Baroness Hale effectively aligned themselves with the importunate dissenters, and for victimisation, elevated the benign motive defence to precedential respectability.

Fourth, another, albeit lesser, danger associated such a defence is the risk of yet another technical error. A tribunal may inadvertently broaden the defence by inverting the question and demanding that for liability the employer must have acted dishonestly *and* unreasonably.[48] Here, the employer need only show that its response was, say, not dishonest even though it was unreasonable (and less likely, vice versa). For instance, an employer may threaten to expose a claimant's extra-marital affair should he or she persist with their claim; or report the worker's suspected fraudulent conduct to the police only after the worker instigated discrimination proceedings.[49] Such responses may be characterised as unreasonable, but not necessarily dishonest.

The distinction between the bringing and the existence of proceedings

The decision in *Khan* relied on this distinction, first aired in *Cornelius v University College Swansea*.[50] The speeches in *Derbyshire* did not question this distinction, with Lord Bingham (a party to the *Cornelius* decision) and Lord Hope citing it with approval.[51] In *Cornelius*, the claimant brought sex-discrimination proceedings against her employer. Pending the outcome the employer refused her transfer request and access to the grievance procedure. Consequently, she brought a separate claim for victimisation. The Court of Appeal rejected her claim, inter alia, because:

> The existence of the proceedings plainly did influence [the employer's] decisions. No doubt, like most experienced administrators, they recognised the risk of acting in a way which might embarrass the handling or be inconsistent with the outcome of current proceedings. They accordingly wished to defer action until the proceedings were over. But that had . . . nothing to do with the appellant's conduct in bringing proceedings under the Act.[52]

This is linguistic nonsense, of course. The futility of this distinction is realised by adding a second protected act to the claim: that the claimant had 'otherwise done

47 *Nagarajan v London Regional Transport* [2000] 1 AC 501 (HL), respectively, 521 (Lord Steyn), 512 (Lord Nicholls).
48 See *Chief Constable of Norfolk v Arthurton* (EAT 6 December 2006) [25].
49 See the US case *Berry v Stevenson Chevrolet* 74 F 3d 980, 989 (10th Cir 1986).
50 [1987] IRLR 141 (CA).
51 [2007] ICR 841, [9] (Lord Bingham), [21] & [23] (Lord Hope).
52 [1987] IRLR 141, 145–146 (Bingham LJ, with whom Sir John Donaldson MR and Fox LJ agreed).

anything under or by reference to this Act'.[53] As well as having *brought* proceedings, she was 'otherwise' continuing their existence. This repeats the error of assuming that one statutory phrase applies exclusively to a number of scenarios more specifically covered by other parts of the provision. The fragility of the distinction was exposed when the employment tribunal in *Derbyshire* made a *third* distinction: that the employer reacted not to the commencement or existence of proceedings, but to their 'continuance'.[54]

Further, this fragile, futile, and nonsensical distinction between the *bringing* and *existing* of proceedings (leading to a third category of 'continuance') frustrates Lord Diplock's plea that the rule of law demands that legislation is 'reasonably understood . . . by those whose conduct it regulates'.[55] Moreover, in this context, it shows a drift away from the 'straightforward' approach adopted by the House of Lords in *Nagarajan v London Regional Transport*, where 'in the application of this legislation', Lord Nicholls urged, 'legalistic phrases, as well as subtle distinctions, are better avoided so far as possible'.[56]

The result of the distinction will always favour the defendant, and shows that, once again, it was devised with the employer's perspective in mind. For the House in *Derbyshire* to endorse it rather undermines a foundation of its decision, that, in light of *Coote v Granada*,[57] the question should be viewed from the claimant's perspective.

Deterring other workers – the 'chilling' effect

A broader issue was left untouched in the *Derbyshire* speeches. The statutory purpose ought to include the deterrent, or 'chilling', effect of the employer's reaction on other workers.[58] Take *Khan* again. Even if it could be said (as the House in *Derbyshire* asserted) that Sergeant Khan himself suffered no detriment, the act of withholding the reference still sent a signal to other workers (most of whom presumably would receive positive or neutral references) making them think twice before complaining of discrimination. As noted above, the House of Lords in *Derbyshire* took recourse to EU law – in particular *Coote v Granada* – to switch the focus to the perspective of the worker. But, given the facts, the judgment in *Granada* went further than that.

Mrs Coote sued her employer following her pregnancy-related dismissal. After those proceedings were complete, the employer refused to give her a reference

53 SDA 1975, section 4(1)*(c)*. See pp 120–121. See now EA 2010, s 27(2)(c).

54 Para 4(e) cited [2007] ICR 841 (HL) [19].

55 *Black-Clawson International Ltd v Papierwerke Waldhof-Aschaffenberg AG* [1975] AC 591 (HL) 638. See further Chapter 2, p 28, text to n 85.

56 [2001] AC 501, 513. In *Pothecary Witham Weld v Bullimore* [2010] ICR 1008 (EAT) [19](2) Underhill J advocated that 'the subtle distinctions advanced in *Khan* as to the different capacities of employer and party to litigation should be eschewed'.

57 Case C-185/97 *Coote v Granada Hospitality* [1999] ICR 100. See below, and p 146.

58 A 'general deterrent' policy has been adopted expressly by some Circuits in the United States: e.g. *Hashimoto v Dalton* 118 F 3d 671 (9th Cir 1997).

and Mrs Coote sued again, this time for victimisation. The question referred to the CJEU was whether the victimisation provisions should protect *former* employees. Predictably, the CJEU ruled that they should, observing:

> Fear of such [reprisals], where no legal remedy is available against them, might deter workers who considered themselves the victims of discrimination from pursuing their claims by judicial process, and would consequently be liable seriously to jeopardise implementation of the aim pursued by the Directive.[59]

Although the refusal of a reference may have caused Mrs Coote a detriment, it could not be said to have deterred *her* because, at the time of the refusal, her pregnancy discrimination claim was complete. So the CJEU's judgment must have been directed at the broader chilling effect of the employer's conduct.

Assuming that *Derbyshire*, being in the House of Lords, was a case of public importance, and that the House chose to broaden the matter beyond the case in hand, by revisiting *Khan* and *Cornelius*, and invoking *Granada*, a failure to identify this aspect was remiss.

Conclusion

Derbyshire was an easy case to decide. The sending of the letters treated the claimants less favourably than other workers, and the effect of this was undoubtedly to their detriment; indeed, it is arguable that the conduct was so serious that it ought have attracted criminal proceedings (for contempt of court).[60] But in attempting to reconcile the decision with an 'honest and reasonable defence' and upholding the futile and fragile distinction between the bringing and existence of proceedings, the House of Lords perpetuated bad law. This obvious and flagrant case of victimisation took several years and a House of Lords decision to decide because of this law, originating in *Cornelius* and *Khan*, which encouraged the employer to think it could bully the claimants with impunity. Indeed, it convinced the Court of Appeal to hold that the employer's conduct *did not* amount to victimisation.[61] Yet, in the face of this, the majority perpetuated the benign motive 'defence'. Moreover, in switching it to another element whilst at the same time holding that it cannot be found in the legislation,[62] it did so in the most clumsy, perverse, and technically flawed manner.

59 Case C-185/97, [1999] ICR 100 [24].

60 See Chapter 7, pp 149–151.

61 *Derbyshire v St Helens MBC* [2006] ICR 90 (CA). For other examples of the 'honest and reasonable defence', see *Croad v UCU* (EAT, 13 June 2012) (conflict of interest caused Union to stop supporting member who sued it); *Abiola v North Yorkshire CC* (EAT, 7 January 2010) (refusal to respond to separate complaints pending trial by African teacher alleging discrimination regarding registration); and further n 64, and accompanying text.

62 [2007] ICR 841 (HL) [65] (Lord Neuberger).

The speeches also fell short of offering clarity on the meaning of victimisation, notably on the chilling effect. The only useful guidance must be *inferred* from the decision. This suggests that normal private negotiations to compromise should be lawful. Any broader guidance, that honest and reasonable conduct by the employer will not cause 'any other detriment', was of limited use, because (1) claimants often could bring claims under the more specific features of employment (e.g. 'access to opportunities for promotion, transfer or training, or to any other benefits, facilities or services'); and (2) 'honest and reasonable' conduct will not necessarily equate with causing no detriment. It was apparent that the courts had a certain sympathy for the employers in these cases, which is evocative of the benign motive 'defence' peddled by the importunate dissenters in the direct discrimination cases. This time, though, the defence was championed by the *majority*.

Underhill J once suggested some efficacy for this defence when observing that it is confined to victimisation cases 'of a very particular type' because the employer was defending litigation; thus, it should not be applied in other scenarios.[63] But there was nothing expressed in the *Derbyshire* or *Khan* speeches to indicate such a limit. Indeed, as if to illustrate the unsatisfactory state of this law, examples of *both* approaches can be found in the law reports.[64] Furthermore, given that 'particular types of case' were not identified in the legislation, this is hardly a sound interpretation of the provisions. In these cases, it would have been much clearer to admit that legislation could not be read to accommodate this sympathy.[65] There was nothing in the EU jurisprudence to suggest such a sympathetic approach (in fact *Granada* suggested the contrary), and so a 'purposive' redrafting along the lines of the *Ghaidan* approach,[66] or *Marleasing*,[67] to *narrow* the scope of the protection would have been wholly inappropriate. And even if the failure of the legislation to accommodate these 'litigation cases' were the result of an obvious drafting error, it was not 'abundantly clear' what Parliament's policy would have been, let alone any specific drafting to implement this, as required to 'fill the gaps'

63 *Pothecary Witham Weld v Bullimore* [2010] ICR 1008 (EAT) [18], defaulting to the guidance from *Nagarajan v London Regional Transport* [2000] 1 AC 501 (HL). Underhill J went to opine ([19](3)–(4)) that and that there was no '"honest and reasonable defence" as such', but then with elastic logic suggested that 'such a litigant could not properly regard as a detriment conduct by the employer which constituted no more than reasonable conduct in defence of his position in the litigation'.

64 *BMA v Chaudhary (No. 2)* [2007] IRLR 800 (CA), [175]–[177] (applying the 'defence' to conduct made in *anticipation* of litigation); *Bayode v Chief Constable of Derbyshire* (EAT, 22 May 2008) (colleagues making notes of, and reporting, incidents in anticipation of a race discrimination claim). Cf *Deer v University of Oxford* [2015] EWCA Civ 52 (distinguishing between conduct in response to litigation and that in response to a 'mere complaint' – see further Chapter 7, p 143); and *Commissioners for the Inland Revenue v Morgan* [2002] IRLR 776 (EAT) (memo mentioning imminent proceedings to the detriment of the claimant was not in defence of the litigation and so *Khan* distinguished).

65 For some drafting possibilities, see M Connolly, 'Rethinking victimisation' (2009) 38(2) ILJ 149.

66 See *Vodafone 2 v Revenue and Customs Commissioners* [2010] Ch 77 (CA) [38]. See p 44.

67 I.e. invoking the doctrine of indirect effect: Case C-106/89 *Marleasing SA v La Comercial Internacional de Alimentación* [1990] ECR I-4135. See Chapter 2, p 36, text to n 139.

under *Inco Europe*.[68] As such, the courts in *Cornelius* and *Derbyshire* ought to have referred the matter to the Court of Justice,[69] or at the very least, signalled to Parliament their concerns over the drafting.

Aside from the messy and unconvincing attempts to reconcile the technical aspects of the law, what stands out in these cases is that those who complain of discrimination should not expect special, or enhanced, protection from retaliation. This is in the face of victimisation provisions that, by their existence, suggest quite the opposite: discrimination complainants are not 'ordinary' complainants. The failure to provide the enhanced protection mandated by Parliament has some unfortunate echoes of the historical common law indifference to matters of equality.

The effect of the Equality Act 2010

As it happens, Parliament has provided a new vehicle upon which the 'honest and reasonable' debate can be had. The victimisation provisions of the RRA 1976 and SDA 1975 were superseded by the Equality Act 2010, section 27:

> (1) A person (A) victimises another person (B) if A subjects B to a detriment because—
> (a) B does a protected act, or
> (b) A believes that B has done, or may do, a protected act.

The main purpose of this revision was to remove the comparative element (*less favourable treatment*), which had caused problems.[70] It also brings the formula into line with that used in the growing number of victimisation provisions in Part V of the Employment Rights Act 1996, which cover areas such as whistle blowing, jury service, health and safety, Sunday working, family leave, and working-time rights.

The abolition of the comparative element simplifies matters and as such is an improvement for both claimants and defendants. But the choice of wording suggests, perhaps inadvertently, codification of the 'honest and reasonable' doctrine as reformulated in *Derbyshire*. It is no longer necessary to prove that the defendant treated the victim 'less favourably', only that the defendant *subjects him to a detriment*. In itself, this may appear to add up to much the same thing. But it enables the courts to redeploy the *Derbyshire* formulation, which was located in the employment provisions, to the actual definition of victimisation. This could resolve one weakness with the *Derbyshire* formulation, that it can be bypassed where the conduct affects a worker in the more specified ways, such as 'opportunities

68 [2000] 1 WLR 586 (HL). See Chapter 2, p 19.
69 *Khan* predated the Race Directive 2000/43/EC.
70 See *Kirby v Manpower Services Commission* [1980] ICR 420 (EAT) overruled; *Aziz v Trinity Street Taxis Ltd* [1989] QB 463 (CA).

for promotion . . . or access to any other benefits, facilities or services'.[71] In *all* cases (not just 'litigation cases'), courts could now consider that they have discretion to assess the reasonableness and honesty of the conduct irrespective of whether it related to 'opportunities' or 'benefits' etc. of employment.

But this seemingly attractive vehicle for the 'honest and reasonable defence' still runs into the problem of equating the employer's conduct with the worker's perspective of a detriment. Such a misconceived notion of detriment not only jars with a literal reading of the statute, but it is also at odds with the statutory purpose, given the legislative history of section 27. In its response to its Consultation, the Government stated:

> We recommended ending the need for a comparator through aligning with the approach in employment law because this offers a more effective, workable system – not one in which it would necessarily be easier to win a case, but one where attention rightly focused on considering whether the 'victim' suffered an absolute harm, irrespective of how others were being treated in the same circumstances.[72]

The final clause ('irrespective of how others were being treated in the same circumstances') suggests that a 'normal', 'reasonable', or 'standard' reaction to litigation (or any other protected act) does not necessarily exonerate the defendant. This is so even where the reaction is one taken against all complainants, whether or not they are complaining of discrimination. Thus 'general policy' reactions, such as the withholding of a reference, or the suspension of a transfer, promotion, or grievance procedure, should attract liability, irrespective of the honesty and reasonableness of such conduct. In effect, it reverses *Khan* and *Cornelius.* This view is sustained by the Explanatory Notes to the Equality Bill and to the resulting Act, which provided this example: 'A woman makes a complaint of sex discrimination against her employer. As a result, she is denied promotion. The denial of promotion would amount to victimisation.'[73] Assuming the 'complaint' amounts to proceedings, the facts of this example are on all fours with *Cornelius*, the only difference being the denial of a promotion rather than a transfer.

Given the courts' obvious sympathy for the employer's position, and their cavalier approach (in *Cornelius*, *Khan*, and *Derbyshire*) to the text of the legislation, it is just as likely that they will not see this as an impediment to their interpretation of the new formula. Moreover, if the UK's secession negotiations fully detach domestic discrimination law from the EU, the courts will have further grounds to marginalise the claimant's perspective and effects of the conduct, as these notions, expressed in *Derbyshire,* were rooted in *Granada.* In any case, the

71 See EA 2010, s 39(2). On the 'bypass' matter, see pp 127–128.

72 Government Equalities Office, The Equality Bill – Government response to the Consultation (Cm 7454, 2008) para 735. See also Department for Communities and Local Government, Discrimination Law Review. *A Framework for Fairness: Proposals for a Single Equality Bill for Great Britain.* A consultation paper (June 2007) para 161.

73 Explanatory Notes to the Equality Bill 2008, para 105. Explanatory Notes to the Equality Act 2010, para 106, and the Revised Explanatory Notes (October 2010) to the Equality Act 2010, para 103.

courts may still continue to use the 'causative' element, *because of*, for the distinction between the bringing and existence of the proceedings. As such, one must fear the new definition provides the courts with as much licence as before to focus on the employer's conduct, despite a Consultation Response and Explanatory Note to the contrary, both of which are standard guides to interpretation.[74]

As suggested in the conclusion on *Derbyshire*, there is another dimension to these cases: the 'parallel' offence of contempt of court. The influence, or otherwise, of the principles of contempt is explored in the next chapter.

Further reading

S Middlemiss, 'Is a claim for post-employment victimisation currently permissible under the Equality Act 2010?' (2014) 14(2) IJDL 117.

M Connolly, 'Rethinking victimisation' (2009) 38(2) ILJ 149.

M Connolly, 'The chilling effect and the most ancient form of vengeance' (2011) 11(3) IJDL 123.

M Connolly, 'Victimising third parties: the equality directives, the European Convention on Human Rights, and EU general principles' (2010) 35 EL Rev 822–836.

Pothecary Witham Weld v Bullimore [2010] ICR 1008 (EAT).

74 See *Deer v University of Oxford* [2015] EWCA Civ 52, [49]–[53] noting, under EA 2010, s 27, the employer's 'ordinary and reasonable' retention of data upon legal advice. See further Chapter 7, p 143. On using Explanatory Notes and extraneous materials see pp 27 and 28, respectively.

7 Victimisation and contempt of court

Introduction

It is apparent from the last chapter that fear of victimisation is a major deterrent to complaining of discrimination.[1] Hence, Lord Steyn has suggested that the victimisation of those who complain of discrimination under the equality legislation should be treated as seriously as discrimination itself.[2] If employees can be denied promotions, grievance processes, transfers, or references because of a complaint, their careers could be frozen for years, or even destroyed. This would undermine the legislation's principal rubrics against discrimination and harassment. Yet, also apparent in Chapter 6, from these earliest days, the courts have given the victimisation provisions a particularly narrow construction. Back in 1993, Miller and Ellis suggested that the resulting 'weak' victimisation provisions could be 'supplemented' with (criminal) contempt of court, by filling the gaps left by the narrow interpretations and, moreover, providing a stronger 'deterrent value'[3] of criminal proceedings.

The notion is not implausible. As Bingham LJ observed in *Cornelius v University College Swansea*, the victimisation provisions had an 'obvious although partial analogy to the law of contempt'.[4] On the assumption, as concluded in the previous chapter, that these were 'weak' (or troublesome) decisions, the notion may provide a solution and thus a reasonable benchmark by which to reference the technical merits of the judgments (and, of course, their prolixity). Indeed, as will be seen below, a textual analysis of the judgments from this perspective reveals that the courts have indeed imported principles of contempt, but not in the way anticipated.

1 This is borne out by research. See e.g. J Gregory, *Victimisation is Discrimination* (1990) 20 EOR 23; EHRC, 'Section 20 investigation into the Metropolitan Police Service', < https://www.equalityhumanrights.com/en/our-work/news/investigation-met-police-reveals-significant-weaknesses-handling-discrimination > accessed 30 March 2018.

2 *Nagarajan v London Regional Transport* [2001] AC 502 (HL), [79].

3 CJ Miller and E Ellis, 'The victimisation of anti-discrimination complainants – is it contempt of court?' [1993] PL 80, 87.

4 [1987] IRLR 141, 145. See also Slade LJ in *Aziz v Trinity Street Taxis Ltd* [1989] 1 QB 463, 484; and Buxton LJ, in *Rhys-Harper v Relaxion* [2001] ICR 1176 (CA) [38], reversed [2003] 2 CMLR 44 (HL).

This study begins by noting the relevant legislation and the Miller and Ellis' 'weak' cases. This is followed by an outline of the relevant principles of (criminal) contempt of court, and then a review of some prominent victimisation cases. This review shows first, how contempt was used to restrict victimisation, second, how it was ignored to fill obvious gaps in the victimisation provisions, and third, that some victimisation cases ought to have been referred for contempt. In each case, it is shown how, once again, relatively easy cases made bad law, this time, with an unexpressed 'on-off' relationship with the law of contempt of court.

The legislation and troublesome cases

Most cases under consideration here were heard before the Equality Act 2010 came into force, with its revised definition of victimisation. (It is addressed below where appropriate.) The first discrimination statutes to carry victimisation provisions were the Sex Discrimination Act 1975 (SDA 1975), followed shortly by the Race Relations Act 1976 (RRA 1976). The legislative formula common to both is set out at the beginning of Chapter 6. In essence, it provided that victimisation occurs when a person is treated less favourably 'by reason that' they did a protected act (such as complaining of discrimination).[5] It will be recalled that both statutes outlawed employment discrimination and victimisation in recruitment; access to opportunities for promotion, transfer, or training, or any other benefits, facilities, or services; dismissal; or by subjecting the person to any other detriment.[6] So, for these cases, the elements for liability appeared to be: (1) the victim did a protected act; (2) the employer treated the victim less favourably in recruitment, or the terms of employment, or access to opportunities etc.; (3) and it did so 'by reason that' the victim did the protected act.

Miller and Ellis identified three cases in particular for criticism. First, in *Cornelius v University College Swansea*,[7] the Court of Appeal held that the protected act of having 'brought proceedings' did not to apply to their existence.[8] In *Kirby v Manpower Services Commission*,[9] an employee at a job centre was moved to less desirable work because he disclosed confidential information regarding suspected discrimination by some employers. The Employment Appeal Tribunal (EAT) rejected his claim of victimisation because any person disclosing confidential information of *any nature* would have been moved to other work. Thus, the EAT held that that treatment was not less favourable. In *Aziz v Trinity Street Taxis Ltd*,[10] a taxi driver was expelled from his association for making secret recordings in support of his existing discrimination claim. In Mr Aziz's subsequent claim for

5 SDA 1975, s 4; RRA 1976, s 2.
6 SDA 1975, s 6; RRA 1976, s 4.
7 [1987] IRLR 141 (CA). See Chapter 6, pp 127–128.
8 An apparent incongruity explored in Chapter 6, 'The distinction between the bringing and the existence of proceedings', p 127.
9 [1980] ICR 420, (EAT).
10 [1989] QB 463 (CA).

victimisation, the Court of Appeal rejected the association's first argument that as it would expel anyone for such a breach of confidence, Aziz had not been treated less favourably; the comparison should *not* include any element of the protected act. As such, it overruled *Kirby*. But the Court then torpedoed any purposive credentials of its judgment by holding that the third limb – 'by reason that' – incorporated an element of conscious motive (and with it, the now familiar benign motive 'defence').[11] (In turn, after Miller and Ellis wrote, the House of Lords disapproved of this aspect of the judgment,[12] *but not* the decision, which was explained as 'causative': in other words, the association acted 'by reason that' Aziz was in breach of confidence, and not that he was pursuing a discrimination claim.)[13]

Criminal contempt of court

Criminal contempt is punishable by a fine and a maximum of two years' imprisonment.[14] It is traditionally a common law offence, although nowadays it is also an offence under a number of statutory provisions,[15] most notably the Contempt of Court Act 1981 (hereafter CCA 1981), which placed strict liability publication contempt on to a statutory footing.[16]

Contempt of court is universal in nature, and can be applied to new and novel situations without apparently widening its scope.[17] Hence, there are many varieties of contempt of court. The analogous one here is the *offence* of conduct interfering with the administration of justice, and in particular this means conduct deterring persons from participating in the legal process; this, loosely at least, is the goal of the victimisation provisions. Given the vast, perhaps infinite, variety of scenarios that could amount to interfering with the administration of justice, it is difficult to pin down the law to anything more than a few general principles.

For parties to the action, private pressure might be justified in a 'common interest that fair, reasonable and moderate personal representations would be appropriate'.[18] But if the conduct is public, the courts are more sensitive, and will not permit 'conduct which was calculated so to abuse or pillory a party to litigation or to subject him to such obloquy as to shame or dissuade him from

11 ibid, 485. This aspect of the judgment (but not the decision) was disapproved in *Nagarajan v London Regional Transport* [2000] 1 AC 501, 512 (Lord Nicholls), 522 (Lord Steyn).

12 *Nagarajan v London Regional Transport* [2000] 1 AC 501, 512 (Lord Nicholls), 522 (Lord Steyn). See M Connolly, 'Rethinking victimisation' (2009) 38(2) ILJ 149, especially 160.

13 ibid. Lord Nicholls referred to the 'conscious motivation' statement merely as a 'dictum', while Lord Steyn considered that *Aziz* was decided on the 'causative approach'.

14 See Contempt of Court Act 1981, s 14(1), limiting imprisonment to two years for both criminal and civil contempt: *DPP v B* [2012] 1 WLR 3170 (CA), [21].

15 See Law Commission, *Contempt of Court* (Consultation Paper No. 209, 2012) Appendix F, p 6, listing 27 statutory offences, and over 50 examples of statutory provisions stating that particular conduct should be treated as if it were a contempt of court.

16 In response to *Sunday Times v United Kingdom* (A/30) (1979–80) 2 EHRR 245. (The 'Thalidomide case'.)

17 *Attorney General v Newspaper Publishing Plc* [1988] Ch 333 (CA), 368 (Sir John Donaldson MR).

18 *Attorney General v Times Newspapers* [1974] AC 273 (HL) 318–319 (Thalidomide).

obtaining the adjudication of a court to which he was entitled'.[19] When deciding if the conduct in question amounted to contempt, 'a court should consider [the facts] in the light of all the surrounding circumstances . . . [including] the nature of any pending litigation and the stage it had reached'.[20]

The courts are concerned principally with the *effect* of the conduct, no matter the intent. It is unsurprising to find that that where intent is required, it need not be the sole reason for the offending conduct.[21] Hence, a newspaper publishing in defiance of a court order can be in contempt even though its principal intention was to enhance its circulation.[22] Similarly, otherwise lawful conduct can amount to contempt if it interferes with the administration of justice. In *Rowden v Universities Co-operative Association*,[23] a witness was suspended and instructed to dismiss his son from the same employer, for having given evidence against their employer. The employer was held in contempt, despite (at the time[24]) its otherwise lawful right to dismiss workers for any reason or no reason: there is no 'greater exercise of power for intimidating witnesses' than furnished in this case; it was a 'gross contempt of Court'.[25]

A deterrent principle also underpins the law of contempt. This is foremost in after-the-event cases, where the conduct, coming later, could not have affected the proceedings in question. *Rowden* is one such example. A more recent example is *Attorney General v Butterworth*.[26] Here, one Greenlees, a trade federation official, gave evidence to the Restrictive Practices Court (RPC) to the effect that a trade agreement made by the Federation was harmful to the public interest. The RPC declared the agreement void, and afterwards, members of the Federation called on Greenlees to answer for his conduct and made various attempts to oust him from his posts as branch treasurer and delegate. Some, but not all, of this conduct was intended to punish him for testifying. The Court of Appeal found the conduct amounted to contempt, even though it came *after* the conclusion of the RPC proceedings.

The underlying policy for this ruling was not only the deterrent effect on the victim,[27] but more importantly, the chilling effect on others. As Lord Denning MR once put it:

19 ibid, 302 (Lord Morris).

20 ibid.

21 *Attorney General v Newspaper Publishing* [1988] Ch 333 (CA) 375 (Sir John Donaldson MR), 383 (Lloyd LJ); *Attorney General v Times Newspapers* [1974] AC 273 (HL) 296, 299 (Lord Reid).

22 *Attorney General v Newspaper Publishing (Spycatcher)* [1989] 1 FSR 457 (Ch), 486.

23 (1881) 71 LT Jo 373 (Ch); 1 Law Cent 161 (Hein Online: *Law-Central*, vol 1, pp 129–184 (1881)).

24 Nowadays, an employer may dismiss a worker of less than 2 years' continuous service for no reason, but may encounter a number of prohibitions if it gives a reason, such as discrimination, jury service, trade union activities, and so on. See Employment Rights Act 1996, s 108(3).

25 ibid. See also *Re Martin (Peter)* The Times, 23 April 1986 (QB); *R v Kellet* [1976] QB 372 (CA).

26 [1963] 1 QB 696 (CA). Applied, *Attorney General v Jackson* [1994] COD 171 (DC), where threatening letters sent by prisoner to witnesses after conviction was held to be contempt.

27 For an instance of purely private after-the-event retribution amounting to contempt, see *Chapman v Honig* [1963] 2 QB 502 (CA).

> If this sort of thing could be done in a single case with impunity, the news of it would soon get round. Witnesses in other cases would be unwilling to come forward to give evidence, or, if they did come forward, they would hesitate to speak the truth, for fear of the consequences.[28]

In a similar vein, Donovan LJ asserted that the administration of justice was 'a continuing thing', meaning: 'It has a future as well as a present; and if somebody pollutes the stream today so that tomorrow's litigant will find it poisoned, does he appeal to the court in vain?'[29] In a brief concurring speech, Pearson LJ agreed that 'such victimisation, because it tends to deter persons from giving evidence as witnesses in future proceedings . . . is an interference with the due administration of justice as a continuing process'.[30]

Although perhaps essential to conduct where the proceedings are complete, the chilling principle can be detected in other forms of contempt. In *Attorney General v MGN Ltd*,[31] a murder suspect under arrest was vilified by some tabloids. Speaking for the three-judge Administrative Court, Lord Judge, LCJ, stated: 'At the simplest level publication of such material may deter or discourage witnesses from coming forward and providing information helpful to the suspect.'[32] And in *R v Socialist Worker Printers and Publishers Ltd, ex p Attorney General*,[33] a three-judge Divisional Court held that publishing the names of blackmail victims in defiance of the trial judge's direction was contempt inter alia because it would deter other victims from coming forward.

The next question – relating to procedural matters – is whether lower courts and tribunals, where most discrimination cases are tried, are recognised as courts for the purposes of contempt and, in particular, contempts occurring out of court. As superior courts, the High Court, Court of Appeal, and the Supreme Court have 'inherent powers'[34] to punish for contempt committed against their own courts, or the lower courts.[35] The procedure betrays just what a unique creature of law that contempt happens to be. Cases usually come before these courts by committal, and not indictment.[36] The cases are tried summarily without a jury, despite the risk of imprisonment and an unlimited fine.

28 ibid, 719. See Borrie and Lowe (4th edn, 2010): para 10.10: 'Therefore, the basis of contempt in this context is that such conduct is likely to deter potential witnesses from giving evidence in future cases.'
29 [1963] 2 QB 502 (CA) 725.
30 ibid, 728.
31 [2012] 1 WLR 2408 (Admin), at [31] (Lord Judge LCJ, Thomas LJ, Owen J).
32 ibid [31].
33 [1975] QB 637 (QB) (Lord Widgery CJ, Milmo and Ackner JJ).
34 *R v Lefroy* (1864) 5 B & S 299; 122 ER 842. See also Borrie and Lowe (4th edn, 2010), para 13.3); Joint Committee on Statutory Instruments, *Eleventh Report of Session 2012–13* (2012–2013, HL Paper 68, HC 135-xi) paras 1.4, < www.publications.parliament.uk/pa/jt201213/jtselect/jtstatin/68/68.pdf > accessed 30 March 2018.
35 *R v Parke* [1903] 2 KB 432 (DC). See the discussion in *Law Society v Otobo* [2011] EWHC 2264 (Ch) [17], citing H Jacob: 'The inherent jurisdiction of the court' [1970] CLP 23, especially 28–29, 48.
36 See *Re Lonrho* [1990] 2 AC 154 (HL), 177, (Lord Keith), noting that the last reported prosecution by indictment of a newspaper for contempt was *R v Tibbits and Windust* [1902] 1 KB 77, a practice 'that ought not to be revived'.

To a degree, the procedure, nowadays laid down by statutory instrument,[37] governs these powers. In particular, the rules recognise the High Court's jurisdiction over contempts made in relation to proceedings in an 'inferior court'.[38] An 'inferior court' has been defined in the House of Lords as a body that 'discharges judicial rather than administrative functions and forms part of the judicial system of the country rather than the administration of the government'.[39]

It would seem unarguable that litigation under the discrimination legislation, wherever it occurs, is more judicial than administrative in nature. Some related examples bear this out. Industrial (now Employment) Tribunals[40] and Mental Health Tribunals[41] have been recognised as 'courts' for the purpose of contempt. For the purpose of vexatious litigant restraints,[42] the Leasehold Valuation Court[43] and Investigatory Powers Tribunal[44] have been recognised as 'inferior courts'. On this logic, it seems certain that the Special Educational Needs and Disability Tribunal (SENDIST) would be included. It was stated *obiter* that SENDIST and even a Local Authority Appeal Panel (dealing with exclusions from schools) exercise 'judicial responsibilities'.[45]

Finally, contempt proceedings normally are brought by the Attorney General, although there are examples of individuals with sufficient interest instigating contempt proceedings with punishment as the goal.[46] To date, no contempt proceedings have been brought in relation to a discrimination complaint,[47] although, as the cases reviewed below suggest, this could be because of a (misplaced) belief that all forms of victimisation are provided for comprehensively by the equality legislation.

This review shows first, how contempt was used to restrict victimisation, second, how it was ignored to fill obvious gaps in the victimisation provisions, and third, that some victimisation cases ought to have been referred for contempt.

37 Civil Procedure Rules 1998 SI 1998/3132, Part 81, s 3.

38 Save for Contempt in the Face. ibid, Rules 81.12–81.14. CCA 1981, s 19, states that '"*court*" includes any tribunal or body exercising the judicial power of the State, and "*legal proceedings*" shall be construed accordingly'.

39 *Attorney General v BBC* [1981] AC 301 (HL), 339H (Viscount Dilhorne); see also 360A (Lord Scarman) holding that it should be a body 'exercising judicial functions [which] can be demonstrated to be part of this judicial system'.

40 *Peach Grey v Sommers* [1995] ICR 549 (QB) 557–559; see also *Harris (Andrews) v Lewisham & Guy's NHS Trust* [2000] ICR 707 (CA), [17], [32].

41 *Pickering v Liverpool Daily Post and Echo Newspapers* [1991] 2 AC 370 (HL).

42 Supreme Court Act 1981, s 42.

43 *Attorney General v Singer* [2012] EWHC 326 (Admin).

44 *Ewing v Security Service* [2003] EWHC 2051 (QB).

45 *R (N) v Independent Appeal Panel of Barking and Dagenham LBC* [2009] ELR 268 (CA), [33].

46 *Connolly v Dale* [1996] QB 120 (QB), at 125; *Raymond v Honey* [1983] 1 AC 1 (HL); *In Re the William Thomas Shipping Company* [1930] 2 Ch 368 (Ch).

47 Two private attempts have failed. In *Edward v Greenwich RLBC* [2017] EWHC 1112 (Admin), the claimant alleged that a housing authority's response to a judicial review application amounted to contempt; it was rejected as 'meritless'. In *Wardle v Northampton BC* [2017] EWHC 1774 (QB), the court placed a General Civil Restraint Order on a claimant (inappropriately) alleging contempt for the way in which the defendant had conducted proceedings in his claims of discrimination and victimisation (which had no real prospect of success).

1 Restricting the scope of the victimisation provisions

When interpreting the victimisation provisions, rather than adopting orthodox rules of statutory interpretation, some cases have relied instead on principles of contempt of court. This is betrayed, among other things, by the use of language. The statutory 'causative' phrase 'by reason that'[48] was key to the decisions in two prominent cases notable for the use of the language of contempt to restrict the reach of the law of victimisation (as seen in Chapter 6). In *Chief Constable of West Yorkshire v Khan*,[49] a reference was refused, and in *Cornelius v University College Swansea*,[50] a transfer and grievance procedure was denied. In both cases these denials were made pending the outcome of discrimination proceedings. And in both, the subsequent claim for victimisation failed.

The Cornelius *distinction*

The judgments in each case relied on a distinction between the *bringing* of proceedings and their *continuance*, or 'existence'. As noted in the last chapter,[51] this is a fragile and futile distinction. The protected act in question, couched under the RRA 1976, section 2(1)(a) ('brought proceedings') is indistinguishable from 'continuing' them. In any case, 'continuing proceedings' would just as readily fall within the protected act of section 2(1)(c), having 'otherwise done anything under or by reference to this Act'. Thus, whether the proceedings were 'brought', or continued, should have made no difference. However, for the purpose of contempt, the stage of proceedings is a relevant factor.[52] If the distinction had any substance at all, it comes from the law of contempt.

Moreover, in addition, the Court of Appeal in *Cornelius* noted that:

> No doubt, like most experienced administrators, they recognised the risk of acting in a way which might embarrass the handling or be inconsistent with the outcome of current proceedings. They accordingly wished to defer action until the proceedings were over.[53]

In likening the conduct to that of 'most experienced administrators', the Court signalled that it considered the conduct to have been reasonable. The House of Lords in *Khan* more obviously expressed a similar sympathy for the employer, stating that '[e]mployers, acting reasonably and honestly, ought to be able to take steps to preserve their position in pending proceedings',[54] and that the refusal of

48 From either RRA 1976 s 2(1), or SDA 1975 s 4(1). See p 121 et al. The statutory formula is set out in Chapter 6, pp 120–121.

49 [2001] ICR 1065 (HL). See Chapter 6, pp 71 and 122–129.

50 [1987] IRLR 141 (CA). See Chapter 6, pp 127–128.

51 See Chapter 6, pp 127–128.

52 See e.g. *Attorney General v Times Newspapers* [1974] AC 273 (HL), 302 (Lord Morris). See text to n 20.

53 ibid [33] (Bingham LJ, for the Court).

54 [2001] ICR 1065 (HL), [31] (Lord Nicholls).

a job reference was 'a reasonable response to the need to protect the employer's interests as a party to litigation'.[55]

Bearing in mind the victimisation provision under consideration, what is revealing here is that this *language*, focusing on the reasonableness of the conduct, rather than its cause ('by reason that'), is so patently out of place; but it is familiar to the law of contempt, which permits a certain degree of 'reasonable' pressure or 'fair and temperate' criticisms between litigants.[56] The sweeping statements were made without reference to either the statutory language or its purpose. Beyond crossing the relatively undemanding and straightforward threshold of less favourable treatment,[57] the victimisation provisions at the time were not concerned with the *gravity* of the conduct. Thus, the reasonableness of the conduct was irrelevant, or at best a minor consideration, for liability. The point is proved in *Khan* itself, where the House of Lords held that the refusal to provide a job reference was less favourable treatment, even though it would have been negative.[58]

The Derbyshire *switch*

In its subsequent attempt to provide a more rational explanation for these decisions, the House, in *St Helens MBC v Derbyshire*,[59] suggested that the 'honest and reasonable defence' in *Khan* was no more than stating that the claimant had suffered no 'detriment', as required by the employment provisions of the legislation, such as RRA 1976, section 4(2)(c).[60] This switching of the 'honest and reasonable defence' from the element of 'by reason that' to that of 'detriment' was an attempt to legitimise the discretion to assess the reasonableness of the conduct (or its effect). As such, it has more to do with the principles of contempt than the statutory definition of victimisation. Apart from the obvious problem that the House in *Khan* expressly held the quite the opposite (that Khan *had* suffered a detriment),[61] this explanation lacks credibility simply because being caused 'any other detriment' need not have played any part in the two cases, as the provision of references, grievance processes, and transfers fall quite readily under the RRA 1976, section 4(2)(b), 'opportunities for . . . transfer . . . or to

55 ibid [59] (Lord Hoffman).

56 See text to note 18, and *Attorney General v Times Newspapers* [1974] AC 273 (HL), 297–298 (Lord Reid).

57 See e.g. *R v Birmingham City Council, ex p Equal Opportunities Commission* [1989] AC 1155 (CA and HL) (grammar schools perceived as better, despite no evidence); *R v Secretary of State for Education and Science, ex p Keating*, The Times 3 December 1985 (single-sex school for girls treated boys less favourably); *Gill v El Vino* [1983] QB 425 (CA), (table service only in wine bar for women denied women a choice).

58 [2001] ICR 1065, [28] (Lord Nicholls), [42] (Lord MacKay), [52] (Lord Hoffman), [76] (Lord Scott). Lord Hutton agreed with Lord Nicholls and Lord Hoffman [61].

59 [2007] ICR 84 (HL). See Chapter 6, p 123 et al.

60 See p 123 et al. The legislation is set out at pp 120–121.

61 [2001] ICR 1065 [14] (Lord Nicholls), [53] (Lord Hoffman), [37]–[38] (Lord Mackay). Lord Hutton agreed with Lord Nicholls and Lord Hoffman [61].

any other benefits, facilities or services',[62] and withholding them, when they are normally provided, was less favourable treatment.

The cases and contempt

Given the fragility of the distinction (between the bringing and existence of proceedings) and the misplaced reliance on the element of 'detriment', these decisions are better explained on the 'reasonableness' basis, which itself was informed by the law of contempt. A consideration of the factual analysis in *Derbyshire* reinforces this view.

In *Derbyshire*, it will be recalled, the employer wrote directly to all 510 members of staff (bypassing their trade union and the claimants' solicitor) stating that should an equal pay claim, pursued by just 39 members, succeed, the resulting cost was likely to cause redundancies. The employment tribunal found as fact that the letter was 'effectively a threat', 'intimidating', and 'directed against people who were in no position to debate the accuracy of the . . . pessimistic prognostications'. The tribunal considered that reasonable reactions could include 'surrender induced by fear, fear of public odium or the reproaches of colleagues'.[63] As a consequence, the 39 claimants brought a separate claim of victimisation, succeeding in the employment tribunal and the EAT, but losing in the Court of Appeal (which followed *Cornelius* and *Khan*). We know that a unanimous House of Lords restored the decision of the employment tribunal, but consider the language used in doing so. Lord Bingham reasoned that *Khan* was distinguishable, because, 'the object of sending the letters was to put pressure on the appellants to drop their claims'.[64] Lord Hope described the employer's conduct as 'while no doubt honest, could not be said to have been reasonable'. Lord Neuberger was satisfied that the employer's conduct did not satisfy the 'honest and reasonable' test.[65] Lord Carswell agreed with Lord Neuberger. Only Baroness Hale steered clear of any 'reasonableness test', holding more simply that the employer's conduct caused the claimants a 'detriment'.[66]

The only distinction between this case and *Khan* was the gravity, or 'reasonableness', of the conduct. Some of the language used betrays this, with references to public odium, pressure, and, indeed, reasonableness. As such, the cases of *Khan*, *Cornelius*, and *Derbyshire* become indistinguishable under the law of victimisation.[67] They are only distinguishable if analysed under the law of contempt.

62 In *Khan*, Lord Mackay alone made this point for the job reference, ibid [37]–[38]. The parallel provision for the SDA 1975 was s 6(2)(b).

63 Para 4(d) of the ET Reasons, cited, [2007] ICR 84 (HL), [38].

64 [2007] ICR 84, [9].

65 ibid [74].

66 ibid [36] & [39].

67 Save for the *type* of less favourable treatment, which was in *Derbyshire* causing a detriment, rather than the withholding of an 'opportunity for a transfer', or a 'benefit'.

It is apparent from this that the courts actually considered the employers' conduct in *Cornelius* and *Khan* to be 'fair and temperate',[68] and not calculated to subject the claimants to obloquy.[69] It will be recalled that when deciding if the conduct was improper (for contempt), 'a court should consider [the facts] in the light of all the surrounding circumstances'.[70] An important circumstance in both cases was the 'general policy' nature of the conduct. The denials of a reference, transfer, or grievance procedure were all standard responses in litigation, thus suggesting again that the conduct was 'reasonable'. This is in contrast to *Derbyshire*, where the letters were intended to pressurise the claimants into a compromise, and had more of an ad hoc flavour about them. Any 'general policy defence' has no place in the law of victimisation, as it would be isolating only responses to discrimination complaints, which is effectively identifying *discrimination*, and leaving the victimisation provisions redundant, breaching a 'cardinal rule' of statutory interpretation.[71] The point for the present purpose is that if this 'general policy' distinction played any part in the rationes decidendi of these cases, it has no relationship to the victimisation provisions, but is consistent with the law of contempt.

Another feature common to these three cases which aligns them to contempt is that they all involved a response to ongoing litigation, rather than conduct short of litigation, such as reporting or complaining about discrimination.[72] The significance of this feature was most flagrantly realised in a single case, *Deer v University of Oxford*.[73] Here, the mishandling of a grievance procedure was held to cause the claimant a 'detriment', as she held a 'legitimate sense of injustice', even though the grievance would have failed in any case. In the same case, the withholding of papers pending (subsequent) litigation was held *not* to cause the claimant a detriment, as it was done on 'reasonable' legal advice.[74]

An example of just how readily courts will consider the irrelevant matter of the reasonableness of the defendant's conduct arose in *Nicholls v Corin Tech*.[75] Here, Mr Nicholls was suing his former employer for disability discrimination. Outside the room where the hearing had taken place for the day, it was alleged that the defendant (owner and director of the employer) with three others approached Mr Nicholls; the defendant then abused him, and threatened physical injury ('I will give you a disability') if he maintained his claim. Mr Nicholls then sued for victimisation. The issue was whether the conduct was related to Mr Nicholl's prior employment, because only then would the victimisation provisions be

68 *Attorney General v Times Newspapers* [1974] AC 273 (HL), 297–298 (Lord Reid).
69 ibid, 302 (Lord Morris). See text to n 16.
70 ibid. See text to n 20.
71 *Re Florence Land Co.* (1878) 10 Ch D 530 (CA), 544 (James LJ). See further Chapter 2, 'Other words and sections of the instrument', p 25.
72 See *Pothecary Witham Weld v Bullimore* [2010] ICR 1008 (EAT), [18]-[19], where Underhill J acknowledged this distinction.
73 [2015] EWCA Civ 52.
74 ibid [48] & [52] respectively.
75 (EAT, 4 March 2008), UKEAT/0290/07/LA.

engaged. Underhill J correctly emphasised that the statutory formula at the time required that the conduct arose out of and was '*closely* connected' to the employment relationship,[76] but then put a gloss on this, directing that the conduct had to be 'intended or calculated to deter Mr Nicholls from continuing with his proceedings'; otherwise it was open for a tribunal to find no liability.[77]

Bearing in mind that the issue in this case was *not* the relationship of the conduct to the proceedings, but its relationship to Nicholls' prior employment, this rider was unnecessary. At the time, the conduct had to be 'by reason that' Mr Nicholls had done a 'protected act' (e.g. having brought proceedings), and for this to bite, the conduct had to be 'closely connected' with the prior employment relationship. If the facts alleged were established, it should not matter whether the conduct was intended to deter Mr Nichols, punish him, done out of spite, or done with no apparent motive.[78] In fact, one would have to concoct quite a scenario where a claim of *employment* discrimination was *unrelated* to the employment relationship. Even if the issue *were* the relationship between the conduct and the *proceedings*, the gloss went beyond anything suggested in *Khan* and was unnecessary. This case was decided after *Derbyshire*, yet no attempt was made to connect the defendant's conduct, or intent, to 'causing a detriment', or any other element of the statutory formula. The judge (even then, experienced in discrimination law and who now sits in the Court of Appeal)[79] made resort to the language of contempt of court for no apparent reason, but the effect of this, once again, was to restrict the scope of the victimisation provisions.

Conclusion

In conclusion, the *Cornelius* 'distinction' and *Derbyshire* 'switch' were intellectually dishonest attempts to judge the cases by a notional standard of reasonableness, a standard that has more to do with the law of contempt than the victimisation provisions. This is apparent from the House's analysis of the facts in *Derbyshire*, the distinctive 'general policy' (*Cornelius*, *Khan*) and 'litigation' cases (*Deer*).

Finally, note that it was argued in Chapter 6 that the new definition of victimisation carried by the Equality Act 2010, section 27, should defeat any 'general policy defences'. In the context of contempt, it should also be noted that the new standard of 'absolute harm' envisaged by the Government introducing

76 Disability Discrimination Act 1995, s 16A(3). Emphasis supplied. See now EA 2010, s 108 as interpreted by *Rowstock Ltd v Jessemey* [2014] 1 WLR 3615 (CA), explained Chapter 2, p 20.

77 (EAT, 4 March 2008), UKEAT/0290/07/LA, [14].

78 See e.g. *Nagarajan v London Regional Transport* [2001] AC 502 (HL), holding that motive had no part in the victimisation provisions and, 512 (Lord Nicholls), 523 (Lord Steyn), overruling an *obiter dictum* to that effect from *Aziz v Trinity Street Taxis Ltd* [1989] QB 463 (CA) 485.

79 In the EAT 2000–2003 (part-time) and 2006–2013. See < https://www.judiciary.gov.uk/you-and-the-judiciary/going-to-court/court-of-appeal-home/coa-biogs/ > accessed 30 March 2018. A Westlaw search up to the date of *Nicholls v Corin Tech* (4 March 2008), indicated he presided over 15 discrimination cases.

the Act,[80] ought to remove considerations of the 'reasonableness' of the defendant's conduct. We wait to see whether the courts will defer to this legislative history or whether they continue to assess victimisation claims by the standards of contempt of court. The cases reviewed here, decided with little deference to the previous statutory formula, suggest the latter will prevail.

But there is perhaps a more serious point lurking here. One must wonder why the judges felt strongly enough to ignore the statutory wording, and import principles from a field of *criminal* law. The parallels with contempt are not enough to explain this, as the next discussion reveals.

2 The limited reach of victimisation – contempt ignored

The cases above demonstrate how the principles of contempt were used to limit the reach of victimisation under equality law. But there are other cases where quite the opposite *ought to* have occurred, but did not. The first hint of this came in *Cornelius*, an example of the 'on-off' relationship with contempt occurring in a single judgment. Here, the principle of 'reasonableness' was imported from contempt to justify the employer's conduct, yet the tenet[81] that the defendant's principal motive was subsidiary to the *effect* of the conduct was absent. Elsewhere, there is a distinct body of case law on post-employment victimisation, where the victimisation provisions could have been supplemented with contempt principles to achieve their obvious purpose.

Post-employment victimisation

It is not uncommon for employers to victimise ex-workers for having brought a discrimination claim, typically by providing no reference, a negative reference, or even supplying unsolicited detrimental comments to the new employer.[82] In these situations, the claim is also a thing of the past, having been won, lost, or settled out of court. As such, these scenarios resemble *Butterworth* and *Rowden*,[83] as after-the-event contempt cases, where there is an interference with justice as a 'continuing process'. However, the equality legislation on this issue has a rocky history.

The original major discrimination statutes[84] were not expressed to cover post-employment victimisation. As noted above,[85] for instance, RRA 1976, section 4(2), outlawed discrimination and victimisation by an employer 'in the

80 Government Equalities Office, The Equality Bill – Government response to the Consultation (Cm 7454, 2008) para 735. See also Department for Communities and Local Government, Discrimination Law Review, *A Framework for Fairness: Proposals for a Single Equality Bill for Great Britain*. A consultation paper (June 2007) para 161. See further Chapter 6, pp 131–133.

81 *Attorney General v Newspaper Publishing (Spycatcher)* [1989] 1 FSR 457 (Ch), 486. The same criticism could be levelled at *Chief Constable of West Yorkshire v Khan* [2001] ICR 1065 (HL) (see pp 122–129), and *Aziz v Trinity Street Taxis Ltd* [1989] QB 463 (CA).

82 *Metropolitan Police Service v Shoebridge* [2004] ICR 1690 (EAT).

83 [1963] 1 QB 696 (CA) and (1881) 71 LT Jo 373 (Ch) respectively. See p 137.

84 I.e. SDA 1975, RRA 1976, and Disability Discrimination Act 1995.

85 Chapter 2, p 20.

case of a person employed by him'. The provisions were gradually amended expressly to cover post-employment victimisation under the influence of a CJEU ruling, in *Coote v Granada Hospitality*, on the basis that such conduct came within the purpose of 'effective judicial control', under the deterrent principle.[86] Subsequent directives extending EU law beyond sex discrimination codified *Granada*.[87]

Before these developments, a post-employment race *discrimination* case came to the Court of Appeal. In a decision that fed subsequent victimisation cases, in *Adekeye v Post Office (No. 2)*[88] the Court gave RRA 1976, section 4 an all-too-predictable unambitious interpretation. A (black) claimant had been dismissed and brought an internal appeal seeking reinstatement. This was unsuccessful and the claimant alleged that the appeal process directly discriminated against her because white workers guilty of similar misconduct were not dismissed.[89] The claim was rejected in three ways, all weighed down with a blinkered adherence to a literal interpretation. First, the 'ordinary and natural' meaning of the phrase, 'in the case of a person employed by him' in section 4(2) referred only to *current* employees.[90] Second, in that case, argued the claimant, as a dismissed employee seeking reinstatement, she became a job applicant. This relied on section 4(1)(a) or (c):

> 4.—Applicants and employees.
> (1) It is unlawful for a person, in relation to employment by him at an establishment in Great Britain, to discriminate against another—
> (a) in the arrangements he makes for the purpose of determining who should be offered that employment; or
> (b) in the terms on which he offers him that employment; or
> (c) by refusing or deliberately omitting to offer him that employment.

Invoking the sidenote to section 4, 'Discrimination against applicants and employees', Peter Gibson LJ held: 'It is unrealistic to regard a dismissed employee seeking reinstatement by an appeal against dismissal as seeking an offer of employment.'[91] Third, the Court rejected as 'extraordinary' the argument that the more broadly worded Equal Treatment Directive 76/207/EEC (covering sex discrimination) could inform a broader interpretation of the concurrent Sex Discrimination Act 1975, which being *in pari materia*, compelled an equally broad interpretation of the RRA 1976.[92]

86 Case C-185/97 *Coote v Granada Hospitality* [1999] ICR 100, [27].
87 Race Directive 2000/43/EC, art 7(1); Framework Directive 2000/78/EC, art 9(1) (religion or belief, disability, age or sexual orientation).
88 [1997] ICR 110 (CA).
89 Her claim against the actual dismissal was out of time.
90 [1997] ICR 110, 118. Disapproved [2003] ICR 867 (HL).
91 ibid, 118–119.
92 ibid, 119. The principle, *in pari materia* ('in the same matter') is discussed in Chapter 2, p 28.

Even after *Granada* was decided, the Court of Appeal rigidly stuck to this line. In 2002, in *Jones v 3M Healthcare Ltd (No. 2)*,[93] it entertained four joined appeals of post-employment discrimination and victimisation under the similarly worded Disability Discrimination Act 1995.[94] Three of the claims involved job references. The Court of Appeal chose a somewhat officious distinction of *Granada*, confining it to sex discrimination, and was dismissive of the impending Directive covering disability discrimination: 'The regimes proposed in the Framework Directives for Equal Treatment . . . augur legislative changes in domestic employment [law] but obviously do not impact on the judicial construction of the 1995 Act.'[95]

At the time, 2002, the Court of Appeal had weighty authority to adopt a different path. Ringing down the courts and tribunals was Lord Bingham's then recent advice that domestic discrimination legislation should be afforded a purposive approach, and that for the trio of Acts with parallel provisions in force at the time,[96] 'it is legitimate if necessary to consider those Acts in resolving any issue of interpretation which may arise'.[97] Thus, it could have readily adopted this purposive approach with the blessing of the House of Lords. Little imagination was required, because the CJEU in *Granada* had already provided a demonstration on how to go about this. The situation was rescued by the House of Lords[98] with a purposive approach adopted in deference to *Granada*.

As if the legislative notion of post-employment victimisation were jinxed, the Equality Act 2010 again omitted it from the provisions, this time, in all likelihood, because of a drafting error.[99] Predictably perhaps, the EAT[100] failed to engage the recently established *Ghaidan* approach,[101] or even to consider the long-standing *Inco Europe Ltd*[102] mechanism (permitting corrections to an obvious *casus omissus*), despite the obvious error in the legislative drafting and its failure to comply with EU law. The matter was rescued, this time by the Court of Appeal.[103]

93 *Jones v 3M Healthcare Ltd (No. 2)*; *Bond v Hackney Citizens Advice Bureau*; *Angel v New Possibilities NHS Trust*; *Kirker v Ambitions Personnel (Nottinghamshire) Ltd* [2002] ICR 1124 (CA). Reversed [2003] 2 CMLR 44.

94 Disability Discrimination Act 1995, s 4(2).

95 [2002] ICR 1124, [28].

96 SDA 1975, RRA 1976, and Disability Discrimination Act 1995.

97 *Anyanwu v South Bank Student Union* [2001] 1 WLR 638 (HL) [2].

98 *Rhys-Harper v Relaxion* [2003] 2 CMLR 44, which also reversed a post-employment sex discrimination case ([2001] 2 CMLR 44 (CA)), and overruled *Adekeye v Post Office (No. 2)* [1997] ICR 110.

99 EA 2010, s 108. See *Rowstock Ltd v Jessemey* [2014] 1 WLR 3615 (CA), [36]. See Chapter 2, p 20.

100 *Rowstock Ltd v Jessemey* [2013] ICR 807, reversed [2014] 1 WLR 3615 (CA). See Chapter 2, p 20.

101 Encapsulated in *Vodafone 2 v Revenue and Customs Commissioners* [2010] Ch 77 (CA) [38]. Permission to appeal refused by the Supreme Court: UKSC 2009/0162 (16 December 2009), < https://www.supremecourt.uk/docs/pta-0910-1002.pdf > accessed 3 April 2018. See Chapter 2, p 44.

102 *Inco Europe Ltd v First Choice Distribution* [2000] 1 WLR 586 (HL). See Chapter 2, p 19.

103 *Rowstock Ltd v Jessemey* [2014] 1 WLR 3615 (CA).

Of course, the law of contempt does not recognise the post-employment boundary in itself, only the sometimes coincidental post-litigation boundary, with its focus on the deterrent principle. In none of these victimisation cases can the principles of contempt be detected, let alone mentioned. Yet, the consequences of these acts of retaliation or punishment were serious for the victims. Although they differ from *Butterworth* and *Rowden*[104] in that the retaliatory acts were not dismissals, they had potential to do comparable, or even more, harm. Former employees may well be able to find alternative work, but with the handicap of no reference, or an erroneous negative reference, they might find only lower-paid, less skilled employment, or no work at all. In the context of negligent misstatement, House of Lords authority is forthright on this matter. In *Spring v Guardian Assurance*, Lord Slynn said: '[I]n many cases an employee will stand no chance of getting another job, let alone a better job, unless he is given a reference. There is at least a moral obligation on the employer to give it.'[105]

Lord Woolf went further and expressed the view, that in respect of some types of employment,

> it is necessary to imply a term into the contract that the employer would, during the continuance of the engagement or within a reasonable time thereafter, provide a reference at the request of a prospective employer which was based on facts revealed after making . . . reasonably careful enquiries.[106]

Further, a post-employment retaliatory act, such as derogatory comments made to the current employer, may lead to a dismissal.[107] Such treatment of former employees, because they had issued discrimination proceedings, was a clear interference with the administration of justice as a continuing process.

Given the potential serious consequences of post-employment victimisation, it is remarkable that the courts found a solution only under compulsion by the CJEU, rather than supplementing the legislation with the principles of contempt, as the House of Lords had done with *Khan* and *Derbyshire*, and the Court of Appeal in *Cornelius* and *Deer*. One distinguishing feature was that these after-the-event cases were not 'litigation cases'. But this makes little difference in the law of contempt. The remaining distinction is that this time, it was the workers, rather than the employers, who would have benefitted from the influence of the law of contempt.

3 Victimisation cases amounting to contempt of court

None of the courts involved in the post-employment cases referred the conduct to the Attorney General for contempt proceedings. *Rowden* and *Butterworth*

104 [1963] 1 QB 696 (CA) and (1881) 71 LT Jo 373 (Ch) respectively. See p 137.
105 [1995] 2 AC 296 (HL), 335.
106 ibid, 354. See also Lord Goff, at 319.
107 *Metropolitan Police Service v Shoebridge* [2004] ICR 1690 (EAT).

suggest that serious consequences for someone's career and its deterrent effect warranted this. In other fields, the courts have not been afraid to 'fill the moral gaps' of legislation by creating an offence,[108] or use public policy to do so with the civil law.[109] Here, even that would not be necessary, because, as noted previously, contempt can be applied to new and/or novel situations without apparently widening its scope.[110] Neglecting to refer these cases effectively condones such conduct as a 'mere civil wrong', reparable with compensation, rather than the more serious criminal interference with the administration of justice, which this conduct often is. Thus, the third and final consideration is whether defendants in many cases of victimisation should have been referred for contempt of court. Aside from the post-employment cases, three examples are considered below.

The first case is *Nicholls v Corin Tech*, discussed earlier.[111] If the accusation of a threat of physical injury were proven, this would be the most serious contempt of the three, warranting imprisonment.[112] The second is *St Helens MBC v Derbyshire*, also discussed previously.[113] The relevant contempt here is, at common law, interfering with the administration of justice, and/or under the CCA 1981, applying to publications, which include 'any speech, writing broadcast or other communication addressed to the public or any section of the public'.[114] The letters sent by the employer were 'publications' for this purpose, while the 510 workers constituted the 'section of the public'.

As a matter of contempt, this case resembles *Attorney General v Hislop*.[115] Here the satirical magazine *Private Eye* published defamatory articles about Sonia Sutcliffe (wife of the 'Yorkshire Ripper') suggesting that she knew her husband was a murderer and gave the police false alibis. Ms Sutcliffe sued *Private Eye* for libel. Before the trial, *Private Eye* repeated the allegations pointing out that Ms Sutcliffe would be cross-examined on them. The Court of Appeal held that the articles were designed to pressurise Ms Sutcliffe to abandon her claim and as such they amounted to contempt at common law and under the 1981 Act. McCowan LJ stated that there is:

108 See e.g. *Shaw v DPP* [1962] AC 220 (HL), *Knuller v DPP* [1973] AC 435 (HL). See generally Chapter 4.

109 See e.g. A Burrows, 'The relationship between common law and statute in the law of obligations' (2012) LQR 235, 248 (Part 6) and the cases cited within, including *Parry v Cleaver* [1970] AC 1 (HL) and *Samuals v Davies* [1943] KB 526 (CA).

110 *Attorney General v Newspaper Publishing Plc* [1988] Ch 333 (CA), 368 (Sir John Donaldson MR). See p 136.

111 (EAT, 4 March 2008)UKEAT/0290/07/LA. See text to n 75.

112 See e.g. *R v William Pittendrigh* (1985) 7 Cr App R. (S) 221, (nine months for threatening 'If you shit on him, you've had it'); *R v Maloney (Grant)* (1986) 8 Cr App R. (S) 123, (six months for 'You're in for a seeing to').

113 [2007] ICR 84 (HL). See text to n 59.

114 CCA 1981, s 2(1).

115 [1991] 1 QB 514 (CA).

> [A]ll the difference in the world between a private discussion between lawyers aimed at bringing to Mrs Sutcliffe's attention that she might be cross-examined about certain matters and holding her up to public obloquy in terms neither fair nor temperate but of abuse, which is what I conclude without hesitation occurred in this case.[116]

And Nicholls LJ observed: 'There is an enormous difference between bringing home to an opponent the strength of one's own position and the weakness of his, and vilifying him in public.'[117]

The circumstances in *Derbyshire* and *Hislop* were alike in many ways. There was private pressure to abandon the proceedings. There was also public pressure (a fortiori on a daily basis, in person, from work colleagues), as well as public 'odium' or 'obloquy'. The difference is that the letters were not misrepresentations (in the ordinary legal sense of misstatements of existing fact), even though the forebodings never materialised. It should be noted though, the editor's belief at the time that the allegations were true was considered irrelevant to liability.[118] More importantly, the emphasis in *Hislop* was not on the untruthfulness of the articles, but on their *effect* upon the claimant,[119] suggesting that untruthfulness is not a necessary ingredient for contempt. In *Hutchinson v AEU*,[120] the *Daily Worker* attacked a litigant who was seeking an injunction to prevent his removal as union president, stating that union members 'will no doubt have no mercy upon those who seek to upset working-class decisions in the capitalist courts'. Goddard J found the newspaper guilty of contempt for the pressure it placed on the litigant as well as possible witnesses. The attack contained no misrepresentations.

In *Hislop*, the Court of Appeal held that as the articles were intended to dissuade Ms Sutcliffe from pursuing her claim, they could not have been made in good faith, and so there was guilt even under CCA 1981, which does not apply to 'public interest' articles published in good faith.[121] The same logic applies here. The reason for the sending out the letters was to pressurise the claimants into abandoning their equal pay claim.

The conduct in *Hislop* was a 'serious contempt'.[122] It was only the editor's contrition and resolution not in future publish comment connected to proceedings to which *Private Eye* was a party that persuaded the Court not to imprison the editor.[123] And in one judge's view, this was only after 'considerable hesitation'.[124] Any conduct coming close to one of the most flagrant and notorious contempts of modern times

116 ibid, 535.
117 ibid, 530.
118 ibid, 526–527 & 531.
119 ibid, 526.
120 *The Times* 25 August 1932 p 4.
121 CCA 1981, s 5.
122 [1991] 1 QB 514 (CA), 539 (Parker LJ), 533 (Nicholls LJ), 536 (McCowan LJ).
123 ibid, 539 (Parker LJ), 533 (Nicholls LJ), 536 (McCowan LJ). The publisher and editor were each fined £10,000, plus 'considerable' costs.
124 ibid, 539 (Lord Parker LJ).

must risk being in contempt of court, and yet in none of the eight speeches involved was it suggested.[125]

The third case is *Commissioner of Police for the Metropolis v Maxwell*.[126] Here, the claimant was a Detective Constable within Specialist Operations Counter Terrorism Command Special Branch of the Metropolitan Police. He is of mixed race and is gay. He had issued proceedings for some 120 incidents of discrimination by his employer and colleagues. In response, one colleague leaked details of 'their side of the story', ridiculing the claim, to *The Sun* newspaper, which in turn informed the claimant's solicitor of its intention to publish. In the event, it did not publish (perhaps fearing contempt proceedings).

This act may have been laced with motives of punishment, revenge, and indignation. But it was most obviously an attempt to hold the claimant out to public obloquy, and thus dissuade him from persisting with the claim. It was not surprising that the employer was found liable for victimisation. Publicly ridiculing the victim's claim would also seem to exceed the 'fair and temperate' thresholds required for contempt, especially given the circumstances: the employer knew the claimant was mentally fragile (he was off sick with stress at the time); he had already suffered several incidents of victimisation before he had issued the proceedings; and the employer was the police, lending exceptional credibility to its side of the story whilst correspondingly undermining his.

The notable feature here is that, apart from being relayed to the claimant's solicitor, the story was never published. Nonetheless, a threat to publish can amount to contempt,[127] and for a few days at least, the claimant must have been in fear of the adverse publicity, creating a real risk (as opposed to a remote possibility)[128] that he might abandon the claim. Even where there is no risk, with sufficient intent, a failed attempt to interfere with the administration of justice can attract guilt.[129] Thus, the leak, and the newspaper's threat to publish, each amounted to a contempt. Alternatively, it has been advanced, *obiter*, that a person can be guilty of attempted contempt,[130] which *inter alia* this surely was.

125 [2007] ICR 84 (HL), [2006] ICR 90 (CA), [2004] IRLR 851 (EAT).

126 [2013] Eq LR 680.

127 *Re Mulock* (1864) 3 Sw & Tr 599; 164 ER 1407.

128 *R v Duffy, ex p Nash* [1960] 2 QB 188 (DC) 200 (Lord Parker LCJ). See also *Attorney General v News Group Newspapers Plc* [1989] QB 110 (QB), 125; *Attorney General v Sport Newspapers Ltd* [1991] 1 WLR 1194 (QB), 1208, 1210.

129 '[I]f the publication created no . . . risk, . . . common law contempt . . . could only be established if those responsible for the publication intended it to have consequences affecting the . . . proceedings which it neither achieved nor was ever likely to achieve.' *Re Lonrho* [1990] 2 AC 154 (HL), 213 [10] (Lord Bridge). See e.g. *Welby v Still* (1892) 66 LT 523, 8 TLR 202, excerpted in Borrie and Lowe (4th edn, 2010), para 10.7). See also, *Re B (JA) (an Infant)* [1965] Ch 1112 (Ch), 1123 (Cross J): 'the mere fact that no harm has been done in this particular case is neither here nor there'. For a similar approach to intending to pervert the course of justice, see *R v Vreones* [1891] 1 QB 30 (Crown Cases Reserved).

130 See *Balogh v St Albans Crown Court* [1975] QB 73 (CA), 85 (Lord Denning MR), 94 (Lawton LJ), although doubted by Stephenson LJ, at 87.

The reason for these oversights is difficult to fathom, especially as they were not addressed in the cases, even by counsel. One possibility flows from the court's reluctance to step into an area of employment law covered by Parliament. This occurred (in)famously in *Johnson v Unisys Ltd*,[131] where the House of Lords held that damages were not available for the *manner* of a dismissal, even though it was in breach of the contractual term of mutual trust and confidence. The reason, in part, was that the House did not want to 'circumvent'[132] the limited remedy[133] provided for the *statutory* right not to be unfairly dismissed. If presented with the argument that the defendant should be referred for contempt, a court might similarly be wary of stepping into an area now regulated by Parliament. The cases are distinguishable though, because *Johnson* was claiming for something he would otherwise not get. In these victimisation cases, liability has been established, and the claimant would gain nothing (financially at least) if the employer were convicted of contempt. Moreover, it is not unusual for one event to lead to civil and criminal proceedings against the same defendant. Road traffic accidents are an obvious example. Thus, a more likely explanation lies in a (misplaced) belief that all forms of victimisation are provided for comprehensively by the equality legislation, and/or that victimisation in discrimination cases is not taken as seriously as it is in elsewhere.

Conclusion

The victimisation provisions may well be drafted too rigidly to account specifically for conduct defending litigation or the 'general policy' cases. In response, the courts have taken the rather odd position of importing principles of contempt to *restrict* the scope of victimisation, but then thoroughly ignoring those principles to find the scope to fulfil its purpose. Only when compelled by EU law did the courts yield on post-employment victimisation (a principle consistent with the law of contempt). As well as ignoring their instincts on contempt to *progress* equality law, these victimisation judgments failed to consider whether the conduct should be referred for contempt. The victimisation provisions cannot have been intended to provide defendants with an air-raid shelter from the criminal law.

Importing principles of contempt undermined the technical merits of many of these cases, notably the mess of *Khan* and its excruciating attempted reinterpretation in *Derbyshire*. Even if it could be argued that those *decisions* were efficacious (based on a notion of 'reasonableness'), they carried little integrity, lacking transparency and fidelity to the statutory wording. The invisibility of this process will muddy the waters for anyone trying to divine some consistent reasoning on the meaning of the victimisation provisions. And even if this opaque process could be 'reasonably understood . . . by those whose conduct it

131 [2003] 1 AC 518 (HL).

132 See e.g. ibid [66] (Lord Hoffman).

133 At the time, £11,000. It generally increases from year to year. Seessss now Employment Rights Act 1996, s 124, and explained ibid [53].

regulates', as the rule of law requires,[134] or by lawyers and non-lawyers alike,[135] such assiduous minds would be dumbfounded again by the inconsistency provided by the on-off association with the law of contempt.

Miller and Ellis' confidence that the law of contempt could 'fill the gaps' and provide a stronger deterrent[136] was somewhat misplaced. Quite reverse has occurred. Of course, the naivety of the proposition was that it relied on the same judiciary to resort to another field of law to undermine their own restrictive decisions. Its on-off use can only be explained other factors apparent throughout this book. These are a cavalier approach to the rules of statutory interpretation and an apparent lack of expertise in the legislation's technical definitions, notably its 'deterrent purpose', which seems obscured by the judges' binary mind-set requiring an at-fault tortfeasor causing harm to an individual victim. One can only conclude from this on-off association with the law of contempt, that the judiciary – and perhaps the Attorney General – do not consider the proper administration of discrimination law to be as important as the administration of justice elsewhere, which may well be explained by a lingering historical judicial negative attitude towards matters of equality.

Further reading

J Gregory, 'Victimisation is discrimination' (1990) 20 EOR 23.

EHRC, 'Section 20 investigation into the Metropolitan Police Service', < https://www.equalityhumanrights.com/en/our-work/news/investigation-met-police-reveals-significant-weaknesses-handling-discrimination > accessed 30 March 2018.

CJ Miller and E Ellis, 'The victimisation of anti-discrimination complainants – is it contempt of court?' [1993] PL 80.

Borrie and Lowe, *The Law of Contempt* (4th edn, 2010).

Chapman v Honig [1963] 2 QB 502 (CA).

Attorney General v Butterworth [1963] 1 QB 696 (CA).

Rowden v Universities Co-operative Association (1881) 71 LT Jo 373 (Ch); 1 Law Cent 161 (Hein Online: *Law-Central*, vol 1, pp 129–184 (1881)).

134 *Black-Clawson International Ltd v Papierwerke Waldhof-Aschaffenberg* AG [1975] AC 591 (HL) 638.

135 Lord Neuberger, 'Open justice unbound?' Judicial Studies Board annual lecture 2011, 16 March 2011, para 5,< webarchive.nationalarchives.gov.uk/20131202164909/http://judiciary.gov.uk/media/speeches/2011 > accessed 1 April 2018.

136 CJ Miller and E Ellis, 'The victimisation of anti-discrimination complainants – is it contempt of court?' [1993] PL 80, 87.

8 Problems with indirect discrimination

Introduction

The next group of cases centres on several elements of the definition of indirect discrimination. In general, indirect discrimination law is group-based and effect-based, and is most closely tied to substantive equality.[1] It is the antithesis of the binary fault-based litigation usually coming before the courts. The handling of four aspects of this law is explored in this chapter: (1) the defendant's facially neutral requirement; (2) the disadvantage required; (3) the comparison required; and (4) the nature of the causative element: proving the *reason why* the group was disadvantaged by the defendant's facially neutral practice.

The facially neutral requirement: the '*Perera* problem'

The original Sex Discrimination Act 1975 (SDA 1975) and Race Relations Act 1976 (RRA 1976) provided a definition of indirect discrimination (since revised) intended to reflect the US Supreme Court's definition given in *Griggs v Duke Power*.[2] This was based on the US Civil Rights Act 1964, Title VII, which simply outlawed discriminatory employment 'practices'. In the seminal case *Griggs*, a unanimous Supreme Court fashioned its indirect discrimination (or adverse impact) theory with the following reasoning:

> Congress has now provided that tests or criteria for employment or promotion may not provide equality of opportunity merely in the sense of the fabled offer of milk to the stork and the fox. On the contrary, Congress has now required that the posture and condition of the job-seeker be taken into account. It has – to resort again to the fable – provided that the vessel in which the milk is proffered be one all seekers can use. The Act proscribes not only overt discrimination but also practices that are fair in form, but discriminatory in operation. The touchstone is business necessity. If an employment practice which operates to exclude Negroes cannot be shown to be related to job performance, the practice is prohibited.[3]

1 Described in Chapter 3, p 65 et al.
2 (1971) 401 US 424.
3 ibid, 431.

More legalistically, this meant that if a plaintiff could prove that a facially neutral employment practice disparately impacted on a racial group, the burden switched to the employer to show that the practice was necessary for job performance.

The inclusion in Britain's anti-discrimination legislation was a direct result of the then Home Secretary's (Roy Jenkins) discovery of *Griggs* whilst on a trip to the United States.[4] Upon his return, the Home Secretary introduced this concept using a late amendment to the Sex Discrimination Bill, which became section 1(1)*(b)* of the 1975 Act:

> 1 (1) A person discriminates against another in any circumstances relevant for the purposes of any provision of this Act if . . .
>
> *(b)* he applies to her a requirement or condition which he applies or would apply equally to a man but—(i) which is such that the proportion of women who can comply with it is considerably smaller than the proportion of men who can comply with it, and (ii) which he cannot show to be justifiable irrespective of the sex of the person to whom it is applied, and (iii) which is to her detriment because she cannot comply with it.

The subsequent Race Relations Act 1976 adopted the same formula with the necessary adjustments for race.[5] Until its revision decades later,[6] the element *requirement or condition* proved frustratingly problematic. The Act demanded that for prima facie discrimination to be proved, the discriminator must have applied a *requirement or condition* that adversely affected the victim's group (as well as the victim). Often that would not be a problem. For example, a job advertisement might read, 'Librarians wanted. Applicants must be over six feet tall.' That would adversely affect some racial groups and women. But if the advertisement were amended to read, 'Librarians wanted. Applicants who are at least six feet tall will be *preferred*', the exchange of the word *must* for *preferred* hints at the trouble to come. Particular racial groups and women would remain disadvantaged by the modified criterion, yet it is arguable that the *preference* was no longer a *requirement or condition*. As we shall see, this argument was well-received in the Court of Appeal. The analysis of this problem takes four perspectives: (1) whether the section should be given a narrow or liberal interpretation; (2) the application of the literal rule; (3) international comparisons; and (4) the role of European Community (EC) law.

4 See Lord Lester's account (he accompanied the Home Secretary on the trip), 'Discrimination: what can lawyers learn from history?' [1994] PL 224, 227.

5 RRA 1976, s 1(1)(b) provided: 'he applies to that other a requirement or condition which he applies or would apply equally to persons not of the same racial group as that other but—(i) which is such that the proportion of persons of the same racial group as that other who can comply with it is considerably smaller than the proportion of persons not of that racial group who can comply with it; and (ii) which he cannot show to be justifiable irrespective of the colour, race, nationality or ethnic or national origins of the person to whom it is applied; and (iii) which is to the detriment of that other because he cannot comply with it'.

6 See p 170.

1 A narrow or liberal interpretation?

A narrow interpretation would create a loophole in this law. Employers could evade the legislation simply by relegating any (indirectly) discriminatory requirements to 'mere preferences'. Consequently, with this element in particular, the role of the judges is stark as well as critical. In this context, there were three ways of approaching this aspect of indirect discrimination. First, there must be a requirement or condition in the sense that it is an absolute 'must' (the first librarian advertisement). Second, there need only be an (employment) *practice* (the second advertisement). These two views envisage a cause and an effect, the cause being the requirement or practice having the effect of disadvantaging the victim's group (and the victim). The third possibility is to look solely for the adverse effect, and from this deduce that there must have been a requirement or practice that caused the effect. This would resemble the 'fair share' theory of discrimination law generally rejected in Western democracies,[7] leaving a choice between the first and second options.

The matter was not helped by the use of language in the first White Paper to explain the intended policy. The last-minute amendment to the SDA 1975 accounts for the omission of any Government policy on indirect discrimination in the preceding White Paper.[8] The opportunity came several months after the passing of the Act, when the Government published its 'parallel' White Paper on Race Relations.[9] At first, the policy seems clear but then the matter becomes confused with a careless use of language, clearly not envisaging how contentious this was to become. This White Paper stated that direct discrimination laws alone could not address the 'practices and procedures which have a discriminatory effect' and 'practices' that are 'fair in a formal sense but discriminatory in their operation and effect'.[10] This is language obviously informed by *Griggs*. Further on, the White Paper outlined the intended legislation. In place of the words *practice* and *procedure* we find *requirement* and *condition*,[11] the words adopted for the legislative formula.

In the early days of the legislation the EAT drew on the American progenitor to identify the purpose or mischief and suggest a liberal interpretation. In *Clarke v Eley (IMI) Kynoch*[12] Browne-Wilkinson J stated *obiter*:

> In our view it is not right to give these words a narrow construction. The purpose of the legislature in introducing the concept of indirect discrimination into the 1975 Act and the RRA 1976 was to seek to eliminate those practices which had a disproportionate impact on women and ethnic minorities and were not justifiable for other reasons. The concept was derived from that developed in the law of the United States which held to be unlawful practices

7 See Chapter 3, p 65 et al, esp p 66.

8 Home Office, *Equality for Women* (Cmnd 5724, 1974).

9 Home Office, *Racial Discrimination* (Cmnd 6234, 1975).

10 ibid, para 35. Note that even within one paragraph there is inconsistent use of terms, *practices and procedures* followed by *practices* alone.

11 ibid, para 55. Lord Lester has recalled how the Home Secretary and he were 'powerless' to secure a less restrictive definition of the Parliamentary drafter's interpretation of *Griggs*: 'Discrimination: what can lawyers learn from history?' [1994] PL 224, 227, n 11.

12 [1983] ICR 165 (EAT).

> which had a disproportionate impact on black workers as opposed to white workers: see *Griggs v Duke Power*. If the elimination of such practices is the policy lying behind the Act, although such policy cannot be used to give the words any wider meaning than they naturally bear it is in our view a powerful argument against giving the words a narrower meaning thereby excluding cases which fall within the mischief which the Act was meant to deal with.[13]

Shortly afterwards, the EAT cited this passage in *Watches of Switzerland v Savell*,[14] where counsel (David Pannick) formulated the employer's practice as a 'vague, subjective, unadvertised promotion procedure which does not provide . . . any adequate mechanisms to prevent subconscious bias unrelated to the merits of the candidates . . . for the post'.[15] The EAT found that the procedure, so formulated, could amount to a *requirement or condition* within the meaning of SDA 1975, section 1(1)*(b)*.[16] These early EAT cases showed an appreciation of the statutory purpose using the legislation's American antecedent, and accordingly attributed a liberal interpretation to the phrase *requirement or condition*.

Things changed abruptly when the Court of Appeal came to the matter for the first time in 1983, just a few months[17] after *Clarke v Eley*. In *Perera v Civil Service Commission (No. 2)*,[18] for the post of legal assistant, candidates were assessed *inter alia* on their command of the English language, experience in the UK, age,[19] and possession of British nationality. Without reference to Browne-Wilkinson's J dictum, or to *Griggs*, the Court of Appeal held that these 'mere preferences' did not amount to a *requirement or condition* within the meaning of the section 1(1)*(b)*. To come within the Act, the Court stated, an employer should elevate the preference to a requirement or 'absolute bar' that *had* to be complied with in order to qualify for the job.

This change of tune was all the more surprising as it upheld the decision of the EAT, with Browne-Wilkinson J presiding.[20] *This* decision predated *Clarke v Eley*,

13 ibid, 170–171, rejecting an argument that 'Condition' included qualifications for the job and not disqualifications to continue holding the job, where only part-timers (all female) were made redundant. See also: *Steel v Union of Post Office Workers* [1978] 1 WLR 64 (EAT), 70–71, where Phillips J cited *Griggs* for 'assistance' in defining the 'heavy onus' of justification, where the preferable rounds were allocated according to length of 'permanent' service, not available to women until 1975; *Snoxell v Vauxhall Motors* [1978] QB 11 (EAT), 29, citing *Griggs*, and another US case which was relevant to the facts ('red circling' defence to equal-pay claims): *Corning Glass Works v Brennan* 417 US 188 (Sup Ct, 1974).

14 [1983] IRLR 141, Waterhouse J presiding. The claim failed because that procedure did not adversely affect women.

15 ibid [17].

16 ibid [23].

17 22 September 1982 to 2 February 1983.

18 [1983] ICR 428.

19 Younger applicants were preferred. Ethnic minority applicants were more likely to have arrived in the UK and/or attained qualifications later in life.

20 [1982] ICR 350, 356. The EAT found that each criterion did not amount to an 'absolute bar' as each could be offset by another. Perera's separate claim that a more specific age requirement (to be under 32) attached to a separate job indirectly discriminated against ethnic minorities was upheld and not appealed: ibid, 358–359.

and one can only surmise that in the meantime the judge had a change of heart in *Clarke* in order to cite *Griggs* in support of a consideration of the statutory purpose and the consequent liberal interpretation; such features were conspicuously absent in his *Perera* speech.

Nevertheless, the *Clarke v Eley* dictum was now history. This was confirmed a few years later when the Court of Appeal followed *Perera* in *Meer v London Borough of Tower Hamlets.*[21] In this case, the employer attached 12 'selection criteria' to an advertised post. One of these was experience in the Tower Hamlets district. That put persons of Indian origin at a disadvantage because a higher than average proportion of them were new to the area. The Court of Appeal rejected Meer's claim of indirect discrimination holding that the criterion (or preference) of Tower Hamlets experience did not amount to a *requirement or condition.* Balcombe LJ acknowledged that this interpretation of section 1(1)*(b)* 'may not be consistent with the object of the Act'[22] and declined to expound upon this statement. He curtly distinguished the *Clark v Eley* dictum as being made 'in a context wholly different',[23] and followed *Perera* as binding precedent.

These were not just simple narrow interpretations rooted in a blinkered adherence to the literal rule. The two Court of Appeal decisions were underpinned with (misplaced) notions of statutory purpose,[24] expressed in defiance or complete ignorance of the *Clark v Eley* dictum and the American progenitor upon which the statutory definition was based. The closest they came to the history was when Stephenson LJ, giving the leading speech in *Perera*, said:

> I appreciate the importance of looking at the way in which what is alleged to be a discriminatory requirement or condition operates, as is clear when one looks at the origin of this provision in the United States and decisions there, on which this statutory provision in section 1(1)*(b)* is based.[25]

This proved to be a meaningless meander, as Stephenson LJ had his own theory, explained thus: '[A] brilliant man whose personal qualities made him suitable as a legal assistant might well have been sent forward . . . in spite of being, perhaps, below standard on his knowledge of English.'[26]

Instead of being related to the statute or its purpose, this is in fact an ideological predilection that employers should be free to choose whom to employ. There is no need for 'special' treatment for minorities. That the 'exceptional' underdog can prosper is proof of that. Of course, the explanation also reveals the technical flaw in the theory, which seriously reduces the statute's efficacy.

21 [1988] IRLR 399.
22 ibid [10].
23 ibid [9].
24 The EAT in *Perera v Civil Service Commission* [1982] ICR 350 expressed nothing in support of its 'absolute bar' interpretation.
25 [1983] ICR 428, 437.
26 ibid, 437–438.

The candidate had to be 'brilliant' to compensate for a racially connected disadvantage: a 'brilliant' black person will obtain a post otherwise suitable for an 'average' white person. The Court of Appeal also failed to address Mr Perera's argument deployed in terms of the Court's logic: that several 'preferences' which could not be complied with added up to an absolute bar. If a candidate lacked a good command of the English language, experience in the UK, youth, *and* British nationality, he stood no chance of being selected. Stephenson LJ merely noted the argument and the EAT's rejection of it for lack of evidence that any such combination had been applied.[27]

A more elaborate underpinning of the 'absolute bar' doctrine was offered in *Meer*. Staughton LJ rejected the appeal because otherwise: 'section 1(1)*(b)*, RRA . . . would have such an extraordinary wide and capricious effect'.[28] This of course overlooks the possibility that 'wide and capricious' discriminatory practices were the mischief intended to be addressed by the legislation. Instead, it evokes a related ideological predilection that equality law is the problem, rather than a solution; it interferes with the individual's liberty to choose whom to employ. This can be seen Staughton's LJ example given in support, which requires quoting in full:

> Suppose an employer takes into account, amongst other things, whether an applicant's surname begins with the letter 'A'. If it does, that is a factor to be taken into account in his favour. Suppose also, and this is not difficult, that the letter 'A' has no relevance to the job on offer and the requirement or factor is not justified – it is just adopted at the whim of the employer. I do not doubt that a racial group could be found somewhere in which the proportion of persons whose surnames begin with the letter 'A' is considerably smaller than the proportion of persons not in that group whose surnames begin with the letter 'A'. There will be a risk that a person from that racial group whose surname does not begin with the letter 'A' will have applied for the job and not been awarded it. The applicant will be able to say that he suffered a detriment in the shape of an inability to take advantage of a factor which would have told in his favour. That is an extreme example in order to make the point clear.[29]

This example reveals two problems. First, with respect, Staughton LJ missed the point because the issue ought not to be the specifications within the whim, but whether or not they amounted to a *requirement or condition* within the meaning of the Act. Second, this employer's 'whim' could conceivably amount to discrimination if a higher than average proportion of a protected group was affected by it. For instance, excluding those whose name begins with the letter 'P', would exclude all Patels, which would be likely to adversely affect those of Indian origin.

27 Ibid, 435.
28 [1988] IRLR 399, [20].
29 ibid [21].

A major feature of indirect discrimination law is its effects-based nature. Yet Staughton LJ failed to appreciate the discriminatory *effect* of the 'whim'.

Staughton's LJ ideological predilection manifested in his speech as a matter of discriminatory intent. The judge used his example in support of his view that otherwise an employer would be exposed to a charge of racial discrimination 'whether or not he had the slightest intention to discriminate on racial grounds and whether or not racial grounds had any effect whatever on his decision'.[30] Staughton LJ is suggesting that section 1(1)*(b)* should be read to exclude cases of unintentional discrimination, thus confining liability to *intentional* discrimination (an ongoing judicial preoccupation with direct discrimination[31]). As well overlooking the provision's antecedent, *Griggs*,[32] and its purpose, the comment has no basis in the statutory wording. For instance, RRA 1976, section 57(3) provided that no damages should be payable in cases of *unintentional* indirect discrimination,[33] a provision rendered meaningless by this opinion. Thus, the comment in support of the narrow interpretation fails to recognise the mischief, adds words to the statute, and renders a part of it otiose, breaching a 'cardinal rule' of statutory interpretation.[34] From a technical viewpoint, implanting an element of discriminatory intent into the inherently effect-based definition of indirect discrimination would alter its character to such an extent that it would no longer resemble indirect discrimination. If such an error were put into practice, it would seriously damage the efficacy of the law of indirect discrimination.

Aside from these distractions, and the American progenitor, there was another reason to afford the legislation the liberal interpretation. The Equal Treatment and Equal Pay Directives[35] were part of the European Community's push to achieve sex equality in employment, expressed in Article 119 of the original Treaty of Rome. As long ago as 1961, the member states had expressed by a Resolution the goal of elimination of all direct and *indirect* sex discrimination in employment.[36] This was cited in the preamble to the Equal Pay Directive. Meanwhile, article 3(1) of the Equal Treatment Directive instructed that the principle of equal treatment meant that 'there shall be no discrimination what-

30 ibid [20].

31 See Chapter 5, 'The importunate dissenters', p 99.

32 '[G]ood intent or absence of discriminatory intent does not redeem employment procedures or testing mechanisms that operate as "built-in headwinds" for minority groups and are unrelated to measuring job capability': (1971) 401 US 424, 432.

33 See also SDA 1975, s 66(3). See, for example, *Orphanos v QMC* [1985] AC 761 (HL). See now, a modified version: EA 2010, s 124(5) (employment) and s 119(6) (other claims).

34 *Re Florence Land Co.* (1878) 10 Ch D 530 (CA) 544 (James LJ). See Chapter 2, p 25, text to n 70.

35 Respectively, Council Directives 76/207/EEC and 75/117/EEC. See now Recast Directive 2006/54/EC.

36 Emphasis supplied. See the account in Case 43/75 *Defrenne v SABENA (No. 2)* [1976] ECR 455, paras 43–56: the 'Resolution of the Conference of Member States of 30 December 1961', to extend a time limit to the end of 1964, was made in frustration at the failure of all member states fully to implement Article 119 by its 'first stage transitional period', which expired on 31 December 1961. (It was held that the time extension in the Resolution had no effect to exonerate a member state from earlier failures to implement Article 119.)

soever on grounds of sex'. Neither this nor any case law suggested anything so restrictive as indirect discrimination applying only to 'absolute bars'. This being the case, it is no surprise that the Court of Justice at the time had not addressed the 'absolute bar' issue (and never has since, of course). But in those early days of discrimination law for the Court, the Advocate General had cited the Resolution in a (successful) argument to expand the scope of the UK's equal pay law,[37] whilst the Court had cited the European Social Charter in support of the principle that the elimination of sex discrimination was a 'fundamental human right'.[38] (One could hardly argue that any lesser principle applied to race.) Given this, and the aspiration to eliminate *all* indirect sex discrimination and the edict requiring no sex discrimination *whatsoever*, it would have been inconceivable for the Court to entertain a restrictive 'absolute bar' rubric, let alone sanction one just for the United Kingdom. Notable here would have been the Court's teleological and schematic approaches, and the principle of uniformity.[39]

When *Perera* was decided, all of this was available to the Court of Appeal. The Equal Treatment Directive applied to sex discrimination in recruitment, and so dictated the meaning ascribed to the SDA 1975. As the SDA 1975 could not be interpreted as requiring an 'absolute bar' for indirect discrimination in employment, nor, one would imagine, could the parallel provision of the RRA 1976, these being statutes *in pari materia*.[40] After all, it would have been inevitable that one day any incongruity between them would be exposed in court.[41] None of this potential was even considered by the Court of Appeal in *Perera* or *Meer*.[42] If it had, the Court would have had another reason to afford the legislation a liberal approach.

In summary, the Court of Appeal maintained that the words *requirement or condition* in section 1(1)*(b)* should be given a narrow interpretation because: (1) employers may not intend to discriminate when using mere preferences;[43] (2) 'a brilliant man' may overcome a disadvantageous preference;[44] and (3) otherwise the section would have 'such an extraordinary wide and capricious effect'.[45] All of this was without reference to the White Paper, which stated the purpose, as noted above, that *direct* discrimination laws alone could not address the 'practices

37 Case 61/81 *EC Commission v UK* [1982] 3 CMLR 384, Opinion of Advocate General Verloren Van Themaat, para 291.

38 Case 149/77 *Defrenne v SABENA (No. 3)* [1978] ECR 1365, para 28 (but Article 119 did not extend to conditions of work or dismissal).

39 See Chapter 3, p 41.

40 See Chapter 2, p 28.

41 It arose in *Falkirk Council v Whyte* [1997] IRLR 560 (EAT). See p 170.

42 Many years later, in *Adekeye v Post Office (No. 2)* [1997] ICR 110, 119, the Court of Appeal rejected such a proposition as 'extraordinary'. *Adekeye* was overruled in *Rhys-Harper v Relaxion* [2003] 2 CMLR 44.

43 *Meer v London Borough of Tower Hamlets* [1988] IRLR 399, [20] (Staughton LJ).

44 *Perera v Civil Service Commission (No. 2)* [1983] ICR 428, 437–438 (Stevenson LJ).

45 *Meer v London Borough of Tower Hamlets* [1988] IRLR 399, [20] (Staughton LJ).

and procedures which have a discriminatory effect' and 'practices which are fair in a formal sense but discriminatory in their operation and effect'.[46] Given that reference to White Papers was at the time commonplace,[47] this omission, in exchange for a number of speculative, spurious, flawed, and ultimately doomed theories, is puzzling, and somewhat remiss, as was the failure to continue the early practice of the EAT and refer to the Act's American antecedents for guidance, or even to consider the certainty of an inconsistent interpretation being given under EU law to the parallel provision in the SDA 1975.

Perera stood as precedent for many years, leading to two notable consequences. On the one hand, tribunals sidestepped its negative connotations. On the other, it had potential to be misapplied, wrecking a claim from the outset.

Side-stepping Perera

It is clear from the facts of these two cases that mere preferences could amount to discrimination in fact. The only escape route open to tribunals, it seemed, was to sidestep *Perera* by finding that criteria expressed as preferences *in substance* operated as absolute bars. This could occur in two ways. First, a list of discriminatory 'preferences' taken together could amount to an absolute bar. That is the case even though each criterion, taken in isolation, would not be so. We saw that argument put forward by Mr Perera and left unaddressed by the Court of Appeal for want of sufficient evidence. Thus, a tribunal finding sufficient evidence could take that line without offending *Perera*.

Second, a criterion *expressed* as a 'mere preference' might be *applied* as an absolute bar. For instance in *Jones v University of Manchester*,[48] a job advertisement stated that the successful candidate would be 'a graduate, preferably aged 27–35 years'. It was alleged this put women at a disadvantage because a larger proportion of women than men obtained degrees as mature students.[49] An industrial tribunal found that although the advertisement expressed age as a *preference*, in practice the employer had applied the age limit as a *requirement*. Thus, the tribunal interpreted section 1(1)*(b)* in accordance with *Perera*, but was prepared to look beyond the form of the criterion to the recruitment *practice*. The Court of Appeal had doubts about the tribunal's interpretation of the evidence,[50] but refused to interfere with its finding of *fact*, that the employer had applied a 'requirement' for the purposes of SDA 1975, section 1(1)*(b)*. With the

46 Home Office, *Racial Discrimination* (Cmnd 6234, 1975).

47 Indeed it was used in a discrimination case by a differently constituted Court of Appeal just a few years earlier: *Shields v Coomes* [1978] 1 WLR 1408 (CA) 1425. See Chapter 2, p 29.

48 [1993] ICR 474 (CA). The claim failed because there was no adverse impact on women. See further p 176.

49 See also *Price v Civil Service Commission (No. 2)* [1978] ICR 27 (EAT) where an upper age limit of 28 years was held to adversely affect women, who were more likely to take time out from work for family responsibilities. Discussed at p 178.

50 See, for instance, [1993] ICR 474, 490–491 (Ralf Gibson LJ).

retrospective blessing of the Court of Appeal, the industrial tribunal sidestepped *Perera* and the obvious consequences of following it. In each of the two examples given, the Act could cover criteria expressed as mere preferences without distorting the statutory words.

Misapplying Perera

Beyond such ingenuity by a willing tribunal given fortuitous facts, there was for a time little escape from *Perera*. Moreover, not only was it a precedent of 'bad law', but also it had the potential to be misapplied, further frustrating the purpose of the legislation. In *Mutemasango v Staffline Recruitment Ltd*,[51] Staffline specialised in recruiting workers who were available immediately or at short notice. Consequently, it targeted the unemployed. But Staffline had a policy of not recruiting those who had been unemployed for more than six months. This was because, it claimed, the long-term unemployed were unreliable. However, the evidence showed that Staffline had recruited those applicants who had given a good reason for being out of work for over six months. It was not the practice of Staffline to ask for such a reason; it only considered the long-term unemployed if a reason was volunteered.

Mutemasango approached Staffline for work. When asked, he stated that he had been unemployed for 15 months. He was rejected without being asked for a reason for his long-term unemployment. He brought a claim of indirect racial discrimination based upon statistics that showed that a disproportionately high amount of the long-term unemployed were from ethnic minorities.[52] The EAT held, applying *Perera*, that the 'six-month rule', being open to exceptions, was a 'mere preference', and not being an 'absolute bar' it was not a *requirement or condition* within RRA 1976, section 1(1)*(b)*.

It is quite alarming that when faced with statistical proof that the policy adversely affected ethnic minorities, the EAT followed *Perera* without considering the implications. If it had done, it would have realised that *Perera* had led it to fail to identify properly the policy under attack. The EAT identified the policy solely as 'not recruiting those unemployed for over six months'. It then noted that that policy was subject to an exception (the 'good reason' explanation). Hence, the logic went, the policy is not an absolute bar to the long-term unemployed, it was only a 'preference'. Of course, the true policy here, for the purposes of a discrimination claim, was 'not recruiting those unemployed for over six months *without good reason*'. Hence, if a person was long-term unemployed without 'good reason' there was an 'absolute bar' to his or her recruitment. If the claimant's racial group had been adversely affected by *this* policy, the burden of justification would have shifted to the defendant and the tribunal would have been able to scrutinise the policy, by asking, for instance, whether Staffline had any evidential or objective

51 EAT 13 May 1996.

52 It seems from the Report that the claimant was 'African' although his individual protected characteristic was not part of the EAT's reasoning.

basis to consider the long-term unemployed unreliable, what Staffline considered to be a 'good reason', and whether the policy was applied uniformly (say, why applicants had to *volunteer* the good reason).

2 The application of the literal rule

The analysis so far is expressed in negative terms, with the implication that under the mischief (or purposive) rule, the statutory words should have been given a 'secondary meaning', interpreted liberally, or even distorted, to address the mischief. But in fact, none of this was necessary to fulfil the statutory purpose.

The crude logic of *Perera* is that the phrase *requirement or condition* equates to an absolute bar, or a 'must'. In fact, this in itself was not seriously harmful. To explain how the harm arises, we should first consider the actual cause of action in these cases, provided by the employment part of the legislation. For instance, RRA 1976, section 4 provided:

> (1) It is unlawful for a person, in relation to employment by him at an establishment in Great Britain, to discriminate against another—
> (a) in *the arrangements* he makes for the purpose of determining who should be offered that employment . . . or
> (c) by refusing or deliberately omitting to offer him that employment.[53]

It was noted above that Stephenson LJ underpinned the decision by stating that the 'brilliant man . . . might well have been sent forward'.[54] In effect, this is stating that the employer's requirements should be an absolute bar *to the job*, which assumes the claim was under paragraph (c). The error here was connecting the requirement to the job, when it should be connected only with the *arrangements* for recruitment, under paragraph (a). No mention of section 4 was made at all in *Perera*, whilst in *Meer*, although paragraph (a) alone was cited, the judgments assumed again that the criterion should be an absolute bar to the job, thus treating the claim as one under paragraph (c).

The drafting may or may not have been intended to cover cases in this sense; it may be that the relevance of paragraph (a) to mere preferences was more fortuitous than foreseen. Nonetheless, these recruitment cases fall readily into paragraph (a), and given that the reasons underpinning *Perera* and *Meer* were spurious, there is nothing to suggest that paragraph (a) should not apply.

Once this is established, the claim can be more properly formulated. Combined with the definition of discrimination, the law thus demanded a requirement or condition in the arrangements for recruitment with which the claimant, and a disproportionate amount of persons of the claimant's racial group (and the claimant), could not comply. Accordingly, in *Perera*, to gain an advantage in the selection process there were requirements to have *inter alia* a command of the English

53 Emphasis supplied. SDA 1975, s 6 was substantially the same. See now EA 2010, s 39.
54 [1983] ICR 428, 437–438. See p 158.

language, experience in the UK, youth, or British nationality. Similarly, in *Meer*, compliance with each of the 12 'arrangements', or selection criteria, would carry credit. Of course, those unable to comply with some might have been compensated by compliance with others. In that sense, each criterion is not a barrier to the job. However, each criterion could be a barrier to obtaining credit in the selection process and this would be to the detriment of the claimant.[55] The requirement is that to gain an advantage in the selection process one *must* comply with any particular criterion. In short, rather than having applied a literal or narrow interpretation, the Court of Appeal in *Perera* exchanged the statutory word 'arrangements' in favour of an imaginary phrase, 'the job'. One could surmise that the Court of Appeal mistakenly judged the case under paragraph (c), but as this was not explained at all in either case, that would be too generous an assumption.

Given that the objections expressed in *Perera* and *Meer* to the liberal interpretation were spurious, and that *this* literal interpretation accords with the purpose expressed in the White Paper and the American antecedent on which the provision was based, these decisions were wrong, not because they took the narrow interpretive option, but because they had no basis whatsoever in any rule of interpretation.

3 International case law comparisons

Had tribunals[56] subsequent to *Perera* looked a little further afield, they would have realised that its doctrine was becoming increasingly an isolated approach to indirect discrimination law. In the United States, for instance, in the wake of *Griggs v Duke Power*,[57] as early as 1972 subjective hiring practices (which would fall outside of the *Perera* doctrine as 'mere preferences', at best) were challengeable under the employment provisions of the Civil Rights Act 1964 (Title VII). In *Rowe v General Motors*,[58] the following promotion/transfer procedure was identified:

(1) The foreman's recommendation was the indispensable single most important factor in the promotion process.
(2) Foremen were given no written instructions pertaining to the qualifications necessary for promotion. (They were given nothing in writing telling them what to look for in making their recommendations.)

55 Under RRA 1976 (or SDA 1975) s 1(1)(b)(iii); see now EA 2010, s 19(2)(c) 'particular disadvantage'. It was not necessary to show a financial loss. A tribunal can make a declaration in recognition of the 'wrong' (RRA 1976, s 56(1)(a); SDA 1975, s 65(1)(a); see now EA 2010 s 124(a)) and award damages solely for injury to feelings (SDA 1975, s 66(4); RRA 1976, s 57(4); see now EA 2010, s 124(6) and (for other claims) s 119(4)).

56 As well as *Mutemasango v Staffline Recruitment Ltd* (EAT 13 May 1996), see e.g. *Meikle v Nottingham City Council* EAT/249/92, (EAT, 14 April 1994) (advertisement declaring that 'experience of grant/funding processes at local and national level and knowledge of urban policies and programmes' was 'desirable', held to be a mere preference); *Barking and Dagenham v Camara* [1988] ICR 865 (EAT), 873 (criterion of continuity or stability in previous employment not a requirement because neither a 'must' nor part of the job description).

57 (1971) 401 US 424. See n 2 and accompanying text.

58 457 F 2d 348 (1972) (CA 5th Cir).

(3) Those standards which were determined to be controlling were vague and subjective.
(4) Hourly employees were not notified of promotion opportunities nor were they notified of the qualifications necessary to get jobs.
(5) There were no safeguards in the procedure designed to avert discriminatory practices.[59]

The Fifth Circuit Court of Appeals held that this 'procedure' amounted to an employment practice for the purposes of Title VII,[60] which adversely affected black workers, who occupied predominantly the 'Hourly' jobs.

Similarly, the Canadian Supreme Court has recognised subjective hiring practices. *Action Travail des Femmes v Canadian National Railway*[61] is a classic example. The defendant railway company discouraged women from working on blue-collar posts with these recruitment practices:

(1) The employer had not made any real effort to inform women in general of the possibility of filling blue collar positions in the company.
(2) Canadian National's recruitment programme with respect to skilled crafts and trades workers was limited largely to sending representatives to technical schools where there were almost no women.
(3) When women presented themselves at the personnel office, the interviews had a decidedly 'chilling effect' on female involvement in non-traditional employment; women were expressly encouraged to apply only for secretarial jobs. Women applying for employment were never told clearly the qualifications which they needed to fill the blue collar job openings.
(4) The personnel office did not itself do any hiring for blue collar jobs. Instead, it forwarded names to the area foreman, and Canadian National had no means of controlling the decision of the foreman to hire or not to hire a woman. (The evidence indicated that the foremen were typically unreceptive to female candidates.)[62]

The Supreme Court of Canada affirmed the decision of the tribunal of first instance that these practices amounted to sex discrimination. Dickson CJ commented:

> [S]ystemic discrimination in an employment context is discrimination that results from the simple operation of established procedures of recruitment, hiring and promotion, none of which is necessarily designed to promote discrimination. The discrimination is then reinforced by the very exclusion of the disadvantaged group because the exclusion fosters the belief, both within

59 ibid, 358–359.
60 See also *Montana Rail Link v Byard* (1993) 260 Mont 331 (Supreme Court of Montana); *Watson v Fort Worth Bank* 487 US 977 (Sup Ct, 1988); *Stender v Lucky Stores* 803 F Supp 259 (ND Cal, 1992); and *Butler v Home Depot* No. C-94-4335 SI, C-95-2182 SI, (ND Cal, 29 August, 1997).
61 [1987] 1 SCR 1114.
62 ibid, 1123–1125.

> and outside the group, that the exclusion is the result of natural forces, for example, that women 'just can't do the job'.[63]

Although the courts in these two cases were not restricted by the statutory words *requirement or condition*, they illustrate the proper reach of indirect discrimination law, which in these cases went beyond even the 'mere preferences' left untouched by *Perera*.

A more precise case for comparison arose five years after *Perera*. The Federal Court of Australia (New South Wales District) entertained a case of 'mere preferences' under the identical statutory phrase *requirement or condition*, given in the Australian SDA 1984, section 5(2).

The case was *Secretary of Department of Foreign Affairs and Trade v Styles*.[64] The complaint concerned a job-selection process. The post was that of a Counsellor in the Department located in London. It was advertised by a circular distributed within the Australian Public Service. Although this post was designated 'Grade A2' journalist, it was quite clear that anyone Grade A1 could apply. Grade A1 was immediately below Grade A2. Twelve members of the Australian Public Service applied; two of them Grade A2 and the other ten Grade A1. Helen Styles was among the Grade A1 applicants. The Department considered only the two Grade A2 applicants and disregarded all 10 of the Grade A1 applications. Of the two Grade A2 applicants, one was considered to be needed elsewhere in Canberra and so the other was chosen. What happened here is clear. The Department preferred a Grade A2 applicant. It may have considered the exceptionally brilliant Grade A1 candidate (but did not). Or, more likely, in the absence of any Grade A2 journalists applying, it would have considered the Grade A1 applicants. In the same way, the employers in *Perera* and *Meer* preferred applicants to have certain characteristics. Helen Styles based her claim on the basis that men were overrepresented (85 per cent) in the category Grade A2. Of course, to support this claim she had to show that the preference for Grade A2 was a 'requirement or condition' so as to come within section 5(2).

In a common judgment Bowen CJ and Gummow J considered *Perera* and held:

> In construing these words [SDA 1984, s 5(2)] it is essential to bear in mind that the concept of indirect discrimination . . . is concerned not with form and intention, but with the impact or outcome of certain practices. . . . to look solely at the terms of the departmental circular is to put misplaced reliance on the formal terms of the criteria for selection, which is both contrary to the legislative intent and would tend to encourage evasion of the operation of the statute. . . . A requirement or condition, therefore, means a

63 ibid, 1139.

64 (1989) 88 ALR 621. Other Australian cases at the time took the same view: *Waters v Public Transport Corporation* (1991) 173 CLR 349 (High Court of Australia); *Australian Iron & Steel Pty Ltd v Banovic* (1989) 168 CLR 165, 185, & 195–197 (High Court of Australia).

> stipulation which must be satisfied if there is to be a practical (and not merely a theoretical) chance of selection.[65]

In contrast to *Perera* and *Meer*, this judgment recognised the purpose of indirect discrimination law, as well as the potential loophole. The closest the Court of Appeal came to this was in *Meer*, with Balcombe's LJ unexplained doubt about the correctness of *Perera*. *Styles* illustrates that the Court of Appeal should not have felt fettered by the language of section 1(1)*(b)*. It might be argued that *Styles* is distinguishable because, rather like the conclusion in *Jones v University of Manchester*,[66] it was found that in practice a requirement had been *applied*: no A1 applicants were short-listed. But this logic is vulnerable to the error that holds that the requirements must be for *the job*, rather than for any aspect of the recruitment process.[67] Moreover, the *Styles* decision was explained as much by the statutory purpose as it was on the specific facts, suggesting that the Australian court would have taken a more generous approach to disadvantages within a recruitment process, such as those evident in *Perera* and *Meer*.

These three international cases, ranging from 1972 to 1989, illustrate not only the increasing international isolation of the *Perera* doctrine in terms of statutory purpose and (in the case of *Styles*) wording, but also how insular the Court of Appeal, and the tribunals that followed it, had become. Further similar indications were to come from EU law.

4 The role of EC law

Given its flaws and increasing isolation, it is surprising that *Perera* stood for 14 years before its decline even began. This was with a predictable consequence of EC law, a Directive passed in 1997. The first indication, if one were needed, that EC law would not countenance the *Perera* approach, came in fact a little earlier in 1994.

Suppose a case parallel to *Perera*, save that the claimant were an Italian national. His claim under the Race Relations Act 1976 would fail presumably because of *Perera*. At the time, there was no Community legislation on racial discrimination, but EC law *did* prohibit discrimination against EC workers on the grounds of nationality.[68] Rather like its American counterparts, no specific formula defining indirect discrimination was provided; it was left for the CJEU to develop. Given that the definition of 'race' in the RRA 1976 included 'nationality',[69] one might have supposed the Court of Appeal to have been aware of the potential for a conflict,

65 ibid [29]. Pincus J [23]–[24] agreed with this point, but dissented [21] on basis that an adverse impact on women had not been proven.

66 [1993] ICR 474 (CA). See p 176.

67 See 'The application of the literal rule', p 176.

68 What is now Art 45 TFEU, ex Art 39 TEC, ex Art 48 EEC.

69 RRA 1976, s 3(4) provided: '"racial group" means a group of persons defined by reference to colour, race, nationality or ethnic or national origins'. See now EA 2010, s 9(1)(b).

which would arise unless the CJEU found a reason to adopt *Perera*'s 'absolute bar' notion. Given that no other comparable court had done so, this was unlikely.

Hence, when a 'mere preference' case came before the CJEU, such an argument was not even on the table. In *Ingetraut Scholz v Opera Universitaria di Cagliari*,[70] Scholz, a German woman who had gained Italian nationality by marriage, applied for one of 21 posts as a canteen assistant with the University. The University applied selection criteria that included two-and-half points merit per year of similar or superior public-sector work experience, and one point per year of other public-service experience. Scholz had seven years' experience as a postal assistant in Germany, which would have placed her eleventh among the candidates, but the University only gave credit for experience gained in *Italy*. Without those seven points, Scholz came forty-fifth, and so was not appointed.

The criterion was not an 'absolute bar'.[71] It merely put candidates at an advantage if they possessed the stated experience. The University would have offered Scholz the job if her lack of Italian experience were offset by other qualifications, or if some of the other candidates did not score so highly, or there were fewer than 22 candidates. Scholz complained that the University's criterion amounted to nationality discrimination. This was not considered as a case of direct discrimination because Scholz was, at the time, an Italian national.[72] However, in the words of Advocate General Jacobs, the selection procedure was

> more likely to affect nationals of other Member States more severely than it affects Italian nationals. That is so because most Italian candidates will have acquired their previous experience (or the greater part of it) in Italy, whereas most candidates from other Member States will have acquired their previous experience (or the greater part of it) in other Member States.[73]

Note here that Advocate General Jacobs is concerned that the criterion was 'more likely to affect . . . more severely' other nationals, rather than 'absolutely bar' them. Accordingly, the CJEU held that 'the Treaty prohibits not only overt discrimination by reason of nationality but also all forms of covert discrimination which, by the application of other distinguishing criteria, lead in fact to the same result.' Consequently, the Court found in favour of Scholz, and signalled, to a British audience at least, it made no distinction between absolute bars and mere preferences. What mattered were the effects of the challenged criterion.

Despite the significance of the case, *Scholz* went unnoticed in the English courts, to be mentioned only in passing in 2015,[74] long after *Perera* ceased to be

70 Case C-419/92 [1994] ECR 1-505. The earliest case in which the CJEU recognised indirect discrimination under Art 48 EEC was Case 152/73 *Sotgiu v Deutsche Bundespost* [1974] ECR 153, concerning a requirement to live in the host country to qualify to 'separation' payment.

71 It is not clear from the reports if the University applied other criteria.

72 Case C-419/92, [1994] ECR 1-505 [AG16]–[AG17].

73 ibid [AG17].

74 *R (Unison) v Lord Chancellor* [2015] IRLR 911 (CA).

an issue. Instead, it was Europe's sex discrimination legislation and the Scottish EAT that first marked the demise of *Perera*. In *Falkirk Council v Whyte*,[75] an employer advertised a post of first-level line manager. One of the selection criteria stated that both 'management training and supervisory experience' were 'desirable'. The three female complainants, each having made unsuccessful applications for the post, alleged that the criteria amounted to unlawful sex discrimination because a considerably smaller proportion of women than men had such training or experience. (The claimants themselves had none.)

The EAT recognised a discrepancy between the SDA 1975 (according to *Perera*) and the Equal Treatment Directive[76] and preferred to follow the Directive for two reasons.[77] First, it distinguished *Perera* as a case under the RRA 1976, not the SDA 1975 in question. Second, if there was a conflict between domestic and European law, the European law must prevail. *Scholz* was not cited, and given that the Directive provided nothing more than a general edict against sex discrimination, and that there was no other CJEU case law on the matter, the tribunal must have had a further reason to decide that European law was different from *Perera*. It did. Citing *Griggs v Duke Power*,[78] it reasoned:

> In many ways this was a classic situation of indirect sex discrimination, with mostly women in basic grade posts, and mostly men in promoted management posts – a vivid example of what the Act and its forerunners in the United States set out to eliminate, i.e. those practices which had a disproportionate impact on women and were not justifiable for other reasons.[79]

For the first time since *Perera*, the EAT looked beyond the Court of Appeal for its understanding of what the law ought to be. The judgment was that *Griggs* was a better guide than *Perera* to the meaning of the Directive and indeed, the meaning of indirect discrimination; the EAT found for the claimants accordingly.

Whyte stated what every discrimination lawyer knew. But this was merely an EAT decision, still theoretically vulnerable to an overruling and carrying limited precedential weight. *Perera*'s fate was sealed soon after in more concrete terms with the Burden of Proof Directive,[80] article 2 of which provided a definition of indirect discrimination, which 'shall exist where an apparently neutral provision, criterion or practice disadvantages a substantially higher proportion of the members of one sex'. This was the clearest possible signal that *Perera* had no place in EC discrimination theory, and in time, successive equality directives carried similar

75 [1997] IRLR 560 (EAT).

76 Council Directive 76/207/EEC. See now Recast Directive 2006/54/EC.

77 [1997] IRLR 560, [5].

78 (1971) 401 US 424. See n 2 and accompanying text.

79 [1997] IRLR 560 (Lord Johnston).

80 Council Directive 97/80/EC of 15 December 1997 on the Burden of Proof in Cases of Discrimination Based on Sex (Burden of Proof Directive) transcribed SI 2001/2260, in force 12 October 2001.

formulas,[81] which in turn fed into to the domestic derivatives, recast nowadays in the Equality Act 2010 (EA 2010), section 19 (set out below on pp 174–175). Given that *Perera* was so at odds with the established definition and purpose of indirect discrimination law (notably nowadays, its goals of substantive equality and equality of opportunity), as well as being internationally isolated, it is unlikely that UK secession from the EC should upset the wording of section 19.

5 Conclusion

Perera and *Meer* provided technically flawed interpretations made on no recognised rule of statutory interpretation. The decisions were laced with misplaced purposes and could not even be described as literal interpretations. They were narrow and myopic. The Court of Appeal's explanations merely disclosed an utter misconception of the nature and purpose of indirect discrimination (including the now-familiar flirtation with fault-based liability), which was not only easily divinable with a little consideration, but had been expressed elsewhere, notably in the White Paper and *Griggs*.

Many subsequent tribunals slavishly following *Perera* failed to show the imagination, wisdom, or simple trade craft (demonstrated in *Styles*, *Whyte*, and *Jones v University of Manchester*) to sidestep *Perera*. Ultimately, the EC came to the rescue of this judicially embarrassing affair. Yet, as the proper literal interpretation showed,[82] *Perera* and *Meer* were easy cases with an easy solution producing good law.

Disadvantage and *Mandla*

The Court in *Perera* may have been influenced by a similarly reductionist judgment on indirect discrimination delivered the previous summer by a differently constituted Court of Appeal (and which was not reversed until after *Perera* was decided). It will be recalled that the RRA 1976, section 1(1)*(b)* stated that the challenged requirement must be such that 'the proportion of persons of the same racial group . . . who can comply with it is considerably smaller than the proportion of persons not of that racial group who can comply with it'.

In *Mandla v Dowell Lee*,[83] Gurinder Singh Mandla, an orthodox Sikh boy, was denied entry to a school because he failed to comply with its dress code, which required short hair and the wearing of a cap. Mandla's religion dictated he kept his hair unshorn and restrained with a turban. His father complained to the Commission for Racial Equality, which pursued the case on their behalf. The Court of Appeal (Lord Denning MR, Oliver, Kerr LJJ) rejected the complaint.

To understand how the court came to the decision, one must first understand the ratio decidendi, which was that Sikhs did not constitute a racial group within

81 See e.g. Recast Directive 2006/54/EC (gender); Race Directive 2000/43/EC; Framework Directive 2000/78/EC (religion or belief, sexual orientation, disability, and age).

82 See above, p 164.

83 [1983] QB 1. Reversed [1983] 2 AC 548 (HL).

the meaning of RRA 1976 (the case predating dedicated religious discrimination legislation). The Act defined 'racial grounds' to mean 'colour, race, nationality or ethnic or national origins'.[84] Adopting the antithesis of the purposive approach, each judge used a dictionary to deliver an interpretation of 'ethnic origins' with the result that as Sikhs could show no common biological characteristic, they could not constitute racial group.[85] Bolstering his resort to the dictionary, Oliver LJ said: 'I do not believe that the man in the street would apply the word "ethnic" to a characteristic which the propositus[[86]] could assume or reject as a matter of choice.'[87]

By reducing the term 'ethnic origins' to a biological test, the Court effectively assimilated the term with 'race', offending the 'cardinal rule' that a statute ought not to be read in a way that renders any of its words otiose.[88] Even without the purposive approach, this alone should have alerted the Court that they were on the wrong path. Further, this scientific approach to identifying a racial group was at odds with a House of Lords dictum. As far back as 1972, in an otherwise restrained interpretation of 'national origins' in the Race Relations Act 1968, Lord Simon had reasoned: '"[R]acial" is not a term or art, either legal or . . . scientific. I apprehend that anthropologists would dispute how far the word "race" is biologically at all relevant to the species amusingly called homo sapiens.'[89]

This part of the judgment was not cited by the Court of Appeal. And, once again, had the Court troubled to look overseas for guidance, it would have found a similar 'anti-scientific' sentiment expressed in the New Zealand Court of Appeal. In *King-Ansell v Police*,[90] Richardson J said:

> [A] group is identifiable in terms of its ethnic origins if it is a segment of the population distinguished from others by a sufficient combination of shared customs, beliefs, traditions and characteristics derived from a common or presumed common past, even if not drawn from what in biological terms is a common racial stock.[91]

The Court's rejection of Sikhs as a racial group was enough to dismiss the appeal. But Oliver and Kerr LJJ ventured further. They held that as Mandla could *physically* comply with the dress code, by cutting his hair, removing the turban, and fitting the school cap, he *could* comply with the dress code. For Kerr LJ, the issue was inevitably tied to the finding that Sikhs did not constitute a racial group. He

84 RRA 1976, s 3(1). See now EA 2010, s 9.
85 [1983] QB 1, 9–10 (Lord Denning MR) 14–15 (Oliver LJ), & 21–22 (Kerr LJ).
86 OED 2016: 'A person from whom a line of descent is derived', < http://oed.com > accessed 1 April 2018.
87 [1983] QB 1, 15.
88 *Re Florence Land Co.* (1878) 10 Ch D 530 (CA) 544 (James LJ). See Chapter 2, p 25, text to n 70.
89 *Ealing LBC v Race Relations Board* [1972] AC 342 (HL), 362.
90 [1979] 2 NZLR 531.
91 ibid, 543.

suggested that as the definition of a racial group is based upon unalterable characteristics; the statutory phrase 'can comply' must be contrasted with 'something approaching impossibility'. Thus, '[i]t was not intended to be measured against criteria of free will, choice, or conscience.'[92] Similarly, Oliver LJ thought the law was aimed at 'impossible' requirements related to things such as 'height, pigmentation, or linguistic or educational qualifications' and not matters 'which some individual members of a group are unwilling to fulfil or may find unacceptable by reason of religious or conscientious scruple'.[93]

Of course, a consequence of such logic would undermine the efficacy of the legislation. Employers would argue that as women had a 'choice' as to marriage and childbirth, 'family-hostile' policies, such as the hiring of only young persons or full-timers, or a last-in-first-out redundancy process, would not even have to be justified, despite their inevitable impact on women.[94] Similarly, a public house would argue that as Romanies could abandon a nomadic 'lifestyle' after seeing a 'No Travellers' sign, they need not be adversely affected.[95]

There is no doubt that all three judges were influenced by the motive underlying the dress code, which was to 'to minimise the divisive differences of race, class or creed, and to serve as a good advertisement for the school'.[96] Oliver LJ considered this 'a perfectly respectable viewpoint and is the sincerely held and responsible opinion of a man who is running a multi-racial school in a difficult area'.[97] As such, the headmaster was 'entirely blameless',[98] or in Lord Denning's MR opinion, not 'at fault in any way'.[99] Meanwhile, Kerr LJ declared: 'This school was demonstrably conducted harmoniously on a multiracial basis.'[100] Although a consideration for any justification defence, none of this is at all relevant to the issues supposedly in question. It suggests, once again, that liability for discrimination must be fault-based. Kerr LJ betrayed another dimension to his thinking when he embellished the decision by telling the young Mandla with a flourish: 'If persons wish to insist on wearing bathing suits they cannot reasonably insist on admission to a nudist colony.'[101] In doing so, as Lord Rodger had done in *JFS*,[102] he brought to his judgment the ideological predilection that the individual's liberty to define his business should not be trumped by meddlesome equality law.

92 [1983] QB 1, 24.
93 ibid, 16.
94 See e.g. *Price v Civil Service Commission (No.2)* [1978] ICR 27 (EAT) 32. In *Mandla*, without giving reasons, Oliver LJ stated that the RRA 1976 should not 'necessarily be accorded the same extended meaning' as the SDA 1975: [1983] QB 1, 16.
95 *CRE v Dutton* [1989] QB 783 (CA), 803.
96 [1983] QB 1, 20.
97 ibid, 17.
98 ibid, 18.
99 ibid, 13.
100 ibid, 25.
101 ibid, 21.
102 See p 113.

Conclusion

The judgment could be characterised as one turning on the literal rule of interpretation. (It was indeed curious to witness Lord Denning, a leading and active advocate of the purposive approach,[103] resort to a dictionary.) But the wider comments suggest that the Court was led by its sympathy for the headmaster, rather than an adherence to a literal rule. Technically, the Court would have done much better to have invoked its sympathy within the justification defence, rather than produce these wholly inadequate models of statutory interpretation.

One could also ascribe to this judgment a broader policy objective, in support of mono-culturalism, despite the unconvincing comments equating the policy (minimising 'divisive differences of race, class or creed') with multiculturalism.[104] Any mono-culture policy objective was at odds with the long-standing political commitment to multiculturalism, which no doubt was an underlying purpose to the Race Relations Act 1976, a purpose totally ignored.[105] More worrying was the confusion of mono- and multiculturalism concepts. This would undermine any attempt, were there one, at a purposive interpretation. Allied to the Court's expressed sympathy for the headmaster and the ('swimwear') admonishment of the schoolboy was of course the now familiar gravitation to the common law's traditional at-fault tortfeasor and victim mind-set.

As a postscript, the Court dedicated over 1,000 words of heavy criticism directed at the Commission for Racial Equality for pursuing the case.[106] The Commission's perseverance was rewarded when the House of Lords rescued the situation by reversing the Court of Appeal on all counts.[107] Nonetheless, the criticism exposed the distance between those who understand this law and this Court of Appeal, and was evocative of the historical negativity, if not hostility, towards matters of equality.

The comparison required

As noted above, the old 'requirement or condition' definition of indirect discrimination gradually gave way to a new formula, consolidated in the Equality Act 2010, section 19:

103 'The literal method is now completely out of date. It has been replaced . . . In *all* cases now in the interpretation of statutes we adopt such a construction as will promote the "general legislative purpose" underlying the provision': *Nothman v Barnet LBC* [1978] 1 WLR 220 (CA) 228 (Lord Denning MR), emphasis supplied.

104 In addition to Oliver's LJ comment, Kerr LJ said: 'the school's aim is clearly to provide a multi-racial approach to the education of all its pupils for life in the present-day multi-racial society of this country', [1983] QB 1, 20.

105 See the argument of Irvine QC, [1983] QB 1, 7.

106 ibid, 90 words, at 13 (Lord Denning MR) 801 at 17–18 (Oliver LJ) and 150 at 24–25 (Orr LJ).

107 [1984] 2 AC 548.

(1) A person (A) discriminates against another (B) if A applies to B a provision, criterion or practice which is discriminatory in relation to a relevant protected characteristic of B's.
(2) For the purposes of subsection (1), a provision, criterion or practice is discriminatory in relation to a relevant protected characteristic of B's if—

(a) A applies, or would apply, it to persons with whom B does not share the characteristic,
(b) it puts, or would put, persons with whom B shares the characteristic at a particular disadvantage when compared with persons with whom B does not share it,
(c) it puts, or would put, B at that disadvantage, and
(d) A cannot show it to be a proportionate means of achieving a legitimate aim.

On the matter of making a comparison for the purpose of establishing the 'particular disadvantage', guidance is provided by section 23(1): 'On a comparison of cases for the purposes of [indirect discrimination] there must be no material difference between the circumstances relating to each case.'

Although establishing the 'particular disadvantage' ought to be easier[108] than establishing that a 'considerable smaller' proportion of persons 'can comply' with the requirement or condition (under the old definition), the formula for the comparison provided by section 23 remains essentially the same.[109] Upon this rubric, case law has developed a method of analysing a pool comprising persons whose circumstances are materially the same, save for the protected characteristic. The pool is analysed to see if the protected group has been put at a particular disadvantage. The analysis is measuring the impact of the provision, criterion, or practice on the claimant's group in comparison with the impact on the others in the pool. Apart from excluding material differences, the courts have been troubled on how to select the pool, as observed by Sedley LJ:

> [O]ne of the striking things about both the race and sex discrimination legislation is that, contrary to early expectations, three decades of litigation have failed to produce any universal formula for locating the correct pool, driving tribunals and courts alike to the conclusion that there is none.[110]

Thus, for Sedley LJ, there is no single principle. It is a question of fact in each case.[111] That may be largely true, but one technical rule, beyond the material

108 The new formula does not require a statistical analysis, where no statistics exist. See e.g. *Homer v Chief Constable of West Yorkshire* [2012] ICR 704 (SC) [14] (Baroness Hale). See p 182.
109 RRA 1976 3(2) provided that the comparison 'must be such that the relevant circumstances in the one case are the same, or not materially different, in the other'. SDA 1975, s 5(3) was substantially the same.
110 *Grundy v British Airways* [2008] IRLR 74 (CA) [27].
111 ibid [31].

differences rubric, is that the challenged factor(s) should not be used in defining the pool, as this would frustrate the purpose of assessing its impact.[112] The problem can be seen in the dissent of Aikens LJ in *Rolls Royce v Unite*.[113] In this age discrimination case, the challenged practice was credit for long service in a redundancy selection procedure: those with longer service were less likely to be made redundant. The majority of the Court of Appeal accepted that this adversely affected younger workers (although it was objectively justified). In his dissent on the adverse effect element, Aikens LJ assembled a pool of workers of all ages who completed the same length of service. He then compared the group of older workers (50–55) with younger ones (40–45), with the inevitable conclusion that the criterion did not adversely affect the younger group.[114] The technical error, of course, was including the challenged practice of length of service (albeit rather unrealistically uniform) in the definition of the pool.

That said, on the whole, the Court of Appeal seemed to have mastered this process. In *Jones v University of Manchester*,[115] the job requirement was to be a graduate aged 27–35. The claimant argued that the age requirement indirectly discriminated against women. She argued that the pool should comprise graduates who had obtained their degree as mature students, i.e. aged at least 25. The Court of Appeal rightly rejected this, as the age factor should be disregarded. The correct pool was *all* graduates. (Then the proportion of female graduates within the age requirement was compared with the proportion of male graduates within the age requirement.)

In another sex discrimination case, *Allonby v Accrington & Rossendale College*,[116] where part-time lecturers were dismissed and rehired through an agency on inferior terms, the part-time factor was disregarded providing a pool of *all* the College's teaching staff. The comparison was between the proportions of female full-timers and male full-timers (i.e. those not dismissed), which was 21 and 38 per cent respectively. A further example of good practice can be seen in the Northern Ireland Court of Appeal. In *McCausland v Dungannon DC*,[117] the claim was that a job requirement to be an existing member of staff indirectly discriminated against Catholics. The other (unchallenged) requirement was a 'standard occupational classification' (SOC) of 1, 2, or 3. The pool consisted of anyone from the whole Northern Ireland workforce with a SOC 1, 2, or 3. (The comparison was between the proportions of Catholics and Protestants from the pool who could comply with the requirement to be an existing member of staff.)

112 'There is no formula for identifying indirect discrimination pools, but there are some guiding principles. Amongst these is the principle that the pool should not be so drawn as to incorporate the disputed condition.' *Allonby v Accrington & Rossendale College* [2001] ICR 1189, [18] (Sedley LJ).

113 [2010] ICR 1 (CA).

114 ibid [142].

115 [1993] ICR 474 (CA).

116 [2001] ICR 1189 (CA).

117 [1993] IRLR 583 (NICA), heard under the Fair Employment (Northern Ireland) Act 1989 (outlawing discrimination on grounds of religious belief or political opinion).

Thus, the Court of Appeal showed a good grasp of the process, with comparisons which were proper, practical, and served to identify whether or not there was any adverse impact. This was thrown into doubt by the majority's pronouncements in the House of Lords case *Rutherford v Secretary of State for Trade and Industry (No. 2)*.[118] In this case, predating the first specific age discrimination legislation,[119] Mr Rutherford was dismissed at the age of 67. At the time, by section 109 of the Employment Rights Act 1996, those over 65 could not claim for unfair dismissal.[120] Mr Rutherford argued that section 109 adversely affected men and so was contrary to EU sex discrimination law. The majority compared men and women over 65 who were in work, and concluded that there was no adverse impact *at all*, because section 109 treated these workers equally, irrespective of sex. Notable in this methodology is the inclusion of a challenged factor (age) in defining the pool. Baroness Hale explained why younger persons should not be in the pool: 'Indirect discrimination cannot be shown by bringing into the equation people who have no interest in the advantage or disadvantage in question.'[121] This does not tally with the exclusion of younger workers, who are advantaged by unfair dismissal rights. Thus, the *decision* could be confined to something narrower than this dictum, which is itself troublesome. The technical problem with its logic is that it supposes a binary pool where every member is either advantaged *or* disadvantaged by the challenged factor. This fails to account for the wider purpose (and efficacy) of indirect discrimination law, which is to address adverse impacts on protected *groups*. In *Griggs v Duke Power*,[122] for instance, the statistics used included all those of post-high-school age in North Carolina, most of whom had no interest whatsoever in working at Duke Power and so were neither (directly) advantaged or disadvantaged by Duke Power's recruitment practices. But the statistics helped show the adverse impact on African-Americans generally. A more realistic explanation for the chosen pool in *Rutherford* might be that the majority struggled to equate an age limit with a condition, such as that for two years' service for unfair dismissal rights.[123] In any case, the claimant's case was relatively simple: as men have a greater tendency to work beyond 65, they are disproportionately affected by section 109. This argument may have led the majority into a rather pointless debate between a pool comprising all citizens over 65 (working or retired) or just all those in work over 65. Both outcomes are wrong for including

118 [2006] ICR 785.

119 Employment Equality (Age) Regulations 2006, SI 2006/1031. See now EA 2010, ss 4 & 5.

120 The bar was lifted 1 October 2006: ibid Sch 8(1) para 25.

121 [2006] ICR 785 [82].

122 401 US 424 (US Sup Ct, 1971). See further p 153. Statistics revealed that 34 per cent of whites completed high school, in contrast to 12 per cent of blacks. Research showed that 58 per cent of whites, in contrast to 6 per cent of blacks, passed the intelligence tests used by Duke Power.

123 See e.g. Case C-167/97 *Seymour-Smith* [1999] ICR 447. In *Rutherford*, Lord Scott said: 'But where the provision in question does not constitute a condition for obtaining a benefit that some employees are able to satisfy and some are not but imposes a disadvantage on those who remain in employment after a specified age, the situation produced presents a rather different picture' ([2006] ICR 785 [15]). Cf *Price v Civil Service Commission (No. 2)* [1978] ICR 27, at p 178.

the challenged (age) factor, rendering the comparisons unable to assess that factor's impact. Disregard the age factor and the pool (crudely) is the nation's entire workforce.[124] Now a proper comparison can be made between the proportions of men and women who cannot meet the condition (to be under 65). In the event, as the minority found, *this* comparison did not show a significant enough difference to suggest that that section 109 adversely affected men.[125] The majority's approach compared only those in the disadvantaged group, with the inevitable result of no adverse impact. Indeed, the impact was *precisely* the same on men and women, a sure sign that their test might have been technically flawed.

This pool, along with Baroness Hale's advantaged/disadvantaged dictum, has led to confusion in three particular ways. It has produced a polarised debate, been honoured in name only, or used to support a fundamentally incorrect pool.

First, *Rutherford* has been taken by some to mean that the pool should be the narrowest possible, which has produced a counter-argument advocating the widest possible pool. This rather polarised debate arose in *British Medical Association v Chaudhary*.[126] Here, the challenged practice was the British Medical Association's (BMA) bar to financially supporting racial discrimination claims by its members against regulatory bodies. While the claimant argued for a pool comprising its total membership, the BMA asserted the other extreme, that it should comprise only those few members wanting to bring racial discrimination claims. The Court of Appeal, *obiter*,[127] applied *Rutherford* and agreed with the BMA. As everyone in that group was disadvantaged (as in *Rutherford*), the claim had to fail.

Some sense was restored in *Grundy v British Airways*,[128] where Sedley LJ in particular, neutralised this debate. He stated that the guiding principle is that provided by what is now EA 2010, section 23(1): *like should be compared with like*. Within this, 'the pool must be one which suitably tests the particular discrimination complained of'.[129] As such, it 'needs to include, but not be limited to, those affected by the term of which complaint is made, which can be expected to include both people who can and people who cannot comply with it'.[130] Note here, the pool need not comprise *only* those 'affected' (i.e. advantaged or disadvantaged) by the challenged factor. Using the old case of *Price v Civil Service Commission*,[131] he offered two extreme examples to defuse notion that either one or the other is correct. In *Price*, the employer stipulated an age limit of 17–27. This was challenged as adversely affecting women.[132] The employer argued for

124 Conceivably this could be refined with factors such as the (then) one-year qualification period for unfair dismissal and unemployed persons who wish to work. But this would make no difference to the outcome.

125 Lord Nicholls and Lord Walker affirming [2002] ICR 123 (EAT) and [2004] EWCA Civ 1186.

126 [2007] IRLR 800 (CA).

127 It was held that the finding of fact below that there was such a practice was perverse; ibid [165].

128 [2008] IRLR 74 (CA).

129 ibid [27].

130 ibid [33].

131 [1978] ICR 27 (EAT).

132 The case predated the dedicated age discrimination legislation.

a pool comprising the nation's entire workforce. Such a pool would 'empty the issue of reality', Sedley LJ observed. On the other extreme, a pool of only those over 27 'would have assumed the legitimacy of the very rule that was in issue'.[133] The correct pool (actually used in that case) was those men and women who were (otherwise) qualified for civil service employment. Accordingly, the correct pool for *British Medical Association v Chaudhary*, suggested Sedley LJ, was those members seeking support for legal claims.[134] This is indeed correct. The challenged factor in *Chaudhary* was 'claims for *racial* discrimination', and so it would be proper to include in the pool those seeking other claims, including other discrimination claims.

The whole court in *Grundy* considered that that the ratio of *Rutherford* was not clear.[135] If *Rutherford* were taken to provide a universal rule, Sedley LJ added, 'it is hard to see how indirect discrimination claims could ever succeed'.[136] These comments and the general guidance should, one would hope, effectively confine *Rutherford* to its own facts, the lawyers' euphemism for it being quietly forgotten.

But that is not to be. More recently, a differently constituted Court of Appeal showed *Rutherford* more deference. This is a second consequence of *Rutherford*. In *Somerset CC v Pike*,[137] teachers returning to work part-time could not make pension contributions, unlike their full-time counterparts. The claimant argued that this indirectly discriminated against women. The employment tribunal decided upon a pool comprising *all* teachers. Apparently applying *Rutherford*, the Court of Appeal reversed, as this was 'bringing into the equation people who have no interest in the advantage or disadvantage in question'.[138] The correct pool, according to the Court of Appeal, was those teachers returning to work. (This showed an adverse impact on women of the part-time factor, as the part-timers were predominantly female by comparison to the full-timers.) Although this is the correct pool, using the advantaged/disadvantaged dictum affords it credibility it does not merit. It worked here by the happenstance of the facts providing a tangible pool readily defined by the (non-challenged) factor of those teachers returning to work. (Of course, applying the actual *decision* in *Rutherford* would have provided a pool of only part-time returnees and a pointless and doomed comparison would follow.) Similarly, in *XC Trains v CD, ASLEF*,[139] the EAT gave an unnecessary nod to *Rutherford* in coming to the correct conclusion. Here it was held that an unsocial hours roster adversely affected women, using a pool of the whole workforce (17 women, 532 men) '[a]s in *Rutherford*', the EAT

133 [2008] IRLR 74 (CA) [32].

134 ibid [30].

135 ibid [23] (Sedley LJ), [43]–[46] (Carnwath LJ), [47] (Waller LJ). See also the similar unanimous opinion in *British Medical Association v Chaudhary* [2007] IRLR 800 (CA) [193], [200] (Mummery, Maurice Kay LJJ, Smith LJ).

136 ibid [27].

137 [2010] ICR 46 (CA). Maurice Kay, Lloyd LJJ, Sir Simon Tuckey.

138 ibid [18], citing *Rutherford (No. 2)* [2006] ICR 785 (HL) [82] (Baroness Hale).

139 UKEAT/0331/15/LA (EAT, 28 July 2016).

reasoned.[140] It gave no explanation as to why this pool resembled anything in *Rutherford*, and rejected the employer's pool[141] of just those who had requested (and been denied) different hours (four men, two women),[142] which would have been a '*Rutherford* pool': it was defined by the challenged factor (denials) and no one apart from these six were advantaged or disadvantaged by the denials. It was not clear whether this was tactful sidestep or a less than full understanding of *Rutherford*.

These cases may have produced satisfactory outcomes, but they left the meaning of *Rutherford* in even more confusion. All that can be said in their favour is that they managed to sidestep its neutralising effects. But that may be better than the third consequence of *Rutherford*, which is to produce fundamentally incorrect pools, with the inevitable result. This can occur either with Baroness Hale's advantaged/disadvantaged dictum or simply by using the challenged practice to dictate the composition of the pool.

An example of the first occurred in *Bailey v Brent Council*.[143] In a challenge to library closures, the Court of Appeal held that the pool should be confined to library users. The consequence of such a comparison was set out by the trial judge:

> In any event, since Asians are the largest ethnic group among the users of Brent libraries, it would be expected that they would be the most numerically disadvantaged. But the Asian users of the libraries were not proportionately more disadvantaged or indeed advantaged than non-Asians. 76% of Asian users and 76% of non-Asian users use the libraries that remain and 24% of Asian users and 24% of non-Asian users use the libraries that will close. Moreover . . . the percentage of users of all Brent libraries who were Asian and the percentage of users of the six to be closed who were Asian differed by 0.04.[144]

These figures, displaying a virtually equal impact, were received by the Court of Appeal without a degree of scepticism. All they tell us is that the impact upon Asians and non-Asians was evenly distributed geographically.[145] They measured the impact on library *users* across the borough, but failed to measure the impact on Asian residents of the borough, who relied on the libraries to a greater degree than non-Asians. Hence, the claimants advanced their case upon a different pool: '28% of the population of the Borough is Asian, 46% of the active borrowers from libraries are Asian. The corresponding figures for whites are 45% population, 29% active borrowers, and for blacks 20% population, 19% active borrowers.'[146]

140 ibid [60].
141 ibid [34].
142 See ibid [21]. Thus, the denials affected 11.6 per cent of the women and 0.75 per cent of the men.
143 [2011] EWCA Civ 1586.
144 ibid [36], citing [2011] EWHC 2572 (Admin) [17] (Ouseley J).
145 This is for the borough overall. The claimant showed *some* local disparities. ibid [28].
146 ibid [24].

A comparison using these figures showed a significant disproportionate impact of the closures on the Asian residents. But these figures were disregarded, using Baroness Hale's logic from *Rutherford* that the pool should not include 'people who have no interest in the advantage or disadvantage in question'.[147] Pill LJ (with whom the Court agreed)[148] bolstered this conclusion by quoting Sedley LJ from *Grundy*, to the effect that being a fact-sensitive exercise, tribunals had considerable discretion in selecting a pool. This selective citation overlooked the point of this part of Sedley's LJ speech, which was that *Rutherford* should *not* be applied as a universal rule otherwise 'it is hard to see how indirect discrimination claims could ever succeed'.[149] Of course, the claimant's figures suggest that no matter how the council went about closing its libraries, an adverse impact on Asians would be inevitable. But that is a matter for justification, not the prima facie case.

Perhaps the most pitiful use of *Rutherford* arose in *Hacking & Paterson v Wilson*.[150] In a case where requests for flexible working by property managers were universally denied, the Scottish EAT held the pool comprised only those who had actually requested flexible working, the rest of the workforce being neither advantaged nor disadvantaged by the practice.[151] So constructed, the pool merely demonstrated that 100 per cent of men and 100 per cent of women had their requests denied. The result was so inevitable that this case was actually an appeal by the employer to strike out the claim for want of any chance of success. But Lady Smith (sitting alone), while advocating this pool, somehow considered that the result was not inevitable. She reasoned thus:

> The fact that all of them did or would have received a negative response to a request for flexible working does not mean that all would have suffered what can properly be characterised as a disadvantage or that the disadvantage to them would necessarily have been the same.[152]

It is difficult to imagine a scenario where women in this pool could show that they suffered a particular disadvantage, that is one compared to the men (if any). It could occur perhaps where the women needed flexible work for childcare, whilst the men needed it to play golf. But even this might not pass muster under Lady Smith's guidance. She suggested that society had 'changed quite dramatically'[153] since 1984 and the case of *Home Office v Holmes*,[154] where, with the approval of the EAT, an industrial tribunal found 'unhesitatingly'[155] that a refusal of flexible

147 [2011] EWCA Civ 1586 [53] & [82] citing [2006] ICR 785, [82].
148 Richards LJ [87], Davies LJ [106].
149 [2008] IRLR 74 (CA) [27].
150 [2011] Eq LR 19 (EAT).
151 There were 16 property managers overall, 9 male, 7 female. ibid [4].
152 [2011] Eq LR 19 (EAT) [27].
153 ibid [28]
154 [1984] ICR 678 (EAT).
155 ibid, 74.

working would disadvantage women. Nowadays, reasoned Lady Smith, women *and* men request flexible working for childcare, 'or to combine jobs, pursue other interests or follow educational courses'.[156] Moreover, mothers may prefer part-time work out of 'choice rather than necessity', and so 'it is difficult to see that it would be correct to talk in terms of that employee being disadvantaged'.[157] Of course, the particular disadvantage here need not be one of the consequences of the denial, such as an inability to spend more time with one's children compared to an inability to play golf (or 'pursue other interests'). Such comparisons would import value judgments (possibly gender-loaded) and risk of bringing the courts into ridicule. The disadvantage would be quite simply the inability to work flexibly. As such, the result is inevitable. Whatever the flavour or relevance of the judge's social commentary, at the heart of this case is the technical error of defining the pool by the challenged practice.

Conclusion

The cases demonstrate that beyond the statutory 'material difference' rubric (EA 2010, s 23), tribunals and courts have to resort to their understanding of discrimination law and its technicalities more generally. After a largely sound start in the Court of Appeal and below, the House of Lords then displayed the least understanding, which, obvious to say, is most worrying. It is sad to report that *Rutherford* has not been quietly forgotten, or confined to its facts, but has created confusion and will be cited before any tribunal or court credulous enough to take it as a universal principle, as occurred in *Bailey* and *Wilson*. As well as showing a worrying lack of expertise, some of these faulty cases demonstrated a considerable indifference to the outcome, evoking once again a negativity towards matters of equality.

The Court of Appeal's *reason why* theory

Section 19(2)(b) of the Equality Act 2010 requires that the challenged practice 'puts' the claimant's group 'at a particular disadvantage', as well as putting the claimant at that disadvantage (s 19(2)(c)).[158] This causative element demands a connection between the challenged practice and the claimant's group. Where there are tangible challenged practices, causation is unlikely to be an issue. It goes without saying that, for instance, entrance exams,[159] last-in-first-out selection for redundancy,[160] or length-of-service benefits[161] will have a tangible impact

156 [2011] Eq LR 19 (EAT) [28].
157 ibid.
158 EA 2010, s 19 is set out on pp 174–175.
159 *Employment: Statutory Code of Practice* (2011, EHRC) para 4.11, < https://www.equalityhumanrights.com/en/publication-download/employment-statutory-code-practice > accessed 1 April 2018. See further below, p 184.
160 *Rolls Royce v Unite* [2010] ICR 1 (CA); *Clarke v Eley (IMI) Kynoch* [1983] ICR 165 (EAT).
161 *Wilson v Health and Safety Executive* [2010] ICR 302 (CA).

on those who respectively, fail the exam, are selected for redundancy, or who have shorter service. In such cases the issue will be whether that impact falls disproportionately upon a protected group (the 'particular disadvantage'), which in these concrete examples is a relatively straightforward task, as there are likely to be statistics available to assess any such impact.

All this was thrown up in the air for some 21 months by an ultimately doomed rewriting of indirect discrimination theory by the Court of Appeal in two cases, *Essop v Home Office*,[162] shortly followed by *Naeem v Secretary of State for Justice*.[163] In two convoluted judgments, the Court of Appeal launched its *reason why* theory, which, in essence, placed an extra and generally insurmountable burden on claimants to explain not only that they *were* disadvantaged by the challenged practice, but also to explain the *reason why*.

1 Essop v Home Office

The facts were straightforward. To be eligible for promotion, employees of the Home Office were required to pass a generic core skills test (CSA). In 2010, a report commissioned by the Home Office found that the pass rates for candidates who were black and ethnic minority (BME), and those who were older (i.e. those over 35), were significantly lower than for white, or younger, candidates respectively. This was confirmed by another report, finding that the selection rate for BME candidates was 40.3 per cent of the white candidate selection rate. For older candidates the rate was 37.4 per cent. In each there was a 0.1 per cent risk that this could happen by chance. Having failed the test, each claimant brought a case of indirect discrimination, either on race or age grounds.

Reversing the decision of the President of the EAT, Langstaff J, the Court of Appeal held that these facts alone (the tests combined with the statistics) were not enough to found a prima facie case under section 19(2)(b) or (c) (respectively group and individual disadvantage). It reasoned that the claimants had to show the reason why the group performed disproportionately poorly,[164] and then the reason why each individual failed the test.[165] In other words, there was a 'known unknown', and the claimants had to identify it to progress their case.

Paragraph (b) – the group 'particular disadvantage'

It will be recalled that the section 19(2)(b) requires that the challenged practice 'puts, or would put, persons with whom B shares the characteristic at a particular disadvantage when compared with persons with whom B does not share it'.

162 [2015] ICR 1063, reversed [2017] UKSC 27.

163 [2016] ICR 289 (CA) overruled on the prima facie case, but note that Supreme Court upheld the employment tribunal's finding that defendant had justified the challenged practice [2017] UKSC 27.

164 ibid [59].

165 ibid [62].

To satisfy paragraph (b), the argument came down to whether it was sufficient to prove the comparative success rates, or in addition, paragraph (b) required the reason behind those rates. The comparative success rates could be proved by statistics alone (combined with the tests). Case law of the CJEU, *Enderby v Frenchay Health Authority*,[166] suggests that statistics alone (in that case combined with a pay structure) can be enough to raise this inference. This explains the statutory Code of Practice:

> 4.11 In some situations, the link between the protected characteristic and the disadvantage might be obvious . . . In other situations it will be less obvious how people sharing a protected characteristic are put (or would be put) at a disadvantage, in which case statistics or personal testimony may help to demonstrate that a disadvantage exists . . .
>
> Example:
>
> A consultancy firm reviews the use of psychometric tests in their recruitment procedures and discovers that men tend to score lower than women. If a man complains that the test is indirectly discriminatory, he would not need to explain the reason for the lower scores or how the lower scores are connected to his sex to show that men have been put at a disadvantage; it is sufficient for him to rely on the statistical information.[167]

It also explains why Langstaff J held that section 19 'does not in terms require members of a disadvantaged group to show why they have suffered the disadvantage, in addition to the fact that they have done so'.[168] Speaking for a unanimous Court of Appeal,[169] Sir Colin Rimer disagreed, holding that this was a 'somewhat literal interpretation' overlooking 'that it is conceptually impossible to prove a group disadvantage . . . without also showing *why* the claimed disadvantage is said to arise'.[170] In this context, he observed: 'Many BME and older candidates did pass the test and there is no logical warrant for an assertion that any who did not pass failed it only because of the disadvantage to the group posed by the CSA.'[171]

There are a number of problems with this reasoning. First, Sir Colin Rimer speaks as if momentarily detached from the common law tradition of proof, which is centred on thresholds, such as an asserted fact being 'more likely than not', or 'beyond reasonable doubt', rather than any notion of 'absolute truth'. Hence, many a defendant has been found liable or convicted upon circumstantial evidence, from which inferences were drawn. It might be conceptually impossible

166 Case C-127/92 *Enderby v Frenchay Health Authority* [1994] ICR 112.

167 *Employment: Statutory Code of Practice* (2011, EHRC) para 4.11, < www.equalityhumanrights.com/publication/employment-statutory-code-practice > accessed 1 April 2018.

168 [2014] ICR 871 (EAT), [24].

169 Comprising Sir Terence Etherton, Lewison LJ, and Sir Colin Rimer.

170 [2015] ICR 1063, [59].

171 ibid [56].

to prove group disadvantage, but it is not *legally* impossible to infer it from the evidence. Aside from any common law tradition, Sir Colin Rimer ought to have heeded a recital in the Race Directive recognising that indirect discrimination could be established on the basis of statistical evidence.[172] Thus, implanting an additional element (and burden) into the definition of indirect discrimination with no consideration of the related rules of proof was a technical shortcoming that would deprive the provision of much of its efficacy.

Second, the Court of Appeal distinguished *Enderby* as a case centred on the meaning of the objective justification defence.[173] This is somewhat misleading. *Enderby* was a case of statistics showing a difference in pay between two occupations, one 63 per cent female (pharmacists), and the other 98 per cent female (speech therapists). The first question asked was whether the employer had the burden of proving that the difference was *not* the result of sex discrimination. This is exactly the point in *Essop*. In the answer to the question, the CJEU held:

> [W]here significant statistics disclose an appreciable difference in pay between two jobs of equal value, . . . Article 119 EEC[174] requires the employer to show that that difference is based on objectively justified factors unrelated to any discrimination on grounds of sex.[175]

Enderby could be distinguished as a case of equal pay, which has a particular framework of proof;[176] but it was a case of indirect discrimination, and shows that the CJEU readily will shift the burden to the employer to objectively justify a disparity apparent from statistics alone.

Third, Sir Colin Rimer's suggestion that the *reason why* is required because some in the claimants' groups passed the test misunderstands a fundamental (and technical) aspect of indirect discrimination law. It is not confined to group *exclusion*, but group *disadvantage*. Otherwise, paragraph (b) would require a 'particular *exclusion*'.[177]

Fourth, another basis of the *reason why* requirement was that as it should be asked for direct discrimination, it should be transposed into the group context of indirect discrimination:

> In indirect discrimination claims, there is also a necessary 'reason why' question but it is of a different nature. It does not go to the employer's motive or intention, whether conscious or unconscious. It is as to why the

172 A point made by Baroness Hale when reversing *Essop*: [2017] UKSC 27, [28]. See Directive 2000/43/EC, Recital 15. See also Framework Directive 2000/74/EC, Recital 15.

173 [2015] ICR 1063, [56].

174 Now Art 157 TFEU (ex 141 TEC).

175 Case C-127/92 *Enderby v Frenchay Health Authority* [1994] ICR 112 [19].

176 Although this did not prevent the Court of Appeal in *Naeem* from citing a body of equal-pay case law in support of the *reason why* theory. See further p 196.

177 See case comment, Tarunabh Khaitan, 'Indirect discrimination law: causation, explanation and coat-tailers' (2016) 132 LQR 35, 37.

> PCP [provision, criterion, or practice] disadvantages the group sharing the protected characteristic.[178]

Given that direct and indirect discrimination are said to be mutually exclusive definitions,[179] making parallels without support is a somewhat precarious undertaking, requiring very persuasive reasoning. The Court presented neither precedential nor other conceptual basis for this proposition. The obvious flaw is the starting point: the suggestion that direct discrimination requires a discriminatory motive or intent (conscious or unconscious), a notion persistently discredited by a number of House of Lords and Supreme Court pronouncements, as explained in Chapter 5. Thus, even the starting point for this notion is illusory.

Fifth, the only possible statutory word on which Sir Colin Rimer could hang the *reason why* theory (he did not try) was the adjective 'particular' attached to 'disadvantage', which appears rather redundant in an otherwise tightly drafted provision,[180] and so open to interpretation. In essence, the phrase 'particular disadvantage' replaced the statistically natured threshold 'considerably smaller', found in the original RRA 1976 and SDA 1975. This was in response to EU Directives, which had themselves evolved from 'substantially higher proportion'[181] to the current phrase. The change was explained by Baroness Hale in *Homer v Chief Constable of West Yorkshire*, as 'intended to do away with the need for statistical comparisons where no statistics might exist'.[182] It was not intended to make it more difficult to establish a prima facie case, 'quite the reverse'.[183] That makes a general (and valid) point, but it does not explain the inclusion of 'particular'. In a judgment post-dating *Essop* (in the Court of Appeal), the Court of Justice stated,

> [T]he concept of 'particular disadvantage' . . . does not refer to serious, obvious or particularly significant cases of inequality, but denotes that it is particularly persons of a given racial or ethnic origin who are at a disadvantage because of the provision, criterion or practice at issue.[184]

This, of course, was not available to the Court of Appeal at the time, but it accords generally with Baroness Hale's interpretation in *Homer* (which was available). It suggests that any disadvantage (such as a disproportionate failure rate) should relate to the particular group, and gives the word a purpose. This may not

178 [2015] ICR 1063, [58]–[59].

179 *R (E) v Governing Body of JFS* [2010] 2 AC 728 (SC) [57] (Baroness Hale).

180 Noted by Tarunabh Khaitan, 'Indirect discrimination law: causation, explanation and coat-tailers' (2016) 132 LQR 35, 38.

181 Burden of Proof Directive 97/80, art 2(1).

182 [2012] ICR 704 (SC) [14].

183 ibid.

184 Case C-83/14 *CHEZ Razpredelenie Bulgaria AD v Komisia za zashtita ot diskriminatsias* [2016] 1 CMLR 14 [109]. See further p 206.

be wholly convincing,[185] as none of this explains why the omission of the word 'particular' would cause problems. But at least it makes sense of the word, and is a lot more persuasive than the *reason why* theory.

Sixth, even if the word 'particular' did not suggest any ambiguity in the statutory definition, one might have thought the Court of Appeal would have looked outwards to some relevant jurisprudence before embarking upon an isolated new theory of indirect discrimination law. In addition to *Enderby*, the Court could have considered *R v Secretary of State for Employment, ex p Seymour-Smith* where the CJEU *and* the House of Lords held that an increase in the qualification period for unfair dismissal rights raised a prima facie case because it disproportionately affected women.[186] Note that in *Enderby*, *some* women were pharmacists and in *Seymour-Smith*, *some* women satisfied the longer qualification period, just as some BME and older workers passed the test in *Essop*.

Of course, a court concerned with pronouncing a theory of indirect discrimination would be remiss in omitting from its consideration the law's progenitor and subsequent case law from a jurisdiction heavily experienced in (class-action) discrimination cases based on statistics. In *Griggs v Duke Power*,[187] the evidence was that 58 per cent of white candidates, in contrast to 6 per cent of black candidates, passed the entrance exams. The US Supreme Court held that it was for the employer to justify its use of the tests. It *did not* hold that the claimants should show *why* black workers disproportionately failed the tests.[188]

The *Griggs* court had the benefit of the background racially disparate educational achievements of the state, a result of historical school segregation. *Griggs* also concerned entrance exams. But the principle persists without such background information, and for promotion exams, as seen in two further US cases. In *Bushey v New York State Civil Service Commission*,[189] a written examination was used for the post of Captain in state prisons. Two hundred and forty three whites and 32 non-whites took the test. One hundred and nineteen (49 per cent) of the whites and 8 (25 per cent) of the non-whites passed the test. Upon this, a prima facie case was made out. In *Bridgeport Guardians v City of Bridgeport*,[190] tests used in the promotion of police officers to the rank of sergeant were challenged, as 68 per cent of whites, 30 per cent of blacks, and 46 per cent of Hispanics, passed the test. Again, a prima facie case was made out. In none of these American cases were the plaintiffs required to demonstrate *why* the minority groups passed at lower rates.

185 For instance, if read narrowly in conjunction with s 19(2)(c) it could *exclude* claims such as *CHEZ* (ibid, and see p 206), as non-Roma had not suffered 'that' disadvantage.

186 Case C-167/97, [1999] ICR 447 [61]; [2000] 1 All ER 857 (HL) 870.

187 (1971) 401 US 424. See also n 2 and accompanying text.

188 Statistics showed disproportionate school completion rates (34 per cent white males/12 per cent black males) but again, these were in non-specific terms, taken for the whole of North Carolina in 1960. See also *Connecticut v Teal* 457 US 440 (Sup Ct, 1982), where a disproportionately low pass rate for blacks in written promotion tests was held sufficient for the prima facie case.

189 733 F 2d 220 (2nd Cir 1984) certiorari denied, 469 US 1117 (1985).

190 933 F 2d 1140 (2nd Cir 1991).

It would seem from *Griggs*, *Bushey*, and *Bridgeport Guardians*, an inference of causation was made from a simple finding of an adverse impact (despite some of the claimant's group passing the tests). What these American cases have in common is proof of (1) an employment recruitment/promotion practice, and (2) a disproportionate success rate for protected groups. Upon this, an inference of causation was assumed. None of these cases demand a *reason why* to establish a prima facie case. Indeed, that was the line taken in *Enderby*. As such, *Essop* is indistinguishable.

The same approach is taken under the European Convention on Human Rights (ECHR). In *DH v Czech Republic*,[191] primary-school children who performed poorly in intelligence tests were placed in a special school for those with learning disabilities. Statistics showed that in one district a Roma child was 27 times more likely to be placed in a special school. The bald result of this facially neutral policy was that over half of Roma and just 1.8 per cent of non-Roma children were placed in these special schools. The European Court of Human Rights (Strasbourg) cited a number of authorities including *Griggs*, and reasoned that 'to guarantee those concerned the effective protection of their rights, less strict evidential rules should apply in cases of alleged indirect discrimination'.[192] In a case of a protected group disproportionately failing tests, the Court accepted statistics as proof of a prima face case of indirect discrimination;[193] the *reason why* was not relevant to this. The similarity to *Essop* is striking. And, of course, it was irrelevant that *some* Roma children would have performed well in the tests. Although the Convention does not afford employment rights per se, the case contributes to the picture of the Court of Appeal being completely isolated in its understanding of indirect discrimination, a picture also including the House of Lords, the CJEU, the Code of Practice, and the antecedent American case law.

Seventh, instead of taking note of all this weighty opinion on the definition of indirect discrimination, Sir Colin Rimer selected a quote from *Homer v Chief Constable of West Yorkshire* in support of his *reason why* theory.[194] The quote requires context. In *Homer*, the challenged practice was a requirement to obtain a law degree, which adversely affected older workers approaching (compulsory) retirement age. As Baroness Hale described:

> Put simply, the reason for the disadvantage was that people in this age group did not have time to acquire a law degree. And the reason why they did not have time to acquire a law degree was that they were soon to reach the age of retirement.[195]

191 (App No. 57325/00) (2008) 47 EHRR 3.

192 ibid [186]. See also *Hoogendijk v Netherlands* (App No. 58641/00) (2005) 40 EHRR SE22 189, para 207; and *Adami v Malta* (App No. 17209/02) (2007) 44 EHRR 3, [77]–[78].

193 ibid [188].

194 [2015] ICR 1063, [60], citing [2012] ICR 704 (SC).

195 [2012] ICR 704 (SC) [17].

In that case, the reason was obvious (to quote the Code of Practice[196]). In *Essop*, and cases like it, the reason is not obvious. Ignoring Baroness Hale's more general observation – that the new formula was intended to make proof easier for claimants[197] – rendered this a selective quote, to say the least. Moreover, the distinction between obvious and not-obvious cases was under the nose of the Court of Appeal. In the EAT below, Langstaff J noted: 'The purpose of the provision – eliminating the adverse effects of "disguised" discrimination – is not advanced, but hindered, by requiring the additional proof.'[198]

Thus, Langstaff's J understanding of the facts and the statutory purpose gave him no reason to depart from the statutory wording. Given this and the alarming statistics, it is somewhat ironic for the Court of Appeal to demean Langstaff's J approach as 'somewhat literal'.

Paragraph (c) – individual 'particular disadvantage'

Section 19(2)(c) demands that the challenged practice also 'puts, or would put, B at that disadvantage'. On this point of ***individual*** disadvantage, the Court of Appeal was even more trenchant. Sir Colin Rimer said that as 'many BME and older candidates did pass the test' there was 'no logical warrant for an assertion' that those who failed did so because of the group disadvantage asserted under paragraph (b). He noted that paragraph (c) alludes to 'that' disadvantage in paragraph (b).[199] (Now it was the Court of Appeal's turn to attempt a literal approach.) Sir Colin Rimer is correct in that paragraph (c) is necessarily linked to the finding of group disadvantage under paragraph (b). The logical consequence is that the meaning accredited to paragraph (c) depends on the interpretation of paragraph (b). Nevertheless, the judge provided two arguments seemingly independent of paragraph (b) in support of the *reason why* theory. The first was precedent, and the second was possibility of *coat-tailers*.

PRECEDENT

First, Sir Colin Rimer considered that '[t]he present case is no different in principle from other types of indirect discrimination claim'.[200] In support he cited four cases where the *reason why* an individual was disadvantaged was (or was not) proven.[201] These were *Home Office v Holmes* (refusal of flexible working and childcare); *Homer* (mentioned previously); *McClintock v Department of Constitutional Affairs* (magistrates' obligation to place children with same-sex couples and 'Christian doubts'); and *Eweida v BA* (dress code and Christian

196 See p 184.
197 [2012] ICR 704 (SC) [14]. See p 186, text to n 182.
198 [2014] ICR 871 (EAT), [28].
199 [2015] ICR 1063, [62].
200 ibid [59].
201 ibid [60].

belief in displaying crucifix).[202] The problem with this rather selective list is that they belong to a type of case where the reason is, or would be, obvious. The latter two failed because of a failure to prove a 'known'.[203] Many cases brought on statistics involve an 'unknown' cause. Authority (*Enderby*, *Seymour-Smith* or indeed *Griggs, Bushey,* and *Bridgeport Guardians*) shows that it is not necessary to prove an individual *reason why*. At the root of this selective citation is the technical shortcoming of a failure to recognise the distinction between the 'obvious' and 'unknown' cases.

'COAT-TAILERS'

A principal trigger for the *reason why* theory for group disadvantage was that *some* of the claimant's group were successful, in the sense they fell into advantaged group. The obverse concern here (for individual disadvantage) is that some of the *un*successful candidates failed tests for reasons unconnected with race, or age, as the case may be (e.g. late attendance resulting in an incomplete test). As claimants, such candidates were dubbed 'coat-tailers', and became a personal predilection of Sir Colin Rimer, who asked: 'But why should a coat-tailer, *if* he can be identified as such, be entitled to succeed? He has, *ex hypothesi*, not satisfied the section 19(2)(c) requirement.'[204] The ideology here seems to be that the meritorious will always get a 'fair chance', which itself relies on a blind faith that employers, given the liberty of choice, will act prudently.

In more practical terms, Sir Colin Rimer's judgment here seems to envisage (to take an extreme example), a ne'er-do-well worker standing before court demanding compensation and a court order for promotion because he failed out of idleness a test that happens statistically to disadvantage people of his protected characteristic: a freeloader, or *coat-tailer*.

This overlooks several things. First, the coat-tailer argument was a purely hypothetical one, put by the employer,[205] yet the existence of one (or more) seemed to be the basis for this decision. This is rather odd in a particularly fact-sensitive part of the formula, and so should have played no part in the actual decision. Second, given the link between paragraphs (c) and (b), a consideration of the ramifications of the *coat-tailer* argument should have signalled that something was wrong with his interpretation of paragraph (b) and the *reason why* theory. Putting such an onus on each individual in the group would render such claims practically impossible, undermining the efficacy of the indirect discrimination provisions. It is one thing to isolate a non-discriminatory reason for failing, such as late

202 Respectively, [1984] ICR 678 (EAT); [2012] ICR 704 (SC); [2008] IRLR 29 (EAT); [2010] ICR 890 (CA) reversed, 57 EHRR 8 under ECHR, Art 9, alone. Only the claims in *Holmes* and *Homer* succeeded.

203 McClintock failed to show that religion had anything at all to do with his disadvantage, while Eweida failed to show group disadvantage.

204 ibid [37]. Emphasis original.

205 See e.g. [2014] ICR 871 (EAT) [29].

attendance. Aside from the absurd theory that BME and older candidates have a propensity for such self-inflicted failure, it is quite another to demand that each proves the *reason why* they failed. Depending on quite what the Court expects as proof, this could involve a huge amount of research beyond the reach of most claimants, encompassing, for instance, cultural, sociological, socio-economic, and educational factors. It could also produce a morass of absurd arguments. What, for instance, would be the evidential value of a (white or young) latecomer having *passed* the test? How would a claimant prove that he or she was diligent? Are there records of candidates' attendance times?

Moreover, the theory bears no consideration of the potential remedies (another technical flaw). One must consider what fear lay behind Sir Colin Rimer's demand to identify coat-tailers. Take the extreme example of a freeloader bringing a claim. The most likely outcome should the claim succeed (i.e. the Home Office fails to objectively justify the test) would be the adoption of a more refined test that better predicted job performance and had the minimal discriminatory impact.[206] Thus, the coat-tailer's only benefit would be the opportunity to sit a test that was better tailored to job performance. Now, the freeloader again fails, but this time the meritorious pass. An award of damages would be most unlikely as he or she could show no tangible or non-pecuniary loss *caused* by the flawed tests. Thus, even in an extreme case of coat-tailing, there are only beneficial effects with no unfair advantage to the freeloader.

Third, of course, the selective use of precedent overlooks that there could be 'coat-tailers' in many a statistical group that is held to have suffered an adverse impact, including *Enderby*, *Seymour-Smith*,[207] *Griggs*, *Bushey*, and *Bridgeport Guardians*. In none of those cases was it suggested that the claimants had to prove that they were *not* coat-tailers. This is another consequence of the technical error[208] of supposing that the principal mischief of indirect discrimination law is group *exclusion*.

Thus, while it is true that paragraph (c) is somewhat dependent on paragraph (b), that itself is reliant on a correct application of paragraph (b). The ramifications of Sir Colin Rimer's interpretation of paragraph (c), and the relevant precedents, ought to have alerted him that his view of paragraph (b) was wrong. None of this is to say that paragraph (c) is otiose: individual disadvantage still depends on a finding of group disadvantage. Further, paragraph (c) serves the purpose of its predecessors[209] of excluding those with no interest at all in the case.

206 This is a remedy available to a tribunal. EA 2010, s 124(3): a tribunal may make 'a recommendation that within a specified period the respondent takes specified steps for the purpose of obviating or reducing the adverse effect on the complainant of *any matter to which the proceedings relate*'. (Emphasis supplied.) (As amended, Deregulation Act 2015, s 2(1)(a), in force 1 October, 2015.)

207 In *Enderby*, for instance, some may have failed their pharmacy exams. In *Seymour-Smith*, some may have been feckless or idle workers who could not hold down a job.

208 See 'Paragraph (b) – the group 'particular disadvantage', p 183.

209 See SDA 1975, s 1(1)(b)(iii); RRA 1976, s 1(1)(b)(iii), and HC Deb 18 June 1975, vol 893 col 1491–1492.

Mixed messages

Despite the general tenor of a conservative judgment, Sir Colin Rimer's speech included some mixed messages. At one point, he suggested that placing 'too high a burden' on the claimants would result in the continuation of unlawful discrimination: 'a social evil which must be stopped'.[210] Elsewhere though, he suggested that Langstaff's J decision gave the claimants 'an automatic ride to victory' (subject to objective justification).[211] Then, in a rather strange twist at the end of the judgment, Sir Colin Rimer wrote: 'I would accept that a statistical report . . . is in principle capable of being relied on by the claimants to prove the group disadvantage caused by the PCP.'[212] He repeated this for individual disadvantage.[213] At this point, it is worth noting section 136(2) and the claimant's evidential burden: 'If there are facts from which the court *could* decide, in the *absence of any other explanation*', it '*must* hold that the contravention occurred' (emphasis supplied). In the unlikely scenario it could be read to do so, this makes clear that the legislation does not permit a court to offer an optional range of evidential standards and burdens. The case was remitted to an employment tribunal to decide. One is left wondering quite what the statistics can show the second time around that they failed to show before this Court of Appeal. Of course, the Supreme Court's reversal saved the tribunal (and many others no doubt) from the torturous task of interpreting and applying this judgment.

Summary

With the startling test results and resulting workplace stratification, and a fixed pool for comparison, this archetypal scenario presented yet another easy case to decide. If the Court of Appeal was unsure of this, there was to hand plenty of consistent House of Lords/Supreme Court, CJEU, Strasbourg, and antecedent American case law for guidance, all reflected in the Code of Practice. But rather than absorb this jurisprudence, it quoted selectively and designed its own isolated definition of indirect discrimination law. The Act's stated ambition 'to increase equality of opportunity' (Long Title) and 'strengthen the law to support progress on equality' (Explanatory Note 10) found no place in this judgment, nor its thinking. Instead, the Court read words into the statute that had no place, conceptually, purposively, and certainly not literally. The judgment made technical errors regarding the standard of proof, group exclusion, obvious and 'unknown' causes, and the remedial consequences for the coat-tailer. If this were not enough, the decision was also unhelpfully ambivalent on the evidential burdens. Rather like *Perera* three decades earlier, it was merely a narrow, isolated, and ultimately doomed interpretation.

210 [2015] ICR 1063, [34].
211 ibid [35].
212 ibid [63].
213 ibid [63]–[65].

The Court of Appeal's unreceptive attitude to the claim was perhaps summed up by its preoccupation with the hypothetical coat-tailers. Given the workforce profile, the test results, and a Home Office in denial, it was ironic, of course, that the Court made no mention of the more likely coat-tailers, who would be those white or younger workers over-promoted on the back of a seemingly flawed test.

2 *Naeem v Secretary of State for Justice*[214]

Just a few months after its decision in *Essop*, the Court of Appeal built on its *reason why* theory to take the law even further away from its purpose, origins, and statutory wording; and in doing so erected another barrier to claimants. Apparently, it was not enough to ***know*** the reason why; that reason had to be 'inherently' discriminatory. Once again, this left the law in a state of confusion until eventually overruled by the Supreme Court, some 15 months later.[215]

The case is also notable for its (mis)use of precedent as an aid to statutory interpretation in place of the standard tools of literal reading and statutory purpose. The panel included one judge from *Essop*, Lewison LJ. He was accompanied by the Master of Rolls, Lord Dyson, and Underhill LJ (who wrote the leading judgment).

In *Naeem*, Muslim prison chaplains were paid less than Christian ones. There were two standout reasons for this: first, a length-of-service pay criterion; and second, no Muslim chaplains were employed before 2002, there being no need, it seemed. Hence, Muslim chaplains tended to have a shorter length of service and registered lower on the pay scale.[216] Upon these bare facts, a Muslim chaplain made a claim of indirect (religious) discrimination, defined, of course, by section 19 of the Equality Act 2010. This case differed from *Essop* because the cause of the disadvantage was 'obvious': it could be traced precisely to the pay criterion, the challenged practice.

The case up to the Court of Appeal

The employment tribunal, the EAT, and Court of Appeal each rejected his claim, albeit for different reasons. At first instance, the tribunal adopted the counsel's submission that 'the claimant need not show *why* the PCP put him at a disadvantage, but *whether* it does'.[217] Thus, the bare facts were enough to establish the prima facie case. But the claim failed because the tribunal found the disparity was objectively justified. In the EAT and the Court of Appeal, the case fell at the prima facie stage, but for different reasons. For the EAT, the case foundered on the

214 [2016] ICR 289 (CA).

215 [2017] UKSC 27. But note that Supreme Court upheld the employment tribunal's finding that defendant had justified the challenged practice.

216 As at 1 April 2011 the average basic pay for Muslim chaplains was £31,847 whereas for Christian chaplains it was £33,811. The average length of service of Muslim and Christian chaplains was 5.76 and 9.43 years respectively. See [2016] ICR 289 (CA) [5].

217 Cited [2016] ICR 289 [31].

comparison. A 'like-for-like' comparison could not include chaplains employed before 2002, as that would be a 'material difference' between the groups.[218] The Court of Appeal found that this 'was not the best route to the right result'.[219] For Underhill LJ, the case centred on another element of indirect discrimination, the *cause* of the disparity, or in the words of section 19(2), whether the criterion 'puts' the claimant and his group at a particular disadvantage. And for this, Underhill LJ presented a two-pronged 'inherent' theory, which is not easy to follow. First, the cause must be 'the legally relevant' one, and second, claimant's group should be already disadvantaged by social circumstances.

In a short concurring judgment, Lewison LJ came to the same result via the Act's burden of proof provisions. It will be recalled that Equality Act 2010, section 136(2) provides: 'If there are facts from which the court could decide, in the absence of any other explanation, that a person (A) contravened the provision concerned, the court must hold that the contravention occurred.' Subsection (3) states that this does not apply if 'if A shows that A did not contravene the provision'. Relying on Sir Colin Rimer's speech in *Essop*, Lewison LJ held that this meant that once the claimant had presented the statistical disparity, 'section 136 then shifts the burden to the employer to prove that the "reason why" was not the impugned PCP'.[220]

Burdens of proof and section 136

It is better to address Lewison's LJ reasoning first, as this can remove one complication from the central 'causation', or *reason why*, issue of the case. The effect of his statement is twofold. First, that the defendant can play a role in the establishment (or not) of the prima facie case. This is a normal process of civil litigation and uncontroversial. For instance, the defendant may produce evidence discrediting the claimant's statistical model.[221] Second, more worryingly, given his agreement with Underhill's LJ reasoning,[222] Lewison's LJ statement implies that section 136 permits the defendant to destroy the prima facie case by producing *a* non-discriminatory cause of the disparity.

The second effect takes the evidential rules into matters of substantive law. This is not itself controversial, especially in the context of indirect discrimination, where section 19 and its progenitor, *Griggs v Duke Power*, integrate law and proof by making it clear that once the claimant has proven the prima facie case, the burden shifts to the defendant to justify the disparity.[223] But the difficulty with Lewison's LJ reasoning is that it assumes that a rule of evidence dictates the

218 See [2014] ICR 472 (EAT) [15]–[31].
219 [2016] ICR 289 [33].
220 ibid [38].
221 See e.g. *Jones v University of Manchester* [1993] ICR 474 (CA), above, p 176.
222 [2016] ICR 289 [39].
223 See now EA 2010, s 19 (see p 224); *Griggs v Duke Power* (1971) 401 US 424. See n 2 and accompanying text.

substantive law; the tail is wagging the dog. Given that section 19 itself provides for the shifting burden, section 136 plays only a complementary role, at best. Its predecessors were introduced by European law[224] and applicable to both direct *and* indirect discrimination, but only because the accompanying definition of indirect discrimination did not allocate burdens.[225] It was not surprising then, that in the UK its principal impact was made on direct discrimination, producing an elaborate and lengthy body of case law.[226] There was no concern at the time that indirect discrimination had any issues with shifting burdens, as this was integrated into the formula from the earliest days of the Sex Discrimination Act 1975.[227] Moreover, the burden of proof rules were introduced (by the EU) to make it *easier* to prove a case.[228] Thus, section 136 can do little to affect section 19 apart from reinforce it. It cannot be used to hold that section 19 permits the defendant to destroy the prima facie case established on significant statistics by pointing to *a* non-discriminatory *cause* or alternative *reason why*. That removes one pillar of the *Naeem* judgment and its requirement for the discriminatory *reason why*. The matter of shifting burdens per se is considered further here, after a consideration of Underhill's LJ cited authorities. The first taken here is *Essop*, followed by a tranche of equal pay cases.

The relevance of Essop v Home Office

Given that his 'inherent' theory was rooted in the *reason why*, it is no surprise that Underhill LJ cited *Essop* in support. At first sight, this might seem rather strange. The Court of Appeal in *Essop* wanted to know the precise cause of the disparity, the *reason why*. One might suppose in a case where the precise reason *was* known, such as the length-of-service criterion, *Essop* would have no application. But for Underhill LJ, *Essop* established that 'it is permissible to consider the reason for the disparity complained of, in the sense of the factors which caused it to occur';[229] this

224 Starting with the Burden of Proof Directive 97/80/EC.

225 ibid, art 2(2): '[I]ndirect discrimination shall exist where an apparently neutral provision, criterion or practice disadvantages a substantially higher proportion of the members of one sex unless that provision, criterion or practice is appropriate and necessary and can be justified by objective factors unrelated to sex.'

226 See e.g. *Igen (formerly Leeds Careers Guidance) v Wong* [2005] ICR 931 (CA) [annex to the judgment]; *Madarassy v Nomura* [2007] ICR 867 (CA); *Appiah v Governing Body of Bishop Douglass Roman Catholic High School* [2007] ICR 897 (CA); *Brown v Croydon LB* [2007] ICR 909 (CA).

227 See e.g. SDA 1975, s 1(1)(b) set out at p 155. For a rare, if only, example of the statutory rubric on the burden of proof being applied in a case of indirect discrimination, see *Bethnal Green and Shoreditch Education Trust v Dippenaar* (21 October 2015), a case post-dating *Essop*.

228 E.g. Burden of Proof Directive 97/80/EC, art 1: 'The aim of this Directive shall be to ensure that the measures taken by the Member States to implement the principle of equal treatment are made more effective, in order to enable all persons who consider themselves wronged because the principle of equal treatment has not been applied to them to have their rights asserted by judicial process after possible recourse to other competent bodies.'

229 [2016] ICR 289 (CA) [30].

tallied with section 19's requirement that the challenged practice 'puts' the claimant's group at a disadvantage: 'The concept of "putting" persons at a disadvantage is causal, and, as in any legal analysis of causation, it is necessary to distinguish the legally relevant cause or causes from other factors in the situation.'[230] Thus, it was open to the employer 'to go behind the bare fact that Muslim and Christian chaplains have different lengths of service and seek to establish the reason why that was so'.[231] Upon this logic, Underhill LJ concluded: 'In my view the only material cause of the disparity in remuneration relied on by the claimant is the (on average) more recent start-dates of the Muslim chaplains.'[232]

Note that, for Underhill LJ, this was the '*only* material cause of the disparity'.[233] It had nothing to do with the length-of-service criterion. This is rather perplexing. It brazenly re-writes the claimant's pleadings and, as such, fails to address the actual claim. It also carries problems of substantive law. First, and most obviously, it overcomplicates the straightforward statutory requirement that the challenged practice 'puts' the claimant's group at a disadvantage. As noted above in the review of *Essop*,[234] there is nothing in the statute, nor the jurisprudence, suggesting the incorporation of the *reason why* theory. Second, although at times it refers to 'causes' (plural), Underhill's LJ judgment gravitates to a single cause. Not only is it unrealistic to suppose that all events have a single cause, it is paradoxical, given that the 'inherent' theory also demands discriminatory social circumstances (discussed later), which can only be an additional contributory, or 'causal' factor to the disadvantage.

This being a case of 'obvious' indirect discrimination, there was no requirement to follow *Essop*. Yet the Court of Appeal chose, without any reluctance, to build upon its already flawed logic, with a predictable result.

The equal pay precedents

The bulk of authority for Underhill's LJ judgment was drawn from the law of equal pay. There is, of course, an obvious parallel with this case, being a discriminatory pay case. But that was not the apparent reason for invoking this body of law, nor the focus Underhill's LJ particular citations, which can be understood to serve three purposes. The first pair of cases (*Cadman* and *Wilson*) was used in support of the 'social circumstances' prong of the 'inherent' theory. The second (*Marshall* and *Wallace*), was used to show that there was no onus of objective justification where the disparity arose otherwise than by discrimination. The third batch of cases (the '*Armstrong* line') was used to show that this '*Marshall* defence' applied to indirect discrimination. These were not perhaps set out in

230 ibid [22].
231 ibid.
232 ibid.
233 Emphasis supplied.
234 See p 182 et al; see also below, p 206.

the most comprehensible order, with the '*Marshall* defence' presumably cited in support of the 'legally relevant cause', the 'first-prong' of the inherent theory.

CADMAN AND *WILSON*

These related cases each challenged different increments of the same employer's pay scales. They bore the closest resemblance to *Naeem*, as the challenged factor was a length-of-service pay criterion. The cases were *Wilson v Health and Safety Executive*[235] and its forerunner, *Cadman v Health and Safety Executive*,[236] and cited principally in support of the Underhill's LJ 'inherent' theory, and the particular meaning he attached to it; this was that a prima facie case required that the claimant's group was already disadvantaged by discriminatory social circumstances.

The first point to make here is that these cases centred on the precise requirements of the objective justification test. The prima facie case was never at issue. The closest anything in the judgments came to this matter was when the Court of Appeal noted in *Wilson* that 'it is common ground that women are often disadvantaged by the use of such a criterion in pay schemes'.[237] That followed a similar line expressed in *Cadman*, by Judge Burke QC, speaking for the EAT:

> It was . . . common ground before the tribunal that the factor which created the differentials complained of . . . i.e. length of service, had a disproportionate impact as between male and female band 2 employees and was, therefore, indirectly discriminatory. This feature occurred because, overall, women in band 2 had shorter service than men. Whether it arose because women joined the service of the employers later, took career breaks or were promoted later, or a combination of those factors, does not matter; the fact of disproportionate impact was not in dispute.[238]

Notable here is the *presumption* that the challenged factor (the pay scales) caused a (gender) disparity. One might think that this supports Naeem's case. But for Underhill LJ, the precedential value of these cases was in the facts presumed to fulfil the prima facie case; these facts were distinguishable because a length-of-service criterion 'had an inherent tendency to put women at a disadvantage because women are liable to start their careers later than men and/or to take career breaks because of family and childcare responsibilities'.[239] It would have been different, the judge opined, that as a result of a change in social attitudes the proportion of women recruited in recent years increased. 'Indeed,' he noted, 'if it were otherwise an employer who made positive efforts to increase the diversity

235 [2010] ICR 302 (CA).
236 [2004] ICR 378 (EAT); [2006] ICR 1546 (CA); Case C-17/05, [2006] ICR 1623.
237 [2010] ICR 302 [35]. See also [2]. (Arden LJ, giving a unanimous judgment.)
238 [2004] ICR 378 [31]. See also [2006] ICR 1546 (CA) [2] (Maurice Kay LJ).
239 [2016] ICR 289 [24].

of his workforce . . . would be making a rod for his own back, at least if length of service were a criterion in his pay system'.[240] Thus, for liability under this 'inherent' theory, there must be some pre-existing social circumstance that is itself (inherently) discriminatory. This theory can be further explored with some similar projections of a change of circumstances. Numerous examples could be made, but three will suffice.

In the first scenario, an employer had on his books 100 machine fitters, all doing equal work. There were 20 women and 80 men, and 5 (25 per cent) of the women and 60 (75 per cent) of the men were at the top of the pay scale, which was based entirely on length of service. Now suppose, as Underhill LJ envisaged, the ratio changes, so that in time, there were 50 women and 50 men, and that 10 women and 25 men were at the top of the scale.[241] Now, 20 per cent of the women and 50 per cent of the men are at the top of the scale. The difference may have closed (from 50 to 30 points), but there remains a significant pay gap. For Underhill LJ, these women would no longer have a prima facie case, because the pay scale no longer has an 'inherent tendency' to put women at a disadvantage. Instead, as with *Naeem*, the cause is the 'more recent start-dates'.[242] Such a conclusion may surprise some, not least, Judge Burke QC who noted that the cause could well be late recruitment, but 'the fact of disproportionate impact' is what mattered. Moreover, the disparity has roots in historical sex discrimination[243] and/or 'social attitudes'. Without this, the preponderance of more recent (lower-paid) recruits would not be female. Thus, this employer would be 'making a rod for his own back' not by recruiting more women, but only if he persisted with a pay scale that was not objectively justifiable.

Underhill's LJ theory is more exposed if applied to an equal *value* scenario. Suppose a car factory where seamstresses (predominantly female) are paid less than fitters (predominantly male). Both jobs are of equal value. Presumably, at one time in the past, the theory would label the policy 'inherently' discriminatory because sewing was considered a 'mere' domestic routine chore of housewives. In modern times, girls are not taught sewing, and women are not expected to mend the clothes. The discriminatory social attitudes have subsided, and because of this the pay gap is now untouchable by equal pay law, because the pay policy is no longer 'inherently' discriminatory.

Those two scenarios are distinguishable from Underhill's LJ example because *historical* discriminatory social circumstances may have been a cause of the current

240 ibid [24] and n 9 (in the judgment). A similar point was made by Elias J in *Middlesbrough BC v Surtees (No. 1)* [2007] ICR 1644 (EAT) [54] (reversed on other grounds: [2000] ICR 133 (CA)) although speculatively made in a search for a justifiable example after explaining it would be difficult for employers to justify any disparity. The example was cited by Smith LJ in *Gibson v Sheffield CC* [2010] ICR 708 (CA).

241 The women's position has not improved because most are newly hired. The men's position has worsened because mainly older workers retired/resigned.

242 [2016] ICR 289 (CA) [22]. See p 196, text to n 232.

243 This might have been a better distinction from *Naeem*, where no historical discrimination was found. See [2016] ICR 289 [9] and n 7 (in the judgment).

disparities.[244] But should that matter? The third projection involves indirect discrimination, but this time, in recruitment, and without any contemporary or historical discriminatory social circumstances. This represents in some senses an obverse scenario, where seemingly innocent practices remain benign for years or even decades until social circumstances change. Suppose at some time in the past a local authority decided that recruits should have resided locally for five years, in an attempt to create greater empathy with the public (although there is no evidential basis behind this). The requirement was benign because there were no immigrants in the area.[245] Decades later, a wave of Bangladeshi immigration changes the racial profile of the area, and the local authority's formerly benign recruitment policy puts these immigrants at a disadvantage. As Underhill's LJ *reason why* theory would have it, the cause is not the council's policy, but the 'more recent arrival-dates' of the recent immigrants. Such an approach would leave the equality legislation impotent whilst for years to come an all-white local authority presided over its mixed-race residents. Yet according the Underhill's LJ reasoning, there is no prima facie case of indirect discrimination to justify because the length-of-residence criterion is not 'inherently' discriminatory. In this sense, this example and *Naeem* are on all fours, in that both the social circumstances were benign.

These three projections of Underhill's LJ 'inherent' theory suggest that his interpretation would leave equality law inadequate to address all but a few select classes of cases. At the least, the application of the theory in the first two scenarios would be a blatant dissent from the avowed statutory purpose of closing the gender pay gap.[246] This alone should have alerted him that his interpretation of *Wilson* and *Cadman* was erroneous and that this theory was flawed. But none of this occurred to the Court, as Underhill LJ continued with his selective citation of equal pay cases.

MARSHALL AND *WALLACE*

The second body of equal pay case law relied on in *Naeem* centred on two 'fair pay' cases and the succeeding judicial commentary. Here, it is said, where there is no sex discrimination, the employer no need to be put to the trouble of proving objective justification. The two 'fair pay' cases were *Strathclyde Regional Council v Wallace*[247] and *Glasgow CC v Marshall*.[248] Underhill LJ cited a well-known speech of Lord Browne-Wilkinson from *Wallace*:

244 This assumes, generously, that there were no lingering effects in Underhill's LJ example.

245 More likely to be new to the district. See e.g. *Meer v London Borough of Tower Hamlets* [1988] IRLR 399 (CA) 'experience in the Tower Hamlets area'. The claim failed because the criterion – expressed as a 'mere preference' – was held not to be actionable under the old definition of indirect discrimination. See p 154 et al.

246 See e.g. Government Equalities Office 'Closing the gender pay gap.' Government consultation and response (February 2016) 43 ('diversity and equality'), < https://www.gov.uk/government/consultations/closing-the-gender-pay-gap > accessed 11 April 2018.

247 [1998] ICR 205 (HL).

248 [2000] ICR 196 (HL).

> [T]he only circumstances in which questions of 'justification' can arise are those in which the employer is relying on a factor which is sexually discriminatory. There is no question of the employer having to 'justify' . . . all disparities of pay. Provided that there is no element of sexual discrimination, the employer establishes a . . . defence by identifying the factors which he alleges have caused the disparity, proving that those factors are genuine and proving further that they were causally relevant to the disparity in pay complained of.[249]

In line with this, Underhill LJ also cited Lord Nicholls from *Marshall*: 'if the employer proves the absence of sex discrimination he is not obliged to justify the pay disparity'.[250] These quotes are intended to demonstrate that Naeem's employer can defeat his prima facie case by pointing to a non-discriminatory cause of the pay disparity, presumably, the more recent recruitment. On the face of these extracts, this appears correct. But put into context, they tell a somewhat different story and provide a more limited authority.

In *Marshall* the claim was by special-school instructors who, for less pay, were doing work equal to that of the teachers. Seven female instructors compared themselves with a male teacher. At the same time, a *male* instructor compared himself with a female teacher. However, there was no sex disparity between the two groups (females made up about 96 per cent instructors and 97 per cent teachers).[251] This was a 'fair pay' claim, and not one for (sex) discrimination law to address.[252]

Wallace is less clear. Here, a national pay structure recognised the post of a principal teacher. However, various national policies stymied the ability of local authorities to promote teachers to this post. As a result, many unpromoted teachers, out of a sense of duty,[253] were doing the work of principal teachers, but, of course, on less pay. These teachers brought equal pay claims, each identifying a male principal teacher as a comparator. The claim eventually failed in the House of Lords, the reasoning provided by the single speech of Lord Browne-Wilkinson:

> The disparity in pay between the (female) claimants and principal teachers has nothing to do with gender. Of the 134 unpromoted teachers who claimed to be carrying out the duties of principal teachers, 81 were men and 53 women. The selection by the appellants in this case of male principal teachers as comparators was purely the result of a tactical selection by these appellants: there are male and female principal teachers employed by the respondents without discrimination. Therefore the objective sought by the appellants is to achieve

249 [1998] ICR 205 (HL) 213.
250 [2000] ICR 196 (HL) 203.
251 A separate argument comparing instructors and teachers from *all* schools was not taken up for being introduced too late.
252 See [2000] ICR 196, 203.
253 [1998] ICR 205 (HL) 263.

> equal pay for like work regardless of sex, not to eliminate any inequalities due to sex discrimination.[254]

It appeared as if the claimant women had hand-picked male comparators without showing any sex discrimination. The difficulty with the case is that no full statistics were reported. With respect to Underhill LJ, these cases cannot be said to support a *reason why* theory of any sort for indirect discrimination. In the context of the equal pay legislative regime at the time,[255] where the definitions of direct and indirect discrimination were not explicit, the cases held that a single-comparator, or 'direct discrimination', claim can be defeated by showing that the lower pay was not because of sex. The evidence for this was the group statistics. The claims were not expressed as indirect discrimination. If they had been, they would have failed in *Marshall* for want of a disparity and in *Wallace* for the want of complete statistics.[256] *Marshall* and *Wallace* were effectively (failed) cases of direct discrimination; all they can demonstrate for the purposes of indirect discrimination is that there must be a gender disparity, a somewhat obvious proposition. Nonetheless, broader propositions have been drawn from these cases and Underhill LJ was keen to exploit them. He characterised them as the '*Armstrong* line of cases'.[257]

THE '*ARMSTRONG* LINE OF CASES'

Underhill LJ began with *Armstrong v Newcastle upon Tyne NHS Hospital Trust.*[258] Here, Buxton LJ said:

> Once disparate adverse impact has been established, the burden passes to the employer in respect of two issues. First, that the difference between the man's and the woman's contract is not discriminatory, in the sense of being attributable to a difference of gender. Second, if the employer cannot show that the difference in treatment was not attributable to a difference of gender he must then demonstrate that there was nonetheless an objective justification for the difference.[259]

254 ibid, 263.

255 Equal Pay Act 1970. The concept of indirect discrimination was provided first in Britain by the SDA 1975, s 1(1)(b).

256 Lord Browne-Wilkinson noted that the majority of the claimants' group (unpromoted teachers) were men. For a claim of indirect discrimination, this was a superfluous observation in the absence of information about the comparators' group. It may well have been that the comparators' group (of principal teachers) contained an even higher proportion of men. In Case C-127/92 *Enderby v Frenchay Health Authority* [1994] ICR 112 (see p 185), even though the comparator group (pharmacists) was 63 per cent *female*, the claimants group (speech therapists) was 98 per cent female.

257 [2016] ICR 289 [28].

258 [2006] IRLR 124.

259 ibid [110]. See also [32]–[33] (Arden LJ).

The introduction ('disparate adverse impact') suggests, of course, that the '*Marshall* defence' applied to indirect discrimination as well. But the phrase 'attributable to a difference in gender' is key here, and rather ambiguous. It could be doing no more than permitting the employer to produce evidence undermining the claimant's statistical model,[260] showing that, in fact, there is no (gender) disparity. This is the narrow view. As noted previously, this is a normal process of civil litigation and uncontroversial. As the CJEU stated in *Enderby v Frenchay Health Authority*:

> It is for the national court to assess whether it may take into account those statistics, that is to say, whether they cover enough individuals, whether they illustrate purely fortuitous or short-term phenomena, and whether, in general, they appear to be significant.[261]

That, of course, concerns the *effect* of the challenged practice, on the one hand. On the other hand, the phrase 'attributable to a difference in gender' may be permitting employers to point to a non-discriminatory *cause* of the (gender) disparity (the wide view),[262] thus destroying the prima facie case. At the centre of the debate are equal pay claims based solely on statistics showing, say, one occupation (predominantly female) being paid less than another (predominantly or exclusively male), where the jobs are of equal value. Here, the employer points to an 'innocent' cause of the disparity, and is then freed from having to objectively justify it. Such a case arose in *Enderby*,[263] where the employer paid pharmacists (63 per cent female) 40 per cent more than speech therapists (98 per cent female). An industrial tribunal found that the respective collective bargaining agreements that had led to the different pay structures for these occupations were in no way sex-tainted and rejected the claim.[264] However, the CJEU held that the statistics alone were enough to oblige the employer to objectively justify the disparity; the 'innocent' cause was a matter for objective justification.[265] The wide view of *Armstrong* holds that such an employer would not now have to justify such a disparity. As such, *Armstrong* must be wrong. *Enderby* demonstrates that indirect discrimination, for equal pay at least, is concerned with *effect* rather than cause. Underhill LJ did not discuss *Enderby*, only noting that, elsewhere, the EAT had found *Armstrong* and *Enderby* consistent.[266]

260 See e.g. *Jones v University of Manchester* [1993] ICR 474 (CA). See p 176.
261 Case C-127/92, [1994] ICR 112 [17].
262 See generally, I Steele, 'Sex discrimination and the material factor defence under the Equal Pay Act 1970 and the Equality Act 2010' (2010) 39 ILJ 264.
263 Case C-127/92, [1994] ICR 112.
264 Paras 10.1–10.5, reported [1991] EAT 382 (EAT) 396.
265 It was held that the collective agreements, although taken in isolation were not sex-tainted, could not be relied upon for justification: Case C-127/92, [1994] ICR 112 [22].
266 Citing *Middlesbrough BC v Surtees (No. 1)* [2007] ICR 1644 (EAT) [24]–[55] (Elias J, recanting, at [46], on his contrary opinion in *Villalba v Merrill Lynch* [2007] ICR 469 (EAT) [131]). In *Newcastle upon Tyne NHS Hospitals Trust v Armstrong (No. 2)* [2010] ICR 674 (EAT) [71] Underhill J did discuss *Enderby* and boldly asserted: 'Even judgments of the European Court of Justice are not to be read like sacred texts; and, as with many cases that break new ground, the precise definition of what was decided in *Enderby* will need exploration as the case law develops.'

Instead, Underhill LJ cited further dicta[267] apparently in support of the wide view, culminating with the Court of Appeal case of *Gibson v Sheffield CC*,[268] where he asserted 'the point was put beyond doubt'.[269] Again, this is drawing a conclusion that is unsupported by the case's facts, result, and dicta of the judges. Of the three judges, only Maurice Kay LJ fully endorsed *Armstrong*.[270] Pill LJ dissented on the point,[271] while Smith LJ offered only a limited approval.

Smith LJ concluded that *Armstrong* was correct, as far as it meant that 'it is always open to an employer . . . to demonstrate that the particular disadvantage apparently demonstrated is nothing to do with gender'.[272] Further, 'it is important that tribunals examine such a contention with great care'.[273] Thus,

> [w]here the disadvantaged group is heavily dominated by women and the group of advantaged comparators is heavily dominated by men (as they were in this case), the inference of sex taint will readily be drawn and it will be difficult for the employer to prove its absence.[274]

This tells us two things. First, Smith's LJ phrase 'the particular disadvantage . . . is nothing to do with gender' suggests the defence is a narrow one: an employer would have to undermine the statistics rather than just point to a benign cause. It also suggests that where significant statistics reveal a disparity, it would be 'difficult' to rebut the 'readily drawn' presumption of discrimination. One wonders why Underhill LJ did not consider this relevant to the significant statistics presented by Mr Naeem.

More telling was the issue at stake in *Gibson*. Predominantly female carers were paid less than predominantly male street cleaners and gardeners, despite doing work of equal value. The difference was attributable, first, to a historically agreed productivity bonus system paid to the street cleaners and gardeners, even though this no longer served the purpose of improving productivity; and, second, to the fact that a similar scheme was inappropriate for carers. Applying (the wide view of) *Armstrong*, both the employment tribunal and the EAT[275] held that these causes were not tainted by sex, and so the employer was not obliged to objectively justify the difference. The Court of Appeal reversed, holding that this was a misapplication of *Armstrong*. For Pill LJ (with whom Maurice Kay LJ agreed on this point),[276] the 'compelling' statistics meant that *Armstrong* did not apply.[277]

267 From the EAT cases, ibid, and *Surtees* (ibid) sub nom. *Redcar and Cleveland BC v Bainbridge* [2009] ICR 133 (CA) [59–60], where Mummery LJ in fact endorsed a very restrictive view of *Armstrong* – where 'the statistical evidence was not very strong or convincing'.
268 [2010] ICR 708 (CA).
269 [2016] ICR 289 [27].
270 [2010] ICR 708 [75].
271 ibid [49].
272 ibid [68].
273 ibid.
274 ibid.
275 UKEAT/0303/08/ZT, UKEAT/0304/08/ZT (EAT 17 February 209) [34].
276 [2010] ICR 708 [75].
277 ibid [51].

For Smith LJ, the mistake was that in looking for a sex-tainted *cause*, the tribunals confused indirect with direct discrimination.[278]

The unanimous decision in *Gibson* was that *Armstrong* was not relevant to the facts. That means, at the least, *Armstrong* is not of universal application in cases of indirect discrimination. As with its *obiter dicta*, the decision does nothing to support Underhill's LJ requirement for an inherently discriminatory practice, while Smith's LJ reversal of the decisions damns the theory for confusing direct with indirect discrimination, a fundamental technical error.

In *Enderby*, the CJEU held that significant statistics will produce an irrebuttable presumption of discrimination for the employer to objectively justify. Underhill's LJ use of case law from the equal pay regime was not only unconvincing, it was hazardous, given the dominance of *Enderby*. In his much vaunted case, *Gibson*, the '*Marshall* defence' was expressly rejected by Pill LJ, and given a lukewarm reception by Smith LJ,[279] leaving just one judge out of three as authority, hardly a precedent to put the matter 'beyond doubt', as claimed.[280]

Overall, the (domestic) equal pay law cited does not support Underhill's LJ requirement for discriminatory social circumstances or an inherently discriminatory cause. It was, of course, completely at odds with the unexplainably sidelined higher authority of *Enderby*.

The shifting (or ambivalent) burdens

Given that so much of *Naeem* (and *Essop*) involved the shifting burdens, it is surprising that this matter was not actually fully addressed. It will be recalled that the Court of Appeal in *Essop* gave some mixed messages regarding the claimant's burden.[281] In *Naeem*, after quoting Sir Colin Rimer's *reason why* dictum from *Essop*,[282] Underhill LJ concluded 'it is permissible to consider the reason for the disparity complained of, in the sense of the factors which caused it to occur'. The passive 'it is' leaves unresolved the matter of *who* has to prove these causal factors. The judgment made it clear that the defendant could *disprove* them but no more than that. The nearest Underhill LJ came to the matter was when he recorded in parenthesis:

> I should note that the passage [from *Essop*] quoted might in isolation be taken as suggesting that the burden of proving the reason is in all cases on the claimant; but it is clear from the later reasoning in his judgment that that was not Sir Colin's view—see in particular paras 63–65 and the reference to the provisions of section 136.[283]

278 ibid [58] & [69]–[70].
279 ibid [49] (Pill LJ), [58] & [69]–[70] (Smith LJ).
280 [2016] ICR 289 [27].
281 See p 192.
282 [2015] ICR 1063 (CA) [57]–[59]. See p 183 et al.
283 [2016] ICR 289 [30].

This merely brings forward *Essop*'s mixed message. It does nothing to clarify the matter. Thus, assuming the ***reason why*** theory were correct, it leaves two broad possibilities:

1 The claimant must identify a practice of the defendant and consequent disparity (by sex, race, religion etc.). The defendant may produce evidence undermining the claimant's case by identifying an 'innocent' cause of the disparity: the *reason why*.
2 The claimant must identify a practice of the defendant and consequent disparity (by sex, race, religion etc.). In ***addition***, the claimant must prove the *reason why* the claimant and the claimant's group were disadvantaged by the practice. If the claimant fails to do this, the case fails at that stage and the defendant has no burden of any sort.

If this case (and *Essop*) means that statistics alone are not enough for a prima facie case, despite being significant (in the *Enderby* sense), it would seem the second interpretation would be the correct one, as, in line with the Equality Act 2010, section 136, such evidence would not be enough 'from which the court could decide, in the absence of any other explanation', that there has been discrimination. But the absence of clarification on this basic point merely exacerbates the confusion caused by the decisions and substantive law dicta.

The comparison in the EAT

As noted in earlier[284], the EAT also found that the claimant had failed to make out his prima facie case, but for a different reason. For the EAT, the case foundered on the comparison. It will be recalled that section 23(1) of the Equality Act 2010 provides: 'On a comparison of cases for the purposes of section 13, 14, or 19 there must be no material difference between the circumstances relating to each case.' According to the EAT (dedicating 16 paragraphs to the issue), a 'like-for-like' comparison could not include chaplains employed before 2002, as that would be a 'material difference' between the groups:

> The PCP in question here could only properly be tested as to its effect by limiting the pool to those persons employed since 2002, from which point forward Muslim chaplains and Christian chaplains had been on a level playing field.[285]

Rather than reject this approach outright as technically incorrect, Underhill LJ presented a rather ambivalent opinion. At one point, he stated: 'Specifically, I agree that it is necessary to consider the impact of the length of service criterion

284 See 'The case up to the Court of Appeal', p 193.
285 [2014] ICR 472 (EAT) [28] (Mr Recorder Luba QC). See generally [15]–[31].

on the actual population to which it is applied.'[286] This comment was made in response to Naeem's argument that the pool for comparison comprised all the Christian and Muslim chaplains employed. By implication, this rejects the EAT's comparison. But later the judge merely found that the EAT's comparison 'was not the best route to the right result', even though this route 'should lead to the same result'. The reason given for this (seemingly contrary) view was that use of section 23 was best confined to arguments over statistical analysis that were not present here.[287] Of course, the EAT's approach was fundamentally the *wrong* route, no matter what the result. The long-established rule (maintained *by* the Court of Appeal) is that any 'pool' for the comparison should not be dictated by the challenged factor, as such a pool could not properly test the impact of that factor.[288] It is of concern that this basic technicality of indirect discrimination law was not clearly identified and reversed by the Court of Appeal.[289]

Statutory interpretation

This case centred on the statutory phrase 'puts, or would put, persons with whom B shares the characteristic at a particular disadvantage when compared with persons with whom B does not share it'. For Underhill LJ, the key here was the verb 'puts'. A plain reading of this does not require a *reason why*, a search for alternative causes, a sole cause,[290] or a prerequisite of discriminatory social circumstances. It simply requires that the challenged *practice* 'puts' the claimant's group at a disadvantage. One of the easiest scenarios to evaluate is where there is a fixed pool (the relevant workforce) and a tangible practice of the employer (a length-of-service criterion). Such a literal reading of the statute accords with the statutory purpose, as the ample body of jurisprudence demonstrates, notably *Enderby*. As with *Essop*, this was largely ignored.

Moreover, unlike the Court in *Essop*, the *Naeem* Court had the benefit of the Court of Justice's decision in *CHEZ*.[291] Here, an electricity supplier placed its meters in a predominantly Roma district higher than in other districts, apparently to prevent tampering. This made it harder for consumers to monitor their use. A central feature of this case is that the complainant was *not* Roma. Nonetheless, the court found, having been inconvenienced by the (discriminatory) practice, she was entitled to complain of indirect or direct discrimination.[292] Underhill LJ

286 [2016] ICR 289 [22].

287 [2016] ICR 289 [33].

288 '[T]he pool should not be so drawn as to incorporate the disputed condition.' *Allonby v Accrington & Rossendale College* [2001] ICR 1189 [18] (Sedley LJ). Discussed at pp 176–177. See also [2017] UKSC 27 [40]–[41] (Baroness Hale).

289 The EAT's pool was expressly rejected by the Supreme Court: [2017] UKSC 27 [40]–[42].

290 As Underhill's LJ demand for discriminatory social circumstances concedes.

291 Case C-83/14 *CHEZ Razpredelenie Bulgaria AD v Komisia za zashtita ot diskriminatsias* [2016] 1 CMLR 14.

292 ibid, paras 50 & 56.

dismissed the case as irrelevant because, 'the issues there considered seem to me to have no application to the circumstances of the present case'.[293]

Again, this was a rather brazen reaction to a decision from a Court that does not operate a strict doctrine of precedent,[294] but whose broader statements *are* law. There were two aspects to *CHEZ* that *were* highly relevant to *Naeem*. First, the spirit of the decision denoted a liberal interpretation of the legislation, in that case, the Race Directive.[295] Hence, the Grand Chamber was 'clear' that the Directive 'cannot, in the light of its objective and the nature of the rights which it seeks to safeguard, be defined restrictively'.[296] Second, it followed that it 'is sufficient that, although using neutral criteria not based on the protected characteristic, it has the effect of placing particularly persons possessing that characteristic at a disadvantage'.[297] The key word here is 'sufficient'. Nothing was added to the sentence to qualify or somehow restrict it, such as demanding an additional *reason why*. Quite why the Court of Appeal came to give the legislation a restrictive interpretation in the face of this is inexplicable. The same could be said of its dismissal of *CHEZ* as irrelevant, save it did not accord with the common law's binary notion of wrongdoer and victim, with the claimant not belonging to a protected group. Of course, these two aspects say little new about the approach of the Court of Justice. But as Fredman (no doubt among others) suggested, *CHEZ* confirms that the Court of Appeal decided *Naeem* and *Essop* contrary to (binding) EU law.[298]

The only possible statutory word on which Underhill LJ could hang the 'inherent' theory (he did not try) was the adjective 'particular' attached to 'disadvantage'. This possibility was discredited previously, in the context of *Essop*.[299] The only difference is that the *CHEZ*[300] opinion on the matter *was* available to the *Naeem* Court. As noted, this is authoritative in negating any suggestion that the additional word 'particular' is intended to require a *reason why*, and with it, any of the other subsidiary demands of Underhill's LJ speech.

Summary

The Court of Appeal missed the opportunity to clarify the law of discriminatory pay beyond the heavily litigated statutory regime of (gender) equal pay. Instead, it handed down a convoluted judgment laced with spurious logic and some basic errors. Whilst sidelining relevant EU cases, such as *Enderby* and *CHEZ*, the Court cited barely relevant authorities, which, if anything, undermined its conclusions.

293 [2016] ICR 289 [35]

294 *R v Henn and Darby* [1981] 1 AC 850, 904 (Lord Diplock). See Chapter 2, p 33.

295 Directive 2000/43/EC.

296 Case C-83/14, [2016] 1 CMLR 14, para 56. See also para 74, setting out the broader aims of the TFEU.

297 ibid, para 62.

298 S Fredman, 'The reason why: unravelling indirect discrimination law' (2016) 45(2) ILJ 231, 236.

299 See p 186, text to n 180.

300 Case C-83/14, [2016] 1 CMLR 14, para 109.

The judgment produced a technically flawed definition of indirect discrimination in that it confused cause and effect, inherence and social attitudes, and direct with indirect discrimination; it could not conceive of multiple causes of a disparity, failed clearly to condemn the EAT's fundamentally incorrect comparison, and failed to clarify a central issue, the shifting burden of proof. This mass of confusion was in the face of the clear, succinct, and correct conclusion at first instance that 'the claimant need not show *why* the PCP put him at a disadvantage, but *whether* it does'.[301]

This was yet another easy case to resolve. A literal interpretation would have served the purpose of the legislation. *Naeem* presented what appeared to be significant statistics to satisfy a prima facie case, notably by the standard of *Enderby*. Section 19 does not require any more than that. Section 136 does not add any substantive law to section 19, and so could not be used to justify the *reason why* theory. At first instance, despite losing the on the prima facie case, the employer successfully justified the practice. Some five years later, the Supreme Court restored both parts of that judgment. That the case then spent so long in limbo was down to the convoluted and erroneous judgments of the EAT and a seemingly zealous Court of Appeal, for which, once again, an easy case produced bad law.

Conclusion

In these cases, senior judges struggled with the effects-based and group-based nature, as well as the technical complexities, of indirect discrimination law. This law, perhaps more than others, exposed the judicial shortcomings. With the *Perera* problem, the Court of Appeal could not marry the legislative text with its purpose. In *Essop* and *Naeem*, the Court of Appeal seemed ignorant of the law's effect-based nature, the judges instead going off instead on a folly of their own. With a blinkered deference to the literal rule, the Court of Appeal in *Mandla* interpreted the statutory words 'can comply' to confine the statutory reach to mutable characteristics, despite the absurd potential. And when given some latitude by the text, in the same case, the Court ignored long-standing political policy and *legal* authority embodied in English and US case law, and instead resorted to a dictionary to define 'race'. All of that, it seemed, was driven by the Court's self-declared, ill-defined notion of multiculturalism (which was in a fact a form *mono*-culturalism). The latitude afforded by the 'comparison' was too much for majority of the House of Lords in *Rutherford*, which produced a precedent that would readily doom most claims, and a misconceived broader formula.

The cases considered in this chapter continue familiar themes of prolixity, poor statutory interpretation, and a lack of a full appreciation of the basic tenets of discrimination law. Most of the Court of Appeal cases (*Perera*, *Meer*, *Mandla*, *Essop*, *and Naeem*) continue the underlying theme that this law's purpose is confined to providing remedies to individual victims against wrongdoers, which is

301 Cited [2016] ICR 289 (CA) [31].

rooted in the common law's binary approach of resolving disputes between two individuals. The Court of Appeal (*Meer* and *Mandla*) even found room to suggest that a discriminatory, or hostile, motive was required for liability, presaging a theme later associated with the importunate dissenters.[302]

A particular feature of these cases is that they ranged from 1983 to 2015. Despite the reversals of the earlier narrow decisions, such as *Perera* and *Mandla* in favour of more liberal definitions, *Essop* and *Naeem* demonstrate that the Court of Appeal in particular, has failed to appreciate that by principle, purpose, precedent, and binding EU law, it is ***obliged*** to eschew restrictive interpretations of this legislation.

Further reading

Lord Lester, 'Discrimination: what can lawyers learn from history?' [1994] PL 224.

Government Equalities Office, 'Closing the gender pay gap'. Government consultation and response (February 2016) 43 ('diversity and equality'), < https://www.gov.uk/government/consultations/closing-the-gender-pay-gap > accessed 1 April 2018.

I Steele, 'Sex discrimination and the material factor defence under the Equal Pay Act 1970 and the Equality Act 2010' (2010) 39 ILJ 264.

S Fredman, 'The reason why: unravelling indirect discrimination law' (2016) 45(2) ILJ 231.

Griggs v Duke Power (1971) 401 US 424 (Sup Ct).

Falkirk Council v Whyte [1997] IRLR 560 (EAT).

Homer v Chief Constable of West Yorkshire [2012] ICR 704 (SC).

Mandla v Dowell Lee [1983] 2 AC 548 (HL).

Grundy v British Airways [2008] IRLR 74 (CA).

Essop v Home Office [2017] UKSC 27.

302 See Chapter 5, 'The importunate dissenters', p 99.

9 Disability-related discrimination

The case of *Malcolm*

The cases explored so far have centred on the 'traditional' concepts of direct and indirect discrimination, as well as victimisation, concepts that date back to the 1970s. A rather newer concept arrived on the British statute book in 1995: disability-related discrimination.[1] Rather than the disability itself, this definition focused on the ***manifestation*** of a disability, such as a guide dog, an eating disorder, absence from work, poor decision-making, a slow typing speed, and so on. In order to establish a prima facie case, a comparison was made with a person without the manifestation in question, i.e. a person without a dog, eating disorder, absenteeism, poor decision-making, or slow typing speed. Various defences were provided, depending on whether the activity engaged was employment, housing, or the provision of services etc. For employment, there was a general justification defence. Other defences were more specific. In a pattern reminiscent of the handling of the comparison required for indirect discrimination,[2] the courts in general dealt with this competently, until the matter came to the House of Lords; the case was *Lewisham LBC v Malcolm.*[3] Although it centred on the housing or 'premises' provisions of the Disability Discrimination Act 1995 (DDA 1995), this judgment, overruling the long-established *Clark v Novacold*,[4] was of great significance to the Act's more litigated coverage of employment, as well as the provision of goods, facilities, and services. Under the DDA 1995, the functional equivalent of direct *and* indirect discrimination was disability-related discrimination,[5] which was defined as less favourable treatment for a reason related to a person's disability, which cannot be justified. The House of Lords undermined two major and established principles of disability-related discrimination. First, for the challenged treatment to be 'related' to the claimant's disability, the defendant must have known, or ought to have known, of the disability at the time of the treatment.

1 Nowadays reformulated as 'Discrimination arising from disability': EA 2010, s 15.

2 See Chapter 8, 'The comparison required', p 174.

3 [2008] 1 AC 1399 (HL).

4 [1999] ICR 951 (CA).

5 'The EA 2010, s 19 (with s 6(3)) introduced a definition of indirect discrimination specific to disability. Direct discrimination (s 13) also applies to disability.

Second (Baroness Hale dissenting), when identifying if the treatment was 'less favourable', the correct comparator was a person in the same circumstances save for the *disability*. Hence, where a restaurant had a 'no dogs' rule, the correct comparator was a sighted customer *with* a dog, or where an employer dismissed a worker who was long-term absent because of his or her disability, the comparator was a worker without a disability who *was* long-term absent.

The facts were as follows. Courtney Malcolm was diagnosed with schizophrenia. In 2002, he exercised his right to buy his flat from Lewisham Council, but completion was delayed for some time. In May 2004, he lost his job and in June 2004, in contravention of his tenancy agreement, he sub-let the flat and moved out. Just after that, he informed the council he wished to complete the transfer on 26 July. It seems his plan was to sub-let after the purchase (which was permissible), but he 'jumped the gun', either because he was unemployed and needed the money, or because his judgment was impaired by his schizophrenia. On 6 July, the council discovered the sub-letting, and gave him notice to quit, in accordance with the tenancy agreement and the Housing Act 1985, section 93, which allowed the council no discretion. Subsequently, both Malcolm's psychiatrist and social worker wrote to the council asking for a reprieve as they feared it would cause him another breakdown. Nonetheless, the council persisted and issued proceedings for possession. Malcolm claimed his eviction amounted to disability-related discrimination.

At first instance, the County Court trial judge found for the council, holding that Malcolm did not have a disability for the purposes of the Act, and that in any case, the reason he sub-let early was to raise money whilst unemployed. It was not a mistake caused by his illness. Thus, the eviction did not relate to his disability. The Court of Appeal reversed,[6] finding that Malcolm's schizophrenia amounted to a disability and that as he had sub-let the flat when his judgment was impaired by his disability, the possession order was related to his disability. Accordingly, he was treated less favourably than a person who did not have schizophrenia and who *had not* sub-let his council flat. The House of Lords restored the County Court decision, holding (by a majority) that Malcolm *did* have a disability, but (Baroness Hale dissenting) he was not treated less favourably because the correct comparator was a person without schizophrenia who *had also* sub-let his council flat (overruling *Clark v Novacold*), and in any case (unanimously) the possession order was not related to his disability.

Before going further, it is worth putting the definition of disability-related discrimination into context. The Act was designed to cover both indirect as well as direct discrimination[7] (these definitions were not employed in the original Act). The conventional model of indirect discrimination was deemed unsuitable because, in contrast to other protected groups such as race or sex, it is unlikely

6 [2008] Ch 129.

7 W Hague, Minister responsible for the Bill in Parliament. HC Deb 24 January 1995, vol 253, col 150. See p 213, text to n 18.

that any facially neutral practice would adversely affect all persons with a disability as a group; the assortment of disabilities is too varied for the conventional model.[8] Instead, in combination with a duty to make reasonable adjustments (which was not in force for the premises provisions in time for this case), the DDA 1995 outlawed 'disability-related discrimination'. This reflected the position under the long-standing disability law in the United States, where, in addition to direct discrimination and a duty to make 'reasonable accommodation', the courts recognised 'discrimination by proxy', which is treatment 'directed at an effect or manifestation of a handicap'[9] such as a wheelchair or service-dog ban. The US courts treated the proxy as a pretext for direct discrimination, although this carried a justification defence.[10] Alternatively, where the evidence showed no pretext, the courts adapted their indirect discrimination model to confine the impact to only those with the same disability. Thus, an 'armlifting' test for postal workers adversely affected those with a similar shoulder injury to the claimant.[11]

The definition of disability-related discrimination was broad enough to encapsulate instances of both direct and indirect discrimination, and in doing so provided a justification defence for either. The definition of the prima facie case was substantially the same for the parts of the Act covering premises, employment, and the provision of goods, facilities, and services.[12] For 'premises', section 24(1) provided:

> [A] person . . . discriminates against a disabled person if (a) for a reason which relates to the disabled person's disability, he treats him less favourably than he treats or would treat others to whom that reason does not or would not apply; and (b) he cannot show that the treatment in question is justified.

Part (a) provided the prima facie case. Section 24 *differed* from the other parts of the Act as section 24(3) provided an exhaustive list of justification reasons, specific to premises. However, this did not include sub-letting (or non-payment of rent). For a prima facie case under (a), there are two elements: the treatment must be for a reason 'related to' the victim's disability and that treatment must be less favourable.

Until *Malcolm*, the established meaning of these elements was set out by the Court of Appeal in *Clark v Novacold*.[13] Writing the judgment of the court, Mummery LJ first of all noted that the DDA 1995, unlike the Sex Discrimination Act 1975 (SDA 1975) and Race Relations Act 1976 (RRA 1976), contained no requirement that in a comparison the relevant circumstances must be the same, or

8 This has now been rectified by EA 2010, s 6(3)(b): 'a reference to persons who share a protected characteristic is a reference to persons who have the same disability'.

9 See e.g. *McWright v Alexander* 982 F 2d 222, 228 (7th Cir 1992). Implemented nowadays by EA 2010, s 6(3)(b), ibid.

10 See e.g. ibid.

11 *Prewit v US Postal Service* 662 F 2d 292 (5th Cir 1981).

12 Respectively DDA 1995, ss 24(1), 3A(1), 20(1).

13 [1999] ICR 951, 964–966.

not materially different.[14] This showed that the 1995 Act adopted 'a significantly different approach',[15] and that the reason for the less favourable treatment need only be *related* to the disability. This should have been enough to settle to matter. But Mummery LJ suggested that definition was 'linguistically . . . ambiguous'[16] and cited *Pepper v Hart*[17] to quote the Minister responsible for the Bill:

> The Bill is drafted in such a way that indirect as well as direct discrimination can be dealt with . . . . A situation where dogs were not admitted to a cafe, with the effect that blind people would be unable to enter it, would be a prima facie case of indirect discrimination against blind people and would be unlawful.[18]

In a similar way, a disabled customer who is told to leave the restaurant because she has difficulty eating as a result of her disability is so treated for a reason *related to* her disability.[19] Accordingly, the choice of comparator differs from that under direct discrimination. In these examples, the comparator is a person without the 'reason' i.e. *without* a dog or *without* an eating difficulty. If it were otherwise, and the comparator were a sighted man *with* a dog, or a person who had difficulty eating for a reason unrelated to a disability (say a coughing fit, or because the food tasted bad), the scope of disability-related discrimination would be drastically reduced, effectively to direct discrimination. It follows that the comparison cannot be made until the reason for the treatment is identified, and the comparator is a person without that reason.

In *Clark v Novacold*, Mr Clark suffered a back injury at work causing soft-tissue injuries around the spine. He appeared to be unable to work for at least 12 months, and after four months absence, he was dismissed. In response to Mr Clark's claim for disability-related discrimination, Novacold argued that it would have dismissed any person unable to work for that long. The Court of Appeal held that that argument used the wrong comparator. First, the reason for Clark's dismissal was his inability to work, which was the 'reason' related to his disability. Therefore, the correct comparator should be a worker with neither the disability *nor* the 'reason', that is a worker without his disability and able to work. Mummery LJ observed that this approach would avoid the problems encountered by the courts in their 'futile attempts' to identify a hypothetical non-pregnant male comparator for a pregnant woman in sex discrimination cases before the CJEU decision *Dekker*, which ruled bluntly

14 ibid, 959 & 963. Under the reformulated version in EA 2010, s 15, no comparison is required, and the matter would not arise.

15 ibid, 963.

16 ibid, 962.

17 [1993] AC 593 (HL). See Chapter 2, p 30.

18 [1999] ICR 951, 964 citing HC Deb 24 January 1995, vol 253, col 150 (William Hague).

19 [1999] ICR 951, citing the Code of Practice on Rights of Access: services to the public, public authority functions, private clubs and premises (1996) para 2.12.

that pregnancy discrimination amounted to direct sex discrimination.[20] It was also consistent with the availability of the general justification defence in this employment case (not generally available for direct discrimination).

The definition of disability-related discrimination was taken a stage further in *Heinz v Kendrick*[21] where Lindsay J suggested that there was no need for the defendant to have had knowledge of the disability. He used two vivid examples to illustrate this point. First, a postman with a concealed artificial leg may be dismissed for being too slow. Second, a secretary with undeclared dyslexia may be dismissed for 'typing hopelessly misspelt letters'.[22] The subsequent Code of Practice supported this view, giving an example of a woman dismissed for persistent absenteeism (as any worker would be) where the employer was unaware that the reason for her absence was her multiple sclerosis.[23] In all these examples, the employer's act amounted to treatment related to the worker's disability (which may or may not be justified).

The House of Lords in *Malcolm* disapproved of these principles. Instead, to identify if the treatment was 'less favourable', the correct comparator was a person in the same circumstances save for the *disability*. Hence, in the examples used earlier, the correct comparator is a sighted customer *with* a dog, a person without a disability but *with* eating difficulties, or a worker without a disability who *was* long-term absent. This overruled *Novacold*.[24] Baroness Hale dissented on this point.[25] Further, for the treatment to be 'related' to the claimant's disability, a unanimous House held that the defendant must have known, or ought to have known, of the disability at the time of the treatment.[26] Lords Scott and Neuberger, carrying the torch of the importunate dissenters, appeared to go a step further, holding that the defendant must have been 'motivated' by the disability.[27]

Malcolm's case actually turned on the finding of fact by the trial judge that the sub-letting was not a result of Malcolm's illness. However, the Law Lords' wider remarks on disability-related discrimination deserve attention because they overruled the long-established *Novacold* interpretation, and applied not only to the housing provisions of the DDA 1995, but also those covering employment, and the provision of goods, facilities, and services.[28]

20 Case C-177/88 *Dekker v Stichting Vormingscentrum voor Jonge Volwassenen (VJV-Centrum) Plus* [1990] ECR I-3941.

21 [2000] ICR 491 (EAT).

22 ibid [25]. See also *Callaghan v Glasgow CC* [2001] IRLR 724 (EAT) 726.

23 *Code of Practice Employment and Occupation* (London: TSO, 2004) para 4.31. Cf *Code of Practice for Employment* (EHRC, 2011) paras 5.3 & 5.13–5.19, https://www.equalityhumanrights.com/en/publication-download/employment-statutory-code-practice (accessed 10 April 2018).

24 [2008] 1 AC 1399, [15] (Lord Bingham) [30]–[40] (Lord Scott), [113] (Lord Brown), [158] (Lord Neuberger).

25 ibid [79]–[80].

26 [2008] 1 AC 1399, [18] (Lord Bingham), [29] (Lord Scott), [163] Lord Neuberger, [86] (Baroness Hale).

27 ibid, respectively [29] & [166]. For more on the importunate dissenters, see Chapter 5, p 99.

28 Either expressly or by overruling the employment case of *Clark v Novacold*: [2008] 1 AC 1399, [15] (Lord Bingham), [28] (Lord Scott), [80] (Baroness Hale), [112] (Lord Brown), [158] (Lord Neuberger). See e.g. *Stockton on Tees BC v Aylott* [2010] ICR 1278 (CA) [64].

1 The correct comparator

It was common ground that the device used to identify if the treatment was less favourable was a comparison. Technically speaking, the problem was whether the 'reason' (for the treatment) at the beginning section 24 was the same reason at the end ('others to whom that reason . . . would not apply'). The 'wide', or in this case, literal (*Novacold*) interpretation supposes that the comparator is *not* endowed with the 'reason' for the treatment.

In addition to the reasons provided by the Court of Appeal in *Novacold*, a plain reading of the provision most obviously points to 'that' reason being the aforementioned (and only) reason in the provision, which is the reason for the treatment. And if the comparator is not endowed with that reason, he or she does not have a guide dog, or an eating disorder, or long-term absence from work. The Court of Appeal's reasoning merely found no basis to deviate from this plain reading of the statute, although it endorsed this using *Hansard*. Thus, any dissent from this view ought to be couched in powerful terms under, say, the golden, mischief, or purposive rule, or in deference to EU law, in order to depart from the plain meaning of the text.

In the House of Lords, the majority's argument was that the 'wide' interpretation would mean that Malcolm's treatment would be compared with a tenant who had *not* sub-let. It would also mean that a worker off sick for a long period because of a disability would be compared to a non-disabled worker *not* off sick. Of course, the council would not evict this tenant nor would the employer dismiss this worker. As such, this test 'would always be met'[29] and is therefore 'pointless'.[30] Lord Scott concluded: 'Parliament must surely have intended the comparison . . . to be a meaningful comparison in order to distinguish between treatment that was discriminatory and treatment that was not.'[31]

This logic enabled the Lords to attack the examples given in *Novacold*. Lord Bingham said:

> A more natural comparison . . . would fall to be made . . . with a person who had a dog but no disability or a diner who was a very untidy eater but had no disability-related reason for eating in that way.'[32]

Lords Scott and Neuberger agreed that a blind person with a dog should be compared to a sighted person *with* a dog,[33] with Lord Scott labelling this the 'common sense' answer.[34]

29 [2008] 1 AC 1399, [14] (Lord Bingham), [112] (Lord Brown). In her dissent, Baroness Hale acknowledged this conclusion, at [71].

30 ibid [32]–[33] (Lord Scott) and [151] (Lord Neuberger).

31 ibid [32], and see Lord Brown at [113].

32 ibid [15].

33 ibid [35] & [155], respectively.

34 ibid [30] & [31].

This reasoning bypasses the literal rule, and, without saying as much, is suggesting that a plain reading of the provision would lead to the absurdity of a pointless comparison. But the conclusion that the test would always be met lacks imagination and misunderstands the concept of disability-related discrimination as the functional equivalent of direct *and* indirect discrimination.

On the first point, for example, using the 'wide' interpretation, the comparator could be a tenant who is being evicted, along with the claimant, because the council wishes to refurbish the block of flats, or perhaps demolish it because it has been condemned unsafe. An 'eviction' could be part of re-housing programme. Similarly, the comparator worker may be dismissed, not because of his or her long-term absence, but because the whole workforce (or a section of it), including the claimant, is being made redundant. In either case, this comparison reveals the treatment was *not* related to the claimant's disability. As such, this wider comparison will not 'always be met' and is not pointless.

Second, as disability-related discrimination was the functional equivalent of indirect discrimination, applying the majority's logic to a classic case of indirect discrimination exposes the inadequacy of the narrow comparator. Suppose entrance exams were challenged as disfavouring black applicants. The 'reason' for their non-selection was the failure of the exam. The correct comparator group would be the white applicants, without that reason, in other words *all* the white applicants.[35] (The respective success rates of white and black applicants can then be identified.) If the 'narrow comparator' theory were applied here, the comparator group would be exactly the same as the claimant group, save for race. In other words, it would include the 'reason' and so consist only of whites who did *not* pass the exam. Of course, no adverse impact would be revealed. This would be a 'pointless' comparison as it would reveal nothing about any discriminatory impact of the exam on black applicants. For disability-related discrimination, the narrow comparison is equally pointless, as it would reveal nothing about any discriminatory impact of the employer's conduct on the person with a disability.

Of course, the difference for disability-related discrimination was that the claimant's group consists only of one person, and this may have led to the mistake. Where the claimant's group contains all of those who *took* the exam, it will comprise, normally, some who failed and some who passed. The 'natural' or 'common sense' (and correct) comparator group of white candidates will contain also some who failed and some who passed. For disability-related discrimination, the claimant's 'group' will comprise one person, and so 100 per cent of this 'group' is disadvantaged by the practice. Thus, it is tempting to project the claimant's identity minus only his or her disability onto the comparator's 'group' (of one), which, in *Malcolm*, would be a person who also sub-let. This is the mistake.

35 See for the US, e.g. *Griggs v Duke Power* 401 US 424 (1971); *Bushey v New York State Civil Service Commission* 733 F 2d 220 (2nd Cir 1984) certiorari denied, 469 US 1117 (1985). For Britain, *Employment: Statutory Code of Practice* (EHRC 2011) para 4.11, < https://www.equalityhumanrights.com/en/publication-download/employment-statutory-code-practice > accessed 10 April 2018.

In the rare conventional indirect discrimination cases where 100 per cent of the claimant's group is disadvantaged by the practice, the comparator's group still discards the 'reason'. In *Greencroft Social Club v Mullen*,[36] only members were entitled to a disciplinary hearing. Women were not entitled to membership, so the proportion of women (either guests or workers) not entitled to the disciplinary hearing was 100 per cent. Nonetheless, the EAT found that a prima facie case had been established. If the *Malcolm* logic were projected onto this case, the comparator group would be men who were not members (the 'reason'), an absurd and pointless comparison.

A third reason why the majority was mistaken reverts attention somewhat closer to the statutory wording. As Baroness Hale explained in her dissent on this issue,[37] the legislative history supports the wider interpretation. When introduced, the Disability Discrimination Bill provided that the comparison should be with 'others who do not have that disability' (clause 4(1)(a)). The drafter then replaced this with the words 'to whom that reason does not or would not apply' in what became section 5(1)(a) (employment) and section 20(1)(a) (services), and 'others to whom that reason does not or would not apply' in what became section 24(1)(a) (premises). When introducing these amendments, the Government explained it now meant that a rejected job applicant who could not type because of arthritis should now be compared with a job applicant who *could* type, rather than an applicant without a disability who could not type. Such a case should not turn on the comparison, but on justification,[38] for instance if typing was necessary for the job.

Baroness Hale then pointed to subsequent amendments made to the employment provisions (to implement the Framework Directive 2000/78/EC), on the basis that *Novacold* was correct. Parliament introduced a specific definition of direct discrimination that was not justifiable to run alongside disability-related discrimination, which *was* justifiable.[39] As the narrow construction reduced disability-related discrimination to direct discrimination,[40] it must be incorrect, otherwise Parliament would have simply repealed its justification proviso, rather than introduce another section.[41] Baroness Hale might have added that reading down a section to render it otiose offended a 'cardinal rule' of statutory interpretation,[42] and that such a construction, being conceptually incoherent, destroyed the provision's integrity and efficacy.

36 [1985] ICR 796 (EAT).
37 [2008] 1 AC 1399, [78]–[81].
38 Minister of State, Department for Education and Employment, Lord Henley, HL Deb 18 July 1995, vol 566, col 120.
39 Respectively DDA 1995, ss 3A(5) 3A(1) inserted by DDA 1995 (Amendment) Regulations 2003, SI 2003/1673.
40 Acknowledged by Lord Brown, [2008] 1 AC 1399, [114]. Lord Neuberger acknowledged that the narrow construction was 'unattractively restrictive' (ibid [119]) and 'very limited' (ibid [141]).
41 ibid [81].
42 *Re Florence Land Co.* (1878) 10 Ch D 530 (CA) 544 (James LJ). See Chapter 2, p 25, text to n 70.

The only criticism one could make of Baroness Hale's otherwise meticulous judgment on this issue was that she had to invoke *Pepper v Hart*[43] in order recite *Hansard*. In doing so, she had to acknowledge that the statutory definition was ambiguous and could lead to 'inconveniences',[44] which, as demonstrated above, was not the case. Of course, as with Mummery LJ in *Novacold*, this may have been a mere pragmatic move to bolster her judgment, and in this case perhaps, persuade her colleagues of their error.

2 Knowledge of the disability

The second point decided by the House (unanimously) was that to be liable, the defendant, when acting, must have knowledge of the claimant's disability. Once again, this is at odds with the concept of indirect discrimination, which is centred on the *impact* of facially neutral conduct, rather than the state of mind of the defendant. It is well established that a person can discriminate without being aware of the victim's personal characteristic, most typically, as noted previously, where entrance exams can disadvantage particular protected groups.[45]

While the 'narrow' interpretation of the comparator reduced disability-related discrimination to the equivalent of direct discrimination (but in some cases, with a justification defence), an additional requirement of knowledge reduced the reach of disability-related discrimination to *less than* that provided by direct discrimination, where it is possible for an employer to directly discriminate without knowledge of the victim's disability. This reinforces the redundancy of the provision[46] under consideration. This (technical) consequence alone ought to have alerted the House that it was astray on this point. If that were not enough, a Code of Practice available at the time offered a supporting example: an employer may advertise internally for a promotion, stating that the post is not suitable for anyone with a history of mental illness, and exclude, unknowingly, a member of staff with a history of schizophrenia.[47] Neither this example, nor the Code, was mentioned. The principle holds at EU level, where public statements by a director that he would not employ Moroccans was held to amount to direct racial discrimination, even though there were no Moroccan applicants.[48] For the CJEU, and the Equality Act 2010,[49] the deterrent effect alone is enough to warrant liability.

43 [1993] AC 593 (HL). See further p 30.

44 [2008] 1 AC 1399 [71].

45 See e.g. p 187.

46 In fact, three provisions, as a separate one existed for each of premises, employment, and the provision of goods, facilities, and services: respectively, DDA 1995, ss 24(1), 3A(1), & 20(1).

47 *Code of Practice Employment and Occupation* (London: TSO, 2004) para 4.11. The Code under the EA 2010 uses the more general example of a public advertisement stating that 'Gypsies or Travellers need not apply': *Code of Practice for Employment* (EHRC, 2011) para 3.12, < https://www.equalityhumanrights.com/en/publication-download/employment-statutory-code-practice > accessed 10 April 2018.

48 Case C-54/07 *Centrum voor Gelijkheid van Kansen en voor Racismebestrijding v Firma Feryn NV* [2008] ECR I-5187.

49 See Explanatory Note 63.

Although these examples show that it is possible to directly discriminate without knowledge of the victim's protected characteristic, they differ from cases such as *Malcolm* because the conduct is facially discriminatory. But, it has been suggested, it is possible for a person to directly discriminate by acting on discriminatory factors of which he or she is unaware. In *Williams v YKK*, Elias J suggested, *obiter*, that an unprejudiced manager's decision may be affected, or tainted, by a report made by a prejudiced supervisor.[50] So, for instance, a manager who is unaware that a worker's absenteeism was due to her disability may be influenced to dismiss her by unfavourable opinions delivered by prejudiced colleagues who were aware of her disability. A similarly innocent landlord may refuse to let to a person with a disability because he has been misinformed by his estate manager that he knows the person to be an unreliable tenant, when in truth, the manager is acting on his prejudice towards the person's disability. This could amount to direct discrimination because the reason for the treatment is the victim's disability: the basis of the prejudiced opinions was disability, rather than absenteeism. This is established in the United States, and known as 'Cat's Paw' theory.[51] The feature of this theory is that the prejudiced subordinate has influence over the decision-maker and so 'poisons the well'[52] from which the decision-maker draws his or her knowledge. More recently in *Reynolds v CLFIS*,[53] the Court of Appeal rejected such a notion (without considering the American jurisprudence). But neither Cat's Paw theory nor *Williams* was considered by the House in *Malcolm*, which was remiss, this being a case of public importance involving the defendant's lack of knowledge of a protected characteristic.

Aside from principle, the demand for knowledge is undermined by considering the provision in context.[54] At the time of the House of Lords' judgment, the DDA 1995 expressly stated, on no less than eight occasions elsewhere, that knowledge *is* required for certain liabilities, one of these even being disability-related discrimination in schools.[55] Thus, the absence of such a rider for the provision in question was a concrete indicator that knowledge was not required.[56]

In summary, the decision on this point conflicted with the concept of indirect discrimination, reduced disability-related discrimination to less than direct discrimination (the technical flaws), was out of step with other provisions of the statute, and failed to address Cat's Paw theory.

50 EAT 22 November 2002 [32].

51 See *Shager v Upjohn* 913 F 2d 398 (7th Cir 1990); see also *Russell v McKinney Hospital Venture* 235 3 F 3d 219, 227 (5th Cir 2000); *Griffin v Washington Convention Centre* 142 F 3d 1308, 1312 (DC Cir 1998); *Burlington Ind v Ellerth* 524 US 742, 762 (Sup Ct, 1998); *Poland v Chertoff* 494 F 3d 1174 (9th Cir 2007).

52 *Sarate v Loop Transfer Inc* No. 95 C 5671, 12 (ND Ill 1997).

53 [2015] ICR 1010 (CA). See further p 100, n 60, and M Rubenstein's criticism [2015] July IRLR, Highlights. There are no signs of an overruling, or even 'second thoughts'. See *Royal Mail Ltd v Kamaljeet Jhuti* [2017] EWCA Civ 1632; *Wilsons Solicitors LLP v Roberts* [2018] EWCA Civ 52 (where *some* doubts about the scope of the restriction was expressed; see [86] (Singh LJ)).

54 *Attorney General v Prince Ernest Augustus of Hanover* [1957] AC 436 (HL) 461 (Viscount Simonds). See Chapter 2, pp 24–25.

55 DDA 1995, s 28B(4).

56 This point was articulated by K Monaghan, *Equality Law* (Oxford University Press 2007) paras 6.153–6.154.

The reasoning behind this part of the decision varied. Lord Bingham and Baroness Hale considered that as disability-related discrimination carried a justification defence, knowledge must be an element, otherwise the defendant would be in no position to justify the challenged treatment.[57] Once again, this overlooks the basic technicalities of indirect discrimination law. In many examples of indirect discrimination, it is perfectly possible that the employer had a justifiable reason for its challenged practice without being aware of the identity of any particular protected group adversely affected. In the context of housing, a landlord without knowledge of his or her tenants' mental illness could justify evicting them for causing a nuisance to their neighbours, even though their behaviour was caused by the mental illness.[58]

Lord Bingham[59] joined with Lords Scott and Neuberger in relating this decision to the availability of damages. For instance, Lord Neuberger observed:

> [I]t would require very clear words before a statute could render a person liable for damages for discrimination against a disabled person, owing to an act which was not inherently discriminatory carried out at a time when the person had no reason to know of the disability which could render the act discriminatory.[60]

Lord Scott was equally convinced:

> But could it really have been intended by Parliament that all employers vis-à-vis their employees, all providers of goods, facilities and services vis-à-vis their customers and all managers of premises vis-à-vis the occupiers of the premises were to be subjected to the risk of becoming statutory tortfeasors and liable to substantial damages claims on account of normal actions taken in understandable pursuit of their respective interests against persons of whose disabilities they were totally unaware? I find it very difficult to accept that that could have been intended by Parliament.[61]

Again, some context is required here, this time a little broader than just the statute in question. A brief perusal of the history of Britain's discrimination legislation would have pointed these judges to a different conclusion. Both the Sex Discrimination Act 1975 and Race Relations Act 1976 originally provided that no damages shall be awarded for indirect discrimination that was unintentional.[62] However, it became clear that this restriction did not comply with EU law, with

57 [2008] 1 AC 1399 [18] & [86], respectively.

58 See e.g. *Manchester City Council v Romano* [2005] 1 WLR 2775 (CA) decided under DDA 995 s 24(3)(a), where tenants unsocial behaviour was held to 'endanger the health' of neighbours, a statutory defence.

59 [2008] 1 AC 1399, [18].

60 ibid [162].

61 ibid [28].

62 SDA 1975, s 66(3); RRA 1976, s 57(3); see e.g. *Orphanos v QMC* [1985] AC 761 (HL).

the CJEU holding that a member state may not make an award of compensation in a sex discrimination case dependent on showing fault on the part of the employer.[63] Consequently, the restriction was dropped and could not apply to any case falling under the equality Directives.[64] The DDA 1995, section 17A(2), provided, like the other equality statutes, that damages may be awarded when a court or tribunal considered it 'just and equitable'.[65] It made no distinction between employment (falling within the Directive) and other matters, and so apparently had the same meaning for all activities covered by the Act. As such, it should have been read to comply with the Framework Directive, and this meant that damages could not be dependent upon fault (or its absence). The legislative history, CJEU jurisprudence, and the text and structure of the statute should have made it plain to these three Law Lords that, indeed, the Act provided very clear words rendering a person liable in damages for no-fault discrimination. It is quite worrying, to say the least, that none of those three opinions using the damages remedy in support of their decisions actually referred to this history, or even the specific provisions of the statute before them.

3 Discriminatory intent

In addition to the requirement that the defendant should have been aware of the claimant's disability, two Law Lords took this a step further and suggested that the defendant should have been *motivated* by the disability.[66] Lord Scott's reasoning was rooted in the consequences should it be otherwise; a landlord should be able to evict for non-payment of rent, for instance, without being liable for disability discrimination. Hence:

> [I]f the . . . disability has played no motivating part in the decision of the alleged discriminator to inflict on the disabled person the treatment complained of, the alleged discriminator's reason for that treatment cannot, for section 24(1)(a) purposes, relate to the disability.[67]

Of course, it might be so that a landlord should be able to evict for non-payment of rent. But the solution to that problem is not a (technical) distortion of the statutory definition of disability discrimination, especially as it would affect other activities covered by the Act, such as the more frequently invoked employment provisions. Moreover, given that this case was heard just a few years after the

63 Case C-180/95 *Draehmpaehl v Urania Immobilien Service ohg* [1997] IRLR 538.

64 At the time, Council Directives 76/207/EEC (sex) 2000/43/EC (race) and 2000/78/EC (religion or belief, disability, age, or sexual orientation).

65 DDA 1995, s 17A(2) inserted by SI 2003/1673, Pt 2, reg 9 (in force 1 October 2004). Nowadays, for unintentional indirect discrimination, damages are awardable only after the court or tribunal has 'considered' other remedies, such as an injunction, or for employment, a declaration or recommendation: EA 2010, ss 119(6) 124(5).

66 [2008] 1 AC 1399, [29] (Lord Scott), [166] (Lord Neuberger).

67 [2008] 1 AC 1399, [29].

Macpherson Report,[68] and its identification of 'unwitting' and 'unconscious' discrimination, and after many *decades* of jurisprudence establishing that discrimination law was not solely fault-based,[69] to use Lord Scott's own words, 'could it really have been intended by Parliament'[70] to confine disability discrimination to fault-based liability?

Lord Neuberger's reasoning requires quoting at length:

> In my view, it is plain that the 'reason' in section 24(1)(a) cannot be confined to the legal ground, because a prospective landlord, under section 22(1) has a legal right to refuse to let as, and on the terms, he chooses. Also, if a landlord voluntarily agreed with all but one of his tenants in a block of flats to vary the user covenants in their leases in some beneficial way, but did not accord that privilege to a tenant because he was disabled, it would be absurd if that was not a 'reason' within section 24(1)(a). Additionally, the fact that knowledge of the disability (including what should be known) is required, supports the argument that one is normally primarily concerned with the state of mind of the alleged discriminator. Crucially, this is also supported by the language of section 22(1): the reference to the 'reason' for the treatment supports the notion that one is concerned with the alleged discriminator's subjective motivation, rather than with the objective legal ground.[71]

This is a rather denser piece of reasoning. Lord Neuberger is arguing that the 'reason' cannot be confined, for example, to the right to evict brought about by sub-letting (the 'legal ground'), and must therefore include a subjective element. He gives three explanations in support. The first (in the second part of the first sentence), makes little sense. DDA 1995, section 22 stipulated that landlords could not discriminate in the letting of premises.[72] Thus, a landlord could *not* refuse to let, or choose to let on (discriminatory) terms of his choice.

In the second sentence, he argues that otherwise, section 24 could not apply where there was blatant or 'inherent' discrimination, such as singling out the sole person with a disability for unfavourable treatment. From here, Lord Neuberger concludes that that section 24 must include subjective motivation. The third, 'crucial support' for this assumes the 'fact' that knowledge of the disability is required. Even if section 24 required this, it would be law, not fact. Labelling an interpretation of a statute a 'fact' gives the proposition an air of truth it cannot merit, as though it were some virtuous principle around which the statute must bend. One must assume that the reference to section 22(1) alludes to the first

68 The Stephen Lawrence Inquiry, Report of an Inquiry by Sir William Macpherson, advised by Tom Cook, the Right Reverend Dr John Sentamu, and Dr Richard Stone. February 1999. Presented to Parliament by the Home Secretary (Cm 4262-I, 1999) at paras 6.1–6.34. See further Chapter 3, p 58.

69 Starting with *Griggs v Duke Power* (1971) 401 US 424. See, in particular, Chapter 5, p 90.

70 [2008] 1 AC 1399, [28]; see p 220, text to n 61.

71 [2008] 1 AC 1399, [166].

72 See now EA 2010, s 33.

reason, as section 22 neither mentions nor hints at the 'reason'. It merely states that landlords may not discriminate; discrimination is defined elsewhere in the statute. As such, the logic of the third reason is as opaque as it was for the first.

This leaves the second reason as the only one reasonably open to scrutiny. It boils down to saying 'if section 24 were objective, it would narrow its scope'. It seems the judge feared a landlord alluding to one 'objective' reason to exclusion of all others. Thus, if the landlord shows that his 'policy was to obtain possession of any property in his portfolio whenever he had a legal ground for doing so', he could always escape liability.[73] This overlooks the *fact* that persons can act for more than one reason, and the long-established *law* that a defendant acting for a number of reasons can be liable if just one was discriminatory.[74]

Lord Neuberger considered this conclusion a 'comparatively generous approach'.[75] This would only be the case if expectations were lowered to the ridiculous proposition that the only reasons included in disability-related discrimination were non-discriminatory ones. This was Lord Neuberger's starting point (his 'legal ground'). Moreover, to interpret a discrimination statute *not* to cover hostile or 'inherent' discrimination would be more than ungenerous; it would be absurd. But to focus on Lord Neuberger's apparent generosity is to distract from his conclusion, which was anything but a generous interpretation, requiring both knowledge of the disability *and* a discriminatory intent. Thus, this technical excursion was flawed from start to finish. To quote the judge's own reasoning, it would require 'very clear words' to upset a fundamental and long-established tenet of discrimination law. It seems that here even clear words were not enough to upset the common law mind-set of fault-based liability or the spirit of the importunate dissenters.

4 Alternative interpretations

Underpinning the speeches was concern for the limited housing stock and waiting lists,[76] and the difficult position of Lewisham Council, which might well have faced judicial review had it not evicted a tenant who was sub-letting.[77] Moreover, there was concern for the position of landlords, public or private, who may never be able to evict a disabled tenant, who, for instance, permanently sub-let, or never paid rent.[78] This, of course, may interfere with a landlord's property rights under the European Convention on Human Rights.[79] Clearly, the majority was afraid, as Lord Neuberger put it, of giving disability-related discrimination 'extraordinarily far-reaching scope'.[80]

73 [2008] 1 AC 1399, [167].
74 E.g. *Owen and Briggs v James* [1982] ICR 618 (CA).
75 [2008] 1 AC 1399, [165].
76 See e.g. ibid [9] (Lord Bingham).
77 ibid [8] (Lord Bingham), [90] (Baroness Hale).
78 ibid [29] (Lord Scott), [102] (Baroness Hale), [158] (Lord Neuberger).
79 First Protocol, Art 1. See ibid [102] (Baroness Hale).
80 [2008] 1 AC 1399, [119].

Although these concerns touch on the true problem, save for Baroness Hale's, none of the speeches addressed it. In the field of premises, justification of disability-related discrimination was limited to an exhaustive list of specific conditions, such as to avoid endangering the health or safety of any person, or that the person with a disability was incapable of entering into an enforceable agreement.[81] None of these conditions covered sub-letting or non-payment of rent. Thus, if for a reason related to his disability a tenant permanently sub-let, or failed to pay any rent, he could never be evicted. This contrasts with the employment field, which provided a general justification defence, amenable to any circumstances.[82] As Baroness Hale explained: 'It may well be that Parliament had not understood that the narrow scope for justification in relation to services and premises would give rise to the problems we face in this case.'[83] For Baroness Hale, the 'simplest solution' would be regulations expanding the list, as permitted by section 24(5).[84] But this falls short of a *judicial* solution, the task before the House.

There was a number of solutions available in this case, and the House of Lords took the worst. It could have resolved the instant case much more simply, either by sending it back to a court to decide if the eviction was related to Malcolm's disability, this time on the basis that Malcolm had a disability, or, more simply, on the trial judge's finding that the premature sub-letting was not a result of Malcolm's illness. But the case was in the Lords as a matter of public importance, and so an interpretation of section 24, at the least, was required. To do this it had ample interpretive tools to hand, and, save for Baroness Hale, the House chose none of them.

The starting point, the literal rule (discussed earlier), points to 'that' reason in section 24 being the aforementioned (and only reason) in the provision, which is the reason for the *treatment*, and not necessarily the disability itself. This envisages, typically, treatment because of a manifestation of a disability, such as slow typing or walking, absenteeism, or the accompaniment of a guide dog. As well as being obvious from the text and structure of the Act, this is supported by the legislative history (as Baroness Hale highlighted) suggesting it represented the intent of Parliament, save for the limited justifications for landlords. The benefit of such a decision would be the signal that an urgent amendment was required. Given the potential interference with property rights by such a literal reading, the signal could have been amplified somewhat if such a decision were accompanied by a declaration of incompatibility.[85] Appropriate amendments could have been made virtually overnight by statutory instrument (under s 24(5)), and so there was no need even to engage the fast-track procedure provided by the Human Rights Act 1998.[86]

81 DDA 1995, s 24(3)(a)–(f).

82 DDA 1995, s 3A(1). To be justified, the reason for the treatment had to be 'both material to the circumstances of the particular case and substantial'.

83 [2008] 1 AC 1399, [80].

84 ibid [103].

85 Under HRA 1998, s 4.

86 The Act provides a fast-track procedure enabling the relevant minister to amend the legislation appropriately either before Parliament or (because of 'urgency') without Parliamentary approval. See HRA 1998, s 10 and Sch 2, para 2.

The immediate effect of the interpretation for landlords could have been ameliorated by returning the case to the trial judge, effectively reducing this interpretation to an *obiter dictum*, although given that it would have been from the House the Lords, this may be a little fanciful. As even this interpretation could have had some unsatisfactory, or perhaps 'absurd',[87] consequences for landlords, a solution beyond the literal one was desirable. Four are considered next.

First, the House could have considered the rule that 'words, and particularly general words, cannot be read in isolation: their colour and content are derived from their context'.[88] The context here was the attachment to section 24 of the exhaustive list of specific defences. This distinguished the premises provisions from the others, notably the employment provisions. Thus, the House could have signalled that its narrow interpretation of section 24 was confined the 'premises' provisions of the Act. This would have avoided the extensive damage done to the more frequently litigated employment provisions.

That, of course, would leave two similar formulas with markedly different meanings. A better approach would be to focus on the drafting oversight itself. This leads to the remaining solutions, the second of which involves the golden rule.[89] Given the absurdity (or, in Baroness Hale's view, the 'inconvenience'[90]) produced by a literal reading, it was open to the courts not to apply section 24 in certain circumstances, notably against the principle of a landlord's essential property rights regarding sub-letting or non-paying tenants. It might be argued that the majority in substance, if not words, applied the golden rule, by avoiding the absurd consequences for landlords. This would be disingenuous for three reasons. First, the majority overruled *Clark v Novacold* and the employment cases. Second, they went far beyond 'disapplying' the statute to the particular absurdity identified. Third, they produced a far greater counter-mischief, especially to the employment provisions.[91]

A third option would be to shape this absurdity in the context of the Human Rights Act 1998, section 3(1), and the landlord's Convention property rights. Given the dramatic consequences of a literal reading of section 24, the risk of judicial review, and the Convention right, it seems obvious this is a drafting error. And given the destructive effect of narrowing the comparison required by disability-related discrimination, it seems equally obvious that the error lies not there, but in the limited justification defences. Instead of a literal interpretation accompanied with a declaration of incompatibility, the *Ghaidan* approach could be considered.[92] Here, it will be recalled, an Act can be interpreted liberally; the precise words used are less important than their substantive effect[93] as long as the interpretation would

87 [2008] 1 AC 1399, [15] (Lord Bingham), [154] (Lord Neuberger).

88 *Attorney General v Prince Ernest Augustus of Hanover* [1957] AC 436 (HL) 461 (Viscount Simonds). See Chapter 2, pp 24–25.

89 See p 21.

90 [2008] 1 AC 1399, [80].

91 The last of Bennion's 'six types of absurdity'. See O Jones, *Bennion on Statutory Interpretation* (6th edn, LexisNexis 2013) Div 5, Pt XX1, s 312. See further p 22, text to n 43.

92 *Godin-Mendoza v Ghaidan* [2004] 2 AC 557 (HL). See Chapter 2, p 44.

93 ibid [35] (Lord Nicholls).

'go with the grain of the legislation'.[94] Thus, Convention compliance could have been achieved by supplementing the list of defences under section 24(3), with something to the effect of 'to enforce a term of the letting agreement'. As it stood, each of the reasons in section 24(3) could be invoked only if it were 'reasonable in the circumstances' for the defendant to hold that opinion,[95] which is broad enough to import a degree of proportionality into the defence, as required by Strasbourg jurisprudence. Alternatively, the supplement could read: 'The reason for the treatment is a genuine one, and appropriate and necessary to enforce a term of the letting agreement.' As the drafting oversight, and the necessary remedy, were 'abundantly clear', a fourth solution exists: much the same the same result could have been achieved using the *Inco Europe* doctrine.[96]

Conclusion

In *Malcolm*, the House of Lords had at its disposal the interpretive tools of the literal and golden rules, *Pepper v Hart*, context, the *Ghaidan* approach, *Inco Europe*, and a declaration of incompatibility. The majority failed even to *consider* any of them, with Lord Scott, it seemed, exchanging all formalities of statutory interpretation for 'common sense'.[97] Instead, the House produced a distorted and inefficacious interpretation, save for Baroness Hale, who, for one of the elements, opted for a less damaging literal one (with the aid of *Pepper v Hart*). Just as worrying was the flirtation with fault-based liability. It managed this 'non-achievement' with five speeches and some 177 paragraphs of sometimes complex, technically flawed, and opaque reasoning. It seems that the notion that this was a case of public importance (being in the House of Lords) was lost on the majority, at least, whose speeches did nothing to clarify the law and everything to distort and damage it, and must have left interested parties, as well as Lord Diplock's 'citizen',[98] quite baffled.

Parliament rescued this situation when enacting the Equality Act 2010 some two years later. It did this by abolishing the comparative element altogether, and adopting a general justification defence. This single definition provided by EA 2010, section 15 ('discrimination arising from a disability') applied to all activities, such as employment and premises. Section 15 also *codified* the 'no knowledge' aspect of *Malcolm*. But the significance of this was marginalised by the introduction of a definition of indirect discrimination specific to disability.[99]

94 ibid [121] (Lord Rodger).
95 DDA 1995, s 24(2).
96 *Inco Europe Ltd v First Choice Distribution* [2000] 1 WLR 586 (HL). See Chapter 2, p 19.
97 [2008] 1 AC 1399, [30] & [31]. A McColgan *Discrimination, Equality and the Law* (Hart 2014) 166, excused this as 'judges not intimately acquainted with the statutory discrimination provisions'.
98 *Black-Clawson International Ltd v Papierwerke Waldhof-Aschaffenberg AG* [1975] AC 591 (HL) 638 (Lord Diplock). See Chapter 2, p 28, text to n 85.
99 EA 2010, s 6(3)(b): 'a reference to persons who share a protected characteristic is a reference to persons who have the same disability'. This replicates the approach taken in *Prewit v US Postal Service* 662 F 2d 292 (5th Cir 1981).

In line with general principle, this requires neither knowledge of the disability nor a discriminatory intent. Thus, the Equality Act 2010 effectively restored the law to the pre-*Malcolm* position.

Further reading

R Horton, 'The end of disability discrimination in employment law?' (2008) 37(4) ILJ 376.

P Roberts, 'Caring for the disabled? New boundaries in disability discrimination' (2009) 72(4) MLR 635.

S Fredman, *Discrimination Law* (2nd edn, Clarendon Law 2011) 171–174.

10 Conclusion

Introduction

In the context of statutory interpretation and equality law, Lord Steyn's observation that 'social welfare legislation and tax statutes may have to be approached somewhat differently'[1] is highly appropriate. At first sight, it would seem from the cases explored here that the judges prefer to treat discrimination law as they would a tax statute, lacking any societal ambition. In some,[2] there is a noticeable absence of the 'sympathetic and imaginative discovery' of purpose urged by Learned Hand J some 70 years ago, and adopted by the House of Lords[3] as a rubric of the purposive approach. But this absence is not aligned with the trends in the development of the 'rules' of statutory interpretation. The cases scrutinised in this book range from 1983 to 2015,[4] a period coinciding with the rise of the purposive approach, and the ever-increasing willingness of the courts to tamper with statutory wording, often, but not always, under the shelter of EU law or the Human Rights Act 1998. Neither is there any apparent relationship between the discrimination cases and the constitutional arrangements of the day, which saw the courts, bolstered by the European Communities Act 1972 and, more recently, by the Human Rights Act 1998, increasingly willing to challenge the executive, and indeed Parliament. Any bravado here failed to infect most of the judgments found in the domestic cases within this book. Less surprisingly perhaps, the establishment of the Supreme Court made no difference to the approach in these cases. From a more political perspective, with no apparent variation, these cases straddled the governments of the free-market Conservatives, the overtly liberal New Labour, and the 'austerity' Coalition. (They all pre-dated the EU secession referendum.)

1 *R (Quintavalle) v Secretary of State for Health* [2003] 2 AC 687 (HL) [21]. See Chapter 2, p 24.
2 Notably, *Perera v Civil Service Commission (No. 2)* [1983] ICR 428 (CA); *Meer v London Borough of Tower Hamlets* [1988] IRLR 399 (CA); *Mandla v Dowell Lee* [1983] QB 1 (CA); *Lewisham LBC v Malcolm* [2008] 1 AC 1399. For imaginative but *un*sympathetic 'discoveries', see *Essop v Home Office* [2015] ICR 1063 (CA); *Naeem v Secretary of State for Justice* [2016] ICR 289 (CA); *Cornelius v University College Swansea* [1987] IRLR 141 (CA); *Chief Constable of West Yorkshire v Khan* [2001] UKHL 48.
3 *R (Quintavalle) v Secretary of State for Health* [2003] 2 AC 687 (HL) [21], citing *Cabell v Markham* 148 F 2d 737 (2nd Cir 1945) 739 (Learned Hand J). See further Chapter 2, p 24.
4 *Perera v Civil Service Commission (No. 2)* [1983] ICR 428 (CA) and *Naeem v Secretary of State for Justice* [2016] ICR 289 (CA) (decided 9 December 2015).

As these factors cannot explain the poor judgments, an explanation must lie elsewhere. The analysis of these cases reveals that the interpretations are more inexpert than merely literal. One does not need to be an authority on discrimination law or statutory interpretation to realise this; the prolixity of many of the judgments are enough for a confident layperson to suspect that something is awry.

It has been demonstrated that the cases in this study were all relatively easy to solve. Assuming this, and that our senior judges are exceedingly good lawyers, one must ask why these judgments are so technically flawed and prolix. The obvious place to start is the apparent absence of expertise within the reasoning. The first thing to note is that the judiciary cannot claim to be unfamiliar with the purposive approach and its antecedent mischief rule, which has been around for centuries. From time to time in the 20th century, notably in the Privy Council, senior judges have shown themselves to be perfectly at ease with a liberal purposive approach.[5] First apparent in 1930, this has occurred long before EEC membership was on the horizon, under which, of course, courts are *obligated* to take that approach.[6]

Of course, familiarity with the purposive rule is no use without familiarity with the purpose of discrimination law. The history shows that the common law has been unwilling and/or unable to apply its vaunted moralistic credentials to matters of discrimination, with attitudes ranging from indifference to outright hostility.[7] The matter is not helped by the paucity of education on discrimination law. To this day, English lawyers receive no compulsory detailed education in discrimination law at their training stages. In English law degrees, the basic definitions may be taught as part of a Foundation subject: either EU Law or Public Law (in relation to the Human Rights Act 1998). Otherwise, discrimination law commonly remains an optional subject, or part of an option, typically Employment Law. By contrast, speak to any lawyer of the United States and you will find them steeped in the parallel definitions of disparate treatment, disparate impact, and retaliation, as the Civil Rights Act 1964 is essential to their legal training.

Given these circumstances, one might have presumed that when the first comprehensive discrimination statutes arrived in the 1970s, with their novel societal purpose and concepts, a programme of judicial training would accompany them. But there is little evidence of judicial training in this area, with only one-day seminars dedicated to the introduction of the Human Rights Act 1998; encompassing the whole of the European Convention on Human Rights (as well as the workings of the Act), it is not even known if these got as far as Article 14.[8] On the one hand, the extensive *Equal Treatment Bench Book*[9] provides some basic

5 See Chapter 2, p 50.

6 See e.g. *R v Henn and Darby* [1981] 1 AC 850 (HL) 904 (Lord Diplock). See Chapter 2, pp 33 and 42.

7 See Chapter 4, p 79 et al.

8 An attendee, Sedley LJ, reflected: 'You cannot teach anyone, even a judge, very much in a day' (M Hill (ed) *Religious Liberty and Human Rights* (University of Wales Press, 2002) Preface, ix–x.

9 February 2018, Appendix A-2, < https://www.judiciary.gov.uk/publications/equal-treatment-bench-book/ > accessed 10 April 2018.

explanations of the key definitions, but goes nowhere near an explanation of the purpose, societal or otherwise, of the Equality Act 2010.[10] On the other hand, there is a wealth of jurisprudence (notably under the progenitor US Civil Rights Act 1964), academic literature, and even extensive guidance,[11] on which to draw. But, as the cases in this study show, these sources were rarely explored.

Hence, on the whole, English judges come to this legislation with little or no expertise in the technicalities or purpose of the legislation. In a range of relatively easy cases, the host of technical shortcomings is evidence of that. Within this, six particular themes can be detected. These relate to technical shortcomings; the absence of basic interpretive tools; prolixity; ideological predilections; binary and fault-based liability; and evolution, stagnation, and regression.

Six particular themes

1 Technical shortcomings

The poor judgments comprise inexpert and technically flawed thinking, undermining the efficacy and integrity of key definitions. With the aid of a dictionary, the Court of Appeal decided that 'ethnic origins' could be defined only by biological origins.[12] Much later, the Supreme Court in *JFS* occupied 65 paragraphs contemplating whether or not a Masorti Jew could be defined as belonging to a racial group by his ethnic origins,[13] in a case in which all that mattered was that the claimant was not an Orthodox Jew.

For direct discrimination, Lord Goff's *but for* test and Lord Browne-Wilkinson's rebuttal were both misstated *and* flawed.[14] Elsewhere judges have assumed that the symmetrical model of direct discrimination facilitated positive action, which was contrary to the all jurisprudence on the matter, the statutory wording and context, and rendered (unknowingly it seems) other parts of the statute otiose.[15]

In the context of indirect discrimination, there was the inclusion of the challenged factor into the pool for comparison;[16] misplaced literal interpretations of

10 The updated (February 2018) edition provides an extended section on definitions, and does at least acknowledge that (ibid, para 15): 'Direct discrimination may be conscious or unconscious. The motive for the treatment is legally irrelevant (though it can be evidentially useful). There cannot be a "good", "benevolent" or commercially justifiable reason for directly discriminating.'

11 For instance, the EHRC Codes of Practice, published for each activity covered by the EA 2010. See < https://www.equalityhumanrights.com/en/advice-and-guidance/equality-act-codes-practice > accessed 10 April 2018. The EA 2010 also carries Explanatory Notes.

12 *Mandla v Dowell Lee* [1983] QB 1 (CA), reversed [1983] 2 AC 548 (HL). See p 171 et al.

13 *R (E) v Governing Body of JFS* [2010] 2 AC 728 (SC). See Chapter 5, p 102 et al.

14 *James v Eastleigh BC* [1990] 2 AC 751 (HL). See Chapter 5, p 92 et al.

15 See e.g. Lord Griffiths in *James v Eastleigh BC* [1990] 2 AC 751, 767, 768; and Lord Brown in *JFS* [2010] 2 AC 728 (HL) [247]. See, respectively, Chapter 5, pp 95–96 and p 110.

16 *Rutherford v Secretary of State for Trade and Industry (No. 2)* [2006] ICR 785 (HL); *Rolls Royce v Unite* [2010] ICR 1 (CA) [142] (Aikens LJ); *Naeem v Secretary of State for Justice* [2014] ICR 472 (EAT), doubted [2016] ICR 289 (CA) but only conclusively overruled [2017] UKSC 27.

the phrases 'requirement or condition'[17] and 'can comply',[18] which would lead to absurd consequences and render other parts of the statute otiose;[19] and an overly liberal justification defence.[20] And, as if these lessons were impossible to learn, as recently as 2015 the Court of Appeal embarked upon another error-strewn and doomed theory.[21] In the heavily litigated field of employment and disability discrimination, the House of Lords needlessly redefined a statutory cause of action to the point of extinction in order to save landlords from penury. Perhaps the most eccentric approach arose in the victimisation cases, where, in addition to the arbitrary and invisible 'on-off' incorporation of the law of contempt, the House of Lords rewrote a precedent in the most clumsy manner in order to preserve an element found nowhere in the legislation; and it did so merely by giving the 'honest and reasonable defence' a different ticket,[22] as if no one would notice.

This summary suggests that the cases were a result of wild and unstructured thinking. To a degree, this is true, and it may be ironic even to gather such a random collection of reasoning under a single heading. But some more tangible underlying themes are detectable.

2 Absence of basic interpretive tools

This book does not presume that the statutory definitions were flawless. It would be surprising if they were, given the relative infancy of discrimination law and its novel and challenging concepts for many areas of civil life. The cases reviewed highlighted drafting problems[23] and the propensity for unpredicted scenarios.[24] Nonetheless, these cases were in the hands of the bench's best legal brains, and identifying and resolving the issues should have been relatively straightforward matters. Instead, they produced unwieldy, unsatisfactory, and, in many cases, unduly narrow judgments. It is perhaps ironic that resort to the legislative text and established tools of statutory

17 See e.g. *Perera v Civil Service Commission (No. 2)* [1983] ICR 428 (CA); *Meer v London Borough of Tower Hamlets* [1988] IRLR 399 (CA). See Chapter 8, p 154 et al.

18 *Mandla v Dowell Lee* [1983] QB 1 (CA), reversed [1983] 2 AC 548 (HL). See Chapter 8, especially pp 172–173.

19 See e.g. *Meer v London Borough of Tower Hamlets* [1988] IRLR 399 (CA). See Chapter 8, p 160; and *Mandla v Dowell Lee* [1983] QB 1 (CA), 9–10 (Lord Denning MR), 14–15 (Oliver LJ), & 21–22 (Kerr LJ), reversed [1983] 2 AC 548 (HL). See Chapter 8, p 172 et al.

20 *Hampson v Department of Education* [1989] ICR 179 (CA) 196. See Chapter 2, pp 39–40.

21 *Essop v Home Office* [2015] ICR 1063 and *Naeem v Secretary of State for Justice* [2016] ICR 289. See Chapter 8, p 183 et al.

22 See Chapter 6, 'The "honest and reasonable defence"', p 123.

23 See e.g. Case C-185/97 *Coote v Granada Hospitality* [1999] ICR 100; *Rowstock Ltd v Jessemey* [2014] 1 WLR 3615 (CA); *Perera v Civil Service Commission (No. 2)* [1983] ICR 428 (CA); *Chief Constable of West Yorkshire v Khan* [2001] UKHL 48; *Lewisham LBC v Malcolm* [2008] 1 AC 1399 (HL).

24 E.g. where a facially discriminatory factor is incorporated into a facially neutral practice: *James v Eastleigh BC* [1990] 2 AC 751 (HL) and *JFS* [2010] 2 AC 728 (SC); standard reactions to litigation: *Chief Constable of West Yorkshire v Khan*, ibid; eviction of disabled tenants in breach: *Lewisham LBC v Malcolm*, ibid; unfair dismissal qualification disadvantaging men: *Rutherford v Secretary of State for Trade and Industry (No. 2)* [2006] ICR 785 (HL).

interpretation would have avoided this, as very often the statutory purpose would have been achieved with a simple literal approach. For instance, of the 12[25] cases singled out for particular attention in this book, judges in nine departed from the literal meaning to produce a narrow interpretation.[26] In five of these, judges departed from the literal rule in order to accommodate a benign motive defence,[27] and in two others to produce a novel and unfounded model of indirect discrimination.[28] In another, the Court of Appeal chose the narrow of two literal possibilities, ignored a House of Lords dictum, ***and*** breached the 'otiose' rule,[29] when providing an ultimately doomed 'scientific' definition of 'ethnic origins', again seemingly under the influence of the defendant's benign motive.[30] With a little imagination, or interpretive skill, three other cases could have avoided unduly narrow results and been resolved purposively without departing from the literal rule.[31]

3 Prolixity

A feature in addition to these technical shortcomings is the prolixity of the judgments. This is unlikely to achieve one particular aim of the literal rule (as well as the rule of law), that citizens should be able to understand the law.[32] The point was made more recently in an extra-judicial speech by Lord Neuberger: '[I]f justice is seen to be done it must be understandable.'[33] Thus (with a coincidental relevance to this book) he pronounced: 'Indeed, the increasing complexity of the law imposes a greater obligation than ever on judges to make themselves clear.'[34]

25 *James v Eastleigh BC* [1990] 2 AC 751 (HL); *JFS* [2010] 2 AC 728 (SC); *Cornelius v University College Swansea* [1987] IRLR 141 (CA); *Chief Constable of West Yorkshire v Khan* [2001] UKHL 48; *St Helens MBC v Derbyshire* [2007] ICR 841 (HL); *Rutherford v Secretary of State for Trade and Industry (No. 2)* [2006] ICR 785 (HL); *Essop v Home Office* [2015] ICR 1063 (CA), reversed [2017] UKSC 27; *Naeem v Secretary of State for Justice* [2016] ICR 289 (CA), overruled [2017] UKSC 27; *Lewisham LBC v Malcolm* [2008] 1 AC 1399 (HL); *Perera v Civil Service Commission (No. 2)* [1983] ICR 428 (CA); *Meer v London Borough of Tower Hamlets* [1988] IRLR 399 (CA); *Mandla v Dowell Lee* [1983] QB 1 (CA), reversed [1983] 2 AC 548 (HL).

26 *James v Eastleigh* (minority, 3–2); *JFS* (minority, 5–4); *Khan* (unanimous); *Derbyshire* (majority 4–1); *Rutherford* (majority 3–2); *Essop* (unanimous); *Naeem* (unanimous); and *Malcolm* (majority, 4–1). All ibid.

27 *James v Eastleigh*; *JFS*; *Cornelius*; *Khan*; and *Derbyshire*, all ibid.

28 *Essop v Home Office* [2015] ICR 1063 (CA); *Naeem v Secretary of State for Justice* [2016] ICR 289 (CA), both overruled [2017] UKSC 27.

29 See e.g. *Hill v William Hill (Park Lane) Ltd* [1949] AC 530 (HL). See further p 25.

30 *Mandla v Dowell Lee* [1983] QB 1, reversed [1983] 2 AC 548 (HL).

31 *Perera v Civil Service Commission (No. 2)* [1983] ICR 428 (CA); *Meer v London Borough of Tower Hamlets* [1988] IRLR 399 (CA); *Mandla v Dowell Lee* [1983] QB 1 (CA) (on the 'racial group' issue), reversed [1983] 2 AC 548 (HL).

32 See e.g. *Black-Clawson International Ltd v Papierwerke Waldhof-Aschaffenberg AG* [1975] AC 591 (HL) 638 (Lord Diplock). See further Chapter 2, p 28, text to n 85.

33 Lord Neuberger MR, 'Open justice unbound?' Judicial Studies Board annual lecture 2011, 16 March 2011, para 5, < webarchive.nationalarchives.gov.uk/20131202164909/http://judiciary.gov.uk/media/speeches/2011 > accessed 10 April 2018.

34 ibid, para 7.

Most notable here is the *JFS* case, where no less than nine Justices of the Supreme Court provided eight separate speeches, occupying 259 paragraphs, in a case of relatively little complexity and importance. In *Meer*, Staughton LJ went off on a whim of his own, exploring irrelevant matters such as discriminatory intent and the potential (misplaced) capriciousness of the law.[35] Taking *Khan*[36] and *Derbyshire*[37] together, the House of Lords alone produced some 160 paragraphs, comprising eight *unanimous* speeches,[38] none of which faced up to the real problem, which was that the statutory formula for victimisation did not provide any sort of defence, notably for those defending litigation. In *Malcolm*, the majority managed its effective destruction of a statutory cause of action with 113 paragraphs bypassing the main issue and any conventional tools of statutory interpretation. The Court of Appeal in *Essop* expended some 70 paragraphs on an unfounded and thoroughly incorrect definition of just the prima facie elements of indirect discrimination.[39] In *Naeem*, the Court managed much the same in just 40 paragraphs, but in doing so failed to identify and properly overrule the EAT's erroneous comparison, which itself occupied some 16 paragraphs.[40]

None of this is inevitable; the analysis in this book has illustrated that the cases were much easier to resolve that their judgments suggest. There is evidence of this in the some of the speeches. In *Derbyshire*, for instance, Baroness Hale's speech stood out as the only one to repudiate the 'honest and reasonable defence'. Moreover, she managed this in just 11 paragraphs, somewhat below the average of 20. And even with a superfluous discussion on the claimant's ethnic identity, her speech in *JFS* was the most germane, clear, and concise, coming in at 18 paragraphs, against the average of 29. Similarly, in a single speech of the Supreme Court, Baroness Hale managed to overrule *both Essop* and *Naeem* and restore the law to its proper position, in just 48 crisp paragraphs. Although these are rare and isolated examples, they demonstrate that such judgments are possible in discrimination cases.

4 Ideological predilections

Whatever their expertise or experience in the area of discrimination law, many of the judges seem enthusiastic to bring to a case ideological predilections at odds with the widely accepted goals of discrimination law. Clues can be found within the judgments, suggesting that the decisions are driven by opinions more personal (and notably populist) than legalistic. In many cases, the

35 *Meer v London Borough of Tower Hamlets* [1988] IRLR 399 (CA). See pp 159–162.

36 *Chief Constable of West Yorkshire Police v Khan* [2001] UKHL 48. Discussed at pp 71 and 122–129.

37 *St Helens MBC v Derbyshire* [2007] ICR 841 (SC). Discussed at p 121 et al.

38 In *St Helens MBC v Derbyshire*, ibid [35]–[36], Baroness Hale dissented on one point (the 'honest and reasonable defence') but not the decision.

39 *Essop v Home Office* [2015] ICR 1063 (CA), reversed [2017] UKSC 27.

40 [2016] ICR 289 (CA); [2014] ICR 472 (EAT) [15]–[31] (Mr Recorder Luba QC), overruled [2017] UKSC 27.

interpretation of the discrimination legislation is being treated as a 'free for all', or as a secondary matter in the process. The most obvious examples here are two pairs of Court of Appeal venturing to rewrite the theory of indirect discrimination without reference to any relevant authority or statutory purpose.[41] But the language deployed betrays this trait as more widely present. Consider these comments (with supplied populist counterparts), which flavour many of the speeches featured in this book:

- 'If persons wish to insist on wearing bathing suits they cannot reasonably insist on admission to a nudist colony . . .'[42] ('People who come to this country should abide by its rules and customs.' Or, 'They come over here . . .'.)
- 'But why should a coat-tailer . . . be entitled to succeed?'[43] ('I'm all for equality, but why should these ethnic minorities get special treatment?')
- This would be 'an automatic ride to victory'.[44] ('It's too easy to claim discrimination these days.' Or, 'This is political correctness gone mad.')
- '[O]ne can't help feeling that something has gone wrong.'[45] ('Political correctness gone mad.')
- '[A] brilliant man whose personal qualities made him suitable as a legal assistant might well have been sent forward . . .'[46] ('This is a fair country where anyone with talent can get on. Race or colour doesn't matter.')
- Requirements 'adopted at the whim of the employer' should not attract liability.[47] ('I am not racist. I should be able to run my business as I see fit, without interfering busybodies.')
- Otherwise, discrimination law would have 'an extraordinary wide and capricious effect'.[48] ('Britain is a tolerant country. Discrimination isn't a problem nowadays.')

The populist parallels, as translations, illustrate that these judicial comments merit no more legal credence than the opinion of the proverbial 'man in the street', or even the 'bloke down the pub' with his ale-loosened inhibitions. Given that they lack legal merit, these pronouncements amount to no more than personal opinions or, more grandly, ideological predilections. Their flavour could be best summarised

41 *Perera v Civil Service Commission (No. 2)* [1983] ICR 428 (CA) and *Meer v London Borough of Tower Hamlets* [1988] IRLR 399; *Essop v Home Office* [2015] ICR 1063 (CA) and *Naeem v Secretary of State for Justice* [2016] ICR 289 (CA), respectively reversed and overruled [2017] UKSC 27.

42 *Mandla v Dowell Lee* [1983] QB 1, 21C (Kerr LJ). See p 171 et al.

43 *Essop v Home Office* [2015] ICR 1063 (CA) [37] (Sir Colin Rimer). See p 183, especially p 190.

44 ibid [35].

45 *R (E) v Governing Body of JFS* [2010] 2 AC 728 (SC) [226] (Lord Rodger) (see p 113, text to n 139). See also ibid [188] (Lord Hope). Both dissenting.

46 *Perera v Civil Service Commission (No. 2)* [1983] ICR 428 (CA) 437–438 (Stephenson LJ). See Chapter 8, p 158.

47 *Meer v London Borough of Tower Hamlets* [1988] IRLR 399 (CA) 403, para 20 (Staughton LJ). See Chapter 8, p 159, text to n 29.

48 ibid.

perhaps, by Lord Diplock's lament over the Race Relations Act 1968, restricting as he saw it 'the liberty which the citizen has previously enjoyed'.[49]

Other statements suppose more overtly to reflect the views of the 'man in the street' (and require no translational counterparts). The first was made without a hint of irony:

- 'I do not believe that the man in the street would apply the word "ethnic" to a characteristic which the propositus[[50]] could assume or reject as a matter of choice.'[51]
- 'To regard a person as acting unlawfully when he had not been motivated . . . by any discriminatory motive is hardly likely to assist the objective of promoting harmonious racial relations.'[52]
- 'To introduce something akin to strict liability . . . is unlikely to recommend the legislation to the public as being fair and proper protection for the minorities that they are seeking to protect.'[53]
- The Objective Justification test should be 'something . . . acceptable to right-thinking people as sound and tolerable.'[54]

These judges have decided what they suppose the 'man in the street' thinks the law should be, or at least chosen to invoke him in support of their own ideological predilections. This, of course, is turning on its head the matter of statutory interpretation (indeed the whole business of declaring the law). The need to explain in plain English what the law actually is becomes especially important with a technical law carrying a novel purpose of societal advancement. Bringing personal, or even populist, opinions to the bench merely adds to the problem inconsistency, or randomness, already a feature of these flawed and complex judgments. Moreover, these statements betray a generally negative, even hostile approach to the group-based societal purpose of this law, an approach redolent of the common law history in these matters. Thus, whether they should be for the benefit of the rule of law,[55] or for 'lawyers of non-lawyers alike',[56] or simply the body of case law, these statements fail to convey anything but misdirection as to the meaning of the law.

49 *Dockers Labour Club and Institute Ltd v Race Relations Board* [1976] AC 285 (HL) 295–296.

50 *OED* 2016: 'A person from whom a line of descent is derived', < http://oed.com > accessed 10 April 2018.

51 *Mandla v Dowell Lee* [1983] QB 1 (CA), 15 (Oliver LJ). Reversed [1983] 2 AC 548 (HL). See Chapter 8, p 171 et al.

52 *Khan v Chief Constable of West Yorkshire* [2000] ICR 1169 (CA) [14] (Lord Woolf MR), reversed on other grounds, [2001] UKHL 48. See also Chapter 3, pp 56–57.

53 *Nagarajan v London Regional Transport* [2000] 1 AC 501 (HL) 510 (Lord Browne-Wilkinson, dissenting).

54 *Ojutiku v Manpower Services Commission* [1982] ICR 661 (CA), 668 (Eveleigh LJ). See Chapter 2, pp 39–40.

55 *Black-Clawson International Ltd v Papierwerke Waldhof-Aschaffenberg AG* [1975] AC 591 (HL) 638. See further Chapter 2, p 28, text to n 85.

56 Lord Neuberger, 'Open justice unbound?' Judicial Studies Board annual lecture 2011, 16 March 2011, para 5, < http://webarchive.nationalarchives.gov.uk/20131202164909/http://judiciary.gov.uk/media/speeches/2011 > accessed 10 April 2018.

5 Binary and at-fault liability

The negativity towards the group-based societal purpose is also apparent in more formal statements, as well as some decisions, that tend to gravitate to the common law tradition of binary litigation supposing the existence of an 'at-fault' defendant corresponding to an individual victim. The theme can be found lurking in the direct discrimination cases. Importunate dissenters continue to champion a benign motive defence[57] (which could also be explained as a manifestation of an ideological predilection of individual liberty[58]), despite a House of Lords' majority emphatically ruling it out as early as 1990.[59] These were not mere polite character references for otherwise liable defendants, or even apologies for reluctantly having to 'apply the letter of the law',[60] they are driving factors in exonerating speeches. More recently, the Court of Appeal *unanimously* rejected the Cat's Paw theory, again suggesting that the defendant must be a 'wrongdoer' to be liable for direct discrimination.[61]

In the field of indirect discrimination, a concept rooted in the notion of no-fault liability, such opinions can be found in unanimous decisions favouring the defendant. In *Meer*, one member of the Court of Appeal suggested that there could be no liability without discriminatory intent.[62] That was back in 1983, and remained unchallenged by the judiciary. Indeed, the notion resurfaced as recently as 2015, when in *Naeem*,[63] the Court of Appeal held that any challenged practice had to be 'inherently' discriminatory.

Similarly, for disability discrimination, a House of Lords four-to-one majority drove the proverbial coach and horses through the statutory wording in favour of its concern for 'innocent' property owners. In the same case, a unanimous House also demanded that for liability, defendants had knowledge of a claimant's disability, while two Law Lords suggested a discriminatory *motive* was required, thus reinforcing the notion of fault-based liability.[64]

For victimisation, there has been an artificial distinction between the *bringing* and *existence* of proceedings[65] and a baseless 'honest and reasonable

57 E.g. *R (E) v Governing Body of JFS* [2010] 2 AC 728 (SC) [182] (Lord Hope), [247] (Lord Brown), each noting the 'utmost good faith' on the defendant's side; *James v Eastleigh BC* [1990] 2 AC 751, 779 (Lord Lowry), 768 (Lord Griffiths).

58 *Dockers Labour Club and Institute Ltd v Race Relations Board* [1976] AC 285 (HL) 295–296 (Lord Diplock). See text to n 49 above; and p 87, text to n 70.

59 *James v Eastleigh BC* [1990] 2 AC 751.

60 E.g. *Khan v Chief Constable of West Yorkshire* [2000] ICR 1169 (CA) [14] (Lord Woolf MR). See text to n 52.

61 *Reynolds v CLFIS* [2015] ICR 1010 (CA). See further p 100, n 60 and Chapter 9, p 219, n 50 and accompanying text.

62 *Meer v London Borough of Tower Hamlets* [1988] IRLR 399, [20] (Staughton LJ).

63 *Naeem v Secretary of State for Justice* [2016] ICR 289 (CA), overruled [2017] UKSC 27.

64 *Lewisham LBC v Malcolm* [2008] 1 AC 1399 (HL). Baroness Hale dissented on the 'comparator' issue.

65 *Cornelius v University College Swansea* [1987] IRLR 141 (CA) 145–146; *Chief Constable of West Yorkshire v Khan* [2001] UKHL 48 [30] (Lord Nicholls), [46] (Lord Mackay), [59] Lord Hoffman, [78]–[80] (Lord Scott); *St Helens MBC v Derbyshire* [2007] ICR 841, [9] (Lord Bingham), [21] & [23] (Lord Hope).

defence',[66] with the subsequent excruciating attempt to reconcile it with the legislation and precedent.[67] These notions, developed in the face of the plain words of the legislation, centred on the 'innocence' or 'reasonableness' of the defendant.

On the other side of the equation, the problem arises with the group-based aspect of the definition of indirect discrimination. In the early days, the Court of Appeal dismissed claims because an exceptional, or 'brilliant', individual from the protected group would be unharmed by the challenged practice.[68] More recently, it held significant statistical evidence to be insufficient to prove a prima facie case; the Court demanded an additional *reason why* the group was disadvantaged by employment skills tests, and further, the *reason why* each claimant had failed, save any 'coat-tailers' were to benefit from the action.[69] In other words, indirect discrimination law served only proven individual victims. As well as being in denial of this law's progenitor, *Griggs*,[70] the Court appeared utterly indifferent to the age and racial profiles of the workplace hierarchy and the most obvious solution; it was instead pre-occupied with any particular wrong done to any particular individual. Moreover, the Court seemed oblivious to the notion of institutional racism articulated in the Macpherson Report. Even the supposedly liberal (majority) decision in *James v Eastleigh*[71] enabled an individual (and atypical) 'victim' to trump group-based benefits. The individualistic aspect of this binary approach is also noticeable in the victimisation cases, which ignored any wider (chilling or deterrent) effect beyond the individual claimant.[72]

6 Evolution, stagnation, and regression

It has been noted that the cases analysed here span a period of some 33 years (February 1983 to December 2015), while the relevant precedents (starting with *Griggs*) date from 1971.[73] Although statutory anti-discrimination law is a relatively recent concept, one reasonably could expect a degree of evolutionary progress. But none is present in the cases reviewed here. Indeed, they represent regression or, at best, stagnation, on the meaning of these key definitions. This was most startlingly evidenced with the baseless logic deployed by the Court of Appeal in *Essop* and *Naeem* in its doomed attempt to launch an unprecedented and regressive theory of indirect discrimination.[74] Similarly, back in 1983, the Court of Appeal in *Perera* regressed from seemingly settled (and correct) EAT

66 *Chief Constable of West Yorkshire Police v Khan* [2001] UKHL 48 [31] (Lord Nicholls).
67 *St Helens MBC v Derbyshire* [2007] ICR 841 (SC). Discussed at Chapter 6, p 121 et al.
68 *Perera v Civil Service Commission (No. 2)* [1983] ICR 428 (CA), 437–438.
69 *Essop v Home Office* [2015] ICR 1063 (CA), reversed [2017] UKSC 27.
70 *Griggs v Duke Power* 401 US 424 (Sup Ct, 1971). See pp 153 and 177.
71 [1990] 2 AC 751 (HL).
72 E.g. *Cornelius v University College Swansea* [1987] IRLR 141 (CA); *Chief Constable of West Yorkshire v Khan* [2001] UKHL 48.
73 *Griggs v Duke Power* 401 US 424 (Sup Ct, 1971). See Chapter 8, p 177 et al.
74 See Chapter 8, 'The Court of Appeal's *reason why* theory', p 182 et al.

pronouncements on indirect discrimination, themselves rooted in the American progenitor, *Griggs*.[75] The House of Lords in *Malcolm* expressly regressed established and correct orthodoxy,[76] while in *Rutherford* it effectively did the same when unknowingly (it seemed), it threw another orthodoxy into uncertainty.[77] In 1982, the Court of Appeal in *Mandla* ignored House of Lords precedent dating from 1972[78] to narrow the scope of the law to immutable characteristics. In the meantime, eight successive House of Lords/Supreme Court judgments dating from *James v Eastleigh* (1990) to *JFS* (2010) merely provided squabbles over the existence of a benign motive defence, with enough importunate dissenters to maintain the argument throughout for direct discrimination (albeit unsuccessfully) and for victimisation (successfully thus far).[79]

Although this does not represent a definitive mini-history of the judiciary and discrimination law, it is consistent with the central theme of this book, that the judgments were made without recourse to the standard tools of statutory interpretation or a full understanding of the key statutory key definitions.

Proposals

The argument of this book has been that many interpretations of the discrimination legislation are technically flawed, overlong, and overcomplicated. The result of the analysis within has been to declutter the judgments of their flaws and prolixity, and show that with a reasonable understanding of discrimination law and the rules of statutory interpretation, such cases are relatively easy to decide, *and* with concise, clear, and technically sound judgments. As such, nothing more need be done to produce a consistent, technically correct, and accessible body of equality case law. Nonetheless, the conclusions point to some fairly obvious, but limited, proposals, which should encourage such good practice.

The first is that the concepts, principles, and theories of equality law should be made a compulsory part of any qualifying law degree, so that all lawyers are familiar with legal aspects of equality, which can arise in any sphere of practice. Notions of equality have a growing influence in Public Law,[80] while a specific rubric is incorporated by the Human Rights Act 1998. Thus, even if Parliament fails to 'convert' all EU rights into domestic law following secession (as promised),[81] the role of equality law in the UK, if anything, is likely to increase in the foreseeable future. As such, all practitioners of the future should be able to raise and articulate

75 See Chapter 8, '1 A narrow or liberal interpretation?', p 156 et al.

76 See Chapter 9.

77 See Chapter 8, 'The comparison required', p 174.

78 *Ealing LBC v Race Relations Board* [1972] AC 342 (HL), 362. See p 172 and further p 103.

79 See, respectively, Chapters 5 and 6.

80 See e.g. *Matadeen v Pointu* [1999] 1 AC 98, 108 (see Chapter 4, p 86). Cited in *R (Rotherham MBC) v Secretary of State for Business, Innovation and Skills* [2015] UKSC 6, [26] Lord Sumption (with whom Lord Hodge agreed).

81 Save for the Charter of Fundamental Rights: European Union (Withdrawal) Bill 2017, cl 5(4). See further Chapter 2, n 159.

equality issues whilst in the longer term some will go on to form the judiciary. This, of course, is long term, and does not guarantee that future judges will ignore their personal views in deference to a proper interpretation, but it would be overly pessimistic to assume it would have no effect.

In relation to the first proposal, the second is judicial training in matters of equality law. One could hope that this would detach entirely the modern bench from the negative historical attitudes, any incompatible ideological predilections, and the 'binary' mind-set. Again, there must be a degree of scepticism about the outcome. As seen throughout this book, a supposed knowledge of the standard rules of statutory interpretation was not enough to compel judges to prioritise even the legislative language, let alone purpose, above their own ideological predilections. But it is likely to produce, to some degree at least, more expert judgments, and given the wider dissemination of expertise, it might provoke the practice, unachievable directly by legislation perhaps, of decisions based on more concurring or even singular judgments.[82]

More generally, there have been some embryonic steps eschewing prolixity. After complaining of needlessly complex and overlong judgments, Lord Neuberger suggested, extra-judicially, that judges should be given training in the 'skill of judgment writing'.[83] There is no evidence that this has been taken up,[84] but at least the matter has been aired at the highest judicial level. It may be that Lord Neuberger's plea was connected to two other developments. The Supreme Court nowadays issues 'judgment summaries',[85] while judges of the Court of Appeal have been 'encouraged'[86] to produce 'short-form judgments' where no point of law is at stake. Of course, these developments fall short in one way or another of the goals of clarity and (appropriate) brevity in all judgments, but they are steps in the right direction. In the meantime, the hand penning the summary or short-form judgment may well absorb the habit when drafting the full or substantive speeches.

82 For a short discussion of the merits or otherwise of 'singular composite' judgments, see Lord Neuberger 'Open justice unbound?' Judicial Studies Board annual lecture 2011, 16 March 2011, paras 26–28, < http://webarchive.nationalarchives.gov.uk/20131202164909/http://judiciary.gov.uk/media/speeches/2011 > accessed 10 April 2018.

83 ibid, paras 5–10 and 27–28.

84 The latest training strategy is set out in very general terms, e.g. 'to provide training of the highest professional standard for judicial office holders' accompanied with the dispiriting rider, 'using methods which represent value for money'. The closest it comes to equality is the definition of 'social context', which 'includes diversity and equality integral to the training programmes. Judges need to relate to and communicate effectively with all manner of people from a variety of backgrounds with different capacities, needs and expectations.' This, of course, does not touch upon legal concepts of discrimination. See Strategy of the Judicial College Strategy 2018–2010 (Judicial College, November 2017) paras 12 and 14 respectively, < https://www.judiciary.gov.uk/wp-content/uploads/2017/12/judicial-college-strategy-2018-2020.pdf > accessed 10 April 2018.

85 Available in video or as a written 'press summary'. See e.g. *Essop v Home Office*, < https://www.supremecourt.uk/cases/uksc-2015-0161.html > accessed 10 April 2018.

86 The 'encouragement' came from Lord Dyson MR and his successor, Sir Terence Etherton MR: *BS (Congo) v Secretary of State for the Home Department* [2017] EWCA Civ 53 [1]; *Frugal v Chief Constable of Nottinghamshire Police* [2017] EWCA Civ 86 [2]; *Cheyne Capital v Deutsche Trustee Company* [2016] EWCA Civ 743 [2].

The third proposal is more concrete: an amendment to all equality legislation, along the lines of that suggested in the Law Commissions' Report for all legislation, *compelling* judges to take a purposive approach to the interpretation of equality law. Again, while this would no doubt improve matters, the equality legislation would remain vulnerable to unduly narrow interpretations. A judge could adopt as the statutory purpose his or her ideological predilections, for instance, by using the 'man in the street' (discussed earlier) as the reference point. As such, it would be prudent to add 'liberal', or 'broad', to the any legislative command.[87] This would reduce the vulnerability to narrow interpretations.

Indeed, the 'conversion' of EU rights into domestic law following secession makes such a command imperative, assuming that the UK is no longer subject to the jurisdiction of the Court of Justice and its binding interpretations. Although this would help avoid a divergence between this proposed shared arrangement of laws and principles, it might not be able to prevent *some* divergence. Much of this debate will be had after the details of secession are agreed. But assuming that the UK is sufficiently detached from the EU not to be bound by its treaty objectives, it is difficult to contemplate an interpretive command to English judges in terms that they must fulfil the objectives of a large foreign neighbour or trading partner. Thus, a legislative command to interpret discrimination law purposively and liberally is about as close as one safely could get to the politically unthinkable direction to adopt the Court of Justice's teleological doctrine with its principal goal of treaty objectives.[88] The second and third proposals could have a near-immediate effect, while the first would take time to feed through. Nonetheless, in isolation, or combined, they ought to underpin good practice.

Epilogue

This book, concerned with discrimination legislation, was prompted by the mystery of why so many easy cases produced so much bad law. Aside from the novel purpose of this law and an absence of technical mastery of the subject, the answer lies, it seems, in much judicial excellence being displaced by a gravitation to the common law's traditional binary approach to litigation and the apparent ability of equality law to provoke ardent personal opinions on what the law should be. These are not the best tools for the task of statutory interpretation, especially with a law designed to *challenge* individual, societal, and institutional assumptions and

87 None of this is particularly fanciful. For instance, Canada's Interpretation Act 1985 mandates a 'fair, large and liberal construction', of all statutes and regulations (consolidated as RSC 1985, s 12) and, with an allusion to the 'living instrument' approach, notes that '[t]he law is always speaking . . . so that effect may be given to the enactment according to its true spirit, intent and meaning' (ibid, s 10). See also the New Zealand Interpretation Act 1999, s 5(1): 'The meaning of an enactment must be ascertained from its text and in the light of its purpose'; Western Australia Interpretation Act 1984, s 18: an interpretation promoting the 'underlying' purpose or object 'shall be preferred'.

88 See further Chapter 2, pp 41–43.

behaviour, as well as patterns of inequality. All of this is against a historical (and indeed quite recent) backdrop of judicial indifference and/or hostility to matters of equality, which seems to have permeated many of the modern cases reviewed here.

On the whole, these were easy cases to decide. Of course, a basic understanding of the wider jurisprudence, technicalities, and societal purpose would help. But this is not asking too much of a judge in the great courts of the land. The primary purpose of this work has not been to promote this or that theory or concept of discrimination law. In any case, there is a loose consensus around the statutory purpose.[89] Indeed, many of the problematic speeches were either in the minority, reversed on appeal, or resolved by subsequent legislation, with mainstream definitions prevailing. The central purpose has been to declutter the case law of the inexpert, prolix, and personal judgments to show that the implementation of any definition expressed in legislation must start with the basics of statutory interpretation combined with a basic understanding of the statutory definitions and purpose. This approach should not only provide much improved decisions, but also it should avoid the upsets, reversals, and repeated litigation that has beset this law. In other words, it was all that was needed to have avoided so much of the bad law produced in these relatively straightforward, or easy, cases.

89 See Chapter 3, pp 75–77.

Bibliography

Alexander L, 'What makes wrongful discrimination wrong? Biases, preferences, stereotypes and proxies' (1992) 141 Penns UL Rev 149

Arai-Takahashi Y, *The Margin of Appreciation Doctrine and the Principle of Proportionality in the Jurisprudence of the ECHR* (Intersentia 2001)

Archbold, *Criminal Pleading Evidence and Practice* (63rd edn, Sweet & Maxwell 2015)

Aristotle, 'Nicomachean Ethics, Vol. 3', in WD Ross and L Brown, *The Nicomachean Ethics* (Oxford University Press 2009)

Asma S, *Against Fairness* (Chicago University Press 2013)

Baker JH, *Introduction to English Legal History* (Butterworths 1979)

Bachmann M, *Core of Conviction* (Senitel, 2011)

Bamforth N, Malik M, and O'Cinneide C, *Discrimination Law: Theory and Context: Text and Materials* (Sweet & Maxwell 2008)

Barbera M, 'Not the same? The judicial role in the new community anti-discrimination law context' (2002) 31 ILJ 82

Barmes L, 'Promoting diversity and the definition of direct discrimination' (2003) 32(3) ILJ 200

Barnard C, 'The ageing model of indirect discrimination' [2007] CLJ 37

Barnard C and Hepple, B 'Substantive equality' (2000) 59(3) CLJ 562

Barton O, 'An analysis of the principle of subsidiarity in European Union law' (2014) 2(1) NELR 83

Bavis CD, '*Vriend v Alberta*, *Law v Canada*, *Ontario v M and H*: the latest steps on the winding path to substantive equality' (1999) 37 Alberta L Rev 683

Bell J and Engle G, *Cross Statutory Interpretation* (2nd edn, Butterworths 1987); (3rd edn, 1995)

Bennion F, *Statutory Interpretation* (3rd edn, Butterworths 1997)

Bilder M, 'The corporate origins of judicial review' (2006) 116 Yale LJ 502

Biko S, *I Write What I Like* (Heinemann 1987)

Blackstone, *Commentaries on the Law of England* (1765–1769)

Breyer S, *Active Liberty: Interpreting a Democratic Constitution* (Clarendon Law Lectures, Oxford University Press, 2008)

Cahill-O'Callaghan RJ, 'The influence of personal values on legal judgments' (2013) 40(4) *Journal of Law and Society* 596

Carney G, 'Comparative approaches to statutory interpretation in civil law and common law' (2015) 36 Stat LR 46

Cockburn C, *In The Way of Women: Men's Resistance to Sex Equality in Organisations* (Macmillan 1991)

Collins H, 'Discrimination, equality and social inclusion' (2003) 66(1) MLR 16–43

Connolly M, *Discrimination Law* (2nd edn, Sweet & Maxwell 2011)

Connolly M, 'Discriminatory motive and the *but for* test: the proper approach to direct discrimination in Britain and the United States (2007) 9 *International Journal of Discrimination and the Law* 3

Connolly M, 'Rethinking victimisation' (2009) 38(2) ILJ 149

Connolly M, 'Statutory interpretation, victimization under equality law, and its "on–off" relationship with contempt of court', (2018) 39(1) SLR 72–90

Connolly M, 'Victimising third parties: the equality directives, the European Convention on Human Rights, and EU general principles' (2010) 35 EL Rev 822

Constitution of the Republic of South Africa 1996, s 10, < www.gov.za/documents/constitution-republic-south-africa-1996 > accessed 10 April 2018

Cook H, 'Against common right and reason: the College of Physicians versus Dr. Thomas Bonham' (1985) 29(4) *The American Journal of Legal History* 301, 317–318

Cooke R, *Turning Points of the Common Law* (Sweet & Maxwell 1997)

Corry J, 'Administrative law and the interpretation of statutes (1936) 1 *University of Toronto Law Journal* 286

Cross F, *The Theory and Practice of Statutory Interpretation* (Stanford University Press 2008)

Cross R, *Statutory Interpretation* (Butterworths 1976)

De Schutter O, 'The prohibition of discrimination under European human rights law: relevance for the EU' (European Commission, 2005) 14–15, < www.migpolgroup.com/public/docs/41.ProhibitionofDiscriminationunderHumanRtsLaw_EN_02.05.pdf > accessed 10 April 2018

De Slooveere FJ, 'Steps in the process of interpreting statutes' (1932) 10 *New York University Press Review* 1

Dicey AV, *Introduction to the Study of the Law of the Constitution* (9th edn, Macmillan 1939)

Dicey AV, *Lectures on the Relation between Law and Public Opinion in England during the Nineteenth Century* (2nd edn, reissue, Macmillan 1962)

Doya NR, 'The drafting history of the Uganda Penal Code (Amendment) Act and challenges to its implementation' (2016) 37 Stat LR 1

Doyle B, 'Enabling legislation or dissembling law? The Disability Discrimination Act 1995' (1997) 60 MLR 64

Edgar SGG, *Craies on Statute Law* (6th edn, Sweet & Maxwell 1971)

Ellis E and Watson P, *EU Anti-Discrimination Law* (2nd edn, Oxford University Press 2012)

Feldman D, 'Human dignity as a legal value' Part I [1999] PL 682

Feldman D, 'Human dignity as a legal value' Part II [2000] PL 61

Finnis JM, 'Directly discriminatory decisions: a missed opportunity' (2010) 126 LQR 491

France A, *Le Lys Rouge* [*The Red Lily*], (1894)Fraser Butlin S, 'The UN Convention on the Rights of Persons with Disabilities: does the Equality Act 2010 measure up to UK international commitments?' (2011) 40(4) ILJ 428

Fredman S, *Discrimination Law* (2nd edn, Oxford University Press 2011)

Fredman S, 'Reforming equal pay laws' (2008) 37 ILJ 193

Fredman S, *Sex Discrimination* (Oxford University Press 2001)

Fredman S, 'The reason why: unravelling indirect discrimination law' (2016) 45(2) ILJ 231

Fredman S, *Women and the Law* (Clarendon Press 1997)

Forshaw S and Pilgerstorfer M, 'Direct and indirect discrimination: is there something in between?' (2008) 37(4) ILJ 347

Gardner J, 'Liberals and unlawful discrimination' (1989) 9 OJLS 1

Gardner J, 'On the grounds of her sex(uality)' (1998) 18 OJLS 167

Gearty C, 'The internal and external "other" in the Union legal order: racism, religious intolerance and xenophobia in Europe', in P Alston, M Bustelo, and J Heenan (eds) *The EU and Human Rights* (Oxford University Press 1999) 327–359

Gibson JL, *Overcoming Apartheid* (Russell Sage Foundation Publications 2006)

Goldsworthy J, *The Sovereignty of Parliament: History and Philosophy* (Oxford University Press 1998)

Graham RN, 'A unified theory of statutory interpretation' (2002) 23 Stat LR 91

Gray CM, 'Bonham's case reviewed' (1972) 116 *Proceedings of the American Philosophical Society* 35

Grayson J, 'Playing the Gypsy "race card"' (2010) Institute of Race Relations, 4 June 2010, < www.irr.org.uk/news/playing-the-gypsy-race-card/ > accessed 10 April 2018

Griffith JAG, *The Politics of the Judiciary* (5th edn, Fontana 2010)

Henriques HSQ, 'The political rights of English Jews' (1907) 19 (4) *Jewish Quarterly Review* 751

Hepple B, *Equality, The New Legal Framework* (Hart 2011)

Hepple B and Szyszczak E (eds), *Discrimination: The Limits of Law* (Mansell 1992)

Hill M (ed), *Religious Liberty and Human Rights* (University of Wales Press 2002)

Holmes E, 'Anti-discrimination rights without equality' (2005) 68(2) MLR 175

Horton R, 'The end of disability discrimination in employment law?' (2008) 37(4) ILJ 376

Hoskyns C, *Integrating Gender* (Verso 1996)

Jones O, *Bennion on Statutory Interpretation* (6th edn, LexisNexis 2013)

Jowell J, 'Is equality a constitutional principle?' (1994) 47 CLP (Part 2, Collected Papers) 1, 91

Kant I, *The Moral Law: Groundwork of the Metaphysics of Morals* [1785] (Hutchinson 1948)

Kendrick Johnson H, *Women and the Republic* [1897] (Bibliobazaar 2006)

Khaitan T, 'Indirect discrimination law: causation, explanation and coat-tailers' (2016) 132 LQR 35

Kirby AC CMG, M (The Hon Justice), 'Towards a grand theory of interpretation: the case of statutes and contracts' (2003) 24 Stat LR 95

Kutscher H, 'Methods of interpretation as seen by a judge at the Court of Justice' Judicial and Academic Conference, 27–28 September 1976, Court of Justice of the European Communities

Lacey N, 'From individual to group', in B Hepple and E Szyszczak (eds), *Discrimination: The Limits of Law* (Mansell 1992) 99–124

Lacey N, 'Legislation against sex discrimination: questions from a feminist perspective' (1986) 14 JLS 411

Lawson A, 'Disability and employment in the Equality Act 2010: opportunities seized, lost and generated' (2011) 40(4) ILJ 359

Lord Ellesmore, 'The Lord Chancellor's Speech to Sir Henry Mountague, when he was Sworn Chief Justice of the Kings-Bench' (1616) Moore KB 826, 828; 72 Eng Rep 932

Lord Irvine, 'Judges and decision-makers: the theory and practice of *Wednesbury* Review' [1996] PL 59

Lord Lester of Herne Hill, 'Equality and United Kingdom law: past, present and future' [2001] PL 77

Lord Lester of Herne Hill, 'The art of the possible – interpreting statutes under the Human Rights Act' [1998] EHRLR 665

Lord Neuberger, 'Open justice unbound?' Judicial Studies Board annual lecture 2011, 16 March 2011, paras 26–28, < webarchive.nationalarchives.gov.uk/20131202164909/ http://judiciary.gov.uk/media/speeches/2011 > accessed 10 April 2018

Lord Phillips, 'Equality before the law' (2008) 161 Law & Just 75

Lord Renton, 'The interpretation of statutes' (1982) 9 J Legis 252
Lord Slynn, 'Looking at European Community texts' [1993] Stat LR 12
Lord Steyn, '*Pepper v Hart*: A re-examination' (2001) 21 OJLS 59
Lord Steyn, 'The new legal landscape' [2000] EHRLR 549
Lord Woolf, 'Droit public – English style' [1995] PL 57
Lustgarten L, *Legal Control of Racial Discrimination* (Macmillan 1980)
McColgan A, *Discrimination, Equality and the Law* (Hart 2014)
McCrudden C, 'Multiculturalism, freedom of religion, equality, and the British Constitution: the JFS case considered' (2011) 9 Int'l J Const L 200
McCrudden C, 'Rethinking Positive Action' (1986) 15 ILJ 219
McGowan MO, 'Engendered differences' (2009) SSRN Library 1361196, < https://papers.ssrn.com/sol3/papers.cfm?abstract_id=1361196 > accessed 10 April 2018
McLachlin B, 'The evolution of equality' (1996) 54 *Advocate* 563
Markesinis B (ed), *The Impact of the Human Rights Act on English Law* (Oxford University Press 1998)
Mayhew L, *Law and Equal Opportunity* (Harvard University Press 1968)
Maxwell P, *On the Interpretation of Statutes* (12th edn, Sweet & Maxwell 1969)
Mead G, 'The role of intention in direct discrimination' (1990) 19(4) ILJ 250
Middlemiss S, 'A licence to discard? Failed sexual relationships in the workplace and sex discrimination' (2007) 78 Emp LB 2 (Westlaw)
Middlemiss S, 'Employers liability for employee references and victimisation' (2012) 34(2) SLR 138
Millett T, 'Rules of interpretation of EEC legislation' [1989] Stat LR 163
Milsom SFC, *Historical Foundations of the Common Law* (Butterworths 1981)
Moon G and Allen R, 'Dignity discourse in discrimination law: a better route to equality?' (2006) 6 EHRLR 610
O'Cinneide C, 'Fumbling towards coherence: the slow evolution of equality and anti-discrimination law in Britain' (2006) 57(1) NILQ 57
O'Connell R, 'The role of dignity in equality law: lessons from Canada and South Africa' (2008) 6(2) IJCL 267–286
O'Donovan K and Szyszczak E, *Equality and Sex Discrimination Law* (Blackwell 1988)
Pannick D, *Sex Discrimination Law* (Clarendon 1985)
Plucknett TFT, 'Bonham's case and judicial review' (1926) 40 Harv LR 30
Plucknett TFT and Barton JL (eds), *St. German's Doctor and Student* (Selden Society, vol 91, 1974)
Radacic I, 'Gender equality jurisprudence of the European Court of Human Rights' (2008) 19(4) EJIL 841
Rawls J, *A Theory of Justice* (Oxford University Press 1972)
Rensen T, 'British statutory interpretation in the light of Community and other international obligations' (1993) 14 Stat LR 186
Roberts P, 'Caring for the disabled? New boundaries in disability discrimination' (2009) 72(4) MLR 635
Robertson D, *Judicial Discretion in the House of Lords* (Oxford University Press 1998)
Rutherglen G, 'Discrimination and its discontents' (1995) 81 Virginia L Rev 117, 127–128
Rutherglen G, 'From race to age: the expanding scope of employment discrimination law' (1995) 24 *Journal of Legal Studies* 491
Samuals A (JP), 'The Interpretation of Statutes' (1980) 1 Stat LR 86
Seawell ME, 'Two suffrage mistakes' (1914) 199(700) March, *North American Review* 366–382

Sedley S, 'Human rights: a twenty-first century agenda' [1995] PL 386
Simpson AWB, *Leading Cases in the Common Law* (Clarendon 1995)
Smith N, *Basic Equality and Discrimination: Reconciling Theory and Law* (Ashgate 2011)
Steele I, 'Sex discrimination and the material factor defence under the Equal Pay Act 1970 and the Equality Act 2010' (2010) 39 ILJ 264
Sunstein C, 'Three civil rights fallacies' (1991) 79 California L Rev 751, 752–753
Thorne SE, 'Dr. Bonham's case' (1938) 54 LQR 543, reprinted in SE Thorne, *Essays in English Legal History* (Continuum 1984) 269
Townshend-Smith R, *Sex Discrimination in Employment: Law, Practice and Policy* (Sweet & Maxwell 1989)
Turner R, 'Gypsies and British parliamentary language: an analysis' (2002) 12 *Romani Studies* 1–34
Vranken M, 'Statutory interpretation and judicial policy making: some comparative reflections' (1991) 12(1) Stat LR 31–47
Ward T, 'Beyond sex equality: the limits of sex equality in the new Europe', in T Hervey and D O'Keeffe (eds), *Sex Equality Law in the European Union* (John Wiley 1996)
Wasserstrom R, 'Racism, sexism and preferential treatment: an approach to the topics' (1977) 24 UCLA L Rev 581
Waters M, 'St. German on reason and parliamentary sovereignty' (2003) 62 CLJ 335
Watt B, 'Goodbye "but-for", hello "but-why?"?' (1998) 27 ILJ 121
Wendell Holmes O, *The Common Law* (ABA 2009)
Whalen C and Whalen B, *The Longest Debate: a Legislative History of the Civil Rights Act* (Seven Locks Press 1985)
Westen P, *Speaking of Equality* (Princeton University Press 1990)
Williams G, 'Statutory interpretation, prostitution, and the rule of law', in CHF Tapper (ed), *Crime Proof and Punishment, Essays in Memory of Sir Rupert Cross* (Butterworths 1981)
Willis J, 'Statutory interpretation in a nutshell (1938) 16 *Canadian Bar Review* 1, 16
Wilson B, 'The making of a constitution' [1988] PL 370
Wintemute R, *Sexual Orientation and Human Rights. The United States Constitution, the European Convention, and the Canadian Charter* (Clarendon Press 1997)
Wintemute R, 'When is pregnancy discrimination indirect sex discrimination?' (1998) 27(1) ILJ 23
Yale DEC, 'St. German's little treatise concerning writs of subpoena' (1975) 10 *Irish Jurist* (NS) 324

Index

For Product Safety Concerns and Information please contact our EU representative GPSR@taylorandfrancis.com Taylor & Francis Verlag GmbH, Kaufingerstraße 24, 80331 München, Germany

Batch number: 10725973

Printed by Printforce, the Netherlands